TRANSNATIONAL TIES
AUSTRALIAN LIVES IN THE WORLD

TRANSNATIONAL TIES
AUSTRALIAN LIVES IN THE WORLD

DESLEY DEACON, PENNY RUSSELL
AND ANGELA WOOLLACOTT (EDITORS)

E PRESS

E PRESS

Published by ANU E Press
The Australian National University
Canberra ACT 0200, Australia
Email: anuepress@anu.edu.au
This title is also available online at:
    http://epress.anu.edu.au/transnational_citation.html

National Library of Australia
Cataloguing-in-Publication entry

Title: Transnational ties : Australian lives in the world /
              editors, Desley Deacon ; Penny Russell ; Angela
              Woollacott.
ISBN: 9781921536205 (pbk.) 9781921536212 (pdf)
Series: ANU Lives
Subjects: Cosmopolitanism--Australia.
              Ethnology--Australia
              Internationalism.
              Australia--Biography.
Other Authors/Contributors:
              Deacon, Desley.
              Russell, Penny.
              Woollacott, Angela.
Dewey Number: 306.40994

All rights reserved. No part of this publication may be reproduced, stored in a retrieval system or transmitted in any form or by any means, electronic, mechanical, photocopying or otherwise, without the prior permission of the publisher.

Cover design by ANU E Press
Cover photograph: Agnes and William Lum Mow, with baby William, Shekki, August 1932.

The editors acknowledge with gratitude the financial support received from The Australian National University's Publications Committee.

This edition © 2008 ANU E Press

The ANU Lives Series in Biography

The ANU Lives Series in Biography is an initiative of the National Centre for Biography in the History Program in the Research School of Social Sciences at The Australian National University. The National Centre was established in 2008 to extend the work of the Australian Dictionary of Biography and to serve as a focus for the study of life writing in Australia, supporting innovative research and writing to the highest standards in the field, nationally and internationally.

Books that appear in the ANU Lives series will be lively, engaging and provocative, intended to appeal to the current popular and scholarly interest in biography, memoir and autobiography. They will recount interesting and telling life stories and engage critically with issues and problems in historiography and life writing.

Table of Contents

Introduction		xiii

Archival fragments

1. The Old Commodore: a transnational life — 3
   Cassandra Pybus

Authority

2. Biography and global history: reflections on examining colonial governance through the life of Edward Eyre — 21
   Julie Evans

3. 'A fine type of Hindoo' meets 'the Australian type': British Indians in Australia and diverse masculinities — 41
   Margaret Allen

4. A British prince and a transnational life: Alfred, Duke of Edinburgh's visit to Australia, 1867–68 — 57
   Cindy McCreery

5. Enacting the international: R. G. Watt and the League of Nations Union — 75
   Nicholas Brown

Intimacy

6. Love, loss and 'going Home': the intimate lives of Victorian settlers — 97
   Maggie Mackellar

7. A journey of love: Agnes Breuer's sojourn in 1930s China — 115
   Kate Bagnall

8. Life stories, family relations and the 'lens of migration': postwar British emigration and the new mobility — 135
   A. James Hammerton

9. 'I'm not a good mother': gender expectations and tensions in a migrant woman's life story — 149
   Alistair Thomson

10. First love and Italian postwar migration stories — 165
    Francesco Ricatti

Intellect

11. The Pacific as rhizome: the case of Sir Henry Alexander Wickham, planter, and his transnational plants — 183
   Ann Lane

12. A transnational imagination: Alfred Deakin's reading lists — 197
   Mark Hearn

Imagination

13. From cosmopolitan romance to transnational fiction: re-reading Jean Devanny's Australian novels — 215
   Nancy L. Paxton

14. Paris and beyond: the transnational/national in the writing of Christina Stead and Eleanor Dark — 229
   Susan Carson

15. Australian 'immersion' narratives: memoirs of contemporary language travel — 245
   Mary Besemeres

16. America and the queer diaspora: the case of artist David McDiarmid — 259
   Sally Gray

Objects of displacement

17. Living in a material world: object biography and transnational lives — 275
   Karen Schamberger, Martha Sear, Kirsten Wehner, Jennifer Wilson and the Australian Journeys *Gallery Development Team, National Museum of Australia*

Contributors — 299

Index — 303

Illustrations

Figure 1.1: Billy Blue, The Old Commodore.	4
Figure 2.1: Eyre and Wylie, one of his Aboriginal companions.	26
Figure 2.2: Edward John Eyre, 1865, the year of the Morant Bay rebellion.	28
Figure 2.3: Edward John Eyre c. 1900	29
Figure 3.1: Otim Singh, an Indian man in business, Kingscote, South Australia.	42
Figure 4.1: HRH Prince Alfred, KG, Duke of Edinburgh in naval uniform.	58
Figure 4.2: The Governor's Ball at the Exhibition Buildings, The Royal Party Dancing the Scotch Reel, 27 December 1867.	60
Figure 4.3: *A Saylore on Horse-backe, ye Adelaide Troops are reviewed bye a Prussian Colonel*, 1868.	63
Figure 5.1: An earnest group: Ray Watt is second from the right in the front row among the delegates at the League of Nations Union Annual Meeting and Conference in Canberra, 28-31 January 1938.	85
Figure 6.1: Murndal Homestead. Samuel Cooke inherited it from his uncle Samuel Pratt Winter in 1878.	98
Figure 6.2: Niel Black, who was born in Argyllshire, Scotland, shared a love of Scottish regalia with Prince Alfred, Duke of Edinburgh.	104
Figure 6.3: Emu Creek, c. 1880, near where the manager of Glenormiston Station, before Niel Black purchased it, led a massacre of the traditional custodians.	107
Figure 6.4: Glenormiston Homestead in 1868. Niel Black waits in Scottish regalia to greet Prince Alfred, Duke of Edinburgh, during the duke's Australian tour.	109
Figure 7.1: Agnes and William Lum Mow, with baby William, Shekki, August 1932.	119
Figure 7.2: 'Water Front, Shekki, Canton, June 1932', taken during Agnes Breuer's visit to China.	121
Figure 7.3: Thomas Lum Mow (front) in the Lum Mow family store, Townsville, c. 1931.	122
Figure 7.4: Agnes Breuer (back centre) and William Lum Mow (back left) picnicking with friends in Townsville, c. late 1931.	123

Figure 8.1: 'Nomads on the Move Again': modern migrants. Since the 1960s migrants have tended to see themselves as inherently mobile and transnational. 137

Figure 9.1: 'The end of a perfect birthday' (caption in photograph album). Dorothy Wright reading to her children, Nicholas and Bridget, at home in Hornsby Heights, Sydney, on Bridget's first birthday, 25 March 1961. 150

Figure 9.2: Caption in Wright photo album, 1960: 'Under our gum tree. 13 weeks old (not the gum tree or Dossie).' 155

Figure 9.3: 'Dorothy on beach by the surf' (caption from family photograph album), Hawks Nest, March 1963. 161

Figure 10.1: Italian migrants at Broken Hill mines, 1953. 166

Figure 10.2: *Il Salotto di Lena*. 167

Figure 11.1: Henry Alexander Wickham. 185

Figure 11.2: (Andre) C. H. Wright, bromeliaceae *Bromelia magdalenae*, 1923. 190

Figure 12.1: Alfred Deakin with book in hand. 198

Figure 13.1: Jean Devanny, 1920s. 216

Figure 14.1: Christina Stead, 1940s. 230

Figure 14.2: Eleanor Dark, ca 1945. 231

Figure 15.1: Cover, John Mateer, *Semar's Cave: an Indonesian Journal*. 247

Figure 16.1: David McDiarmid, *Alphabet City*, 1983–84. 263

Figure 16.2: David McDiarmid, *Juicy fruits: Ralph, Joe, Frank…*, 1978. 266

Figure 16.3: David McDiarmid, *Disco Kwilt*, c. 1980. 270

Figure 17.1: This Latvian national dress was made and worn by Guna Kinne (nee Klasons) in Latvia, Germany and Australia in the second half of the twentieth century. 280

Figure 17.2: The front and back of the jacket made by Guna Kinne, and the pattern book illustrations used to trace the designs. 283

Figure 17.3: Guna Kinne wearing her Lativan national dress in Wangaratta in 1955. 285

Figure 17.4: The bonnet from Guna Kinne's national dress. 286

Figure 17.5: Good Neighbour Council group in their national costumes waiting to greet Princess Alexandra, in Wangaratta, 1959. 287

Figure 17.6: Guna Kinne wearing her Latvian national dress in Melbourne in 1970.   288

Figure 17.7: The *dàn tre*, a 23-stringed bamboo musical instrument.   290

Figure 17.8: Minh with the *dàn tre* at his home in Sydney, March 1990.   293

Introduction

Desley Deacon, Penny Russell and Angela Woollacott

Born in New York in the turbulent eighteenth century, African-American Billy Blue fought with the British against France and America, led a press gang in Deptford, lumped cargo on the Thames, was transported to Australia for pilfering and became a ferryman on Sydney Harbour. In Sydney, he flourished for some years as a man of property, on terms of friendship with Governor Macquarie. Cassandra Pybus speculates that this friendship, which helped secure Blue's stature in Sydney society, might have owed something to an earlier acquaintance when both men served in the same campaigns in America.

Guna Kinne was at high school in Latvia when she began making her national dress in 1939. She took the unfinished dress with her when she fled the country ahead of the Soviet invasion of 1945. She finished the jacket in Germany while living in the Russian Zone, unable to find her family and in continual fear of deportation. When she tried to escape across the border, Russian soldiers threw her from the train. The dress, carefully packed in her suitcase, rolled with her down the railway embankment; she had it still as she clawed her way back on to the last freight wagon, which rattled and lurched to the comparative safety of the English Zone. The outfit came with her to Australia, holding within its folds as many memories of movement and displacement as of the Latvia of her childhood.

Minh Tam Nguyen invented his *dàn tre* on a tea plantation in the Central Highlands of Vietnam, where he was doing hard labour in a Vietcong 're-education' camp. The stringed bamboo instrument, inspired by the traditional musical instruments of the region, symbolised the culture and tradition of a Vietnam he had lost. He made a second *dàn tre* in a refugee camp in the Philippines, where he lived with his son for more than a year before being transferred to Australia in 1982. He brought the second instrument with him. Like Mrs Kinne, he had crafted the object with love while building a life out of displacement. Like her, he later donated this treasured and culturally resonant object to the National Museum of Australia.

Cassandra Pybus and the National Museum's gallery development team tell the stories of Billy Blue, Guna Kinne and Minh Tam Nguyen in the two chapters that begin and end this volume. Chronologically, they neatly bookend the span of 'white' Australian history. Geographically, they offer just a taste of the far-flung lives—of adventure or displacement—that have been lived by many 'Australians' before they ever reached Australia. In so doing, they remind us that white Australia has never existed in isolation from conflicts and crises elsewhere around the globe. Australian lives are intricately enmeshed with the world, bound by ties of allegiance and affinity, intellect and imagination.

Australian historians—and still more Australian politicians—have been perhaps too inclined to forget this obvious fact. Although certain international relationships demand acknowledgment, it has been tempting to seek 'Australian' identity in what is at once unifying and distinctive: the fabric, as Ann Curthoys suggests, of national histories.[1] The nation is a comfortable frame for historical inquiry: one, as Curthoys further observes, that ensures historians a 'large, interested audience and enables our historical work to count in current debate'.[2] The more we speak in terms that are generally applicable across the nation, the wider will be the audience we reach—and historians, like politicians, depend on an audience for professional validation. The quest for Australian identity therefore contains an inherently homogenising impulse: it is a quest for sameness, not diversity. Seeking what is held in common, it is tempting to smooth over the chequered world of difference, held by fragile bonds, that inevitably defines a society built primarily on migration.

Increasingly, however, scholars are attempting to escape the straitjacket of such nation-based inquiries. The borders of modern nationhood are culturally contingent, Homi Bhabha points out: away from 'the psychosis of patriotic fervour', we find 'a more transnational and translational sense of the hybridity of imagined communities'.[3] Transnational history, then, encompasses diaspora, imperialism, exile and conflict. It allows analytical space not only to nations defined by political and geographical boundaries, but to the oceans and the wild spaces and borders that divide them. It is a dynamic history, a history of journeys as well as moments of departure and arrival, crossings and exchanges, 'movements, flows, and circulation'.[4] Transnational history, writes Sven Beckert, takes as its starting point 'the interconnectedness of human history as a whole, and while it acknowledges the extraordinary importance of states, empires, and the like, it pays attention to networks, processes, beliefs, and institutions that transcend these politically defined spaces'.[5] Or, we might add, those that flow around, beneath and through them.

In a settler nation such as Australia, a history of connectedness is not altogether new. The continuing relationship with Britain, the place of the vulnerable colonies and fledgling nation in the Asia-Pacific world and the growing cultural diversity of an immigrant population have produced recurrent preoccupations with issues of defence, derivation and distinctiveness. For Australians, the concept of 'transnational history' represents a shift of emphasis, not of substance. There is, however, more to transnationalism than the history of an immigrant culture. The essays in this volume trace not only the movement of people across the globe, but also the imaginative reach of individuals, including those who physically stay in one place. The flow of people helped shape Australia's distinctive character; the flow of ideas connected Australians to a global community of thought.

Biography, and the study of life stories, can contribute greatly to our understanding of such patterns of connection; but to explore the possibilities of transnationalism tests the limits of biography as an intellectual, professional and commercial practice. When delegates came together in July 2006 at a conference on 'Transnational Lives', held at the Humanities Research Centre at The Australian National University, they were prepared to transgress, rework and critique disciplinary as well as national boundaries. Representing an eclectic mix of disciplines and professions—history, literary criticism, museology, art and writing—they explored and challenged hierarchies of authority, definitions of race and constraints of gender. In the closing session of the conference, the National Museum of Australia gallery team even offered a provocative challenge to the assumed distinction between personal subjects and material objects, arguing that biography could be written of things as well as people. What united the papers was their exploration of a central question: what it means to research and represent a 'transnational life'. This collection of essays takes that exploration further.

The premise of the conference was that biography, in the words of Jill Matthews, 'allows the transnational historian to prise their subject out of the death grip of the national'.[6] Indeed, only sometimes—perhaps only when the identification is drawn from them by exceptional circumstances—do individuals understand themselves first and foremost as citizens of a particular nation. Sporting contests can do it, so can war, so can revolution, so can travel or exile. Other subjective identities, however, draw strength from categories or communities either much narrower, or much wider, than the nation. Individuals identify themselves by family and kinship networks, religious faith, political affiliation, intellectual community or friendship. The communities to which they belong might be those of neighbourhood, town, or city; they might be organisations or churches with an international reach; they might be untidy networks that sprawl across the globe, held together only by fragile ties of communication or affection. Pursuing a life story, it is almost unnecessary to look, in Robert Gregg's words, for 'the global buried within the local'.[7] It lies exposed; one cannot help but stumble over it.

When we bend our frame of inquiry away from the nation, different stories emerge. When the focus is on an individual life, the differences multiply; and the assumed boundaries of the nation are transgressed so many times—and so unthinkingly—that the boundaries themselves begin to seem almost meaningless. We can follow a life across and between nations and continents. We can contain within a single narrative the trauma of disruption and the fragile pleasures of reattachment that mark the transition from one home to another. We can trace the attractions, but also the dislocations, of a wandering life, whether that is the life of a migrant, a traveller, an explorer, an artist, a convicted criminal or a committed activist. We can observe the shifts in allegiance and attachment that flow from the varied cultural exchanges of a life, even when lived within a single country; and we can understand, in Lambert and Lester's terms, the circulation and global evolution of ideas and practices.[8] Of indefinite provenance and infinite outcomes, ideas have flowed around the globe, contained in books and print media, in people's minds, in the very structure of cultural and political institutions. The history of that movement could never be fully narrated, but the focus on an individual life might allow us to follow some stages of the journey.

When tracing an individual life, transnationalism often, therefore, appears less an analytical category than a commonsense descriptor of human experience—and yet the shadow of the nation clings to biography. Personal archives can be preserved and made accessible on the basis of an individual's perceived contribution to the political, social or cultural life of a nation, creating practical difficulties about tracing and assembling material that is distributed in fragmented collections across the globe. The subjects most often chosen for biographical study are—still—towering national figures. The largest compendia of life stories are dictionaries of national biography, which define even the most peripatetic life by reference to its contribution to one nation in particular. Publishers, with their acute commercial antennae, are often wary of publishing the biography of a subject who made equal impact in, say, three different countries. To the aspiring author's optimistic expectation of thus attracting three different markets, they counter the cautious concern that they might fail to capture any. The issue of classification and shelving in bookshops and libraries underlines the problem, with the same volume finding a different home in different countries, according to the perceived national significance of the individual whose life is told therein. What qualifies a book for inclusion in that popular category 'Australian biography', for example? In part, the dilemmas of marketing simply reflect the symbiotic relationship between commerce and nation: arguably it was modern marketing as much as modern politics that necessitated the nation-states of the nineteenth century, and even in a globalised world the national market is still the simplest to define and therefore to reach.[9]

Perhaps, though, the classifications and marketing strategies of publishers and booksellers reflect, as much as they shape, the instilled preferences of readers. We read to lose ourselves in a foreign world, or to learn more about our own. The pleasure of reading might lie in the burst of recognition of shared experience in a national life, or in the tug of curiosity about difference—but we like to know which to expect. Perhaps we are especially habituated to narratives of quest or adventure, where the venture into a foreign world is balanced and resolved by the return to a more secure identity, to 'home', at the end. A life story that crosses nations follows a different narrative arc. It draws us into one social world only to abandon it abruptly when our subject moves on to new circumstances. There is no return: the stable base of 'home' no longer serves as an anchor, but itself moves with the subject. This could be as unsettling for the reader as for the subject. Even on the more pragmatic level of intellectual inquiry, such works can challenge, because they fail to meet, our habitual criteria of relevance: what teacher of Australian history has not struggled to persuade students to read more than the 'Australian' chapter in a transnational work? 'There is something sacrosanct about certain aspects of culture,' observes Jill Matthews, 'that triggers the protective, exclusive, mutual embrace; that constitutes a settled "us" against the nomadic hordes of "them".'[10] Even the fiction of a coherent life story cannot always overcome the reflex of indifference.

There have always been some readers who have looked beyond the boundaries of nation for an alternative or transcendent sense of community—as Mark Hearn shows, for example, in his analysis of Alfred Deakin's reading habits. There are also signs that more and more readers' preferences are moving in the same direction, in response to a globalising world. The life stories traced in this volume help us to understand why this should be so. In particular, James Hammerton's study of changing patterns of British migration suggests that emigrants no longer necessarily expect to uproot and resettle only once. More and more people are moving on rather than simply out and back. They find their communities of belonging not in a particular locale but in far-flung family ties, or in a sense of being 'citizens of the world'. The technologies of modernity, too, increase our capacity to take ourselves into the world or bring the world into our homes, and strengthen the sense of belonging to a wider community.

The essays in this volume respond to both the limitations and the continuing draw of the nation, acknowledging the erratic mobility and imaginative reach of lives in the world but also considering their significance as 'Australian' lives. Here, however, we encounter a paradox: for on what standard do we judge them to be Australian? Not length of residence, for some came to Australia only late in their adventurous lives; some paused here only briefly amid an administrative or scientific career that spanned the empire. Not the requirement of citizenship, for that was denied to many, and never clearly defined until well into the twentieth century. Not, certainly, a resemblance to the 'typical' Australian, for that beer-swilling, football-loving larrikin has no presence in these pages. Not, even, a primary identification as 'Australian', or a commitment to building a future here: for that criterion, too, would rule out many, though not all, of the individuals whose lives we trace in this volume. Indeed, perhaps the only thing that unites these lives is that they were lived—however briefly—in Australia.

Yet there is, after all, something more. For many, perhaps all, of the individuals in this book, 'being Australian' was a series of questions rather than an emphatic declaration. All of them, in different ways, encountered and asked those questions: what did it mean, for the country and for themselves, that they had lived in or visited Australia? How did that experience entangle with their sense of belonging—tangible, imaginative, nostalgic or aspirational—in a wider world? The writers in this volume pose these questions about individual lives. They are questions that historians—and politicians too—must continue to ask, if we are to better understand Australians' place in a changing world.

Mapping transnational lives

This book focusses on 'lives', yet few if any of the essays in this book recount a life story from birth to death, mapped across a shifting geography of place. Rather, they offer glimpses of a life in motion, or of imaginations at work to bridge physical distance and bring the 'world' and 'Australia' closer together.

Such bridges can be built in many ways. Most obviously, they are forged by the mobility of bodies into and out of Australia: acts of travel, migration or exploration. They are also built from words, structures, ideas and emotions. The essays in this volume are grouped to give emphasis to attachments forged from, and through, acts of authority, intimacy, intellect and imagination.

The section on 'Authority' considers the ways Australians are tied to the world by structures of law, policy and administration. Laws and policies secure power, and act to exclude and define as well as unite. The patterns of colonial authority could cement hierarchical structures and facilitate professional mobility for its officials and administrators, as Julie Evans shows; it could also act to restrict the movements and divide the families of subaltern subjects, unwanted in a 'White Australia'. As Margaret Allen shows in her study of such subjects as Otim Singh, masculinity as well as race was at stake. Cindy McCreery and Nicholas Brown explore the evolving patterns of external authority over and in Australia. McCreery's study of the first royal visit to Australia in 1867 shows how it provoked a shock of awareness on both sides: how strong, on the one hand, were the structures and habits of allegiance; and how strange, nevertheless, were the colonies and their prince to one another. In the twentieth century and a post-colonial age, new structures facilitated a politics of internationalism, and Brown shows how R. G. Watt transcended his Australian location and modest social status to further internationalism as an ideology.

Alongside, and threaded through, such formal ties were the intangible yet powerful bonds of love. Australians were tied to the world by kinship, nostalgia, habit and imagination. Each generation of Australians since 1788 has included many whose first attachments were formed in another place—for whom, therefore, living in Australia, let alone 'being Australian', was a matter of negotiation across rupture. The 'intimate empire', as Gillian Whitlock has argued, is one of 'pleasure, dismay, ambivalence—rarely indifference', and her insights

Introduction

can be extended beyond the empire to encompass a wider diasporic world.[11] It is perhaps not surprising that all the stories of 'Intimacy' in this volume are also stories of migration. The legacy of their attachments was complicated, but hardly obliterated, for succeeding generations. Exploring these complexities, the essays in this section make clear that migration is not simply a story of settling into one place. Maggie Mackellar shows how early Western District settlers continually negotiated the idea of 'home', and sharply reminds us that all their creations were built on, but generally ignored, the destruction of Aboriginal homes that preceded them. Kate Bagnall explores the unhappy marriage of a woman who followed her husband to China; James Hammerton tells the stories of migrants who have followed family around the world, moving on without disrupting familial ties; Alistair Thomson shows the continuing importance of letters to and from family for a British postwar migrant; and Francesco Ricatti explores the place of nostalgia in Italian migrant stories of home and first love. Going out, returning home, moving on, staying still—all entailed cultural tensions, adjustments and divisions, within families and across generations.

Intimacy in a transnational life was often sustained by the exchange of letters and photographs. The section on 'Intellect' considers further how transnationalism was fostered by the circulation of print, and by the sharing of language and culture, within and beyond the empire. The taxonomies of Enlightenment science facilitated botanical adventuring, as Ann Lane shows with her story of the imperial entrepreneur Henry Wickham and his passion for the transplanting and acclimatisation of plants across the globe: rubber, tobacco and the fibrous arghan. Not all intellectual adventurers travelled as widely as did Wickham. The empire of literature was even more powerful. Australians could feed their intellectual curiosity about the world, and foster their cultural awareness and cultural attachments through the world of books—as Mark Hearn shows in his analysis of Alfred Deakin's eclectic and far-ranging reading habits.

The next section on 'Imagination' explores how creative artists have, in Hannah Arendt's memorable words, 'trained their imagination to go visiting'. Reaching out to the world or attaching themselves to communities outside Australia, these artists have—with varying degrees of success—used the force of imagination to develop the 'enlarged empathy' Arendt considered necessary to become 'world citizens'. Nancy Paxton and Susan Carson examine how three noted modernist novelists—Jean Devanny, Eleanor Dark and Christina Stead—explored the relationship between 'home' and 'away'. Mary Besemeres highlights a neglected aspect of travel writing by demonstrating, with reference to works by Gillian Bouras, Sarah Turnbull and John Mateer, the complex power dynamics of 'language travel' that inhibit the traveller's ability to 'go visiting'. Finally, Sally Gray shows how artist David McDiarmid had already inhabited the transnational community of the queer diaspora in his imagination before he joined it in New

York and developed a life and an art that was both mobile and located, neither 'Australian' nor 'American'.

Other themes, not flagged by our section titles, may be traced through many of the essays in this volume. Gender shapes, and is shaped by, particular ways of connecting to the world. The worlds of intellect and authority are not inhabited exclusively by men, but perhaps men have been more inclined, historically, to understand their connection to the world through those frames. The worlds of intimacy and imagination are not inhabited exclusively by women, yet perhaps they have presented women with more opportunities to escape the demands of their local environment than have more public structures of power. Ethnicity emerges, unsurprisingly, as another key issue in the study of transnational lives. Never simple, the negotiation of new attachments and identities was particularly fraught for those coming from outside the Anglo-Saxon world, whose background was strange to the normative 'Australian' and whose right to settle, in every sense of the word, into an Australian life was more open to question and challenge.[12] The essays by Allen, Bagnall, Pybus, Ricatti and the gallery development team explore the negotiation of such cultural crossings.

Tendrils of thought, emotion and experience attached 'Australian' lives firmly to the world. Colonial and national authority have been embedded in global networks of ideas and people; a society of immigrants carries within its heart intricate and intimate attachments to loved people and places across the globe; the world of science and ideas is enmeshed in imperial and global cultures; and Australian imaginations are forged within a realm of fantasy and literature that extends far beyond national boundaries. *Transnational Ties: Australian lives in the world* offers some unexpected answers to the question of what it might mean to be 'Australian', and in so doing opens new perspectives on the nation's transnational history.

Notes

[1] Curthoys, Ann 2003, 'We've just started making national histories, and you want us to stop already?', in Antoinette Burton (ed.), *After the Imperial Turn: Thinking with and through the nation*, Duke University Press, Durham and London, p. 85. See also Curthoys, Ann and Lake, Marilyn (eds) 2005, *Connected Worlds: History in transnational perspective*, ANU E Press, Canberra, pp. 13–15.

[2] Curthoys, 'We've just started making national histories, and you want us to stop already?', p. 86.

[3] Bhabha, Homi K. 1994, *The Location of Culture*, Routledge, London and New York, p. 5.

[4] Hofmeyr, Isabel 2006, 'AHR conversation: on transnational history', *The American Historical Review*, vol. 111, no. 5, December, p. 1444.

[5] Beckert, Sven 2006, 'AHR conversation: on transnational history', *The American Historical Review*, vol. 111, no. 5, December, p. 1459.

[6] Matthews, Jill Julius 2005, 'Modern nomads and national film history: the multi-continental career of J. D. Williams', in Ann Curthoys and Marilyn Lake (eds) 2005, *Connected Worlds: History in transnational perspective*, ANU E Press, Canberra, p. 167.

[7] Gregg, Robert 2003, 'Making the world safe for American history', in Antoinette Burton (ed.), *After the Imperial Turn: Thinking with and through the nation*, Duke University Press, Durham and London, p. 171.

[8] Lambert, David and Lester, Alan (eds) 2006, *Colonial Lives Across the British Empire: Imperial careering in the long nineteenth century*, Cambridge University Press, Cambridge, p. 25.

[9] Richard White (1981, *Inventing Australia*, Allen and Unwin, Sydney, p. 108) argues, for example, that just as Federation was motivated by the desire to unify and access national markets, there was a direct link between the 'nationalist credentials' and 'economic self-interest' of the professional group of writers and artists in late nineteenth-century Australia.

[10] Matthews, 'Modern nomads and national film history', p. 169.

[11] Whitlock, Gillian 2000, *The Intimate Empire: Reading women's autobiography*, Cassell, London and New York, p. 2.

[12] See Schech, Suzanne and Haggis, Jane 2000, 'Migrancy, whiteness and the settler self in contemporary Australia', in John Docker and Gerhard Fischer, *Race, Colour and Identity in Australia and New Zealand*, University of New South Wales Press.

Archival fragments

Chapter 1

The Old Commodore: a transnational life

Cassandra Pybus

'The world is all of one piece,' according to the narrator of *All The Kings Men*, the iconic novel by Robert Penn Warren that was the centrepiece of my doctoral thesis on memory, history and narrative. I reprise it here in order to flag my fascination for the interconnectedness of human experience and my desire to transcend the limitations of the national narrative. For the past decade, my historical inquiry has focused on the lives of expropriated Africans throughout the Anglo-colonial world during the long eighteenth century. My subjects are obscure, illiterate and largely forgotten historical actors, whose lives I try to recover through a hybrid methodology that combines micro history and its attention to the small local archival details with biography that emphasises the primacy of personal agency and individual experience in the push and pull of historical forces. I persevere at this eye-straining and vastly time-consuming process because it is an article of faith that individuals make history, even if they cause no revolutions to be forged, create no dynasties, strike no great poses, and write no books. Without knowing the stories of such people, how can we comprehend our part in the world?

In this chapter I explore the life of one obscure African-American man whose long and varied career carried him many places and concluded in the remote colony of New South Wales. In painstakingly recovering his story from the vast detritus of the archives in three continents, I have sought to present a singular biography of a unique individual that can serve also as a window on the shifting constructions of race and class in the complex, interconnected sphere of the British colonial world.

My narrative does not begin with William Blue's birth, about which I know nothing, though I presume it to have been in New York about 1736.[1] Rather, the narrative begins when Blue was in his early twenties in the spring of 1761. I picture him somewhere in Europe, scrambling across the steep, rocky shore of an unfamiliar island in a futile attempt to storm a heavily fortified enemy garrison, while about him his fellow marines are being cut to pieces by enemy gunfire. With 500 marines dead or captured, the survivors were rowed back to the waiting British ships. Two weeks later, using the advantage of fog cover, the marines led a second, successful assault on an even more inaccessible cliff face. Blue was lucky not to have been one of the 700 killed, though he was probably one of many wounded. Bloodied and traumatised, he still had no idea where he was.

Figure 1.1: Billy Blue, The Old Commodore.

Charles Rodius, 1834. National Library of Australia: nla.pic-an6016496 .

I was able to reconstruct this minor incident from the fag end of the Seven Years War by following clues in the short and inchoate autobiography that Blue left to posterity. In 1823, when he was an old man living on another rocky shore at Sydney Cove, Blue hired an amanuensis to write a petition to Governor Thomas Brisbane. The petition stated:

> Petitioner is now 89 years of Age was in the service of his Majesty King George the third at the time he was crowned And went as a Marreen on the first expedition after his Crownation to Germany, Pet^r was at Queabeck with General Wolf when he was killed, also with Major Andrews when he was taken, And with Lord Cornwallace at Little York in Virginea as a Spie or Guide for his Army, and was also for a considerable time, a Serj^t of Pineneers on the continent. Pet^r was his whole Lifetime in his Majestys Service untill Pet^r came to this colony.[2]

A second version of the petition added that Blue had been twice wounded. Nine years later, Blue explained in his own words to the Magistrate's Court that he had served with General Wolfe and General Howe.[3]

Those historians who have considered Blue's petition have dismissed this illiterate black man's claim to an illustrious military career as strategic lying in order to curry favour with the governor.[4] Certainly, it was not possible for Blue to have been a marine in Germany; the war in Germany was finished by the time George III ascended the throne. I was, however, inclined to take Blue's account at face value because I was familiar with the career of Gustavas Vassa (known to us as Olaudah Equiano), slave-servant to a British naval officer during the Seven Years War, who wrote one of the most famous autobiographies of the late eighteenth century. In *The Interesting Narrative of Olaudah Equiano The African*, he described how his ship sailed into Spithead in October 1760 to join a 'large fleet that was thought to be intended against the *Havannah* [*Hanover*]', and he went on to explain that 'about that time the king died', so the expedition was aborted. The ship and crew waited idly at the Isle of Wight 'till March 1761, when our ship had orders to fit out again for another expedition'.[5] Military records confirm that just a week before the demise of George II, 8000 men were embarked for a secret expedition to Germany, but they disembarked when they received news of the allied defeat at Kloster Kampen. Six months later, after George III had become king, these same troops, including two marine battalions, embarked once more, on 29 March 1761, headed for an unknown destination that many still believed to be Germany. It was only some time after they had taken control of an enemy garrison that their destination was revealed to be Belle Isle, an island off the coast of France. The heavily fortified island proved to be of no strategic value and subsequently the Belle Isle campaign was largely ignored in accounts of the Seven Years War. By 1823 there could be no advantage gained from inventing participation in such a long-forgotten episode.

While no surviving musters or pay lists survive to verify Blue's employment as a marine, the circumstantial evidence strongly supports his claim. A search of the surviving records of the marine divisions reveals that the strength of the marine companies was seriously compromised by mass desertion during the long wait and, immediately before the fleet departed, a ruthless press was instigated.[6] Blue was a stranger to England who had probably arrived as a seaman, without any legal or community protection—all of which made him a perfect fit for the press-gang.[7] He was easily mistaken in geography; as an illiterate man from America, he probably never understood that Belle Isle was not in Germany. He might not have lingered long enough to find out the name of the place. Given the extraordinarily high casualty figures among marines, this was probably one of the occasions when Blue was wounded and so was sent straight back to England to be discharged as unfit.

If Blue is to be believed, this was not his first bloody battle, as he claims to have been at the earlier battle of Quebec, where General Wolfe was killed on 13 September 1759. Blue was originally from New York, a colony that raised independent companies of more than 9000 men for the war.[8] Inevitably, blacks found their way into these companies as free men who willingly signed up for the bounty paid, as slaves substituting for reluctant whites or as slave runaways who had absconded to enlist.[9] This explanation does not, however, allow for Blue to have arrived in England by the time of King George III's ascendance to the throne. It is far more likely that he was one of the many African-Americans recruited as seamen.

The sudden and hurried dispatch of a massive British fleet to the St Lawrence River in February 1759 left many ships shorthanded. In April 1759, Rear Admiral Charles Holmes was sent to New York specifically to find additional recruits.[10] A black man in his early twenties, slave or free, was an ideal recruit, whether a volunteer or a victim of the 'hot press'.[11] Blue could have been recruited as a boatman, as these were in great demand, or as a cook, barber, tailor or fiddler. He could have been one of the many officers' servants, just like Gustavas Vassa, who was engaged in the earlier siege of Louisbourg on the St Lawrence. All these ship's 'idlers', as they were called, were used in active combat during the siege: they fed the cannons that pounded the French defences, carried troops and supplies from place to place, acted as scouts for the army and were used as the decoys that distracted the French at the final assault. After the capitulation of Quebec, the ships left on 21 September 1759. Since the official documentation tended to identify only the warships and rarely the names of any of the many transport ships, frigates, brigs and sloops, it is impossible to locate the muster lists for the majority of the fleet, so we cannot know for certain whether Blue was aboard. If he were, he would have arrived in England to be paid off just before the death of George II, on 25 October 1760.[12]

The Old Commodore: a transnational life

What then of Blue's claim to have been 'with Major Andrews when he was taken, And with Lord Cornwallace at Little York in Virginea as a Spie or Guide for his Army'? These slivers of autobiography place him at two of the most famous episodes of the American Revolution: the capture and execution of Major André as a British spy in New York in 1780 and the ignominious defeat of Lord Cornwallis in Virginia in 1781. In addition, Blue's verbal account of having served under General Howe places him in America as early as 1776, when William Howe was the British Commander-in-Chief. What happened to him between 1761 and 1776 and what is the evidence for Blue's military service in those years?

Blue's sense of temporal sequence was about as good as his geography. The answer can be found in his final claim to being 'for a considerable time, a Serj^t of Pineneers on the continent'. At first, this made no historical sense until I chanced upon a clue that showed Blue's enigmatic claim provided the key to the veracity of his account. I knew that a British expeditionary force was raised from among troops at Belle Isle to fight alongside the Portuguese army in 1762. When I was searching among the sparse documents relating to this episode, I found a request from the Portuguese commander for non-combatants to provide logistical support services to the British force.[13] In response to this request, two officers who had resigned their regimental commission in order to be attached to the Portuguese army raised a company of 100 'pioneers' in Britain. This corps of pioneers was quasi-military and not part of the formal army structure, so there were no records—regimental, departmental or otherwise—to indicate who was recruited and what happened to them. Few people, other than those directly involved, would have known that this irregular corps was deployed on the Continent in the last months of the Seven Years War or that, along with the British officers, they stayed with the Portuguese army for many years after. So, once again, Blue was providing information known only to those directly involved.[14]

In May 1775 the first wave of the British army invaded the American colonies, led by three brigadier generals: Henry Clinton, a political appointment; John Burgoyne, a veteran of Belle Isle and Portugal; and William Howe, who had served at Quebec and Belle Isle. Howe's order book clearly indicates that a pioneer corps was attached to the army. Nearly one year later, Howe led a massive assault of British troops and Hessian mercenaries to take New York.[15] Howe's order for the occupation of Manhattan on 18 October 1776 stated that 'the Pioneers of the Army are constantly to march at the head of each brigade'.[16] This is obviously how Blue came to return to America and presumably he stayed within the huge British garrison in New York until 1780. In late September of that year, the dashing Major John André was sent up the Hudson River to secretly negotiate with the American turncoat Benedict Arnold. When André was captured and subsequently executed as a spy, the entire British army was

7

plunged into shock and grief. The young officer's charisma, as well as his gallantry in the face of ignoble death, even won the admiration of his captors. Popular songs celebrating the bravery of 'Major Andrews' were sung on both sides of the ideological divide. Of course, Blue could not have been present at André's capture, since André was alone at the time. Blue could, however, have been a member of a corps of pioneers attached to the British garrison at Stony Point, which was just near the place on the Hudson River where the fateful meeting and later arrest took place. Whether Blue was on duty at Stony Point, or in the garrison at New York, the emotional effect could have been so profound that 50 years later he believed that he was part of these dramatic events.

His claim that he was 'with Lord Cornwallace at Little York in Virginea as a Spie or Guide for his Army' is also easily resolved. He would have gone to Virginia at the beginning of 1781, when the turncoat General Arnold was dispatched to Virginia with a force of 1600 men to establish a naval base at Portsmouth. For this operation in enemy territory, Arnold wanted black spies who would blend unobtrusively into the local population. Certainly, he took black pioneers with him from New York and he recruited others in Virginia, all of whom were later transferred to the army of Lord Cornwallis on the march through Virginia to catastrophe at the garrison Cornwallis established on the bluff above the York River.[17] After Cornwallis's ignominious surrender, this besieged garrison was instantly memorialised as Yorktown. Very few people outside Virginia ever knew that the small town Cornwallis chose for the British garrison was originally known as Little York. It is very telling that it was this anachronistic name that Blue used in his 1823 petition.

The Articles of Capitulation signed by Cornwallis stipulated that nearly 9000 soldiers and sailors be detained in Virginia as prisoners of war, and only officers were paroled. HMS *Bonetta* was permitted to sail immediately for New York with Cornwallis's dispatches and several ships were allowed to take the officers. Cornwallis arranged for the black spies and guides to be secreted on these ships and taken to New York to avoid retribution.[18] It was certainly not safe for Blue to stay in America once the British began to leave and he would have left New York for England during the hasty evacuations of 1782 and 1783, probably working as a seaman on one of the British ships desperate for crew. Such was the chaos of the Loyalist evacuation of some 150,000 people that no proper records were kept.

Like many other black seamen, Blue fetched up in Deptford, an impoverished maritime district of London that was geared towards serving the needs of the huge naval dockyard, where warships were built, refitted and supplied. Many merchant ships also moored off Deptford, even though the cargo had to be unloaded upriver, on the north side of the river, where the customs houses were. Even before the American Revolution, Deptford had a noticeable black presence, which swelled rapidly with the discharge of thousands of African-American seamen from the Royal Navy and the privateers in 1783 and 1784.[19] In the period immediately after the American Revolution, the two Deptford parishes registered a tenfold increase in the number of black adult baptisms.[20] Within a year or so of arrival, almost all were out of work and living by their wits in an alien and uncongenial environment.

It was a desperate predicament to be unemployed in England in 1784, when the labour force was swamped with demobilised soldiers and sailors. The black refugees from America who flooded the city had no support networks on which they could draw, and their situation was worsened because they did not fit easily into the existing framework of the Poor Laws. Blue joined an indigent black community eking out a precarious existence without access to poor relief. The bitter winter of 1784–85 was especially cruel for those struggling to survive on whatever could be begged, borrowed or stolen.[21] The plight of indigent black people in London became a matter of public concern in 1786, when the Committee for the Relief of the Black Poor was formed to provide a relief payment of sixpence a day, paid weekly out of Treasury coffers. Blue was one of the first to sign on for the bounty of three shillings and sixpence, travelling across the river to Mile End to collect it. He was listed as number 50 of the 659 people to whom payments were made throughout August 1786.[22] As many of these black refugees were unhappy about finding themselves marooned in a destination they had not chosen, the idea took root among the committee members to relocate them to a new colony to be established in Sierra Leone, on the west coast of Africa. Blue chose not to join the emigration to Africa. After 4 September 1786, his name no longer appeared among those listed as receiving the bounty.

Nor did Blue choose to willingly immigrate to the colony being established at exactly the same time at the opposite end of the globe. Like most early settlers to New South Wales, Blue was an immigrant who arrived in chains, having been sentenced in 1796 to seven years' transportation for stealing sugar. At that time, England was engaged in an exhausting war with France, but Blue had not enlisted in the army or navy, as he was too old to serve. When he was arrested, he was working as a lumper on the West Indian ships. Why then did he insist he had always been in His Majesty's service before his transportation?

In attempting to resolve this conundrum, I literally stumbled over the crucial evidence in the National Archives when I was searching for the meaning of Blue's nickname. It had always been assumed that 'the Commodore' referred to his long employment as the ferryman at Sydney Cove, but Blue himself suggested the moniker predated his time in the colony. 'I got the name of the Commodore for being in charge of the old *Enterprise* at Tower-hill,' he told the Magistrate's Court in Sydney in 1832.[23] A search of the National Maritime Museum database established that in the 1790s HMS *Enterprise* was a hospital ship moored on the

River Thames, just below the Tower of London. The musters of the *Enterprise* at the museum, however, yielded next to no information: each book had only a few pages listing the 20 or so crew, none of whom were named Blue.

Old muster books are very heavy and very dirty items, rarely consulted by historians. As I was lugging one filthy book back to the counter, I stumbled slightly and it fell open at the back pages where I saw hundreds of names listed under the heading 'Supernumerary'. Looking closely, I realised that these were the names of sailors who were aboard for one night only. Beside their name was written the letter 'P' and the name of a naval lieutenant. There were five such lieutenants named in the lists. By cross-searching the admiralty records, I established that these were the half-pay officers responsible for the operation of London press-gangs. I realised I had stumbled onto the records of an impressment ship. Ten muster books later, I had counted more than 34,000 men impressed on that one ship between 1792 and 1796.[24] I could see no connection between press-gangs and Blue's nickname until I searched the Old Bailey online for the use of the term 'commodore'. Here I found multiple references to a non-naval use to refer to the man in charge of gangs of men labouring in the warehouses lining the Pool of London, or as a term used by seamen to describe the leader of a gang of sailors ashore. In this context, it became apparent that Blue was indeed in the king's service: he must have been in charge of one of the press-gangs of the *Enterprise*. It was disreputable, casual work, but it could be profitable. Deptford was a very promising hunting ground for a press-gang. From 1793, business was brisk and the money earned would have been good. By September 1796, however, this source of income was severely reduced by the introduction of the *Quota Acts* that required each city to provide a set number of men for service. London's quota was achieved largely by reprieving convicted criminals. By the time the Impressment Service returned to strength, Blue was a member of a different gang: the chain gangs put to work raising gravel from the bed of the River Thames.[25]

In order to make ends meet, Blue took on the dangerous seasonal work as a lumper on the ships that carried merchandise from the West Indies. Lumpers unloaded the cargo of the merchant ships that moored side by side in the Thames in tiers of seven or eight. All cargo was offloaded onto lighters and taken to the riverside warehouses. Lumpers were among the lowest-paid workers in London; shipowners did not even provide them with food or drink, requiring them to go ashore for their unpaid food breaks. Compensation for the poor lot of the lumper was the toleration of small-scale plundering, referred to in the business as drainage, spillage or leakage—hence the other connotation of the word 'lumper': a pilferer of cargo. A couple of regular trips ashore during the day for sustenance gave lumpers the opportunity to relieve the cargo of small quantities of merchandise, a practice that was customarily regarded by all parties as an element of the wage.[26] Generally, merchants allowed up to 2 per cent of the shipped weight to disappear as spillage. It was a fine balance. Small quantities taken regularly were acceptable, but larger amounts were regarded as plunder, which was how Blue came to grief. Even though he protested the customary rights of spillage on his arrest, claiming that 'all the lumpers had some sugar', he was singled out because he took too much, too often.[27] Four times on 26 September as he was leaving the *Lady Jane Halliday* to go ashore, the mate had taken a 20-pound (9 kilogram) bag concealed under the voluminous smock worn by Blue.

Blue was just the type of lumper of whom West Indian merchants deeply disapproved: someone engaged in vertical integration, able to create a commercial opportunity from lowly, life-threatening labour on their ships. As he explained in his deposition, Blue also traded in Deptford as a chocolate maker. Almost certainly he lumped on the West Indian ships that imported cocoa beans from plantations in Jamaica, where he would have found the large quantity of beans required. For 80 pounds (16 kg) of sugar, he would need 100 pounds (45 kg) of ground cocoa, which together would have produced as much as 180 pounds (82 kg) of chocolate—nothing less than a serious commercial enterprise. When the case came before the Kent Assizes, the judge and jury were reasonably well disposed to the defendant, although they did not believe that Blue was guiltless. He was found guilty of only one charge of stealing sugar and sentenced to seven years' transportation to New South Wales. He spent nearly five years on the prison hulks before he finally embarked on the *Minorca* for New South Wales in 1801.

A search of the Colonial Secretary's correspondence reveals that Blue received his conditional pardon in 1803. The *Sydney Gazette* indicates that he moved into a small house located in the steepest part of The Rocks, where he applied his energy to various small-time enterprises, including the collection and sale of oysters.[28] At that time, at least half a dozen ships from London, New York, Providence, Calcutta, Madras and China were always at anchor in Sydney Cove.[29] In the shadow of these large sailing ships, which represented the infant colony's lifeline to the outside world, there were several smaller colonial vessels that plied the coastal routes between Sydney, Newcastle and Hobart. Among the hulls of these seagoing vessels, a plethora of small craft bobbed and weaved over the water, transporting people and goods hither and thither. In this unregulated watery space, Blue sought to make his mark, setting himself up as a waterman, ferrying passengers and goods from ship to shore and back again.

By July 1804, Blue was living with Elizabeth Williams, a woman of about thirty, who arrived in Australia at the end of June that year on the female transport *Experiment*. Governor King encouraged free men to look for partners among the new arrivals as a way of accommodating the relatively small number of female convicts arriving in the colony and Elizabeth moved directly into Blue's small dwelling in the turbulent Rocks. They married on 27 April 1805, and their witnesses were Edwin Piper, a former convict who had been with Blue on the *Minorca*, and his wife, Dulcibella, who was free. Blue's daughter, Susannah, was born shortly after.[30]

From his work in the cove, Blue could look up and see his house. On the morning of 31 July 1805, he was 'tugging at the oars' when he sensed something amiss at home. He hurried to his house to discover his wife had been raped, or so he said in his charge against a man named in the *Sydney Gazette* as McKay. The case was heard by the judge advocate, who was assisted by a bench that included the collector of the jail fund, John Harris, a man who held other important colonial positions. Blue explained to the bench that on the day in question 'looking towards his house he saw his wife struggling with someone'. On rushing back to the house, he found his wife 'walking about with the baby in her arms', and she told him that 'McKay had carnal knowledge of her without her consent'. Elizabeth Blue maintained that McKay called at her house and after some conversation pulled her to the floor and raped her. Dulcibella Piper was visiting at the time, and her testimony contradicted this, claiming only that McKay 'took [Elizabeth] by the waist and she fell down and some conversation passed between them'. George Darling, who claimed to have been with McKay at the time, supported Piper's evidence. If a rape had occurred, 'he must have seen it', he said, emphatic that he saw no such thing. A neighbour gave evidence that he overheard the incident and further reported that McKay wanted to send Blue to jail and that Blue was looking for revenge. Finally, Chief Constable John Redman reported that Blue told him that, on entering the house, 'he saw his wife lying on the floor with her petticoat up'—a different story from that offered to the court.[31]

Daniel McKay lived close to Blue. He made his money retailing spirits in a public house that was kept by his convict wife, who had arrived with Elizabeth Blue on the *Experiment*.[32] This man was well placed to threaten Blue with jail: he was the town jailer, possessing a well-deserved reputation as a hard man. John Harris was a close business associate of McKay and the witnesses were all indebted to him one way or another and had good reason to give overly consistent testimony that contradicted Blue's evidence. The *Sydney Gazette* reported that the case against McKay was dismissed and concluded that the attempt to frame the innocent McKay 'left no doubt that Mr Blue's centre was several shades darker than his superficies'.[33] There were, however, significant people in Sydney who regarded Blue's challenge of McKay as a sign of his moral integrity. One of them was the new governor, William Bligh. One of Bligh's first actions in the colony was to remove Harris from of all his offices and to incarcerate McKay in his own jail.[34] Bligh, who was not known for his soft heart, explained that he had removed McKay 'out of motives of humanity'.[35] Blue, in contrast, suffered no retribution other than the scorn heaped on him by the *Sydney Gazette*, and his economic and social standing saw a marked improvement. The *Sydney Gazette* of 2 August 1807 carried an advertisement that William Blue was 'the only waterman licensed to ply a ferry in this harbour'.[36]

Where Blue found grace and favour with the new governor, few others did. On 26 January 1808, Bligh faced his second mutiny when the NSW Corps placed him under arrest. For a day or so, soldiers were kept busy escorting people to the barracks to sign the ex post facto petition imploring the military to arrest Bligh. Among the 150 signatures, written in neat and fluent letters, was the name 'William Blue'. Someone had forged this name, probably without Blue's knowledge or consent, since he was completely illiterate and could sign only his mark. Rather than join the chorus of assent, Blue was more likely to have kept his head down and his opinions to himself, waiting for the inevitable recriminations to begin.

Blue emerged as a winner from the new order that took shape when Lachlan Macquarie stepped ashore on the morning of the last day of 1809. On 17 August 1811, the governor announced that Blue was appointed the watchman and waterborne constable of Sydney Cove.[37] With the new position came a hexagonal stone house built at the edge of the governor's domain, where Blue and his growing family lived rent-free for the next eight years.[38] By 1814, it was well known that Blue had become a favourite of Macquarie. Blue personified the governor's vision of the reformed convict, the figure who would become the backbone of the orderly and respectable society he aimed to create in New South Wales: a hardworking entrepreneur who had, with all propriety, married his convict partner and bestowed legitimacy on his children. There was, however, something more profound in the governor's friendship with this illiterate ferryman: a bond of shared experience.

Macquarie began his military career at age fifteen, and he saw service immediately in America in a regiment raised in New York from veterans of a Highland regiment from the Seven Years War. By 1781 he was a lieutenant in the Seventy-First Regiment of Foot, another Highland regiment, which first saw action in the invasion of New York in 1776 and later served at the garrison at Stony Point, where Blue might also have been stationed. Several companies of the Seventy-First marched away with Cornwallis to disaster at Yorktown. It is feasible that Macquarie and Blue were caught in the dreadful siege and were among the lucky few evacuated by ship to New York. Blue provided a glimpse of this relationship with Macquarie in evidence he gave in a court case in 1832. He and the governor 'were always together', he explained, and it was a relationship of equals: 'I was just the same as the governor. He never countermanded any orders of mine…he built the little octagon house at the corner of the domain for my especial accommodation.' The sense of intimacy was captured in Blue's observation that 'the Governor had a bit of the "old brown" in him'.[39]

This reminiscence also provided Blue with the opportunity to describe the exchange in 1814, when he asked the governor to give him land for his ferry terminus at Millers Point:

> 'Please your honour,' says I, 'I want a landing place.' 'Well come,' says he, 'Show me the place.' And so, when I showed him the place, 'Jemmy,' says he to [Surveyor] Meehan, 'run the chain over the Commodore's land.' Lord bless you. We were just like two children playing.[40]

Blue ended the intriguing vignette by dissolving into laughter, which might have encouraged the magistrates to think it was a piece of tomfoolery. Not so. In the colonial secretary's correspondence is a letter from Macquarie dated 23 April 1814, giving instructions that Blue should receive a grant of 80 acres (32 hectares) of land. Other evidence locates the land in question at Millers Point. In January 1817 Blue received another 80 acres on the opposite side of the cove, now a notable landmark called Blues Point. These grants made him a relatively substantial and very well-appointed landowner; the number of his little ferryboats had grown to seven.[41]

Blue had clandestine sources of income in addition to his public duties, ferry business and farms on his land on either side of the harbour. This became apparent in the early hours of the morning of 10 October 1818 when he was arrested for smuggling 120 gallons (546 litres) of rum. The *Sydney Gazette*'s report of the case hummed with outrage about 'this unfortunate man Blue…a man of colour with a very large family, who has been very much indebted to the humane feeling with which his Excellency the governor has for many years been pleased to view him'. In the editor's view, the crime 'was more than usually criminal', as Blue was a constable, appointed 'for the purpose of *detecting* or *preventing* smuggling'. Blue was clearly the victim of the entrepreneur who possessed the capital, contacts and infrastructure to run a successful smuggling enterprise. The pity was he steadfastly refused to give any names. When the constables tried to persuade Blue to inform on the person who had inveigled him into carrying smuggled goods, he drew the side of his hand across his throat in a quick motion, saying, 'I would suffer this first.'[42]

Blue's determined silence might be read as the loyalty of a member of the criminal class to his accomplices, but an examination of the commercial world of Sydney in 1818 suggests a rather different reading. The captain of the suspect ship had come to the attention of the authorities before for engaging in contraband trade. At the time of his first offence, his employer had been a business partner of D'Arcy Wentworth, the superintendent of police and one of those who sat on the bench in judgment of Blue. Another of Wentworth's partners was the magistrate Alexander Riley, whose brother Edward was an agent for the importation of Bengal spirits. Besides the partnership with Riley, Wentworth had a longstanding commercial arrangement with the third magistrate, Simeon Lord, described by a previous governor as a notorious smuggler. So, many of the plausible contenders for smuggler-in-chief were sitting before Blue, passing judgment on the man and his crime, and relying on his silence. As the hand across the throat signified, he knew silence was the most sensible strategy for long-term survival and comfort. The magistrates submitted the case to the governor with a forceful recommendation for mercy and Blue suffered no custodial sentence, though he was evicted from the pleasant stone house.[43]

In his disgrace, Blue still possessed his ferry business and his land. He even managed to regain the friendship of the governor in the few short years before Macquarie's recall in February 1822. Once Macquarie quit the colony, the sharks began to circle Blue's enterprise. A wealthy free settler successfully demanded of magistrates Riley and Wentworth that the ferry be put in the hands of more a trustworthy person. Blue fought back with a petition to Governor Thomas Brisbane, on 28 October 1823, protesting the gentlemen's use of 'arbitrary power' and emphasising his age, his illustrious military record and his service to Governor Macquarie. On inquiry, the colonial secretary was persuaded by the argument that the north shore was a magnet for escaped convicts, ships' deserters and stolen goods, and that Blue was 'the principal agent in carrying into effect this system of plunder, smuggling and escape'. Blue, however, persisted in asserting his rights and, on 25 January 1825, the *Sydney Gazette* announced he had regained use of his ferry service.[44]

In March 1827, Blue was a widower with six children to support when he again petitioned the governor to take his sons into an apprenticeship at the shipyard, as a carpenter and a shipwright. When this was refused, the wealthy merchant Simeon Lord stepped into the breach, taking both boys as apprentice weavers, even though Blue was too poor to purchase their indentures. Perhaps Lord recalled with gratitude Blue's stubborn silence in the smuggling case nine years before.[45] It was about this time that Blue took to walking about Sydney wearing a travesty of a naval uniform with a top hat, twirling the carved stick he always carried and calling out in a peremptory fashion to all and sundry that they must acknowledge him as 'the commodore'.

Blue was far from senile, as he showed in 1827, when he won a writ for £12 against a Sydney gentleman for unpaid ferry fees. Nor did the magistrate's bench think he had lost his wits when it issued a summons against him for harbouring a runaway convict in early July 1829. Understanding, perhaps, that notoriety was his best defence, Blue became increasingly ostentatious in his displays of eccentricity. On 15 December 1829, the *Sydney Gazette* noted that 'Billy Blue, the Commodore of Port Jackson, has of late grown uncommonly eloquent; scarcely a morning passes without a loud oration from his loyal lips'. He had also adopted the habit of boarding ships that arrived in the harbour, wearing his tattered uniform and top hat, to welcome the captain in his official capacity as commodore. As such, Blue expected to receive 'suitable homage from all of His Majesty's subjects, as befitted a man of his position', the *Sydney Gazette* explained. Twirling his stick and declaiming, 'True Blue forever,' the old man demanded that men salute, children doff their hats and women curtsy. Any who failed to respond suffered a cascade of salty abuse. This highly subversive performance, calculated or not, had the curious effect of endearing Blue to all levels of Sydney society.[46] When Baron von Hügel landed in Sydney in 1834, he was confronted by an old black man standing in the middle of the street with a sack over his shoulder, 'saying something crazy in a loud voice at every passer by'. On inquiring about this disreputable apparition, the European aristocrat could scarcely believe his ears when he was told that this was 'the old commodore whom Governor Macquarie appointed port captain'.[47]

Within days of Blue's death on 6 May 1834, the *Australian* newspaper announced that J. B. East's fine portrait of the old commodore was on public view. East was a painter of some renown who had exhibited at the Royal Academy and his painting captured a tall, graceful man with intelligent eyes and a beatific smile, dressed in rag-tag clothing with a cloth bag slung over his shoulder and carrying a carved stick. East positioned his subject beside Mrs Macquarie's Chair in the Domain, an obvious acknowledgment of Blue's patron, Governor Lachlan Macquarie, with distant harbour views to remind the viewer of Blue's position as the commodore. It was the view of the *Australian* that the portrait 'ought to be preserved in Government House or some other institution'.[48] Two colonial newspapers wrote affectionate obituaries, but it was the *Sydney Gazette*, in which Blue had often been vilified, that produced the most glowing tribute. The paper dedicated two full columns to 'the gallant old commodore', extolling Blue as a founding father of New South Wales, whose memory would be 'treasured in the minds of the present generation, when the minions of ambition are forgotten in the dust'. Indulging in high-flown prose, the editor told the readers of the *Sydney Gazette* that 'the reign of Billy is coeval with the foundation of the colony'.[49]

For the modern historian, it is utterly incongruous that such extravagant praise, the use of the word 'reign' and a commemorative portrait meant for Government House should be reserved for a disreputable ex-convict and multiple offender who was poor, illiterate and black as the ace of spades. It runs counter to everything our national history would lead us to expect. The transnational biography of Billy Blue is a fine example of how an individual life, examined in grainy detail, can confound what we historians like to think we know about the past.

Notes

[1] It was said Blue was aged between ninety-seven and ninety-nine years at his death in 1834. The evidence of Blue's place of birth comes from Susannah Scofield, granddaughter of Blue, who provided a document reproduced in the *Star* (21 September 1808) stating that Blue had told her father that he was born in New York.

[2] 'The Humble Petition of William Blue...', State Records of New South Wales (hereafter SRNSW), 17 November 1823, CS R6052, 4/1764, p. 21; and 21 and 28 October 1823, CS R6017, 4/5783, pp. 438–40.

[3] Blue's later claims are made in evidence given in the civil case *Martin v. Munn*, reported in *Sydney Gazette*, 25 October 1832

[4] See Duffield, Ian 1999, 'Billy Blue: power, popular culture and mimicry in early Sydney', *Journal of Popular Culture*, vol. 33, no. 1 (Summer); and Swords, Meg 1979, *Billy Blue*, North Sydney Historical Society, Sydney.

[5] Carretta, Vincent 2005, *Equiano, the African: Biography of a self-made man*, University of Georgia Press, Athens, pp. 68–70.

[6] Marine recruitment for Belle Isle, The National Archives of the Government of the United Kingdom (hereafter TNA), WO1/16, ADM 2/1157, WO1/165.

[7] The coronation of George III took place after the fleet had sailed, but Blue was not to know that; it was enough that he knew George III was the new king.

[8] For the evidence of New York's contribution, see Anderson, Fred 2000, *Crucible of War: The Seven Years War and the fate of empire in British North America, 1754–1766*, Faber & Faber, London, pp. 227, 318–21, 473, 529, 795.

[9] Runaway-slave notices of the period mention slaves absconding to enlist: see *New York Gazette*, 30 May 1757. See also Hodges, Graham Russell and Brown, Alan Edward (eds) 1994, *'Pretends to be Free': Runaway slave advertisements from colonial and revolutionary New York and New Jersey*, Garland, New York.

[10] The reference to Holmes' ships in New York, as well as ships being 'weak-handed', is contained in the letter of General Wolfe to the Admiralty, 6 June 1759, quoted in Wood, William Charles Henry (ed.) 1909, *The Logs of the Conquest of Canada*, Champlain, Toronto, p. 110. For information about the wide-scale recruitment of sailors in New York, I am indebted to Matthew Ward at the University of Dundee, author of *The Battle for Quebec, 1759: Britain's conquest of Canada* (2005, Tempus, London).

[11] For information on the crisis in maritime labour in 1759 and the regular resort to the 'hot press', see Gradish, Stephen F. 1980, *The Manning of the British Navy During the Seven Years War*, Royal Historical Society, London.

[12] The musters are held in TNA, ADM 36.

[13] Ligonier to Townshend, 26 June 1782, TNA, SP 89/57.

[14] See Francis, A. D. 1981, 'The fantasy war of 1762–63: the campaign in Portugal', *Journal for the Society for Army Historical Research*, vol. 59, no. 237, (Spring).

[15] For the evacuation, see 'William Howe's General Order Book', TNA, WO 36/5.

[16] Kemble, Stephen 1883 [reprint], 'The order book of Lt. Col. Stephen Kemble, Adjutant General of the British forces, 1775–1778', *Collections of the New-York Historical Society for the Year 1883*, vol. 16, New-York Historical Society, New York, p. 389.

[17] See 'Memorial of Walter Harris', TNA, PRO AO 12/99/33; and 'Mary Willing Byrd to Jefferson' in Boyd, Julian P. (ed.) 1954, *The Papers of Thomas Jefferson. Volume 4*, Princeton University Press, Princeton, pp. 690–92.

[18] Walter Harris and Thomas Johnston each gave the Loyalist Claims Commission an account of being smuggled out on the *Bonetta*: see TNA, AO 12/99/334; and AO 13/ 70b1/301–2.

[19] The majority of the black claimants to the Loyalist Claims Commission were seamen from the Royal Navy.

[20] There is no doubt that Blue was baptised, but I have not found his baptismal notice in England. He was probably baptised in America.

[21] For the death of indigent blacks, see Braidwood, Stephen J. 1994, *Black Poor and White Philanthropists: London's blacks and the foundations of the Sierra Leone settlement 1786–1791*, Liverpool University Press, Liverpool, p. 32.

[22] Payment lists, 14 August – 4 September 1786, TNA, T1/635.

[23] The quote is from *Martin v. Munn*, Supreme Court of New South Wales, 22 October 1832, reported in the *Sydney Gazette*, 25 October 1832.

[24] For the records of the *Enterprise*, see TNA, ADM 102.208, ADM 36/15418–28.

[25] The records of Old Bailey trials also suggest that the press-gangs in London were less aggressive in the period 1796–97; see www.oldbaileyonline.org

[26] My understanding of lumping and customary spillage owes much to Linebaugh, Peter 1992, *The London Hanged: Crime and civil society in the eighteenth century*, Cambridge University Press, New York, pp. 416–25.

[27] Indictment of William Blue, Kent County Archives (hereafter KCA), Q/SIW 422; Deposition of William Blue, 29 September 1796, KCA, Q/SB 225.

[28] Blue's emancipation is listed in the *Register of Pardons and Tickets of Leave*, SRNSW, vol. 1/540–41. In 1804, Blue gave evidence in two court cases concerning violent disturbances between his neighbours in The Rocks, both reported in the *Sydney Gazette*.

[29] For shipping in Sydney, October–November 1803, see *Historical Records of New South Wales* (hereafter *HRNSW*), vol. 5, p. 288.

[30] Marriage and Baptism Register of St Philips Church, Sydney.

[31] Trial of Daniel McKay, Judge Advocate's Bench, 17 August 1805, SRNSW, R 656, 601.

[32] Daniel McKay arrived on the *Royal Admiral* in 1792. In 1810, he petitioned the colonial secretary for amelioration of sentence for his common-law wife, Judith Quinlan, from the *Experiment*.

[33] *Sydney Gazette*, 18 August 1805.

[34] Harris to King, 25 October 1807, *HRNSW*, vol. 6, p. 343.

[35] Bligh to Castlereagh, 30 June 1808, *Historical Records of Australia*, vol. 6, p. 533. The men were immediately reinstated after Bligh's arrest.

[36] Blue's ferry was the first of its kind in the port; *Sydney Gazette*, 2 August 1807.

[37] Notice, 17 August 1811, SRNSW, CS SZ758, Reel 6038, 226.

[38] 'The Humble Petition of William Blue…', 17 November 1823, SRNSW, CS R6045, 4/1735, 151.

[39] This was not a racial reference; it expressed the sense that Macquarie shared some of the qualities of poor folk. In the argot of the late eighteenth century, a 'brown' was a copper halfpenny.

[40] The quotes from *Martin v. Munn* were reported in *Sydney Gazette*, 25 October 1832.

[41] For Blue's various grants and appointments, see SRNSW, CS R6048, 4/1742, 42, and R6045, 4/1735, 151.

[42] Case against Blue, Court of Criminal Jurisdiction, 'Informations, Depositions and Related Papers', 10 October 1818, SRNSW, COD 445, SZ795, 421–35.

[43] John Wylde to Lachlan Macquarie, 16 October 1818, SRNSW, CS R6047, 4/1741, 47–50; John Wylde to Lachlan Macquarie, 30 October 1818, SRNSW, CS R6047, 4/1741, 76–7.

[44] William Gore to Edward Wollstonecraft, 23 September 1824, SRNSW, CS R6056, 4/1765; Blue's petitions to Governor Brisbane are from 28 October 1823, Reel 6017; 4/5783, pp. 438–40, and 17 November 1823, SRNSW, CS R6045, 4/1735, p. 151; Colonial Secretary to Wollstonecraft, 6 December 1823, SRNSW R6011 4/3509.

[45] 'The Humble Petition of William Blue…' to Governor Darling, 12 March 1827, SRNSW, Box 4/1926, Item 27/2898.

[46] Other descriptions are from Blue's obituary in the *Sydney Gazette*, 8 May 1834.

[47] Baron von Hügel (*New Holland Journal*) is quoted in Flannery, Tim (ed.) 1999, *The Birth of Sydney*, Text Publications, Melbourne, p. 251.

[48] *Australian*, 8 May 1834.

[49] *Sydney Gazette*, 8 May 1834.

Authority

Politics and the law have been core components of Australians' connections beyond colonial and national boundaries. Life stories offer vivid insights into the ways colonial careers, the rule of law, governing men, political ideologies and movements, and repressive policies all connected residents and visitors in Australia to other parts of the world. Julie Evans' careful scrutiny of the writings of Edward John Eyre forms the basis of her argument that colonialism not only impelled officials to move around the empire, it undergirded connected hierarchical structures that unified the British colonies even as they varied. Margaret Allen looks at governance from the perspective of subaltern lives restricted by racist immigration policies, particularly the White Australia Policy in its first decades. The men whose stories she has recovered, such as Otim Singh, divided their lives between Australia and India, often at the cost of separation from their families and restriction on their movements, as well as assumptions about their inferior masculinity. Cindy McCreery unpacks accounts of the 1867–68 visit of the Duke of Edinburgh to Australia to demonstrate that British royalty had its own particular transnational connections, and that imperial loyalty to Britain itself was one part of colonials' sense of themselves as globally situated. The dedicated internationalist R. G. Watt, Nicholas Brown reveals, exemplified the early twentieth-century belief that bodies such as the League of Nations and the United Nations offered the best hope to avoid repeating the catastrophes of the world wars. Through his organisational building, talks and promotion, Watt transcended his Australian location and modest social status to further internationalism as an ideology. These chapters reveal individuals whose lives linked Australia to other parts of the world through authority in its multiple facets.

Chapter 2

Biography and global history: reflections on examining colonial governance through the life of Edward Eyre

Julie Evans

Edward John Eyre (1815–1901) is in many ways the iconic Australian explorer. Against all odds, he walked across the vast Nullarbor Plain, battling the vagaries of the desert climate and the unforgiving landscape to 'open up' the country from Adelaide to Albany. Although he was born into a very different life in England, by his early twenties he had already made a name for himself as an overlander of sheep and cattle half a world away in the Antipodes, forging stock routes through the outback of the south-eastern colonies in the 1830s. Uncharacteristically for the times, he gained a reputation for befriending Aborigines, a practice that helped him survive that extraordinary 'journey of exploration' for which he is still best known within conventional accounts of Australia's past.[1] The naming of the Eyre Highway and Lake Eyre still commemorates his feat of endurance on maps and landmarks although its precise historical significance is perhaps diminishing within the popular imagination.

This familiar narrative places Eyre fairly easily within local explorer historiography, in the company of other ambitious young men from the 'old world' who were intent on making better futures in the 'new'. Few of these explorers, however, acknowledged so openly the role of the Aborigines in supplying vital food and water or engaged so willingly with their different ways of knowing the world. While their personal dispositions might have differed, all these men were nevertheless representatives of European civilisation and progress, reporting back to investors and settlers in burgeoning towns along the coast—as well as in distant England—the potential of the surrounding country to support pastoral expansion, to be wrested from the so-called strictures of primitive land use and be converted into productive private property. Accordingly, the lives of these individuals can no more be seen in parochial terms than can the histories of the nations whose foundations they establish.[2] They were men who, in living out their hopes and dreams in the colonies, were also the ferrymen of the global market economy.

In seeking to look beyond the constraints of the nation when considering the life of an individual, *Transnational Ties: Australian lives in the world* invites us to reflect, too, on the possibilities that biography presents for the writing of global histories. This mix of genres might seem odd in that it seeks to bring together two apparent oppositions of conventional social inquiry: is it the individual agent or the broader social structure that should be accorded priority in explaining human experience?[3] Such calls to bridge the divide regarding 'the forces that have shaped the modern world'[4] are of course by no means new. The historian Morris Cohen argued 60 years ago (with the class and gender assumptions of the time intact) that

> in studying the individual life of an outstanding man, we may be studying social forces in their clearest expression. The real problem is not whether history is to be written as the biography of great men or as a tracing of social forces, for the great men are precisely the points of intersection of great social forces.[5]

The sociologist C. Wright Mills similarly exhorted us to adopt an integrated approach, although the intention in his case was to advance prospects for social justice by empowering individuals through their appreciation of the significance of their historical position and its relationship with their present circumstances:

> We have come to know that every individual lives, from one generation to the next, in some society; that he lives out a biography, and that he lives it out within some historical sequence. By the fact of his living he contributes, however minutely, to the shaping of this society and to the course of its history, even as he is made by society and by its historical push and shove.
>
> The sociological imagination enables us to grasp history and biography and the relations between the two within society. That is its task and its promise…No social study that does not come back to the problems of biography, of history, and of their intersections within a society, has completed its intellectual journey.[6]

If grasping the relationship between history and biography has the potential to enhance understanding of enduring social inequalities, it is difficult to conceive of a field of inquiry in which the task is more urgent than the history of settler societies, such as those Eyre helped advance at the beginning of his career. In the Australian case, Indigenous peoples continue to fare far worse in the contemporary era than the majority of the population on every indicator of social disadvantage, a characteristic that is common to the native peoples of New Zealand and North America, who share a similar history of dispossession and dislocation.[7] Meanwhile, heated debates about the telling of the national story[8] have seen revisionist and post-colonial critiques[9] drawn ever more controversially into the public domain. While issues of sovereignty, self-determination and land rights in settler societies remain contentious internationally and domestically,[10] however, the problems arising from settler colonialism seem to excite far less interest in the former heart of empire, where mainstream imperial historiography remains relatively detached.

The historian Nicholas Dirks commented recently that '[w]hen imperial history loses any sense of what empire meant to those who were colonised, it becomes complicit in the history of empire itself'.[11] Dirks was drawing particular attention not only to the recent popular books and television productions of Niall Ferguson, whose robust advocacy of Western civilisation radically discounts past colonial violence and oppression, but to that level of academic distance that characterises conventional texts such as *The Oxford History of the British Empire*. Such influential accounts of Britain's past, Dirks claims, not only ignore the empire's troubling legacies in the present; they fail to acknowledge the reciprocity of empire whereby European economies and ideologies developed in response to, rather than in isolation from, colonialism.[12]

That such anxieties and presumptions about colonial pasts appear themselves to be specific to time and place further highlights the need to appreciate more fully the consequences of European expansion from the late fifteenth century to the present. In this sense, Eyre would be a rich subject for historical inquiry even if he had simply stayed in Adelaide and had been content to build up his holdings and prestige in the local community, which was so assiduously extending its control beyond the initial settlement. Eyre proceeded, however, to develop a career in colonial administration that took him from a modest post in 1842 as Resident Magistrate and Protector of Aborigines (a reward for his journey of exploration) to a number of increasingly important government appointments in New Zealand, St Vincent, Antigua and Jamaica, where his repressive policies culminated in his violent suppression of the Morant Bay rebellion in 1865 and eventually led to his recall to England. The notorious 'Eyre controversy' prompted three years of public and legal disputes over his actions in Jamaica. His 'trans-colonial' experience therefore makes Eyre that much more fruitful as a subject of analysis in that the story of his life does not simply represent the generalised concerns of capital in a settler society such as Australia. It also forces us to acknowledge that his role in Australia's constitution as a nation—to say nothing of Britain's role as coloniser—was simply part of the vast and multifarious imperial endeavour in which Europe was engaged as it set about normalising and universalising its interests abroad.

Accordingly, as I have argued in more detail elsewhere, Eyre's personal readings of the colonial encounter throughout his career help clarify the nature and purpose of colonial governance by locating in time and place its characteristic discursive features, its responsiveness to specific economic imperatives and its association with particular modes of violence and coercion.[13] That is, my broader research on Eyre's interventions in Australia, New Zealand and the Caribbean engages centrally with the questions of agency and determination that have long preoccupied the social sciences.[14]

I focus my present reflections on how two conventionally separate styles of historical writing, biography and global history, might be helpfully enmeshed to examine the strategies and techniques of colonial governance—while also alerting us to their contemporary manifestations—through the life of Edward Eyre.

Methodological considerations

Given the title of this book, it is perhaps important to note that I understand my methodological approach to be comparative rather than 'transnational'—a term I have been reluctant to employ in the colonial context where its use seems anachronistic in the sense that it anticipates a status that is still in the process of formation.[15] I argue that it is this formative stage of nationhood that demands closer scrutiny, particularly in terms of explaining how and why Britain's commitment to the rule of law was so severely tested—and indeed could break down completely—while sovereignty was still in the process of being secured. In seeking further detachment from the 'comfortable frame' of the nation,[16] my use of comparative historical inquiry also directs attention to the common and distinctive ways in which racialised laws and practices were called on to fulfil European ambitions in the lands of others.

In facilitating analysis of how the nation is constituted in different colonial contexts, a comparative approach must also do more, of course, than simply extend the bounds of geographical inquiry. Each site should be clarified mutually through the comparison so that detailed examination of their substantive similarities and differences demonstrates how broad-based economic and ideological factors were expressed locally. For instance, historical analysis has the unique capacity to specify the complex circumstances in which race develops, to unearth detailed evidence of how such ideas about social differentiation are grounded in very material concerns and in association with particular disciplinary regimes. Moreover, in relation to colonial governance in the British Empire, it seems additionally important to be able to say how and why ideas about race took different forms in different colonies and performed different functions in Britain than elsewhere.[17]

In his book *The Comparative Imagination*, George Frederickson describes his approach to comparative history as one that 'combines elements of cultural contrast and structural analysis' involving 'the interaction between the peculiarities of culture and ideology on the one hand and the recurrent and generalisable structural factors on the other'.[18] To this end, I argue that Eyre's contrasting perceptions of the colonial encounter in Australia and the Caribbean reflect the particular nature of the economic interests that were at stake in each place and the different modes and rhetoric of governance he considered necessary to uphold them.

The following thoughts about my way of understanding Eyre's career focus on the operations of two key concepts of colonial governance—race and the rule of law—and conclude by considering their continuing significance as primary measures of social justice in Australia and elsewhere.

Biography, historiography and global history

In terms of the relationship between biography and history, my work on Eyre sets out to examine how the idiosyncratic characteristics of one individual interacted with the more general economic, social and political interests that he was employed to pursue.

Although Eyre came from a respectable background—his father was vicar at Hornsea and Long Riston in East Yorkshire—the family's straitened economic circumstances limited his prospects for advancement in England. Rather than pursue a career in the army, Eyre opted for a life of adventure in the colonies and, in 1833, at the age of seventeen, he found himself in New South Wales learning all he could about farming in the outback. By 1839, Governor Gawler of South Australia asked him to explore the regions around Adelaide and, within two years, Eyre felt honoured to be leading the expedition to the northern reaches of the Flinders Ranges and eventually across the Nullarbor Plain towards the west of the continent. He was proud, too, of his subsequent appointment as Resident Magistrate and Protector of Aborigines at Moorunde, outside Adelaide, which formally recognised his contributions to colonial development and seemingly vindicated his decision to fulfil his ambitions abroad.

On his return to England, Eyre's experiences in the Australian colonies led him to feel optimistic about a career in colonial administration. Conscious of his economic vulnerability within Britain's class structure, his modest social status still worried him but seemed set to improve with his appointment as Lieutenant Governor in New Zealand in 1847. He was delighted when Miss Adelaide (Ada) Fanny Ormond, whom he had met through his fellow explorer Charles Sturt, set sail from Plymouth to become his wife. Dark clouds were, however, on the horizon. Ever alert to the significance of petty distinctions in the colonies, the local elite scorned Eyre's entry into polite society. Judge Chapman commented, for example: 'In person he is tall, very thin, and not well made—with a tip-toeing awkward gait. He is narrow chested and has a bad tailor which makes things worse. His countenance is not agreeable and he has what phrenologists call a bad head.'[19] Charlotte Godley also derided Ada's apparent pretensions when hosting a ball: 'At the top of the room was a sofa on which Mrs Eyre sat, without rising to receive anyone, bowing to some, and shaking hands with the more illustrious (such as ourselves).'[20]

Figure 2.1: Eyre and Wylie, one of his Aboriginal companions.

Gordon H. Woodhouse, c. 1910 – c. 1950. Colour glass lantern slide. State Library of Victoria. Image no. b13773.

While such local snobberies were relatively trifling, more serious rifts soon appeared in Eyre's relationship with his superior, Governor George Grey. In time, professional and personal disagreements overwhelmed their relationship until Grey virtually withdrew Eyre's authority and his prospects for promotion looked bleak.[21] It is not difficult to see why Eyre's experiences in New Zealand did little to lessen his sensitivity to criticism, especially when he felt misrepresented and misjudged. As Charlotte Godley again observed, 'He seems a very good sort of person only rather wanting in tact and very anxious to do the right thing by everyone.'[22] Indeed, throughout his career, Eyre wrote copiously and often to the Colonial Office, defending his actions against a range of detractors. He was by no means alone in this practice, but the persistent indignation of his correspondence sets him apart.

After waiting two years for his requested transfer, Eyre was offered a post as Lieutenant Governor in the Caribbean colonies. He arrived on the island of St Vincent with Ada and their two children in 1854. Ada did not, however, adjust well to the tropical climate, so when they returned to England on leave in 1857 she decided to stay there with the children. Eyre continued on in the Caribbean alone, writing his memoirs in his tiny, spidery script[23] and trying to overcome his disappointment on hearing that Sir George Bowen had been made Governor of Moreton Bay in 1859, a position for which he felt uniquely qualified and that he had dearly wanted for himself and his family. After a brief period as Lieutenant Governor in Antigua, and many requests to the Colonial Office for promotion and extended periods of leave in England, he was finally rewarded with the acting governorship of Jamaica in 1862.

Ada joined him this time and, with five children now in tow, they embarked on the most turbulent period of their lives. In the next few years, Eyre would be embroiled in a number of public controversies and would turn increasingly to repressive measures to secure his authority. After the so-called Morant Bay 'rebellion' in October 1865, Eyre declared martial law, but the prolonged display of violence that followed prompted a Royal Commission into his actions. Eyre was dismayed by this turn of events, given the strong support he had formerly received from the British Government and his conviction that he had acted to prevent a massacre of the white population. As Henry Taylor from the Colonial Office later observed, Eyre would have been quite 'unconscious of the view…taken by the public and the press in this country. By this time [early December] it will have dawned on him.'[24]

Figure 2.2: Edward John Eyre, 1865, the year of the Morant Bay rebellion.

Copy print, carte de visite. Mitchell Library, State Library of NSW: CY3190Ae99.

Figure 2.3: Edward John Eyre c. 1900

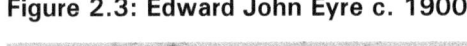

Silver gelatin print. Mitchell Library, State Library of NSW: CY3190Ae911

Though Eyre was never formally indicted, he faced years of action in the courts.[25] His career had come to an ignominious end and he retired to Devon until his death in 1901, the year of Australia's nationhood. Ada and their five children survived him.

How can we best analyse historically these seemingly straightforward biographical details of Eyre's life as an explorer and administrator in the British Empire? Just as Eyre's personal notoriety after the Morant Bay rebellion drew attention away from the issues that fuelled it, the subsequent historiography can inhibit analysis of the implicit violence of colonialism and its continuing ramifications in the present.[26] Nation-bound studies, for example, often sensationalise Eyre's career, describing him either as a heroic explorer and advocate for the Aborigines in Australia or as a brutal and racist governor in Jamaica. Where the full range of his experiences is remarked on, scholars tend to regard Eyre as an individual whose sense of personal duty explained his actions, or as the personification of certain race, class, gender and religious interests that played out reciprocally in England and the colonies.[27]

While acknowledging these important insights, my intention has been, rather, to de-centre the powerful figure of Eyre the individual in order to bring the more commonplace violence of colonialism more fully to the fore. Accordingly, my comparative analysis suggests that Eyre's individual preoccupations—as a person and as an administrator—at once increased his personal vulnerability to criticism and undermined British interests by exposing rather than concealing the coercive techniques of governance that were deployed throughout the empire.

The comparative model

Eyre and colonial governance in the Australian settler colonies

As Patrick Wolfe has explained, settler colonialism is a unique colonial formation wherein settlers seek to 'replace' natives on their land. Unlike in plantation colonies, in settler colonies Europeans sought a permanent stake in the land, rather than the more detached opportunity simply to exploit its resources.[28] Accordingly, in the Caribbean colonies, Britain's interest lay in securing a cheap labour force (initially through slavery but, post-emancipation in 1834, through waged labour), but in the Australian colonies, the priority was wresting exclusive control of the land.[29] Within this comparative structural framework, Eyre's administrations highlight the central issues at stake in the colonial governance of settler and plantation economies.

In the Australian case, Eyre's writings demonstrate how the Indigenous population's claims to sovereignty could threaten British intentions if they could not be suitably diminished. That is, while his *Journals of Expeditions of*

Discovery[30] put forth the case for Aboriginal sovereignty, his later pronouncements outline a system for ensuring its rapid demise. In the remote desert regions, Eyre came to depend on Aborigines for his very survival. While some explorers might have been less willing to expose themselves in this way,[31] Eyre's openness to expressing his vulnerability led him to seek other ways of knowing the land, enabling him to survive in extraordinarily harsh circumstances by locating mounds of edible eggs among the desert dunes, for example, or collecting early morning dew from native bushes. It was during this period that Eyre came to appreciate more fully Aboriginal peoples' attachments to land and the 'injustice…of the white man's intrusion upon [their] territory'. Explaining their actions in defending their sovereign presence, Eyre asserted that 'our being in their country at all is, so far as their ideas of right and wrong are concerned, altogether an act of intrusion and aggression'.[32] In recognising that 'our presence and settlement, in any particular locality, do, in point of fact, actually dispossess the aboriginal inhabitants', Eyre makes a further plea against settler violence against them:

> That as we ourselves have laws, customs, or prejudices, to which we attach considerable importance and the infringement of which we consider either criminal or offensive, so have the natives theirs, equally, perhaps, dear to them, but which, from our ignorance or heedlessness, we may be continually violating, and can we wonder that they should sometimes exact the penalty of infraction? [D]o we not do the same? [O]r is ignorance a more valid excuse for civilized man than the savage?[33]

Eyre openly dismissed the universalist pretensions of the law of nations (as international law was then known) as 'a law that provides not for the safety, privileges, and protection of the Aborigines, and owners of the soil, but which merely lays down the rules for the direction of the privileged robber in the distribution of the booty of any newly discovered country'.[34] Once he became Resident Magistrate and Protector, however, Eyre soon reined in the troubling implications of his earlier outspokenness. In assuming more direct responsibility for colonial interests, Eyre not only set about 'pacifying' the overland route so that more and more settlers could arrive from the east. He also wrote a companion volume to his journals entitled *Manners and Customs of Aborigines and the State of their Relations with Europeans*.[35] In contrast with his earlier criticisms, Eyre now sought to bolster British sovereignty in two key ways: through the discursive containment of Aboriginal claims and the administrative regulation of their lives and culture.

Eyre explained that only the elders were legitimate sovereigns. While lamenting the 'fatal and melancholy effect which contact with civilisation seems ever to produce upon a savage people',[36] only Aborigines 'in their natural state' could retain a sovereign presence in the Australian colonies. It was 'a matter of deep regret', he continued, 'to see them gradually dwindling away and disappearing before the presence of the Europeans'.[37] Meanwhile, those Aborigines who were no longer able to live a traditional lifestyle would be subject to management by the State, whose 'duty' was to break down Aboriginal culture: 'I cannot persuade myself, that any real or permanent good will ever be effected, until the influence exercised over the young by the adults be destroyed, and they are freed from the contagious effects of their example.'[38] State control of Aboriginal people could be achieved through their isolation on reserves. If found in Adelaide without permission, they 'should be taken up by the police and slightly punished', although they would be rewarded for sending their children to school or for giving up 'the performance of any of their savage or barbarous ceremonies upon their children'.[39]

In their entirety, Eyre's Australian writings indicate that British and Aboriginal claims to sovereignty—understood as exclusively European under international law—were incommensurable.[40] His ultimate rejection of Aboriginal sovereignty was based on the idea of an authentic Aboriginality that racialised Indigenous peoples in such a way as to reduce their challenge to British interests. As others have also elaborated, this powerful notion still informs the operations of race in the Australian context, where recent recognition of native title favours the state by limiting eligibility to those who can prove continuous attachments to land and culture after generations of dispossession.[41] Eyre's recommendations for encouraging cultural breakdown, meanwhile, were eventually reflected in the type of bureaucratic regulation that would characterise Aboriginal peoples' lives in Australia well into the twentieth century and beyond.[42] Laced here and there with a menacingly mundane coercion, such procedures made a mockery of Britain's claim that, no matter their lack of political rights, Aborigines were British subjects who were nevertheless entitled to the equal force and protection of the law.

Eyre and colonial governance in the plantation colonies of the Caribbean

Eyre's quite different understanding of the challenge to British sovereignty in the Caribbean, on the other hand, reflects the structural distinctions between colonies of settlement and colonies of exploitation. As observed above, in plantation economies, British economic interest lay in controlling the labour rather than the land of the colonised population. Moreover, whereas the urgency to defend British sovereignty in settler colonies such as Australia commonly diminished over time, as settler hegemony increased, the end of slavery in the middle decades of the nineteenth century served to further destabilise governments in the Caribbean. Emancipation had not only required Europeans to reformulate labour relations, it meant facing the fact that while Europeans had always been outnumbered in the Caribbean, the people they had once enslaved had been notionally transformed into free, fully sovereign individuals who could potentially vote them out at the ballot box. A history of riots and rebellions had long unnerved the local elite, but once freedpeople (as ex-slaves were known) could no longer be openly coerced, their demographic strength had to be reckoned with in different ways.

When Eyre arrived on St Vincent in 1854, 20 years after emancipation, it was clear that freedom meant little more than a simple release from servitude. There were few changes in the political order, while freedpeople who wanted to establish themselves as an independent peasantry were forced by colonial governments to labour for wages in the faltering plantations. Eyre's sensitivity to the need to entrench British rule, already well honed through his experiences in Australia and New Zealand, was heightened by evidence of growing discontent in the community and his consciousness that Europeans formed such a small minority. As conditions worsened, Eyre decided that exercising his authority at the least sign of resistance would not only demonstrate his worthiness as a representative of the British Crown, it might be the only way to stem a more generalised rebellion that risked bringing down British sovereignty altogether. Throughout his administrations in the Caribbean, as we have already seen in the Australian case, the limits of a disinterested, universal rule of law would once again be tested and race would similarly be deployed in the defence of British interests.

When Eyre became responsible for governing the larger and more volatile colony of Jamaica in 1862, tensions were already widespread. In the next few years, economic depression exacerbated the hardships of the people. Eyre extended sentences for poverty-related crimes such as theft and vagrancy, authorised the use of whipping and the treadmill, and established voluntary militias 'which could at any time be called out in aid of the civil power to suppress any riot or disturbance'.[43] Eyre's relentless enforcement of his authority, however, ironically reduced its effectiveness, openly displaying to a disaffected population the government's ultimate dependence on force. Public opposition to Eyre's repressive measures gathered momentum.

Eyre's growing insecurity was also evident in the way he spoke of freedpeople. In 1864, he described ex-slaves as a peasant 'class' who would be eligible for equality once they could demonstrate 'civilised' values. He trusted that with help from the missionaries they would soon become 'as industrious as honest as truthful as virtuous as are the peasantry of any other Country'.[44] By the next year, however, as protests about social conditions in Jamaica increased, Eyre described them as a 'race' of people 'only just emerging from...a state of barbarism', whose antisocial behaviour appeared impervious to reform. Accordingly, their economic distress—and Jamaica's decline—might well be due not so much to external circumstances as to 'something very wrong and defective both in the habits and the character of the people'.[45] This shift from the social category of class to the biological category of race indicated that freedpeople's inferiority, which had once been evident in their slavery, was now considered to be immutable, effectively reinstating their susceptibility to repression.

The British Government and the local elite supported Eyre's administration despite protests by some clergy and missionaries that the widespread distress in the colony had to be addressed by other measures. By October 1865, in Morant Bay, when armed protesters burnt down the court house, liberated prisoners and murdered local officials, the European population's long-held fears of a widespread rebellion prompted Eyre's declaration of martial law. Once the extended display of deaths, floggings and house burnings could no longer be condoned in England, however, Eyre relied yet again on race to justify his actions. In evidence to the Royal Commission, he described freedpeople as 'a race little removed in many respects from absolute savages'.[46]

By the time Eyre left the colony early the next year, prospects for more a democratic social order in Jamaica seemed more remote than ever. In the aftermath of Morant Bay, the assembly had decided to stem once and for all the uncertainties of representative government post emancipation, by voting to revoke its own powers and revert to the perceived safety of crown colony rule.

Sovereignty, race and the rule of law

The disinterested principles of the rule of law purported to distinguish the British Empire from the more brutal undertakings of its rivals. When analysing the 'transnational' dimensions of Eyre's career within the comparative framework adopted above, however, Eyre's writings in Australia and the Caribbean appear consistent in their defence of interests that were far from universal.

As I have argued elsewhere, calls to suspend the rule of law for Aborigines alone accompanied the spread of pastoralism throughout the Australian continent.[47] Indeed, colonial law helped shore up British sovereignty and secure the transfer of the land by countenancing a host of discriminatory provisions otherwise condemned in law. These consisted not only of the types of bureaucratic repression outlined above, they included legislation that made Aborigines subject to summary justice with no rights of appeal, the banning of testimony and the condoning of exemplary executions, and even outright declarations of martial law—and all of this quite apart from the unregulated violence of the frontier.

Meanwhile, although Eyre's apparently exceptional resort to maximal repression in Jamaica has tended to dominate historical inquiry into his Caribbean administrations, a comparative approach places such so-called 'emergencies' in a global historical context and demonstrates their relative ubiquity in colonial situations.[48] Such an analysis identifies the real extent of racialised violence that was deployed in upholding British interests throughout the empire, while also directing attention to the very notion of emergency—no less now than in the past—in justifying the suspension of the rule of law and the use of discriminatory procedures.

Eyre's participation in these broader practices attests to his awareness of the strategic significance of law and race in supporting British sovereignty and authority at critical points of colonial development. In Australia, his use of the notion of 'authenticity' underscored his proposals to deny Aboriginal peoples' culture and sovereignty and authorise their subjection to British rule. In the Caribbean, on the other hand, his construction of the alleged 'immutability' of freedpeople's inferiority helped deliver them up for renewed repression, thereby reconciling their troubling sovereign subjecthood to the demands of the plantation economy in the post-emancipation era.

Moreover, while the capacity of the rule of law to tolerate exceptional provisions on the basis of race is particularly clear in the colonies, such techniques of governance are, of course, by no means confined to the past. In the Australian case, in recent years, race and law have once again acted as prominent signals of discrimination against Indigenous peoples,[49] asylum-seekers, refugees and other minority groups in the defence of the national interest. Similarly, Eyre's abandonment at the hands of the British Government, which had condoned his actions in Jamaica until his exposure of the law's violence was no longer tolerable domestically, is also telling in the present. As Terry Eagleton recently observed in relation to the demonising force of the notion of 'terrorist', for example, the classic idea of the 'scapegoat' makes it possible for the law, and the nation's citizens who put their faith in that law, to turn a blind eye to structural injustice:

> The scapegoat is a living image of society's polluted and disfigured humanity, at once guilty and innocent: guilty because it subsumes to itself the crimes of society as a whole that are off-loaded onto it, but innocent because the more it does that, the more it frees society from guilt and therefore the more morally admirable it is.[50]

Finally, analysing the relationship between biography and history with reference to the concepts of race and the rule of law helps clarify the European-ness of present-day understandings of sovereignty, whose lineage is enmeshed not merely in the British context we have discussed here, but in centuries of broad-based Western expansion. As long as sovereignty's history as a 'discourse of conquest'[51] can still be transcended in law, and its exclusivist claims remain unchallenged, nation-states will continue to call on its legitimising force to deny the aspirations of Indigenous peoples, and other minority groups, to exercise their sovereignty. We need look no further than the refusal of Canada, Australia, New Zealand and the United States to adopt the UN *Declaration on the Rights of Indigenous Peoples*, for example, to understand the contemporary import that questions of indigenous sovereignty still hold for settler states. By seeking to look beyond the self-serving confines of nationalist frameworks, however, it becomes possible to appreciate just how comprehensively, and for how long, indigenous disadvantage has been manufactured to serve the interests of others.

Notes

[1] I am grateful to Patricia Grimshaw for her thoughtful reading and suggestions and to the editors and anonymous referees for their comments.

Eyre was always eager to meet with local people when passing through their country. His expeditions also comprised a number of Aborigines including Wylie, Cootacah, Neramberein, Joshuing, Unmallie, Kour and Warrulan. Originally from King George's Sound, Wylie was the only person to complete the long westward journey with Eyre. Wylie went on to become a native constable in the area and Eyre eventually arranged for him to receive government rations. Wylie was another of the King George Sound travellers whom Tiffany Shellam discusses in Shaking hands on the fringe: negotiating the Aboriginal world at King George's sound (2008, PhD Thesis, The Australian National University); and 'Manyat's "sole delight": travelling knowledge in Western Australia's southwest, 1830s', in Desley Deacon, Penny Russell and Angela Woollacott (eds), *Transnational Lives* (under review). Warrulan was the son of Tenberry whom Eyre met at Moorunde. Drawings of Wylie and Tenberry and his family are included in Eyre's *Journals*. At the end of 1844, Eyre undertook to educate Kour and Warrulan in England, where, unfortunately, Warrulan died. Kour later returned to Australia. Little further is known of Eyre's relationships with these individuals, or of their attitudes or those of their families to accompanying Eyre on his expeditions or to England. Aboriginal people played a largely unacknowledged role in exploration, acting as guides, interpreters and emissaries. See Reynolds, H. 1990, *With the White People: The crucial role of Aborigines in the exploration and development of Australia*, Penguin, Melbourne; and Schaffer, K. 2001, 'Handkerchief diplomacy: E. J. Eyre and sexual politics on the South Australian frontier', in L. Russell (ed.), *Colonial Frontiers: Indigenous–European encounters in settler societies*, Manchester University Press, Manchester, pp. 134–50.

[2] For a comparative study of the effects of dispossession in the settler societies of Australia, New Zealand, Canada and South Africa, see Evans, J., Grimshaw, P., Philips, D. and Swain, S. 2003, *Equal Subjects, Unequal Rights: Indigenous peoples in British settler colonies, 1830s–1910*, Manchester University Press, Manchester.

[3] Carr, E. H. 1961, *What is History?* Macmillan, London, p. 25.

[4] Fredrickson, G. M. 1997, *The Comparative Imagination: On the history of racism, nationalism, and social movements*, University of California Press, Berkeley, p. 9.

[5] Cohen, M. R. 1961, *The Meaning of Human History*, The Open Court Publishing Company, Chicago, p. 221.

[6] Mills, C. W. 1970, *The Sociological Imagination*, Penguin, Middlesex, p. 12.

[7] The 1991 Royal Commission On Aboriginal Deaths In Custody and *Bringing Them Home: Report of the national Inquiry into the Separation of Aboriginal and Torres Strait Islander Children from Their Families* (1996), together with landmark judgments such as *Mabo v. Queensland* (1992), unequivocally relate Indigenous disadvantage to the historical experiences of colonisation and dispossession.

[8] In Australia, a recent conservative backlash has called for the return of a more celebratory view of the nation's foundations. See, for example, Windschuttle, Keith 2002, *The Fabrication of Aboriginal History. Volume 1. Van Dieman's Land 1804–1847*, Macleay Press, Paddington; and Connor, M. 2005, *The Invention of Terra Nullius: Historical and legal fictions on the foundation of Australia*, Macleay Press, Paddington. For responses to this, see Macintyre, S. and Clark, A. 2003, *The History Wars*, Melbourne University Publishing, Carlton; and Manne, R. (ed.) 2003, *Whitewash: On Keith Windschuttle's Fabrication of Aboriginal History*, Black Inc., Melbourne.

[9] Early examples include Rowley, C. D. 1970, *The Destruction of Aboriginal Society*, Penguin, Melbourne; 1970, *Outcasts in White Australia*, Penguin, Melbourne; and 1971, *The Remote Aborigines*, Penguin, Melbourne; Reynolds, Henry 1982, *The Other Side of the Frontier: Aboriginal resistance to the European invasion of Australia*, Penguin, Melbourne; 1987, *Frontier: Aborigines, settlers and land*, Allen & Unwin, Sydney; and 1987, *The Law of the Land*, Penguin, Melbourne; Carter, P. 1987, *The Road to Botany Bay: An essay in spatial history*, Faber & Faber, London; and Thomas, N. 1994, *Colonialism's Culture: Anthropology, travel and government*, Melbourne University Press, Melbourne.

[10] In February 2008, in the 'spirit of reconciliation', newly elected Australian Prime Minister, Kevin Rudd, issued a national apology to members of the Stolen Generations who had been 'separated' from their families (see Endnote 7). Meanwhile, the previous conservative federal government's 'intervention' in the Northern Territory continues (see Endnote 49) with certain modifications. In June 2008, the Canadian Prime Minister, Stephen Harper, also apologised for a century of boarding school policies and practices, which similarly sought to break down indigenous cultures. Unlike his Australian counterpart, Harper promised $2 billion in compensation.

[11] Dirks, N. B. 2006, *The Scandal of Empire: India and the creation of imperial Britain*, Belknap Press, Cambridge, Mass.,p. 332.

[12] Ibid., pp. 330–2. For accounts that deal with the reciprocity of empire, see, among others, Armitage, D. 2000, *The Ideological Origins of the British Empire*, Cambridge University Press, Cambridge; Cooper, F. and Stoler, A. L. (eds) 1997, *Tensions of Empire: Colonial cultures in a bourgeois world*, University of California Press, Berkeley; Hall, C. 2002, *Civilising Subjects: Metropole and colony in the English imagination, 1830–1867*, Polity, Oxford; and Lester, A. 2001, *Imperial Networks: Creating identities in nineteenth-century South Africa and Britain*, Routledge, London. It is worth noting that Seeley reminded his students at Oxford more than a century ago that 'the expansion of England involves its transformation' and that 'England owes its modern character and its peculiar greatness from the outset to the New World'; Seeley, J. R. 1883 [1931], *The Expansion of England: Two courses of lectures*, Macmillan & Co., London, pp. 93, 102. See also Elliott, J. 1991, *National and Comparative History, An inaugural lecture delivered before the University of Oxford, 10 May 1991*, Clarendon Press, Oxford.

[13] See Evans, J. 2002, 'Re-reading Edward Eyre: race, resistance and repression in Australia and the Caribbean', *Australian Historical Studies. Special Edition. Challenging Australian Histories*, vol. 24, no. 120, (June), pp. 411–34; and 2005, *Edward Eyre, Race and Colonial Governance*, Otago University Press, Dunedin.

[14] Key figures in the social sciences including Herbert Spencer, Karl Marx, Emile Durkheim and Max Weber engage theoretically with these questions. For examples in history, see Thompson, E. P. 1963, *The Making of the English Working Class*, Victor Gollancz, London; and 1978, *The Poverty of Theory, and Other Essays*, Monthly Review Press, New York. In sociology, see, for example, Giddens, Anthony 1976, *New Rules of Sociological Method: A positive critique of interpretative sociologies*, Hutchinson, London; and 1984, *The Constitution of Society: Outline of the theory of structuration*, Polity, Cambridge. For a joint analysis of Thompson and Giddens, see Sewell, Jr, William H. 1990, 'How classes are made: critical reflections on E. P. Thompson's theory of working-class formation', in H. J. Kaye and K. McClelland (eds), *E. P. Thompson: Critical perspectives*, Temple University Press, Philadelphia, pp. 50–77.

[15] Alternative views are discussed in Lake, M. 2003, 'White man's country: the trans-national history of a national project', *Australian Historical Studies*, no. 122, (October), pp. 346–63.See also Curthoys, A. and Lake, M. (eds) 2006, *Connected Worlds: History in transnational perspective*, ANU E Press, Canberra; and Darian-Smith, K., Grimshaw, P. and Macintyre, S. (eds) 2007, *Britishness Abroad: Transnational movements and imperial cultures*, Melbourne University Press, Melbourne.

[16] See the Introduction to this volume.

[17] My broader work on Eyre engages with this in more detail: see Endnote 13. See also Wolfe, P. 2003, 'Land, labor, and difference: elementary structures of race', *American Historical Review*, vol. 106, no. 2, (June), pp. 866–905.

[18] Fredrickson, *The Comparative Imagination*, p. 9. See also Cooper, F. and Stoler, A. L. 1997, 'Between metropole and colony: rethinking a research agenda', in Cooper and Stoler, *Tensions of Empire*, pp. 1–56.

[19] Cited in Dutton, G. 1982, *In Search of Edward John Eyre*, Macmillan, Melbourne, p. 57.

[20] Ibid., p. 62.

[21] I discuss the details of Eyre's administration in New Zealand in *Edward Eyre, Race and Colonial Governance*.

[22] Cited in Lawson, I. 1954, An examination of the administration of Edward John Eyre as Lieutenant Governor of the Province of New Munster, New Zealand, 1848–53, MA Thesis, Victoria University College, p. 68.

[23] Eyre, E. J. 1859 [1984], *Autobiographical Narrative of Residence and Exploration in Australia, 1832–39*, Edited and with an introduction and notes by J. Waterhouse, Caliban Books, London.

[24] Henry Taylor to Mary O'Brien, 2 December 1865, Henry Taylor Papers, Folio 65, Bodleian Library, Oxford.

[25] See Semmel, B. 1962, *The Governor Eyre Controversy*, Macgibbon & Kee, London.

[26] Semmel's work on Morant Bay is an exception. See also Guha, R. 1994, 'Dominance without hegemony and its historiography', in R. Guha (ed.), *Subaltern Studies VI: Writings on South Asian history and society*, Oxford University Press, Delhi, pp. 210–309.

[27] See Dutton, *In Search of Edward John Eyre*, and Dutton, G. 1977, *Edward John Eyre: The hero as murderer*, Penguin, Melbourne, first published as *The Hero as Murderer: The life of Edward John Eyre, Australian explorer and Governor of Jamaica, 1815–1901* (1967, Collins, Sydney); and Stokes, E. 1993, *The Desert Coast: Edward Eyre's expedition 1840–41*, Five Mile Press, Melbourne. See also Hall, *Civilising Subjects*, and Hall, C. 1996, 'Imperial man: Edward Eyre in Australasia and the West Indies, 1833–66', in B. Schwarz (ed.), *The Expansion of England: Race, ethnicity and cultural history*, Routledge, London, pp. 130–70; and Lorimer, D. A. 1978, *Colour, Class, and the Victorians: English attitudes to the negro in the mid-nineteenth century*, Leicester University Press, Leicester.

[28] Wolfe, P. 1999, *Settler Colonialism and the Transformation of Anthropology: The politics and poetics of an ethnographic event*, Cassell, London, pp.1-7.

[29] This is not to say that Aboriginal labour was not also called on to support settler interests in certain times and places. See, for example, May, D. 1994, *Aboriginal Labour and the Cattle Industry: Queensland from white settlement to the present*, Cambridge University Press, Melbourne; Berndt, R. M and Berndt, C. H. 1987, *End of an Era, Aboriginal Labour in the Northern Territory*, Australian Institute of Aboriginal Studies, Canberra; and McGrath, A. 1987, *Born in the Cattle: Aborigines in cattle country*, Allen & Unwin, Sydney.

[30] Eyre, E. J. 1845 [1964], *Journals of Expeditions of Discovery into Central Australia, and Overland from Adelaide to King George's Sound, in the years 1840–1; Sent by the Colonists of South Australia, with the Sanction and Support of the Government: Including an account of the manners and customs of the Aborigines and the state of their relations with Europeans*, 2 volumes, T and W. Boone, London [Libraries Board of South Australia, Adelaide, facsimile edition](hereafter *Journals Vol. 1* or *Journals Vol. 2*).

[31] See Carter, P. 1990, 'Plotting: Australia's explorer narratives as "spatial history"', *The Yale Journal of Criticism: Interpretation in the humanities*, vol. 3, no. 2, (Spring), pp. 91–107, at 93.

[32] Eyre, *Journals Vol. 1*, pp. 167–8.

[33] Ibid., pp. 167–8.

[34] Ibid., p. 175.

[35] Although published contemporaneously in 1845, the journals were written in 1840–41.

[36] Eyre, *Journals Vol. 2* , p. 412.

[37] Ibid., p. 415.

[38] Ibid., p. 430.

[39] Ibid., pp. 488–9.

[40] For an introduction to the 'doctrine of discovery' that rendered indigenous peoples non-sovereigns in international law, see Anghie, A. 2005, *Imperialism, Sovereignty and the Making of International Law*, Cambridge University Press, Cambridge.

[41] See Motha, S. 2002, 'The sovereign event in a nation's law', *Law and Critique*, vol. 13, pp. 311–38; and Wolfe, P. 1994, 'Nation and miscegeNation: discursive continuity in the post-Mabo era', *Social Analysis*, no. 36, (October), pp. 93–152.

[42] See Haebich, A. 2000, *Broken Circles: Fragmenting indigenous families 1800–2000*, Fremantle Arts Centre Press, Fremantle; and Nelson, E., Smith, S. and Grimshaw, P. (eds) 2002, *Letters from Aboriginal Women in Victoria, 1867–1926*, History Department, University of Melbourne, Melbourne.

[43] Eyre to Newcastle, no. 195, 19 August 1863, CO 137/374, The National Archives (hereafter TNA), London.

[44] Eyre to Newcastle, no. 94, 9 March 1864, CO 137/380, TNA.

[45] Eyre to Cardwell, no. 90, 19 April 1865, CO 137/390, TNA.

[46] Eyre to Cardwell, no. 321, 8 December 1865, CO 137/396, TNA.

[47] See Evans, J. 2005, 'The rule of law in the settler–colonial encounter: the case of Western Australia', in P. Brand, K. Costello and W. N. Osborough (eds), *Adventures of the Law: Proceedings of the British Legal History Conference, Dublin, 2003*, Four Courts Press, Dublin, pp. 161–76.

[48] See Simpson, A. W. B. 2001, *Human Rights and the End of Empire: Britain and the genesis of the European convention*, Oxford University Press, Oxford; and Hussain, N. 2003, *The Jurisprudence of Emergency: Colonialism and the rule of law*, University of Michigan Press, Ann Arbor.

[49] For responses to the Northern Territory intervention, see Altman, J. and Hinkson, M. (eds) 2007, *Coercive Reconciliation: Stabilise, normalise, exit Aboriginal Australia*, Arena Publications, Melbourne.

[50] Eagleton, T. 2006, 'Terror and the law', *Arena Magazine*, 83, (June–July), pp. 42–6, at 43. I thank Tallace Bissett for alerting me to this observation. Eagleton's comments are elaborated in *Holy Terror* (2005, Oxford University Press, Oxford).

[51] Williams, R. 1990, *The American Indian in Western Legal Thought: The discourses of conquest*, Oxford University Press, New York.

Chapter 3

'A fine type of Hindoo' meets 'the Australian type': British Indians in Australia and diverse masculinities

Margaret Allen

In about 1881, a young Punjabi Sikh from a landowning family, Otim Singh, left his home in Moga in the Punjab and began a journey that would take him to Sumatra, where he would work for five years, supervising Indian workers on an English-owned tobacco plantation, and where he also served with the British Mounted Police. He returned home to the Punjab and purchased land, but shortly after went to Batavia (Jakarta) to visit his brother. Thence he made the journey to Australia, arriving in Melbourne in 1890.[1] He was to live in Australia for the rest of his life and was able to prosper and make his way there, initially as a hawker and later as the owner of a large general store in Kingscote on Kangaroo Island.[2] Like the colonial gentlemen discussed by Cindy McCreery in this volume, Singh came to Australia in search of prosperity.

Otim Singh was one of the many British Indian men who were in Australia in the late nineteenth and early twentieth centuries. A. Palfreeman estimated that there were up to 7637 Indians in Australia during the first decade of the twentieth century,[3] while A. T. Yarwood set the 1901 population at 4681, declining by 1911 to 3653 and by 1921 to 3150.[4] These men and their part in Australian history have been virtually ignored and under-researched. In an Australian history conceptualised within the bounds of 'White Australia', these men were irrelevant to the national imaginary. With a transnational and non-racial lens, they can instead be seen as constituting the first wave of migration to Australia from the Subcontinent.

Studies of gender have become influential in the 'new imperial history'. In 1990, Jane Haggis called for a focus on 'gender as a relational dimension of colonialism'.[5] More recently, Angela Woollacott has noted the 'central role of gender in the British imperial enterprise'.[6] Much of the new scholarship in this field has emerged from the work of feminist post-colonial historians, who began by examining the role of white women in colonialism, and in particular their relationships with colonised women. The domination of white men in imperial spaces has also been examined by a number of scholars.[7] Philippa Levine has written that '[t]he British Empire always seems a very masculine enterprise, a series of far-flung sites, dominated by white men dressed stiffly in sporting and hunting clothes, or ornate official regalia'.[8]

Figure 3.1: Otim Singh, an Indian man in business, Kingscote, South Australia.

H.T. Burgess (ed) 1909, *Cyclopedia of South Australia*, volume 2, p. 1019.

The masculinities of colonised men must also, however, constitute an important element in understanding the workings of imperialism. The connectedness of these various categorisations is crucial, as Catherine Hall has recently elaborated of colonial discourse: '[I]n demarcating black masculinity they enunciated white masculinity, in demarcating brown femininity, they elevated white femininity. Colonial discourses were critical to this process of mutual constitution.'[9] Mrinalini Sinha has delineated the colonial notion of the inferior masculinity of Bengali men, the 'effeminate Bengali',[10] against which was opposed the constructions of other Indian men as particularly martial and manly.

The Indian men under discussion here were framed by and addressed a number of different and at times contradictory notions about their masculinity, 'race' and ethnicity as they moved between Australia and India and within the varied situations and groups they encountered. Indeed, they existed within and related to diverse discourses about masculinities and, of course, as much as they were made and confined by such notions, they also negotiated them and made their own way in relation to them.

Richard White has demonstrated how the white man came into his own in the Australian colonies of the late nineteenth century and in early federated Australia.[11] Marilyn Lake also shows that the new nation—for the white 'race'—was inaugurated 'in a radical act of racial exclusion'[12] of those deemed inferior to the whites, who were destined, in this formulation, to carry the nation's destiny. Lake notes, furthermore, that this clear demarcation occurred amid 'postcolonial apprehensions' as the white man observed the rising power of colonised masculinities and anticipated 'white masculine humiliation'.[13]

This chapter explores some of the notions of masculinity with which the Indian men engaged and by which they were framed, examining these in relation to specific incidents and to the histories of particular men. Administrative practices such as those of the White Australia Policy, with which these men had to engage, also embodied these discourses. Of course, ideas of masculinity were also interwoven with ideas about race, ethnicity and religion. In drawing together understandings of Indian masculinities within the Australian environment with those relating to Australian men, this chapter furthers the 'goal of the trans-national…to unsettle national narratives'.[14] By viewing these men and their masculinities within a transnational context, the pervasiveness of colonial discourses around race and gender become apparent. Such a perspective makes clearer the fact that these men had stories and histories in the Subcontinent as well as in Australia. In naming and giving agency to individual hitherto nameless subaltern figures in the Indian diaspora to Australia, this chapter contributes to a greater understanding of Australia's transnational history.

It should be noted from the beginning that 'Indians' is a highly problematic term. Many of the men who came to Australia hailed from the Punjab, parts of which are now in Pakistan. In Australia, they were often referred to, erroneously, as Afghans. Of course, they were also 'colonials' or Australians, but they were apparently not referred to or viewed as such. In exploring their histories within a different policy framework and historical period, I seek to locate them as Australian colonials who, like the other settlers in nineteenth and early twentieth-century Australia, sought to make their way in the new country.

The 'manly Sikh'

Otim Singh's departure from his village, and his lengthy period abroad, must be understood in part in terms of indigenous categories, of the people and region from whence he came. It seems likely that he was from a landowning family that had a number of sons and could not provide 'for all members of the family at an adequate standard of living from the property group's holding in the village'.[15] Emigration for a short or longer period on the part of one or two members was a strategy adopted by such families to enable them to improve their land holdings and thus their ability to support sons and provide for daughters' weddings.[16] During the 1880s, men such as Singh who had worked in South-East Asia or had contacts there picked up news from other Sikhs that *Telia* (Australia) was open and that there were opportunities to be had there.[17]

Tom Kessinger has noted the potential of such emigration to repair family fortunes in the Punjab village of Vilyatpur. In 1903, 35 men, or approximately one-third of the men of working age, had gone to Australia.[18] The wealth that they brought or sent back into the village had a noticeable impact on land prices and the standing of particular families. In 1896, fourteen-year-old Isher Singh went to Australia with his uncle Naraung, himself only eighteen years old. These young lads were to be very successful:

> Isher's stay in Australia was fruitful. When he returned in 1908 he had sufficient funds to take about eight acres by mortgage. By 1922 he had purchased six acres, which doubled his property group's holding. Naurang never returned to the village, remaining in Australia until his death many years later. He sent enough money through the government post office in the first ten years after his departure to put the property group into the mortgage market. His brother added three acres to the holding by 1922 and constructed a good-sized brick house in the village.[19]

As Kessinger points out, 'Migration was a group effort.' Although the individual man left the village, he did this in the interests of the whole group. Leaving his village 'meant separation from family, community, and, in most cases, the impossibility of producing legitimate heirs'. Given Punjabi values, Kessinger notes, 'the cost to the migrant was high. His only return was achievement for his family.'[20]

Otim Singh worked as a hawker and, like other Indian hawkers in Australia, he would have sent money back regularly to his family by means of postal orders or through trusted friends. He had no children. He was a successful businessman and, when he died in 1927, his estate was worth £10,000.[21] On the death of his Australian wife, the balance was to be sent to his heirs, his nephews Sundar, Eishar and Kham Singh of Bhgalawalla Village, Ferospur District, in the Punjab. His many years of work in Australia, as a hawker and subsequently as a shopkeeper, benefited his property group in his village.

In thinking about such men's transnational lives, it is important to keep in mind the fact that they related to and were framed by differing and even contrasting notions of masculinity in Australia and in their home country. Therefore, while men such as Singh were working to lift their family's *izzat* (their honour) back in their home community, in Australia they were at times reviled and seen as outcasts on the lower rungs of a hierarchy of masculinities.

When Singh arrived in Melbourne in 1890, he learnt how to be a hawker from a compatriot and proceeded to work in the Western District of Victoria and across into the south-east of South Australia. While hawkers were often represented as being of great assistance to outlying settlements and welcome friends at scattered farms,[22] there was a certain amount of hostility towards itinerant hawkers in the Australian colonies during the 1890s.[23] Racial prejudice was central to this social anxiety. Indian hawkers, although they were British subjects, were marginalised in emerging white Australia because of their race. While the controversy in Victoria seemed to focus only on Indians, in South Australia the authorities refused in 1893 to renew hawking licences for Afghans, Assyrians and Chinese.[24] Popular understandings tended to push all those seen as not white into an inferior category. As an Adelaide *Register* columnist candidly admitted:

> With true British arrogance we virtually regard all such, whether Chinese, Afghans, Syrians, Hindus, or Persians, as the scum and offscouring of the earth. They have committed the unpardonable sin of being coloured, and although they were not consulted in the choice of their complexion they must perforce be Ishmaelites.[25]

Itinerant hawkers were outside society in a number of ways: they had no fixed address and they were racialised. L. F. Benaud, the editor of the *Richmond River Times* in New South Wales, declared in 1896 that 'no greater pest is to be met in the country than the objectionable dirty Hindoo hawkers who infest many districts'.[26]

Hawkers were represented as a threat to women alone on farms, whom they would pressure strongly to buy their goods. A NSW Member of Parliament is quoted in the 1890s as saying they 'become a menace to the safety and comfort of the inmate of the house' and use 'most insulting language'.[27]

Singh was more successful than many other hawkers. He became a property holder, establishing a store and enlarging it on a number of occasions. An enterprising businessman, he built up a large trade across Kangaroo Island, supplying townspeople, the farming community and the large summer-holiday trade.[28] His story of hard work and personal initiative from modest beginnings to prosperity was outlined in the *Cyclopedia of South Australia* in 1909, echoing most of those in this volume. These short biographical accounts of mainly white settlers told many stories, if not of 'rags to riches', then of the self-made man who had built his own prosperity.

Singh, however, as an Indian man, had to negotiate the problem of being seen as too successful. With the establishment of a federated white Australia from 1901, his position became more marginal. Federation was, after all, 'the coming of age of a white Australian masculinity'.[29] While some reviled the Indians when they were hawkers, critics also saw their movement into other occupations as equally threatening. In 1911, therefore, the NSW Minister of Lands, Niel Nielsen, noted of Indians gaining land in northern New South Wales:

> The Hindoo applicants are undesirable settlers in many ways and in any community of white settlers are regarded with much disfavour amounting almost to complete aversion. The majority of the Hindoos in this state have started as small hawkers or pedlars and saved a fair amount of money; they are naturally acquisitive.[30]

In response to such charges, Singh might have been able to deploy a powerful colonial discourse by which the British had categorised and defined his people. Sinha, David Omissi and Thomas Metcalf have written about the categorisation of various Indian masculinities by British rulers. Certain groups were deemed to be 'martial races'—namely, the Sikhs and the Ghurkas. The former were often referred to as 'the manly Sikh' or 'the loyal Sikh'. Others, such as the Western-educated Bengalis, were termed 'effeminate Bengalis'.[31] Such categorisations could be limiting, but could also be productive for the individuals thus categorised.[32] Indeed, Singh often referred to his family's loyalty to the British Raj, emphasising their military involvement—possibly a strategy for alleviating anxiety around his material success.

In the entry he contributed to the *Cyclopedia of South Australia*, therefore, we read: 'In earlier life he had a great ambition to join the British Army in India, and whilst in Sumatra served four years in the British Mounted Police.'[33] In his obituary in the *Kangaroo Island Courier*, we read that: 'His father and uncles were soldiers and fought with the British forces during the Indian Mutiny of 1857/8.'[34] Singh did not emphasise his British military links in the same dramatic manner as did Sowar Saut Singh on one occasion in Singleton, New South Wales. When the governor, previously the commanding officer of his regiment in the Indian Army, visited Singleton, Sowar turned up 'in full regimentals', presenting 'an impressive figure'.[35] Otim Singh could, nevertheless, usefully deploy the late nineteenth-century construction of Sikhs as particularly martial and loyal. He seems to have been successful in this, as his obituarist noted that he 'belonged to that fine type of Hindoo known as Sikhs'.[36]

The 'effeminate Bengali'

Such categorisations of the relative manliness and 'essential' qualities of various 'races' of Indian circulated widely throughout the British Empire and were so normalised that they were accepted as part of general knowledge. An incident when Nunda Lall Doss, a Bengali Christian, visited Australia in 1888, demonstrates the categorisation, pointed out by Sinha, of the Bengali as effeminate.[37] A journalist from the *Adelaide Observer* who interviewed Doss was determined to represent him as an example of such an 'effeminate Bengali'. In this remarkable interview, Doss can be seen resisting the deployment of this category against himself and other Indians. They had been discussing Chinese immigration and 'coolies' in general. Indeed, during the previous month, Doss had observed the great uproar that ensued in Sydney when some Chinese tried to land from the *Afghan*.[38] In Adelaide, the issue of the use of Chinese labour in the Northern Territory was being debated. The journalist, employing contemporary discourse around 'racial types', suggested that 'the Indian coolies [were] physically inferior to the Chinese'.[39] Doss disagreed, offering mock combat: 'Look at me, don't you think I am quite as strong as yourself?' The journalist rejected this trial of strength, admitting that Doss was 'physically, at any rate, my superior'. Determined to pursue the notion of the 'effeminate Bengali', however, he queried whether Doss was 'a specimen of the average Hindu'. Doss replied, 'Yes I am a fair specimen of the Hindus from the north of India. We have some very fine men amongst us.' Not convinced, the journalist asked finally: 'Are you a pure native?' Doss laughed outright at this suggestion and, with a little jibe about British drinking habits, replied, 'Yes I am glad to say that my ancestors never had a drop of spirits of wine in their veins', and he continued, after this assertion of his 'pure' lineage, deftly to link Indian and British ancestry: 'I have no British blood; but our native vernaculars when compared with your [W]estern languages show that after all the Indians and the British are very nearly related.'[40]

Here, Doss skilfully turns the discussion towards a claim of longstanding affiliation between the British and Indians by his reference to 'the theory of a common Aryan origin of Europeans and Indians', effectively deflecting the journalist's efforts to render him a mere object under surveillance.[41] Supporters of the London Missionary Society, which brought Doss to Australia, were affronted by the journalist's aggressive and denigrating line of questioning and sprang to his defence. This defence was, however, itself couched in terms of 'racial types', alluding in a patronising manner to the notion of the ridiculously verbose Bengali that was part of the colonial characterisation of the effeminate Bengali:

> The admission of *physical superiority*, unwittingly, no doubt, carried with it the implication of *mental inferiority*. With Mr Doss there is nothing artificial in thought and utterance. Whoever has heard him cannot but have noted the wonderful adroitness with which he picks his way along the stepping stones of English expression, and the exceedingly apposite and erudite manner in which he clothes his evidently *own* thinking in the garb of an alien tongue.[42] (Emphasis in the original.)

Restrictive legislation and masculinity

Doss was a brief visitor to Australia, unlike those Indians who lived in the country for many years and made their living here. With the passage of restrictive immigration acts in some colonies in the late nineteenth century and in particular with the passing of the national *Immigration Restriction Act* (*IRA*) in 1901, their situation worsened. The *IRA* deemed Indians to be prohibited immigrants, despite the fact that they were British subjects, and they had to contend with an array of administrative practices. Such discursive practices 'articulated and organized particular sets of relations', as Hall puts it, 'through the workings of knowledge and power'.[43]

After Federation, in general, no new immigrants from India were allowed to enter Australia and a whole system of surveillance and regulation of the lives and movements of British Indians in Australia was developed. This related chiefly to movements outside Australia and re-entry to Australia, and Indians domiciled in Australia found their mobility and the freedom to come to and go from Australia at will was restricted.[44] An identity document, the Certificate Exempting the Dictation Test (CEDT), was created in order to regulate the movement of Indians and other 'Asiatics' domiciled in Australia as they left and re-entered the country. The certificate involved the use of photographs—front and profile—a description of the holder and the taking of hand-prints and later of thumb-prints. A bureaucracy was created to oversee, regulate and register the movements of domiciled people from the classes of prohibited immigrants. Through such practices, these non-white men (and a few women) were rendered objects to be watched over, administered and controlled. In order to gain a CEDT, they had to provide references from members of the European community as to their character, and the local police checked with their referees and made inquiries into their activities and financial standing.

Such administrative processes inherently positioned these men as untrustworthy. A CEDT was therefore given to the applicant only when he was on board ship and about to leave port. Indeed, for each ship that entered and left a port, customs officers counted and listed the numbers of non-white passengers and crew. For such accounting, the passengers were regularly mustered on deck.[45] Information about the movements of non-white people was conveyed from customs at one port to the next with the special responsibility of the customs officer at the last port of call to note the departure of such passengers. When the person returned to Australia, the CEDT was taken back by the customs authorities and stored in the 'Strong Room' at Customs House. This was presumably to ensure that no other person could make illegal use of it to gain entry to Australia.

Indians protested against the policies and administrative processes of the White Australia Policy on a number of fronts. They drew up petitions, demanding that their rights as British subjects be honoured. Just as Sowar Saut Singh sought to bypass colonial authority by calling attention to his links with the Governor of New South Wales, the Indians' protests and petitions were often addressed across national boundaries to the British Colonial Office or the India Office in London or even to the Viceroy in India. Others directed their complaints to the Indians Overseas Association, which had its headquarters in London. Within Australia, some individuals contested the application of the discriminatory processes to their movements. I have discussed elsewhere the struggle of Sher Mohmad for exemption from thumb-printing and from the requirement to get references each time he wished to visit India.[46] In 1929, he wrote testily to the officials administering the legislation, asserting his right to be treated as a person, a modern citizen and a businessman who had contributed to the making of Australia: 'I have already furnished the Customs with many such certificates and my character is proven beyond any doubt. The process of obtaining the certificates is most painful and humiliating and not necessary in my case.'[47]

The undignified and un-manly character of hand-printing was eventually recognised by an alteration to these requirements, allowing them to be omitted for some more prominent 'Asiatics'. The Customs Officer therefore wrote in 1912 of Rochimull Pamamull, who had a shop in Coles Arcade in Melbourne: 'As Mr Rochimull Pamamull is a well known business man, the handprints need not be taken.'[48] Similarly, when the businessman Marm Deen left Melbourne with his wife and children in 1912, only a family portrait was taken to allow them to re-enter Australia. Deen's status was such that he seemed to correspond directly with Attlee Hunt and other senior officials. Perhaps it was felt that to treat him in an undignified manner would be demeaning to these prominent white men with whom he dealt.[49]

After 1919, British Indians resident in Australia were permitted to apply to bring their wives and minor children to live with them in Australia, thus making it possible for the families to also gain resident status. This allowance was curious given that Indians were not seen as appropriate settlers. Indeed, it came because of the pressure exerted on Australian authorities by imperial authorities as a result of India's great contributions in terms of fighting men and funds to the British war effort. An applicant, however, had to satisfy a number of requirements before his family could join him. He had to prove that it was *his* wife and children who would enter Australia and that the children were indeed minors. Most important was the requirement that the authorities be satisfied that the applicant had sufficient funds to support his family and a suitable home in Australia to house them in an appropriate manner. Many if not most applications seem to have been rejected.

This new policy was run through with paternalism. Some Indians were refused permission to admit their family because their residence was not seen as suitable. Police would make an inspection of the Indian applicant's house and inquire into his financial position to determine whether he could support a wife and children in a suitable manner. Implicit in this practice was the belief that the 'white standard' of civilised behaviour had to be affirmed and that an Indian man might not know how to look after his wife and family in a manner appropriate to a 'civilised' community.[50] Implicit also was the notion of the 'Bengali man as effeminate and incapable of caring for his own dependants'.[51] There were not many applications for wives and children to join men in Australia, and they were often refused on grounds that were presented as solicitous and gentlemanly official concern for the woman.

Gola Singh, who worked as a labourer in the Clarence River district of New South Wales, was the first to apply. In 1918, just as the agreement with the Indian Government was being finalised, he sought permission to bring his wife, Harman Kor, to Australia when he returned from India.[52] The officials made a number of inquiries, asking what occupation he would follow in Australia and how he planned to support his wife and make a home for her. Gola Singh understood the drift of these questions, informing them that he planned to take a farm on lease on the Clarence or Richmond Rivers: 'I do not want to work about like before.' The officials rejected his application, advising him 'to defer bringing your wife to Australia until after you have carried out your intentions of leasing a farm or until you have re-established your self in some suitable occupation that will enable you to provide a satisfactory home for your wife in Australia'.[53]

Sirdar Singh, a South Australian hawker and businessman and a veteran of the Indian and Australian armed forces, was more successful when he applied in 1936 to bring his wife to Australia. An inspector from the Investigation Branch of the Attorney-General's Department looked into his situation, discussing his affairs with one of his referees, a representative of G. & R. Wills, the import and export company with which Singh dealt. The inspector concluded: 'Applicant is well-spoken and a good business man. It is unlikely that he would be unable to satisfactorily provide for his wife.'[54]

Otim Singh went back to India only once, in 1927. He applied for permission to bring his nephew from India as a substitute, to take his place in the store and help his wife during his absence. The policy of substitutes allowed for a man who was planning to return to India for a year or two to temporarily bring out a close relative to look after his business interests in his absence. As was normal with such applications, the Investigation Branch was asked to assess Singh's worth and his standing in the community and also whether 'his white wife would be able to manage the business during her husband's absence'. The officers made inquiries 'of principal business houses in Adelaide and at Kingscote'.[55] The local police at Kingscote also made inquiries and the report read, 'Otim Singh had an old established business as a General Storekeeper at Kingscote, Kangaroo Island and is well spoken of by residents of good standing there.' They also checked if Susannah Singh would be supported in her husband's absence. The implication here was that an Indian man might just leave and abandon his wife, that he might not know how to behave in an appropriately masculine manner. Something of Susannah Singh's feelings about such inquiries can be heard in the official report of her reply: 'Mrs Singh intimated that if her husband left Australia he would do so with her full knowledge and consent and that she had no reason to doubt that she would be fully provided for.'[56]

Most of those Indian men who lived out their days in Australia had to spend their declining years alone, dependent only on other old men who, like them, were virtually relics of a previous more relaxed immigration regime. There are a number of files that demonstrate the strict and cruel administration of the regulations, which were designed to limit the growth of non-white populations in Australia. These regulations made it impossible for such men to enjoy the comforts of fatherhood. Khair Deen was share-farming with Joe Khan on a banana farm at St Helena's, Bangalow, in New South Wales. He had been in Australia since 1891, apart from making some trips home to visit his family. He had some property in Australia: his share of the farm was worth about £100. In 1941, he applied for his son Biroo, born in 1921, to come to Australia to live with him.[57] His solicitors in Lismore forwarded his application, noting that he had been back to India in 1920–22 and 1935–37. His application for his son to join him was refused, as the customs officials had no record of his going to India in 1920–22. They claimed that he went to India in 1914–19 and therefore assumed that Biroo was either no longer a minor and eligible to enter Australia or that he was not Deen's son. While a number of these Indians were rather vague about the dates of their visits to India and the ages of their children, it is also possible that Deen sought to deceive the authorities so that he could have the comfort of his son's company in his declining years and see his property in Australia passed on to his kin. Although his solicitors asked for the decision to be reconsidered, it was once more rejected. He applied again in 1942, noting that '[a]t the present time my eyesight is failing and I am finding it somewhat difficult to carry on without help'. This application also appears to have been rejected.[58] Deen died alone in Australia. In 1944, Biroo wrote from the Punjab seeking to know about this father's estate.

A crucial element in the foundation and maintenance of the White Australia Policy was the attitude of organised labour to 'coloured' labour. The first issue on the 'Fighting Platform' of the Australian Labor Party in the early twentieth century was 'Maintenance of a White Australia'.[59] British Indian workers in Australia had to contend with the view that they were taking away white men's jobs. During a 1919 industrial dispute in Queensland about the rights of Indians to work cutting sugar cane, the Australian Workers' Union (AWU) secretary for far north Queensland sent a telegram to the Industrial Arbitration Court in Brisbane, pointing out that cane growers were defying the court's direction to employ white labour:

> Hambledon growers engaging coloured gangs as usual. This certain [to] cause trouble as large number of men are unemployed…Number [of] coloured gangs also engaged for South Johnstone. Members [at] Johnstone refuse [to] crush cane harvested by aliens.[60]

In a letter of protest addressed to the British Secretary of State for India in 1934, a Brisbane man, S. W. S. Ismail, outlined the great power that the union movement had to deny him and his former compatriots work, even though they had been in Australia for up to 40 years and had children—'our unfortunate offspring'—to support. He wrote:

> I beg to ask your influence about us in Australia, the hardship us Indian subjects in Australia. We are outclass still. Certain liberty we had here not half enough 100 married Indian in Australia. We having very rough passage. Even we can't get A.W. U. ticket from the Australian Workers Union. Other nation[alities] can join and can get a ticket and go where is works are valuable [available]. In our case we go to the employer for work first, they ask us, have you any ticket. That mean A.W.U. if we say no, he advice [sic] us to get a ticket and work are waiting for us. and we go to so call union, pay the money, whatever is due. They simply refuse us.[61]

Good citizens

While the organised labour movement could marginalise some Indian men, making it difficult for them to earn a living, others were accepted in the wider community in other ways. Some Indian men were drawn into sections of the

Australian community as good citizens and trustworthy businessmen. Here, the emphasis was on their honesty, probity and public-spiritedness. These values were recognised and acknowledged, despite 'racial' differences. Judith Brett has argued that in the first half of the twentieth century,

> citizenship was not primarily a status conferred by the state but a capacity of individuals to subordinate self-interest to the common good. This broader concept of citizenship was expressed through people's participation in the voluntary activities for the social good.[62]

Pam Oliver, for example, has discussed how Japanese people living in Sydney before World War II gained social acceptance through their involvement in community and voluntary activities.[63]

Otim Singh's life on Kangaroo Island can be understood in this light. In his obituary, his public-spiritedness was emphasised, and we read that he 'interested himself in local affairs, always being willing to assist in any movement for the good of the town and district'.[64] Singh took part in social activities befitting his business position. He appears to have been a member of the Freemasons in the Kingscote Lodge of the Royal Ancient Order of Buffaloes. In 1911, when the first Kangaroo Island Agricultural Show was held, he was on the committee and part of the group of leading citizens who dined with the governor, appearing in a photograph taken to commemorate the occasion.[65] He was also involved with the local Vigilance Committee, a group of businessmen seeking to advance the interests of the township of Kingscote. He spoke at valedictory dinners for departing bank managers and other prominent citizens.[66]

A close reading of the local newspaper for 1916–17 reveals that he was often a generous donor to fundraising activities. Late in 1915, therefore, he contributed prizes to the Kingscote School prize-giving. During the war years, he made contributions to the Wounded Soldiers Club and the South Australian Soldiers Fund. On New Year's Day 1916, he presented an 'ambulance car', presumably a toy, for an Art Union that raised £1.16. When some South African soldiers had a rifle-shooting match against the Kingscote Club, Singh presented £1.1 to the highest scorer in the match.[67] Such demonstrations of loyalty to the British Empire not only asserted his public spiritedness, they emphasised his common cause with other members of the local community.

There are other examples of Indians resident in Australia being generous philanthropists and good and respected citizens. In 1913, when Rahma Khan, a hawker from around Moama, New South Wales, was going on a visit to his homeland after some 20 years in Australia, his business colleagues wrote warm references for him. One local merchant wrote that he trusted 'as he leave these shores he will enjoy the blessing', and Mr W. Williams, a former chair of the local hospital board, noted that Khan 'has given valuable assistance to many charitable institutions including the Echuca Hospital'.[68] Similarly, in 1912 the Mayor of Bendigo wrote of Jumee Khan as 'a most respected citizen of this city', and two local businessmen expressed the 'hope [that] he will have a pleasant voyage to his native home "India" and a safe return'.[69]

Conclusion

The social location of British Indian men in Australia is complex and contradictory, as is their location within Australian history. They had to carefully negotiate a multiplicity of meanings around masculinity. While honouring notions of manhood learnt in their communities of origin, they might have found themselves positioned as unmanly and suspect as they plied the trade of hawker in the Australian countryside. The discourses of empire and the categorisation of certain types of Indians could disadvantage them but could also be used to claim respect within the Australian community. While the policies and administrative practices of the White Australia Policy restricted their opportunities to be husbands and fathers and denied their humanity, some could demand recognition of their rights as British subjects by emphasising Indian contributions to British military successes and could seek to be exempted from the more humiliating aspects of the procedures. While the aggressive masculinity of the organised labour movement attacked their presence in the labour market, there were other opportunities, especially for successful businessmen, to be accepted as good citizens. Fortunately, some Indian men, such as Otim Singh, were able to manipulate these contradictions and turn them to their advantage.

Notes

[1] Burgess, H. T. 1909, *Cyclopedia of South Australia. Volume 2*, Cyclopedia Company, Adelaide, pp. 1019–20.

[2] See Allen, Margaret 2008 (forthcoming), 'Otim Singh in White Australia', in N. Bierbaum et al. (eds), *Something Rich and Strange*, Wakefield Press, Adelaide.

[3] Palfreeman, A. 1967, *The Administration of the White Australia Policy*, Melbourne University Press, Melbourne, p. 146.

[4] Yarwood, A. T. 1967, *Asian Migration to Australia*, Melbourne University Press, Melbourne, p. 163.

[5] Haggis, Jane 1990, 'Gendering colonialism or colonising gender?', *Women's Studies International Forum*, vol. 13, no. 1–2, p. 113.

[6] Woollacott, Angela 2006, *Gender and Empire*, Palgrave Macmillan, Basingstoke. p. 1.

[7] Ibid., pp. 59–73.

[8] Levine, Philippa 2004, 'Introduction: why gender and empire?', in Philippa Levine (ed.), *Gender and Empire*, Oxford University Press, Oxford, p. 1.

[9] Hall, Catherine 2004, 'Of gender and empire: reflections on the nineteenth century', in ibid., p. 50.

[10] Sinha, Mrinalini 1995, *Colonial Masculinity: The 'manly Englishman' and the 'effeminate Bengali' in the late nineteenth century*, Manchester University Press, Manchester and New York.

[11] White, Richard 1981, *Inventing Australia*, George Allen and Unwin, Sydney, p. 79.

[12] Lake, Marilyn 2003, 'On being a white man in Australia, circa 1900', in Hsu-Ming Teo and Richard White (eds), *Cultural History in Australia*, University of New South Wales Press, Sydney, p. 98.

[13] Ibid., p. 102. See also Allen, Margaret 2008 (forthcoming), 'Through colonial spectacles', in K. Douglas and G. Bastin (eds), *Journeying and Journalling*, Lythrum Press, Adelaide.

14 Ghosh, Durba 2005, 'National narratives and the politics of miscegenation', in Antoinette Burton (ed.), *Archive Stories Facts, Fictions, and the Writing of History*, Duke University Press, Durham and London, p. 32.

15 Kessinger, Tom G. 1974, *Vilatpur 1848–1968: Social and economic change in a North Indian village*, University of California Press, Berkeley and London, p. 138.

16 Ibid., pp. 163–77.

17 McLeod, W. H. 2000, 'The first forty years of Sikh migration', *Exploring Sikhism: Aspects of Sikh identity, culture and thought*, Oxford University Press, New Delhi, p. 250.

18 Ibid., p. 92.

19 Ibid., p. 170.

20 Kessinger, *Vilatpur 1848–1968*, p. 171.

21 Last will of Otim Singh, Probate Registry Office, Supreme Court, Adelaide, No. 48675/1927.

22 Datta, S. K. 1924, 'India and racial relationships', *Young Men of India*, vol. 35, no. 8, August.

23 See Brewster, Athol 1978, The Indian hawker nuisance in the colony of Victoria 1890–1900, Hons History Thesis, University of Melbourne. My thanks to Dr Andrew Brown-May and Athol Brewster for access to this thesis.

24 See reports in *Register*, (Adelaide), 22 April, 1 May, 5 and 7 July 1893.

25 *Register*, (Adelaide), 5 July 1893, p. 4.

26 *Richmond River Herald*, 10 January 1896, quoted in Potts, Annette 1997, '"I am a British subject, and I can go wherever the British flag flies": Indians on the Northern Rivers of New South Wales during the federation years', *Journal of the Royal Australian Historical Society*, vol. 62, September, p. 105.

27 S. T. Whiddon, MP, in *NSW Parliamentary Debates*, vol. 85, p. 3962, quoted in Potts, '"I am a British subject"', pp. 105–6.

28 See Allen, 'Otim Singh in White Australia'.

29 Sinha, Mrinalini 2004, 'Nations in an imperial crucible', in Philippa Levine (ed.), *Gender and Empire*, pp. 181–202, esp. p. 184.

30 Enclosure in No. 37, NSW Minister of Lands, Colonial Office (CO), 886/4/21, Public Records Office (London); Niel Nielsen wrote this minute in 1911.

31 Sinha, *Colonial Masculinity*; Metcalf, Thomas R. 2007, '"A well selected body of men": Sikh recruitment for colonial police and military', in Kevin Grant, Philippa Levine and Frank Trentmann (eds), *Beyond Sovereignty: Britain, empire and transnationalism, c 1880–1950*, Palgrave Macmillan, Hampshire, pp. 146–68; Omissi, David 1991, '"Martial race": ethnicity and security in colonial India, 1858–1939', *War and Society*, vol. 9, no. 1, pp. 1–27.

32 Indeed, Metcalf (in '"A well selected body of men"') has argued that a number of Indians sought to be included in the category 'Sikh' because of the opportunities for employment it offered. Angela Woollacott (2007, 'Rose Quong becomes Chinese: an Australian in London and New York', *Australian Historical Studies*, no. 129, pp. 16–31) has discussed how Rose Quong could use orientalism to make a career performing 'Chineseness'.

33 Burgess, *Cyclopedia*, p. 1020.

34 *Kangaroo Island Courier*, 10 December 1927.

35 Green, W. C. 1961, 'The Indian hawkers of the Upper Hunter', *Scone and Upper Hunter Historical Journal*, vol. 2. p. 213.

36 *Kangaroo Island Courier*, 10 December 1927.

37 Sinha, *Colonial Masculinity*. Woollacott (*Gender and Empire*, p. 88) has noted: '[T]he plasticity of colonial discourse meant that other Indian men could be included in the slur.'

38 See Allen, Margaret 2006, '"The Chinaman had no fault except that they were Chinese": an Indian view of Australia in 1888', in S. K. Sareen (ed.), *Australia and India Interconnections: Identity, representation and belonging*, Mantra, New Delhi, pp. 202–17.

39 'Chat with an Indian missionary', *Adelaide Observer*, 30 June 1888.

40 Ibid.; all quotations from the interview are taken from this source.

41 Sinha, *Colonial Masculinity*, p. 20. On the circulation of the notion of Aryanism, see Ballantyne, Tony 2001, *Orientalism and Race: Aryanism in the British Empire*, Palgrave Macmillan, Basingstoke.

42 *The Christian Weekly & Methodist Journal*, Adelaide, 29 June 1888, p. 1. Although dated after the *Observer* interview, it refers back to it.

[43] Hall, Catherine 2004, 'Of gender and empire: reflections on the nineteenth century', in Philippa Levine (ed.), *Gender and Empire*, pp. 46–76, esp. p. 50.

[44] Allen, Margaret 2005, '"Innocents abroad" and "prohibited immigrants": Australians in India and Indians in Australia 1890–1910', in Ann Curthoys and Marilyn Lake (eds), *Connected Worlds: History in transnational perspective*, ANU E Press, Canberra, pp. 111–24. See also Jones, Paul 1998, Alien acts: the White Australia Policy, 1901–1939, PhD Thesis, University of Melbourne.

[45] See Day, David 1996, *Contraband and Controversy: The customs history of Australia from 1901*, AGPS, Canberra, pp. 70–1.

[46] See Allen, Margaret (forthcoming), '"He has been a good citizen": Sher Mohamad and his finger prints', in Ralph Crane, Anna Johnston and C. Vijaysree (eds), *Empire Calling*.

[47] Sher Mohamad, National Archives of Australia (hereafter NAA), PP4/2 1936/801.

[48] Roehumull [sic] Pamamull, Certificate of Exemption from Dictation Test, NAA, B13 1912/5677.

[49] Mr and Mrs Marm Deen and Family, Readmission to Australia, NAA, B13 1922/7393.

[50] Lake, 'On being a white man in Australia', p. 108.

[51] Hall, 'Of gender and empire', p. 51.

[52] Gola Singh, Readmission, NAA, A1 1919/14322.

[53] Ibid.

[54] Sirdar Singh, NAA, D596 1936/162.

[55] Re Singh, Otim, NAA, D1915 SA 1589.

[56] Ibid.

[57] Khair Deen (Indian), Application for Admission into Commonwealth of son Beer (Biroo) Deen, NAA, SP42/2 C1945/1260.

[58] Ibid.

[59] Markus, Andrew 2003, 'Of continuities and discontinuities: reflections on a century of Australian immigration control', in Laksiri Jayasuriya, David Walker and Jan Gothard (eds), *Legacies of White Australia: Race, culture and nation*, University of Western Australia Press, Perth, p. 186.

[60] See file on Indians in Queensland 1912–23, L/E/7/1246, in File 2754, India Office Industries and Overseas Department, Oriental and India Office Collection, British Library.

[61] S. W. S. Ismail, Brisbane, to Right Hon. Samuel Hoare, Secretary of State for India, London, in L/P & J/8/189 (Collection 108 2A: Indians in Australia, 1928–1947), Oriental and India Office Collection, British Library.

[62] Brett, Judith 2003, *Australian Liberals and the Moral Middle Class: From Alfred Deakin to John Howard*, Cambridge University Press, Cambridge, pp. 63–4, quoted in Oliver, Pam 2007, 'Japanese relationships in white Australia: the Sydney experience to 1941', *History Australia*, vol. 4, 1 June 2007, pp. 5.1–5.20.

[63] Oliver, 'Japanese relationships in White Australia'.

[64] *Kangaroo Island Courier*, 10 December 1927.

[65] Photograph, 'Official Show Dinner, 1911', in Cordes, Neville 1986, *Kangaroo Island, 184 Great Years: A history in photographs, 1802–1986*, Island Press, Kangaroo Island. The original photograph is on display at Hope Cottage, National Trust Museum, Kingscote, Kangaroo Island.

[66] *Kangaroo Island Courier*, 9 May 1916, p. 4; see also 13 June 1908, p. 7.

[67] *Kangaroo Island Courier*, 29 April 1916, p. 5.

[68] Rahmatt Khan, Application for Certificate of Exemption for Dictation Test, NAA, B13 1913/2065.

[69] Jumee Khan, Certificate Exempting Dictation Test, NAA, B13 1912/16684.

Chapter 4

A British prince and a transnational life: Alfred, Duke of Edinburgh's visit to Australia, 1867–68

Cindy McCreery

The voyages of Alfred, Duke of Edinburgh (1844–1900), offer a useful entrée to understanding transnational lives in nineteenth-century Britain and Australia. Alfred crossed borders and nationalities as a prince and serving officer in the Royal Navy. His visit to Australia in 1867–68, the first by a member of the British royal family, attracted considerable attention.[1] Examining official and private accounts of the visit enables us to consider the transnational dimensions of Alfred and his Australian hosts, as well as those of contemporary Britons and Australians in general. Indeed, employing a transnational perspective enriches our historical understanding of such 'British' institutions as the Royal Family and the Royal Navy. Alfred's visit to Australia demonstrates how contemporary individuals, families and societies were seen, and saw themselves, as transnational. Furthermore, while much of this experience took place within the British Empire, much of it took place beyond it.

A British prince

At first glance, it might seem odd to describe the second son of Queen Victoria—that most secure and relatively sedentary of British monarchs—as leading a transnational life. Surely the only identity that really mattered, in Alfred's eyes and others, was his status as the Queen's son and heir, the second in line to the British throne?[2]

Alfred's royal status was certainly made much of in Australia. His familial relationship with Queen Victoria and his status as her proxy were stressed throughout his visit. Colonists sang 'We love thee for thy father's fame…And for thy mother's sake!' and noted that Alfred's presence provided them with the 'opportunity of expressing our devotion to Her Majesty's throne and person'.[3] Queen Victoria was also anxious that her son's royal position be properly acknowledged.[4] As we will see below, however, while Alfred could insist on strict protocol, he preferred to avoid it.

Figure 4.1: HRH Prince Alfred, KG, Duke of Edinburgh in naval uniform.

Photographic print: albumen silver *carte-de-visite*, on *carte-de-visite*. State Library of Victoria. Image no. a15044.

Alfred's dislike of pomp reflected his own shyness and his awareness of the ambiguous position of minor royals within Britain. While there was public delight at their births and marriages, the cost of supporting the Queen's numerous children caused increasing resentment. When combined with frustration at Victoria's own absence from public affairs after the death of her husband, Prince Albert, public dissatisfaction with the royal family ran high. While Alfred wished to appear as a prince, he did not want to appear (and the British Government did not want him to appear) as a grasping one. Whatever the duke's own views on his royal status, it was clear that at least some colonists considered him suitable monarch material. In 1863 the Victorian Premier, John O'Shanassy, proposed that Alfred become 'King of Australia'. As Anita Callaway notes, this idea was revived in a transparency displayed in Melbourne during the duke's visit.[5]

While he often downplayed his royal status, Alfred emphasised his connections with one particular part of his mother's kingdom: Scotland. This had nothing to do with his place of birth or family background (he was born in Windsor to Anglo-German parents), but everything to do with the royal family's projection of themselves as British. In the early nineteenth century, the unpopular Anglo-German George IV fell in love with Highland Scots culture. Although the English population detested George for his excessive spending and shoddy attempt to divorce his German wife, they readily embraced his interest in tartans. George did more than set a new fashion: he attempted to create a new historical tradition. Even more dramatically, his niece Victoria and her German husband, Albert, embarked on a lifelong love affair with Scotland with the purchase of an estate at Balmoral.[6] It was here that the couple chose to spend private time with their children, who grew up with firsthand (albeit selective) knowledge of Highland culture. Scotland represented a physical escape from English critics of their Germanness, and a means to consolidate their own claim to Britishness. For the royal family, then, Britishness, to an extent, was something that could be acquired, or at least assumed, via public display and private practice.

Alfred's recently bestowed title of Duke of Edinburgh further cemented his connection with Scotland, but he seems to have pursued Scottish pastimes out of genuine interest.[7] Scottish dancing, for example, featured prominently in Alfred's entertainments ashore and aboard HMS *Galatea*. Numerous cartoons published in *Sydney Punch* and *Melbourne Punch* displayed Alfred's enthusiasm, along with colonists' often ludicrous attempts to keep up with him. In *The Duke of Edinburgh's Visit. Design for ye Illumination of ye Town Hall*, for example, 'Ye Mayor-Elect Practiseth ye Sword Dance'.[8] Dressed in pseudo-Highland garb, the unfortunate politician manages to pierce his bagpipes with his sword while attempting to dance over crossed swords. Similarly, in *Preparations for the Prince*, 'Miss Clementina Jones practices the Scotch Reel before the Gentleman borrowed from the Tobacconist. N.B.—She finds the prevailing fashion rather in the way.'[9] Here a young woman's desperate attempt to learn Scottish dancing in front of a kilted statue is handicapped by her overly long gown. Rather than demonstrating her dancing skills, she reveals her own vanity. Colonial women's vanity was a popular theme of newspaper articles and cartoons, which widely ridiculed their attempts to impress the duke. In fact, of course, these Australian colonists were simply imitating the royal family's own 'invention of tradition'. This is one instance in which colonial attempts to identify with British culture largely failed. Other attempts would prove more successful.

Transnational Ties

Figure 4.2: The Governor's Ball at the Exhibition Buildings, The Royal Party Dancing the Scotch Reel, 27 December 1867.

Samuel Calvert. Print: wood engraving. State Library of Victoria. Image no. b49420.

National ties

While Alfred's genealogy and his tastes confirmed him as a British prince, he developed associations with other nations. In 1862, for example, Alfred was proposed as the new king of Greece. This honour reflected his German as well as his British bloodline. German princes, who were often relatively poor and landless, were often put forward to occupy vacant European thrones. Indeed, after the British Government turned down the Greeks' request for Alfred, his German Uncle Ernest of Saxe-Coburg Gotha was placed on the throne.[10] While Alfred never became a Greek prince, arguably he always remained a German one. Although his mother's father's family had lived mostly in Britain since the early eighteenth century, the rest of his family was based in Germany. His father, Prince Albert, left Saxe-Coburg Gotha to marry Queen Victoria, and in turn Alfred became heir to this duchy. Alfred's future as well as his past thus lay more in Germany than in Britain.

Alfred's German identity was more than a little problematic in contemporary Britain. As Richard Williams pointed out, since the accession of the Hanoverians to the British throne in 1714, complaints were made that the royal family was more German than British. Queen Victoria was judged to have made things even worse, first by her marriage to a German prince, and, latterly, by encouraging her children to marry German spouses. For example, her beloved eldest daughter, Vicky, married the heir to the Prussian throne in 1858. Arguably, only after Albert's sudden death in 1861 did the crown's Englishness become secure. Doubts, however, remained. The Duke of Edinburgh's first voyage to Australia in 1867–68 was sandwiched between two episodes of bitter anti-German and in particular anti-Prussian feeling in Britain. In the 1864 Schleswig-Holstein affair and the 1869–70 Franco-Prussian War, Queen Victoria was widely criticised for allegedly attempting to influence British foreign policy to support Prussia.[11] In many ways, Alfred's visit provided a timely opportunity to demonstrate the royal family's Britishness.

Alfred's behaviour in Australia both supported and complicated these claims to Britishness—for while the prince emphasised his Scottish links, he also drew attention to his German connections. In Adelaide, Melbourne and Sydney, for example, the duke warmly greeted *liedertafel*: male torchbearers dressed in German national costumes, who serenaded him with German songs. Indeed, in Melbourne, Alfred jocularly urged the mayor to finish his long speech so that he could go and listen to the *liedertafel*: 'Cut it short, Mr Mayor—the Germans are burning their fingers.'[12] Despite this display of partiality, and even though it allegedly caused 'great jealousy in certain press circles, because there was to be a "Leidertafel" [sic] and not an Australasian-tafel as well', Australians apparently accepted Alfred's expressions of his Germanness without public comment.[13] This even extended to the prince's adoption of German military uniform. In Sydney, Alfred wore 'the uniform of a general officer of Saxe-Coburg-Gotha' at the local military review.[14] At the Adelaide and Melbourne reviews, he dressed as a Prussian colonel.[15] For a British prince (and captain in the Royal Navy) to take part in British military ceremonies wearing German uniform (even if, as heir to a German duchy, he was entitled to wear such uniform) seems astonishing. The adoption of Prussian uniform in particular might have been expected to raise a few eyebrows. While Saxe-Coburg Gotha (Alfred's ancestral home) remained an obscure German state, Prussia (with which he was linked only through his sister's marriage) was fast becoming Britain's economic and military rival. In Australia at this time, however, loyalty to Germany was evidently seen as compatible with loyalty to Britain.[16] If colonists were worried by such behaviour, they did not express this concern publicly. One exception was a satirical sketch made by George Gordon McCrae, entitled 'A Saylore on Horse-backe, ye Adelaide Troops are reviewed bye a Prussian Colonel'.[17] In it, a stiff Alfred, resplendent in shiny Prussian uniform, sits astride a gawky steed, while HMS *Galatea*'s presence in the background gently reminds the viewer of the prince's proper, British occupation. This exception might, however, prove the rule: McCrae's drawing was not published, and it seems to have reflected a minority viewpoint, or at least one that was not aired publicly.

Even the most anti-British elements within the colonies appeared unperturbed by these dual identities. Sydney's *Freeman's Journal* drew particular attention to Alfred's German connections, describing him as a 'young Anglo-German gentleman' who probably had an ear for music, since 'most Germans have some'. This paper, which a few months later proudly described its policy as remaining 'truly and unflinchingly, Irish, National, and Catholic', was being deliberately provocative in describing the son of the British monarch as a foreigner. It nevertheless accepted that Alfred could combine English identity with German, in the same article referring to him as 'this young Englishman'. For nationalist Irishmen, of course, an Englishman was as much a foreigner as a German. The *Freeman's Journal* therefore distinguished its constituency from 'Anglo-Saxons', whom it characterised as having 'an innate vulgarity'.[18] Pro-British sources also noted, however, that Alfred combined English and foreign elements. According to the British émigré Samuel Curtis Candler, who was soon to become friendly with the duke in Melbourne, 'his pronunciation is peculiar, something between that of an English gentleman and of a foreigner who had been taught English perfectly'.[19]

For the *Freeman's Journal* and its Irish Catholic constituency, there was no contradiction in Alfred being English and German. Instead, the paper distanced itself from those who were 'preparing to give him a reception betokening the esteem in which they hold *their* sovereign' (my italics). The problem lay not with multiple national identities, but with the assumption that as the son of the British monarch, Alfred should be worshipped by Australian colonists: 'We are not aware that the aforementioned sovereign has done anything particular to win the gratitude of the Australians.' Rather, Alfred was simply a 'young stranger' whose presence demanded respect, due not to his royal birth but for his polite behaviour: '[T]hough we feel no inclination to honour the coming guest simply because he happens to be a prince, we would, at all events, respect him, because we know he is a gentleman.'[20] Candler also emphasised the importance of Alfred's behaviour as a gentleman, and claimed that it was a welcome surprise to learn that 'one may sometimes put one's trust in Princes'.[21] As we will see below, Alfred also put much stock in appearing as a gentleman.

Figure 4.3: *A Saylore on Horse-backe, ye Adelaide Troops are reviewed bye a Prussian Colonel*, 1868.

George Gordon McCrae. Drawing: pen, ink and wash. National Library of Australia: nla.pic-an6330424

Alfred's expression of dual loyalty was accepted in colonial Australia because colonists recognised, and to a certain extent approved of, the existence of multiple loyalties. In other words, Alfred was not alone in combining loyalty to Britain with loyalty (or at least affection) for another state or culture. German–British loyalty was particularly comprehensible in South Australia, which boasted a large German immigrant population (although, as many migrants had fled religious persecution and economic marginalisation in Pomerania, it was a population that owed little gratitude to the Prussian State). Just as British colonists in Tasmania gave the duke a wheelbarrow that combined Australian blackwood with the British heraldic flowers of rose, thistle and shamrock, the German colonists in South Australia gave Alfred 'a well-executed imitation of a flaming torch made of rope in blackwood, and inlaid with thirty-two different species of colonial woods, which were supplied by Dr. Schomburg of the Botanic Gardens'.[22] Both gifts were emblematic of colonists' assertion of the botanical metaphor—namely that the seeds of the old country flourished in colonial soil.

Such a relaxed attitude to dual German–British loyalty would not last long. After Prussia's 1870 victory in the war with France and its emergence as the leading state within the new German Empire, many Australians, like Britons, came to see it as an aggressor state. In 1867, however, while the *Pax Britannica* still held, and Prussia's military threat to Britain was not yet explicit, the adoption of foreign military uniforms was not necessarily associated with any particular ideological commitment or conflict of national interests. People did put on and discard uniforms more casually in this period than later in the nineteenth century. This was probably even truer in the colonies than at home (it is hard to imagine Alfred escaping public criticism had he worn a Prussian uniform while reviewing troops in London, for example). In Australia, where the European population faced many invasion scares but to date no real attack, the wearing of foreign uniforms offered an amusing diversion for the general public as well as the prince.

In fact, the wearing of uniforms was seen to have an aesthetic as well as a military function. At the duke's entry to Melbourne, for example:

> In order to make the whole affair as impressive as possible, all the military force in the colony was brought into requisition…and rendered most effective service, not only as regards the general picturesque effect in lining the streets, but also in the important duty which they undertook in…keeping the thoroughfares clear for the procession to pass along.[23]

The prince also displayed his love of military-style dress when he landed in Sydney wearing 'light trousers with a black military stripe'.[24] Moreover, Alfred was not afraid to mix and match German and British insignia; in Adelaide therefore, his Prussian colonel's uniform was 'ornamented by the badge of KG, and other marks of honourable distinction'.[25] This reflected the prevailing sartorial convention that 'more was more', as well as Alfred's own love of ornamentation. In Melbourne, observers commented on the gold rings the duke wore:

> He had eleven altogether on the two hands yesterday—large massive gold affairs—such as a lucky reefer, or puddler, might wear. They were so thick that he could not close his fingers—making his hands, as Sir Redmond remarked, like the fins of a turtle. In addition to these ornaments he wore a gold bracelet…it may be a delicate recognition of the fashion of wearing bracelets in Australia.[26]

While it might seem far-fetched for a British prince to emulate a gold-digger's taste in jewellery, in fact, Alfred seemed to enjoy following colonial fashion (or at least, what he perceived was colonial fashion). Sailors, like gold-diggers, were also known for wearing ostentatious jewellery and clothing ashore. Perhaps, like these men, Alfred relished the opportunities provided in the colonies to escape naval discipline.

Similarly, the extravagant dress worn by NSW ministers at the duke's arrival drew attention. The ministers' decision to order elaborate uniforms at a cost of £70 each was ridiculed as a 'childish whim' by the *Freeman's Journal*, which attributed it to a desire to do proper honour to the son of 'their Queen'.[27] These costumes, however, demonstrated colonial pride as much as individual vanity or loyalty to Britain, for the British Government had recently given colonial ministers the same status as ministers 'at Home', which meant that they were entitled to wear the same dress. By wearing these costumes in the duke's presence, then, New South Wales' ministers demonstrated their equality with their British counterparts.

Many other colonists wore costumes during the duke's visit. Some, such as the members of the *liedertafel*, wore national dress to express their identification with their homeland. For others, dressing up in foreign outfits provided an opportunity to display past, future or just wished-for transnational experience. At the Civic Fancy Dress Ball held to welcome Prince Alfred to Melbourne, for example, French, German, Italian, Swedish, Russian and Dutch costumes, including several military and naval uniforms, were on display. This reflected the international nature of the gathering—with several foreign consuls present—but also the outward-looking orientation of the Australian colonists themselves. The prominence of foreign naval costumes at local entertainments also reflected elite colonists' frequent contact with visiting navies. Dinners and dances for the officers were held in gentlemen's clubs such as the Melbourne Club as well as in private homes. These visits provided amusement for the visitors, boosted hostesses' egos and facilitated cultural exchange. To commemorate the 1870 visit of the Italian frigate *Garibaldi*, which brought the Duke of Genoa to Tasmania, for example, F. Fiorani inscribed a musical score with a dedication to the writer, artist and musician Louisa Anne Meredith. Such naval visits also appealed to the general public. One month after the Duke of Edinburgh departed Sydney, for example, the local papers were full of enthusiasm for the visiting French transport *Aveyron*. A report published in the *Illustrated Sydney News* suggested that Australian men and women were as keen to visit a French warship as a British one.[28] Indeed, when it came to public entertainment, any nation's warships would do, and the bigger the better.

Just as British colonists greeted foreign visitors enthusiastically, many non-British colonists queued up to honour Alfred. Loyal addresses were presented to him from 'the Hungarian residents of New South Wales', for example, as well as from the Chinese community in Castlemaine, Victoria.[29] Presenting loyal addresses was a well-established way for minority groups to assert their identity in a non-threatening way. This was particularly important for the Chinese community, which was viewed with much suspicion in Australia, as elsewhere. Still, their right to present their own address (albeit with the assistance of a trusted European translator) to the son of the British monarch was widely accepted, and exercised.[30] The press attention given to loyal addresses provided excellent publicity for many of these groups. Indeed, the Melbourne Chinese community's celebrations of the duke's visit attracted great interest, not least from the duke himself. So too in Sydney, the decoration of the steamer *Yamba* to resemble a dragon was widely admired.[31]

This image of multiple ethnic groups coexisting in harmony was, however, overly simplistic. The Irish Catholic community in particular was disaffected. Despite the fact that Catholics represented approximately one-quarter of the colonial population, the Irish Catholic clergy stayed away from official functions during the royal visit. While the *Freeman's Journal* expressed the hope that 'the day is not distant when the cause of the continued absence of the Catholic body from public receptions will be removed and they will be able to join with these acts of loyalty with their fellow colonists', such hope was in fact premature.[32] For while transparencies displaying Irish greetings such as '*Ceade mille failtha*' welcomed the duke, other messages stirred up sectarian hatred.[33] Protestant Orangemen's provocative reference to the Battle of the Boyne in one Melbourne display exacerbated tensions with Irish Catholics, and led to a fatal shooting. Tensions worsened with the shooting of the duke at Clontarf in March 1868. While this attempted assassination was the work of one unbalanced Irish Australian, it was initially blamed on the Fenian Brotherhood, an Irish republican movement. Moreover, in the eyes of the rabidly anti-Catholic NSW Colonial Secretary, Henry Parkes, all Irish Catholic Australians were potential Fenians. So, far from providing an opportunity to cement their ties to the polity, the duke's visit to Australia only isolated Irish Catholics further.[34] In colonial Australia, then, maintaining loyalty to Britain and Ireland (or Australia and

Ireland) clearly proved more problematic than maintaining loyalty to Britain and Germany. Not all combinations of national loyalty worked in the Australian context.

The Royal Navy

While Alfred might have mixed and matched his military uniforms, combining various German uniforms with British insignia, he seems to have treated his naval uniform with greater respect. His captain's uniform was certainly his uniform of choice throughout his Australian tour—at official functions in port as well as aboard HMS *Galatea*. While to an extent this simply reflects the fact that Alfred visited Australia as a serving naval officer, and naturally was expected to wear his uniform, it also reflects his great pride in the navy.[35] The fact that most of the '*carte-de-visite*' photographs circulating in the colonies depicted Alfred in naval uniform suggests that this is how Alfred himself wanted to be seen there.[36] In any case, this is certainly how many Australian colonists wanted to see him. Dozens of transparencies decorating buildings as well as flattering and unflattering cartoons published in the colonial press all depicted Alfred in naval uniform. When colonists noted that 'we know him from his portrait', they could have been describing Alfred's uniform as much as his facial features.[37] Alfred's decision not to wear his naval uniform on one occasion in northern Tasmania even drew press comment:

> Had he but appeared in naval uniform when holding his levee on Thursday, he would certainly have gratified many, and particularly some old naval officers who feel prouder, if possible, of the cloth—the navy blue—since they have had a Prince of the blood Royal in the service.[38]

As this account suggests, the uniform was seen to make the man. More than any other factor, Alfred's naval career confirmed his Britishness in the eyes of his Australian audience. Even the transparency decorating Sydney's Prussian consulate made reference to Alfred's maritime association, depicting Neptune escorting the prince over the ocean.[39] Alfred's 'true-blue' loyalty to the Royal Navy helps to explain further why Australians did not find his German connections disquieting.

For all the apparent Britishness of the Royal Navy, however, it was the navy that gave Alfred much of his transnational experience. On HMS *Galatea* alone, Alfred visited five continents. Similarly, many Australian colonists first saw the world from (or below) the deck of a Royal Navy ship—as officers, crew, soldiers or transported convicts. Even free emigrants who travelled directly between Britain and Australia on commercial vessels often stopped off in other places en route. In short, for many British and Australian men and women in the mid to late nineteenth century, life was transnational.

Colonists liked to see Alfred dressed as a naval officer because the navy was seen as Britain's 'wooden walls'. By choosing a naval career, therefore, Alfred demonstrated his commitment to protect the Mother Country and her colonies. In 1859, at a time when the navy was trying to recruit men, 'Admiral Punch' pointed to the young Alfred, recently entered as midshipman on HMS *Euryalus*: 'There, Boys! There's an Example for You!'[40] Just as Alfred's participation was seen to improve the navy, participation in the navy was seen to improve Alfred. As a fulsome article in a Tasmanian paper put it:

> In selecting his profession Prince Alfred gave convincing proof that he 'scorn'd luxurious ease', and no one can look at him without being further convinced that he, young as he is…has 'lived laborious days'. The result is a sound constitution, nerves firm as steel, an independent, self-reliant, candid spirit, a thorough knowledge of an honourable profession, and a laudable pride in the possession of that knowledge. He can navigate his course ashore as well as afloat, and would live and thrive in any condition of life. Even if stripped of his high rank he would ascend in the social scale, when a mere lordling or court puppet would sink or starve.[41]

By wearing his naval uniform in Australia, therefore, Alfred discarded the trappings of a prince and displayed the very qualities prized by colonists. While Alfred enjoyed many special privileges, his naval background did provide him with some common experience with gentlemen migrants to Australia.[42] Both spent months and years away from home, often in relatively Spartan conditions, exposed to the extremes of weather and reliant on letters and newspapers for news of home.[43] Alfred also seems to have shared many emigrants' desire to leave the tensions of home and seek adventure abroad.[44]

The Melbourne Club

In Victoria, for example, the duke quickly developed friendships with Samuel Curtis Candler and Frederick Standish, members of a circle of colonial gentlemen who entertained him at the Melbourne Club. Misfortune in Britain (Candler suffered ill health and Standish lost huge amounts of money gambling) left them with uncertain prospects. They migrated to Australia, where they built up solid lives in Victoria. Like Alfred, they enjoyed long careers in government service—Candler as coroner and Standish in the police force. While Alfred made his home for many years in the navy, Candler and Standish found homes in the Melbourne Club. Indeed, the Melbourne Club was Candler's residence for more than 50 years.[45]

While each of these three men used his career to establish his individual reputation, each also sought comfort, privacy and relative anonymity in the all-male environments provided by the navy or the Melbourne Club. Aboard ship, or behind the closed doors of the Melbourne Club, Alfred, Standish and Candler could relax with like-minded gentlemen. Candler rejoiced in Alfred's desire to be treated as any other club member: 'In short his bearing expressed as plainly as words could have done "Gentlemen, I am an Honorary member of your club. I perceive that you do not intend to treat me with ceremonial and we will be on the same footing if you please."'[46]

Alfred appears to have found the Melbourne Club's relative informality a welcome change from Victorian vice-regal society. Piqued at Governor Sir Henry Manners Sutton's excessive formality, the prince allegedly gave him a taste of his own medicine by making him and his family remain standing in his presence.[47] Similarly, aboard his ship, Alfred's word was law. Candler described Alfred's request to a Melbourne Club whist party that his own mistakes be pointed out to him while playing. In contrast, Captain Taylor of the *Galatea* assured Candler that 'if I won a hundred from him I should never think of letting him fancy it was from wrong play'.[48]

Like most immigrants to the colonies, Alfred made considerable efforts to fit into local society. Candler records that Alfred picked up colonial slang quickly, and used it frequently while off duty in the Melbourne Club. Similarly, rather than setting fashion trends, Alfred followed:

> He was quietly dressed and not in the extreme of fashion…I also noticed that his white hat was not [?] so much as I had been led to expect. It was of precisely the same shape, height and build of my own—indeed I fancy it was probably bought here in Melbourne.[49]

So delighted was Alfred with his Melbourne Club friends that he chose to spend Christmas Day 1867 with them. It is significant that Alfred chose to spend this holiday, so closely associated with family and 'home', ashore with men he had met only weeks before, as well as a few trusted companions from the *Galatea*. For most of the men at the table, 'home' was Britain. According to Candler, however, Alfred described a sense of dislocation on returning home:

> Talking of living in Melbourne I said I would rather live here on my small income than in Manchester, Birmingham or any of the large towns of England. The Duke said it was a very good place indeed and was inclined to agree with me…Also told us how difficult he found it on getting back from a voyage to London to pick up his old friends.[50]

Alfred's closeness to Candler and the other members of the Melbourne Club should not be exaggerated, nor should his apparent preference for egalitarian treatment. In fact, the duke could and did insist on his royal status when piqued, as his treatment of the Victorian governor and his family demonstrates. Alfred enjoyed the freedom of playing prince one day, captain of HMS *Galatea* another, and Melbourne Club member the next. Moreover, to be a member of the

Melbourne Club was to be a privileged member of colonial society indeed! For their part, Candler's and Standish's diaries reveal their habit of introspection and their enjoyment of solitude, away from their Melbourne Club cronies. Nevertheless, for all three men, all-male society based around the navy or the club played an important role in their lives. It provided the opportunity to reinvent themselves, and to re-present themselves as they chose, free from ordinary social obligations. It is telling that Alfred and Candler seized the opportunity to go incognito when it arose. At the Fancy Dress Ball in Melbourne, the duke changed from his naval uniform into disguise as an old man, and was delighted that very few people recognised him. For his part, Candler enjoyed dressing up as a Knight of Malta.[51] Though very different, both costumes suggest that their wearers relished the opportunity to display their masculine independence.

Colonial Australia also provided young men the freedom to escape the familial, social and moral constraints of Britain. Here was a place to reinvent oneself, while still maintaining some recognition of British class divisions. Like the navy, Australia provided an enjoyable and relatively well-remunerated alternative for young men who did not fit into successful middle-class British society. This allowed men to delay or avoid family responsibilities. Removal to Australia made postponement of marriage, and indeed failure to ever marry, much more likely. As Peter McDonald has pointed out, in the late nineteenth century, 20 to 30 per cent of Australian men had never married by the age of fifty—a higher proportion than in Britain.[52] Whether this was due to lack of opportunity (in most parts of Australia, men considerably outnumbered women) or desire, it is clear that, as Beverley Kingston has argued, contemporary Australian masculine society was ambivalent, to say the least, about marriage with Australian women.[53] Standish remained a bachelor his entire life and, as Penny Russell points out, his diary entries reveal his dislike of what he saw as 'fast' colonial women.[54] While Candler eventually married Laura Ellen Kennedy, who had borne him four children, he lived apart from them. Indeed, his Melbourne Club colleagues apparently learned of Mrs Candler's existence only after his death.[55] Even the duke married only in 1874, more than a decade after his elder brother the Prince of Wales. These examples provided further evidence that what John Tosh termed 'the flight from domesticity' applied to colonial Australia and to institutions such as the Royal Navy as well as to Victorian Britain.[56] From this perspective, Alfred's transnational life took him away from 'home' in more ways than one. For Alfred, as for numerous other British men of his generation, close male friendships and delayed marriage went hand-in-hand with a transnational life.

Conclusion

In a toast delivered shortly before the Duke of Edinburgh departed Tasmania, Governor Thomas Gore-Brown asserted that Tasmanians embodied Horace's maxim that 'they who cross the seas change their climate, but not their feelings'. Tasmanians were 'Britons to the back bone...whose loyalty and attachment to the Queen and her Royal family has not been chilled either by time or the distance which separates them from the mother country'. In his response, Alfred joked that he had in fact changed his feelings, for he had not expected Tasmania to be so wet.[57] Jokes aside, governor and duke had a point. Alfred's visit to Australia demanded that the prince and the locals display their loyalty to the British throne, affection for the Royal Navy and their adherence to British protocol. This involved asserting the Britishness of Alfred and the majority of colonists. Other cultural elements, however, were not easily forgotten, and the visit highlighted how transnational Australian society, as well as the British monarchy, really was. Like the Tasmanian weather, the loyalties of a British prince and Australian colonists were not always predictable. Moreover, the duke's experience with Victorian colonists led him to develop new loyalties.

Alfred's visit reminds us that post-gold-rush Australia was by no means a wholly British or even wholly English-speaking domain. The coexistence of multiple nationalities did not necessarily imply tolerance, of course. Irish and Chinese communities, among others, faced hostility that sometimes spilled over into violence. Neither, however, could the presence of these and other nationalities be wholly ignored or downplayed. The Duke of Edinburgh's visit provided a superb opportunity for national groups to advertise their contributions to colonial Australia, as well as (with the notable exception of the Irish Catholic clergy) to profess their loyalty to the British Crown.[58] Ironically, Alfred's attempted assassination greatly enhanced the opportunities for displays of loyalty, and led to an outpouring of extravagant assertions of submission and devotion.

Alfred's royal birth distinguished him from Australian colonists in many ways. In his choice of career and his travels to Australia and other colonies, however, he followed a path trod by thousands of other privileged young men seeking their fortunes beyond Britain's borders. At times, these men wore the uniforms of British officers and/or gentlemen, while at other times they slipped easily into the dress and manners of local elites. Such men often remained single for many years, and seemed most comfortable in the company of other immigrants and travellers. Their experiences, and those of their counterparts in Britain, demonstrated that Victorian masculinity was often performed outside of, and in resistance to, the domestic sphere. Alfred's transnational life allowed him to share in the colonial experience, albeit that of a privileged minority of men. Examining Alfred's life helps us to understand better his own complicated identity, and in turn those of colonial Australians. Finally, Alfred's visit to Australia helps illuminate how many men and women—within and beyond the British Empire—lived transnational lives.

Notes

[1] See Gibbney, H. J. 1972, 'Edinburgh, Duke of (1844–1900)', *Australian Dictionary of Biography. Volume 4*, Melbourne University, pp. 128–9.

[2] As is appropriate for a man who saw himself, and was seen by others, in different guises, Alfred will also be referred to in this essay as 'the Duke of Edinburgh' and 'the prince'.

[3] Meredith, Louisa Anne 1868, 'Welcome to Prince Alfred', *Prince Alfred Preparation Committee. Programme of the Torchlight Aquatic Procession and Serenade, To Welcome H.R.H. the Duke of Edinburgh on his arrival in Tasmania*, Printed at the Mercury Steam Press Office, Macquarie Street, Hobart Town, p. 11; 'Loyal address of directors of the Launceston and Western Railway Company', quoted in *Cornwall Chronicle*, 18 January 1868, p. 2.

[4] *Sydney Morning Herald* (hereafter *SMH*), 22 January 1868, pp. 4–5.

[5] Callaway, Anita 2000, *Visual Ephemera: Theatrical art in nineteenth-century Australia*, University of New South Wales Press, Sydney, p. 38.

[6] As with George IV, Victoria's activity boosted the popularity of Highland Scots culture within England. See Trevor-Roper, Hugh 1992, 'The invention of tradition: the Highland tradition of Scotland', in Eric Hobsbawm and Terence Ranger (eds), *The Invention of Tradition*, Cambridge University Press, Cambridge, pp. 15–41, at p. 39.

[7] For example, Alfred attended the annual Caledonian gathering in Melbourne 'and at his request the race in Highland costume, and the dance, Gillie Callum, were competed for out of their order in the programme'; *Argus*, reprinted in *Launceston Examiner*, 7 January 1868, p. 3.

[8] *Melbourne Punch*, 31 October 1867, p. 137.

[9] *Melbourne Punch*, 14 November 1867, p. 156.

[10] Callaway, *Visual Ephemera*, p. 38.

[11] Williams, Richard 1997, *The Contentious Crown: Public discussion of the British monarchy in the reign of Queen Victoria*, Ashgate, Brookfield, Vt, p. 154.

[12] *SMH*, 23 November 1867, p. 5, quoted in Van der Kiste, John and Jordaan, Bee with a foreword by Aronson, Theo 1984, *Dearest Affie…Alfred, Duke of Edinburgh: Queen Victoria's second son 1844–1900*, Alan Sutton Publishing, Gloucester, p. 63.

[13] Samuel Curtis Candler, 'Notes about Melbourne, and diaries' (hereafter 'Candler Diary'), 1848–[19—], 1 December 1867, State Library of Victoria, MS 9502, p. 301.

[14] *SMH*, 25 January 1868, p. 5.

[15] Candler Diary, 26 December 1867, p. 342.

[16] The same was not true in the 1890s. Questions were raised in the British Parliament and the German Reichstag about Alfred's suitability to lead a German state given his status as a British prince, a member of the Privy Council and a naval officer. See Van der Kiste and Jordaan, *Dearest Affie*, pp. 148–54.

[17] McCrae, George Gordon 1868, 'A Saylore on Horse-backe, ye Adelaide Troops are reviewed bye a Prussian Colonel', drawing, pen, ink and wash, in his *Album of Drawings*, National Library of Australia, nla.pic-an6330424.

[18] *Freeman's Journal*, Saturday 12 October 1867, p. 8; 25 April 1868, p. 2; 12 October 1867, p. 8.

[19] Candler Diary, 1 December 1867, p. 307.

[20] *Freeman's Journal*, 12 October 1867, p. 8.

[21] Candler Diary, 1 December 1867, p. 305; 14 January 1868, p. 354. In Tasmania, however, Louisa Anne Meredith employed the original, biblical version—'put not ye trust in Princes'—to comment on Alfred's apparent failure to support her petition to the Queen for a pension. See Robson, Lloyd 1991, *A History of Tasmania. Volume II. Colony and state from 1856 to the 1980s*, Oxford University Press, Melbourne, p. 18; and Rae-Ellis, Vivienne 1990, *Louisa Anne Meredith: A tigress in exile*, St David's Park Publishing, Hobart, pp. 217–18.

[22] *Cornwall Chronicle*, 15 January 1868, p. 6; 'From the *South Australian Register*, 2d November', *SMH*, 15 November 1867, pp. 5–6. Other Germans in Australia seem to have focused solely on their shared German heritage with Alfred. See, for example, the verses presented by Louis Kölling, *Fackelträger* (torchlight procession bearer), to Alfred in Melbourne (Gieh. Archiv QQ XVI I. 305, Thuringian State Archives, Gotha, Germany).

[23] 'Public entry into Melbourne' [from the *Melbourne Herald*], *SMH*, 29 November 1867, p. 6.

[24] *SMH*, 30 January 1868, p. 2.

25 *SMH*, 15 November 1867, p. 2.

26 Candler Diary, 2 December 1867, p. 316.

27 Among other cartoons, see 'The great "clothes" question; or, the prince and the ministry', *Sydney Punch*, vol. 7, 7 September 1867, p. 123; *Freeman's Journal*, 12 October 1867, p. 8.

28 Russell, Penny 1994, *A Wish of Distinction: Colonial gentility and femininity*, Melbourne University Press, Melbourne, p. 76; Fiorani, F. [18—], 'Tasmania: remembrance of the Italian frigate *Garibaldi*: romance', Musical score, Giannini, Napoli, Tasmaniana Library, CRO.E 780.9946 TAS, State Library of Tasmania; 'A visiting day on board the French transport ship "Aveyron"', *Illustrated Sydney News*, 16 May 1868, p. 364. Colonists flocked to visit the duke's ship, too; in Adelaide, 20,000 people were reported to have visited the *Galatea*; *SMH*, 15 November 1867, p. 5.

29 *SMH*, 6 April 1868, p. 24; *Argus*, 18 November 1867, p. 5.

30 Chinese communities throughout Australia, Asia, South Africa and the Pacific presented loyal addresses. See, for example, addresses from Malacca (Gieh. Archiv QQ XVI VII. 41) and Otago, New Zealand (Gieh. Archiv QQ XVI VI. 37), now held in the Thuringian State Archives, Gotha.

31 Candler Diary, 2 December 1867, pp. 311–12. The dragon motif seems to have been inspired by Chinese designs; *SMH*, 21 January 1868, p. 5.

32 *Freeman's Journal*, 8 February 1868, p. 1. *Sydney Punch* also commented on the Catholics' absence in 'What we may expect to see. As the head of only one religious denomination "assisted" at the last review, Mr Punch respectfully offers the above suggestion as an improvement in the next one', *Sydney Punch*, vol. 8, 1 February 1868, p. 74.

33 *Cornwall Chronicle*, 15 January 1868, p. 5. Victorian Governor, Sir Henry Manners Sutton, commented on the sectarian tensions in a memorandum on a loyal address submitted by the Orangemen to Alfred, which he advised accepting in order to maintain the peace (16 November 1867, Gieh. Archiv QQ XVI I. 510, Thuringian State Archives, Gotha).

34 Inglis, K. S. 1974, *The Australian Colonists: An exploration of social history 1788–1870*, Melbourne University Press, Melbourne, pp. 94–7.

35 Alfred could also have been making amends for his earlier behaviour. Candler contrasts the rumour of him being told off for wearing *mufti* in South Africa (which he visited immediately before Australia) with his apparently blameless behaviour in Gibraltar; Candler Diary, Christmas Day 1867, p. 338. Naval discipline aboard HMS *Galatea* in the latter voyages (1869–71) seems to have been maintained strictly, according to the notebook of Lieutenant John William Ramsay (University of Cambridge Library, Manuscripts Collection, Add. 9279).

36 In addition to numerous photographs in Australian and British collections, Alfred appears in naval uniform in two *carte-de-visite* photographs, dated 1858 and c. 1862 respectively, held in the National Library of South Africa (Cape Town Pictures, ARC 54 [6630] and Album 1 [5]), as well as in several photographs detailing his 1867 visit to Cape Town (photograph album, Wits University Library, Reference A1552). My thanks to Michele Pickover and Idah Makukele for sending me details of the Wits album.

37 See, for example, 'Australia Supplex and the "real" Australian Australian Ladies' Ball; or, gin-uine "Blue Blood"', *Sydney Punch*, vol. 8, 28 March 1868, p. 139, and vol. 7, 9 November 1867, p. 194.

38 While decades later the duke was chastised for spending too little time on his naval duties, when he was a young man, the navy was clearly the centre of Alfred's world; Van der Kiste and Jordaan, *Dearest Affie*, pp. 28, 40, 54–5; *Cornwall Chronicle*, 18 January 1868, p. 2.

39 *SMH*, 23 January 1868, pp. 5–6.

40 'Men for the fleet! Punch', in M. Lemon (ed.) n.d., *Punch: The first fifty years*, London, p. 238.

41 *Cornwall Chronicle*, 18 January 1868, p. 2.

42 Numerous criticisms were made of Alfred's tardiness and frequent expressions of boredom at official events—for example, Candler Diary, 29 November 1867, p. 301. Had he not been shot in March 1868, it is likely that these criticisms would have increased.

43 In his diary entry for 2 December 1867 (pp. 312–13), Candler describes the duke joining in a conversation at the Melbourne Club about pests such as fleas and cockroaches. Alfred was clearly no stranger to physical discomfort while travelling.

44 Van der Kiste and Jordaan, *Dearest Affie*, pp. 54–6.

45 Cooke, Simon 2005, 'Candler, Samuel Curtis (1827–1911)', *Australian Dictionary of Biography. Supplementary Volume*, Melbourne University Press, pp. 63–4; Legge, J. S. 1976, 'Standish, Frederick Charles (1824–1883)', *Australian Dictionary of Biography. Volume 6*, Melbourne University Press, pp.

172–3 (online edition viewed 1 August 2007); McNicoll, Ronald 1988, *Number 36 Collins Street: Melbourne Club 1838–1988*, Allen & Unwin/Haynes and Melbourne Club, Sydney, pp. 143–4. Candler's and Standish's diaries record the sexual and social adventures of the duke and his entourage in Melbourne. In a forthcoming piece entitled 'Colonial hospitality', I argue that these adventures constituted an unofficial tour that ran parallel with the official tour, illuminating the hypocrisy and the flexibility of elite colonial society's responses to gender, race and class.

[46] Candler Diary, 2 December 1867, p. 314.

[47] The frosty atmosphere in Government House can be gauged by an undated note written by Sir Henry Manners Sutton to his royal guest on the Saturday morning of an official function, pointing out the need to leave the residence in time to arrive punctually (Gieh. Archiv QQ XVI I. 457, Thuringian State Archives, Gotha).

[48] Candler Diary, 2 December 1867, p. 314; 28 December 1867, p. 344.

[49] Candler Diary, 1 December 1867, p. 305.

[50] Candler Diary, Christmas Day 1867, p. 339.

[51] Candler Diary, 23 December 1867, p. 336.

[52] McDonald, Peter F. 1975, *Marriage in Australia: Age at first marriage and proportions marrying, 1860–1971*, The Australian National University, Canberra, pp. 105, 107, cited in Kingston, Beverley 1988, *The Oxford History of Australia. Volume 3, 1860–1900 Glad, Confident Morning*, Oxford University Press, Melbourne, p. 119.

[53] Kingston, *The Oxford History of Australia*, pp. 119–21.

[54] For example, Candler Diary, 23 September 1867, cited in Russell, *A Wish of Distinction*, pp. 110–1.

[55] Legge, 'Standish, Frederick Charles', pp. 172–3; McNicoll, *Number 36 Collins Street*, p. 144.

[56] Tosh, John 1999, *A Man's Place: Masculinity and the middle-class home in Victorian England*, New Haven and London, p. 187.

[57] *Launceston Examiner*, 16 January 1868, p. 5.

[58] The Irish Catholic community (including the priesthood) did profess its loyalty to the royal family after the attempted assassination of Alfred at Clontarf in Sydney in March 1868. I discuss this episode, and its implications for colonial expressions of loyalty and identity, in a forthcoming essay.

Chapter 5

Enacting the international: R. G. Watt and the League of Nations Union

Nicholas Brown

Introduction

As Julie Evans, Margaret Allen and Cindy McCreery have argued in this section of *Transnational Ties*, concepts of empire provided powerful ways of mediating the 'authority' of trans-colonial governance, images of gender and competing identities for Australians in the nineteenth century. Moving into the twentieth century, however, and with the accelerating pressures of mobility, communication and consumption—in short, of modernity—empire became a less exclusive way of experiencing the authority of Australia's transnational ties. Akira Iriye has noted the extent to which an idea of international society came to define forms of conduct, activism, intervention and accountability early in the twentieth century. These forms in turn seemed—so H. G. Wells observed—to summon 'a new kind of people', a 'floating population' of figures associated with an increasingly formalised sector of international organisations.[1] The authority these figures invoked in their ideals, and exercised in setting 'standards' and 'processes', continues to underpin much of the discursive power of the 'international' and the experience of transnationalism.

Just as 'empire' had particular meanings for Australia as a sequence of settler colonies, so did the 'international' as a space associated with new civic modes framed by concepts of nationhood and state experimentation. A good deal has been written about 'international citizenship' as it informed essentially voluntary social movements associated with labour and women's rights from the late nineteenth century onwards, and comprehending issues of destiny and solidarity. The transition into more institutionalised, and later professionalised, forms of action is less studied—except as a loss of that earlier vitality, or as a break between distinct identities and experiences.[2] After World War I and the recognition of Australia at the 1919 Paris Peace Conference (explicitly) and the Russian Revolution (implicitly), these new modes of the international—as an ideal of world regulation or global (potentially violent) transformation—required development and recognition.

For some commentators, these modes served to defuse the challenge of a type of nationalism with no goal beyond its own insular, radical tendencies.[3] These modes were also seen to demonstrate political 'maturity'. In acquiring 'special dominion' responsibilities at Paris, so Harrison Moore argued in 1933, Australia remained within the compass of the British Empire but with enhanced capacities for independent state action. Such capacities, John Latham added, also recast the wider sphere in which civil society must be imagined. By entering into the conduct of 'international relations', Latham stated, Australians must accept that, 'in any intelligible sense', the main currents of society can exist only 'between men organised in States and not between unorganised masses of men, or between any State and such a mass'.[4] Less defensively, W. K. Hancock observed that the British Empire itself had proven more a laboratory for, than simply a precursor to, the recognition of the kind of 'international problems'—especially of economic, cultural and racial diversity—that so characterised the twentieth century.[5]

Translating such thinking into reality, while also fleshing it out as imaginary, was a rather different matter, and one that still—through the inter-war years—required self-conscious adaptation. A figure such as Jessie Street might negotiate such a transition fairly seamlessly. Her privileged family background (with a fair degree of 'empire' providing structure and opportunity) was a considerable, largely unquestioned asset, and brought an element of continuity to campaigns that were underpinned by extensive travel and spanned from prewar feminism and peace and disarmament to post-1945 concepts of human rights.[6] For others, however, this was much less the case. To become the 'new kind of person' Wells identified was an experimental and perhaps risky affair. Frank Moorhouse has conveyed much of this process in the figure of Edith Campbell Berry, the heroine of his novels *Grand Days* and *Dark Palace*. Leaving Sydney to take up her position as clerk, Internal Administration, Division 1, Class B, in the League of Nations, Berry soon finds herself in a Geneva café, 'testing herself to see if she indeed felt international'. Did she move or behave like a stranger or tourist? Was there some distinction in comportment between being an 'international woman', a 'European' or a 'cosmopolitan', and how might such a persona be accessible to an Australian, accustomed only to the 'brand new'?[7]

I want to look now at one such process of experimentation, noting what was invested in it as a transition between the worlds of 'empire' and 'international' with which we are much more familiar, and particularly by registering the risks involved. 'Missing links' are not always edifying creatures, but they do help us understand as historically conditioned much that we otherwise take for granted. At a time when the 'international' is invoked so potently—as threat, benchmark or the selective domain of intervention by 'the willing'—it is particularly useful to look back at how that space first came to be 'peopled'.

'Idealism, energy and persistence': making space for the international

Unlike Edith Campbell Berry, Raymond Watt (1889–1967) lived his transnational life largely at home, in Sydney. He shared, however, much with her in testing himself through the forms of activism he adopted as an advocate for international causes from the 1920s to the 1940s. His was not the transnationalism of travel but of conscience, of an intellectual and personal investment in understanding issues defined as being of significance beyond the nation, and in that new space for international engagement caught ambivalently between social movements and the functions of states.[8] Watt's outlook was formed not through encountering differing societies and cultures; it was a product of working to establish standards against which such differences might be judged. His outlook was shaped in part by a creative engagement with the changing media available to bring the world, in authoritative ways, to popular attention. His apparent altruism was in itself a cultural artefact of his time, the brittleness of which was evident in his experience, even his personality. For these reasons, his is a useful life to reclaim from obscurity, not necessarily to place in the ranks of 'significant figures' alongside, say, Jessie Street, but to understand as a symptom of how contingent are the ways in which we care for our world.

Born in Gosford, New South Wales, in 1889, Watt was the fourth of nine children in a strict Congregationalist family. Five of eight sons served in World War I. Ray, however, stayed at home, abandoning study at Camden Theological College and the University of Sydney (where his courses were English, Greek, economics, philosophy and psychology) to help his father's business as a manufacturer's agent. Watt was ambiguous in his stance towards conscription in a poem written in 1917, but clear in espousing the glory of military sacrifice. A manifesto of 1918 declares his commitment to ensure there would be no return to the carnage of World War I, and 'to work so that others will not have died in vain'. His sense of the war was thus tinged with an awareness of opportunities denied, of honour in service and of advancement in education. Perhaps by way of compensation, his manifesto saw in the war an emblem of what could be achieved through other forms of dedication, and in the synergy of technology, the State and social mobilisation. The war had, he observed, 'heightened the emotional tone of the community'; its effect should be to 'force everyone nearer to those verities which are fundamental'.[9]

Accordingly, in 1921, Watt became a foundation member of the NSW branch of the League of Nations Union (LNU) and was elected its general secretary in 1926. He saw in the new sphere of the international, as represented by the League of Nations, the prospect of idealised order or calamitous disorder. It was a sphere that carried all the potentialities of modernity, redeemed from the mires of nationalism but shadowed by unprecedented economic instability and military destruction, now with the capacity to engulf the globe.[10] He was not an 'internationalist' in the sense of envisaging a universality of culture—a view that might be associated with one of his Sydney LNU colleagues David Stead. Stead's daughter, Christina, conveyed elements of her father's philosophy in her portrait of Sam Pollitt in *The Man Who Loved Children*: Pollitt advocated the 'monoman', embodying 'world peace, world love, world understanding, based on science and the fit education of even the meanest, most wretched' person.[11] Watt was more attuned to another prominent LNU leader and parliamentarian Littleton Groom, who characterised the league as an experiment in a new 'technique of government': deliberative and representative.[12] In Watt's own words, the league offered a mechanism to achieve 'regulation' across nations 'on the basis of consent'.[13]

In 1930, Watt was a founder of the Federal Australian League of Nations Union, and served as its national secretary until 1945. He was therefore organiser and publicist for the union at a state and national level while also assuming a number of closely related responsibilities, including as honorary correspondent for the International Labour Organisation (ILO). His work had many dimensions, as did the union itself. As one among a network of associations that characterised inter-war intellectual engagement, centring mostly on precepts of social improvement through enlightened fellowship, the union depended on commitments sustained through regular meetings, addresses, subscription drives and public events, the circulation of information and the crafting of forms of concern and activity that were appropriate to pre- or proto-professional engagement with international issues. If the league itself represented the quest for 'world government', the union was a lobby group for this cause and an embodiment of the forms of citizenship appropriate to that ideal.

The most prominent issues on the league's agenda spanned from the objectives of disarmament, the arbitration of international conflict and the collective enforcement of peace to the oversight of colonial mandates, the setting of standards and conditions for labour, health and migration, and the equitable distribution of economic progress and access to justice. Bold 'political' causes, such as disarmament, might have been the first appeal of the league, and those that fell most quickly into disillusion, but it was the latter causes—'non-political' matters of 'technique' and 'regulation' focused on social and economic reform—that more enduringly held the interest of those who looked to the league as a way of comprehending the foundations of insecurity and articulating principles of international justice. In this guise, the league's challenge was one of political imagination, and often seemed to supersede the conventional political divisions of the period. So, for example, Sir Otto Niemeyer, stern emissary from the Bank of England, agreed with Watt to give an address for the union during the mission in which he famously condemned Australians for the financial recklessness evident in their exposure to the Great Depression. Humanitarian responsibility, Niemeyer insisted in Sydney in 1930, was integral to international economic interdependence. A member of the league's finance committee since 1922, he had been associated with the resettlement of refugees in Greece and Bulgaria. As Niemeyer informed his Sydney audience, these were 'severely practical' questions that 'touch even distant Australia' and perhaps placed local over-indulgence in a new light.[14]

Watt's work demonstrated that the relationship between the forms of civic action that sustained the union and the causes associated with the league were often unsteady.[15] This relationship was, however, (as Frank Moorhouse's novels attest) integral to the power of the inter-war international community as a field of commitment.[16] Although a less colourful character than Edith Campbell Berry, Watt nonetheless sought to 'enact' the international in ways that extended the boundaries of intellectual and moral engagement. In this sense, he 'lived' the international through one phase of its troubled emergence, at a time when few other sources of informed opinion and political influence were available, and in relation to the sphere of largely voluntary organisations that figured so centrally in transnationalism.[17] It was his 'idealism, energy and persistence' that was most admired by Peter Heydon, for example, who as one of Australia's early career diplomats later recalled the open, critical engagement Watt had fostered—an engagement Heydon thought became rare in more polarised debates after World War II, and hard to sustain amid the pressures of official work that he knew so well.[18]

'A fiery orator': finding a voice for international awareness

Watt certainly became a ubiquitous figure in inter-war Sydney, exploring and exploiting opportunities to present the league and build its constituency. His ideal of 'regulation by consent' was influenced heavily by issues of equity in distribution—of power, finance, resources and wealth—among nations, primarily in a restive Europe, but encompassing a world internationalised through the legacies of nineteenth-century imperialism and facing disintegration through class-based unrest, the restraint of trade and the lure of ideologies that fed on such distortions.[19] The schemes he proposed could be complex, such as a 1932 system of international tariff discounts that would reward countries adopting social reforms: a 10 per cent discount given to the produce of a state that implemented the 40-hour week; 5 per cent off for those that legislated against night work for women and children; another 5 per cent if children under 12 were kept from work.[20] They were, however, delivered in an accessible, engaging style: 'Why don't we?' 'What if?' He was a regular commentator on radio stations 2KY, 2CH, 2BL and 2GB, at public lectures and meetings associated with the union (in city, suburban and country centres), in the press and in classes of the Workers' Educational Association [WEA]. An intense, restless man, Watt was remembered by J. D. B. Miller (later a leading international relations scholar) as 'a fiery orator' around the city: 'a man of very deep convictions' who 'made the League of Nations Union…a significant body'.[21]

Miller's first memories of Watt come from the time when, as a schoolboy, Miller regularly visited the union's office in Castlereagh Street. Perhaps Miller's interest had been kindled by the recitation of Sir Walter Murdoch's 'Credo', inserted by the union in the NSW Department of Education's *School Magazine*: 'I believe that all human beings are members of one family', all races having the 'same right to life and happiness and a fair share of the earth and of the things which the earth produces'.[22] Schools were a favoured recruiting ground for the union, and Watt drove such initiatives hard (membership campaigns, badge distributions and international 'pen friend' programs, which by 1940 had garnered 25,486 subscriptions to the Correspondence Scholars International scheme).[23] Whether in classrooms or public ceremonies, with precisely timed programs of speeches interspersed with musical and poetry recitals, Watt made certain the league had a ready appeal. On the radio, he carefully framed a persona serving the same purpose, with evident success: '[T]he listener feels you are able to be trusted,' testified one letter of appreciation; '[Y]ou are not puffed up with your own vanity,' noted another.[24]

A marked ambiguity, however, surrounded Watt's work with respect to his official role and its 'advocacy' dimensions—and these aspects in themselves reflected the fragility of the international as an area of social engagement. Watt was essentially the first fully salaried official of the League of Nations Union (Constance Duncan was appointed to a similar position for the Victorian branch in 1934, but shared it with other responsibilities, including to the Bureau of Social and International Affairs, a more exclusive and privately funded body devoted to exploring the origins of international conflict).[25] As such, Watt was to organise and (as he increasingly saw it) speak for an organisation that was of its essence voluntary but had to develop engagement with issues that demanded expertise and state action. In selling pamphlets and booklets, he was in part raising funds that met his salary, buying time to broach such work, as well as supporting an ideal.

Skilled in public relations—and sharing with his wife, Eileen, an interest in the psychology of commerce—Watt was inventive in devising schemes of social participation. A 100-car treasure hunt across northern Sydney, for example, ending in fireworks and community singing, was publicity for the union while also supporting Ray and Eileen's travel to the Brussels World Peace Congress in 1936 (the third and last time he left Australia).[26] In public speaking, he was drawn increasingly into questions of interpretation, tactics and style that were personalised: *his* point of view, *his* integrity, *his* opinion. Watt's activities were therefore caught between an ethic of association that was essentially collective and patterns of organisation and commentary that were becoming increasing specialised.

This was not an unchallenged position. David Stead—stoically idealist and president of the NSW branch of the LNU in 1930–31—held that there should be no paid official for such a body: the task was a calling not a job.[27] Other union colleagues expressed similar views, reflecting their own opportunities and the ambivalent placement of international concern between solidarity and expertise. Janet Mitchell, for example, served as education secretary for the Young Women's Christian Association (YWCA) in 1924–26, then as director of the thrift service of the Bank of New South Wales (1926–31), and in 1925 was an Australian delegate to the first Institute of Pacific Relations conference in Honolulu. Frustrated in testing the boundaries of such new fields of instruction, she left in 1931 to work as a journalist in Harbin, China, with feelings of bitterness that Australia had failed to recognise her talents (she returned in 1933 as acting principal of the Women's College, University of Sydney). Before departing, she closely scrutinised Watt's sincerity, diagnosing a failure of his early, if 'simple-minded', idealism as he became more immersed in the LNU. Mitchell had grown 'uncomfortable' with Watt's pursuit of a 'political' dimension to what should have remained matters of 'publicity'.[28] His ego, she judged, had compromised a cause that should have reflected selflessness and devotion.

Watt's papers include many photographs of his activities with the Student Christian Union and the WEA: they are images of groups at study, at picnics, on rambles—of fellowship. If the LNU began with elements of the same ethos, it soon acquired other imperatives. As a personality, but also as an official, Watt marks these transitions. In contrast with Mitchell's increasing distrust, Eleanor Hinder, who pioneered industrial welfare in Australia as superintendent of staff welfare at Farmer's department store before travelling to undertake similar work in China and later at the ILO, sympathised with Watt's fruitless search for a 'place where your social vision could express itself'.[29] Hinder saw a continuity with the religious vocation and university studies Watt had given up to assist his father's troubled business, only to face again in the LNU the frustration of his personal capacities to make a difference. His importance to Hinder—and not to her alone—in building a sense of mission was implied in letters that closed with 'love to you—that's the kind of thing one doesn't say to a man, if one is a woman'. From Shanghai, she wrote, '[Y]ou seem to be so real a factor these days in my life.'[30] In addition to a personal closeness, there is a move beyond the bonds of fellowship in the qualities that define a cause. 'We have the belief,' another supporter wrote, 'that you will make good and be a leader of men.'[31]

Personal dedication and motivation were clearly sensitive issues in this context—perhaps they always are in transnational lives: what explains a move beyond the ready, local identity? If inter-war communist internationalism, according to Eric Hobsbawm, centred on an ethic of 'transcending selfishness', its liberal variations similarly 'reprioritised loyalties' in their own terms—although Watt's idealist philosophy was more attuned to self-realisation than subscription to the laws of history.[32] Hinder and Mitchell had acted on their belief in international causes but in ways that reflected the particular opportunities available to them, in part arising from earlier feminist internationalism. Unmarried and mobile, they made careers in work that offered an intersection between gendered roles and international opportunities.[33] Watt, from 1926 married with children and living (ironically) in Anglo Street, Chatswood, stayed at home, seeking the authority of a public commentator. Scrutiny of his motives—of the fit between his personality and the task of winning public 'trust'—was recurrent.

Even his much younger brother Alan questioned Watt from his college in Oxford, where he had travelled on a Rhodes Scholarship (the brothers' circumstances in education, and career, were to prove very different). 'Before I left,' Alan probed in 1923, 'the virtues that I saw in you seemed clouded. You seemed to feel that sacrifices on your part should be recognised; almost to suggest that unless they were so recognised, they would not be justified.' Ray, Alan wrote from his Balliol study, needed to find humility, whereas for Alan—complaining of the 'ghastly' strains of his final examinations—philosophical reflection gained the legitimacy of academic study: '[W]e must seek the conditions of beauty and holiness,' Alan counselled, 'along the path of economic reconstruction.'[34]

What lay behind such scrutiny? In these exacting assessments of Watt's claims to speak for international causes there are tests of authority similar to those observed by Evans, Allen and McCreery in the context of 'empire'. For Watt, however, they are informed by registers of secularisation, modernity and personality. Watt's theological interests had transferred to psychology as a way of understanding the bases of international unrest. He concurred with one of his mentors at the University of Sydney, Professor Francis Anderson, for many years also president of the NSW LNU, who maintained that 'the world passes from one crisis to another in the attempt not to forestall poverty, but to prevent the threatened prosperity' that modernity might confer in aspirations and opportunities to be shared among humanity.[35] To catch this popular sensibility required the tailoring of a certain appeal. In seeking to dispel the disillusions of colleagues, Watt could argue that

> the world always had its plethora of money-grubbers, its political power-seekers and its bovine masses. Surely they only *seem* to be more numerous now-a-days simply because this age has, what other ages did

not have (not at any rate so widespread!) the pinnacles of new ideas from which to regard them...Certainly, to me, the purview of people these days seems very much more comprehensive than that of those amongst whom I spent my early years[36]

The challenge was to push such 'new ideas', and to create and capture enthusiasm.

The LNU was for Watt a career—if one with a salary that at certain points could be guaranteed only for three-month periods, and always needing supplementation.[37] More than once he threatened resignation, either because he felt there was insufficient support for his work, insufficient payment for him as a 'breadwinner' or intolerable compromise to his mission. 'I am not at all easy in my mind,' he confided to Stead in 1931, given the failure of the union to address the extent to which international tension reflected incipient class rather than national conflict, requiring 'coordinated action on economic and financial matters' and, as such, sustained research and representation to governments.[38] Frustrated, and sometimes labouring his discontent, he still strove to build a position from which it was possible to speak convincingly for international issues beyond the cycles of crisis.

'Let's imagine Geneva': evoking the international

However scrutinised by elements within the LNU, Watt was not alone in his aspirations. The union became a prominent organisation at a time when the pursuit of social and political causes through publicity, discussion and the distribution of information had an importance unimaginable to us in an age of mass electronic communication. Such activities in themselves, however, imposed a considerable burden. The Victorian Bureau of Social and International Affairs, which provided a joint secretariat for the Victorian LNU and the rather more restricted membership of the Institute of Pacific Relations, the Melbourne Round Table group and Royal Institute of International Affairs branch, reported in 1930 that 'by far the most claims on [our] time and attention' were made by the LNU, with its growing membership and many activities.[39] Between 800 and 1000 full adult members had initially joined the NSW branch ('war memories turned people into crusaders'), but by 1925 membership had fallen to 200. Numbers quickly recovered, however, when Watt became a full-time officer (1417 members by 1929, 1555 by 1930, 3560 by 1938). While membership fluctuated, it was assumed, in response to international events and perceptions about the league's relevance (declining to 1036 in 1934, amid the Sino–Japanese crisis, up to 3138 in 1935 after Italy's attacks on Abyssinia), even lean years saw intense activity (more than 200 lectures were given in metropolitan Sydney in 1934).[40] 'The first answer to every citizen who wishes to help the League is "Join the League of Nations Union"'—this appeal from Sir Edward Grey, heading

Australian application forms, was not merely gratuitous but expressed a meaningful connection between the union's programs and the League of Nations. How was Watt to represent or enable that connection?

As a voluntary body, the LNU thrived on sociability—on acts of meeting, modes of discussion, codes of commitment. Its leading, or most prominent, members formed a solid core and a distinct social stratum: overwhelmingly Protestant (Anglicans by far the dominant group, followed by Presbyterians), academically educated (law being the largest disciplinary background) and frequently academics by profession.[41] About 40 per cent of members were women—an association encouraged perhaps by the league's constitutional commitment to non-discrimination. Association with the union was often one affiliation among many others, including with the English Speaking Union, the Student Christian Movement, the Victoria League, the United Service League, the Town Planning Association, the Racial Hygiene Association—the list was extensive. The international, in these contexts, was in part defined through networks and ways of 'performing' concern in meetings, speech and action. If prominent members led such activities, they were joined, watched and listened to by many others who contributed their labour, time and money.

One of the heights of the union's calendar, for example, was an international ball. Watt claimed to have conceived this function, held first at the Palais Royal in 1926, then at the new Trocadero, which usually attracted more than 1200 people. Other branches, even those in the United Kingdom, soon adopted the ball.[42] Complete with vice-regal patronage, these were national-costume or themed affairs, including a pageant in which bonds of art, science, industry and friendship were personified. The Adelaide pageant was especially famous for its elaborate staging: in 1929, actors represented characters including 'Peace', 'Public Opinion', 'Self-Interest', 'Goodwill', 'Time', 'Necessity', Experience' and 'Humanity'. The Sydney branch was more modest in performance, but equally earnest: 250 people in 1930 represented a spectrum from 'Music' and 'Architecture' to 'Law', 'Agriculture' and 'Commerce'.[43]

Very effective in raising money, these pageants were the lighter end of a continuum of activities that defined the LNU's claim to speak for the advancement of people across the world. George Rich, a justice of the High Court since 1913 and an initially cynical delegate to the 1922 league conference, returned from Geneva as if from a 'revivalist meeting'. He was struck by the behaviour of 'shrewd, practical, able and conciliatory men of the world, meeting together to solve in a commonsense way problems that baffled nations'.[44] This face-to-face emphasis indicated a desire to establish credentials, to secure accountability, to ground the abstraction of issues in the display of virtues and to enable an exchange between people accorded the status of delegates of their societies, representing interests rather than states. In this sense, there seemed to be a thread running from sociability at the lunchtime talk or the evening lecture to the promise of the international in a high diplomacy not confined to officials. Douglas Copland, then a young and enthusiastic professor of commerce at the University of Melbourne, recorded in his notebook that the importance of the league lay in tracing the 'growth of government', adding the aphorism that 'the history of the evolution of civilisation is the history of the evolution of *social groups*'.[45]

Figure 5.1: An earnest group: Ray Watt is second from the right in the front row among the delegates at the League of Nations Union Annual Meeting and Conference in Canberra, 28-31 January 1938.

The others are: front row, right to left, W.A. Woods (Tas.), RGW, R.J.F. Boyer (Qld), Sir Robert Garran (president), M.M. Rischbieth (WA), Professor F. Alexander (WA); back row, right to left, O. Smith (Tas.), Eileen Watt (NSW), Constance Duncan (Vic.), E.M. Boyer, W. Macmahon Ball (Vic), Rev Norman Lade (SA), L. Littlejohn (NSW), F.E. Barraclough (NSW), Captain F. O'Sullivan (Qld) and Ruby Rich (NSW). Raymond Watt Papers, National Library of Australia, courtesy Gabrielle Watt.

Modelling 'regulation by consent', Watt was indefatigable in facilitating such social groups, always present, sometimes a speaker—although at the most prominent occasions a higher dignitary would preside (Watt, after all, was not quite of the right stratum). When Watt did get such roles, however, there was an almost palpable sense that he could push too hard at suitable codes of conduct. So, for example, when Watt attended the 1936 league conference as an Australian delegate, S. M. Bruce, as official government representative, would allow him only to 'submit in writing any brain waves that might occur to me'; otherwise

'I'm to be put in cold storage in case my enthusiasm should raise the temperature in Europe'.[46] Watt's busy-ness could irritate office holders who had jobs elsewhere ('Frankly, Raymond,' Fred Alexander wrote from the University of Western Australia regarding a conference on postwar reconstruction that Watt was keen to organise in 1945, 'I am extremely pressed'), just as his need to raise funds by selling his services beyond the LNU was a matter of sensitivity for those who gave their time for nothing.[47]

Watt's work extended beyond organisation. His extensive papers are sorted into hundreds of folders of press clippings organised by theme, country, issue or organisation, drawn from the local and international press (prominently the *Christian Science Monitor*, Manchester *Guardian* and London *Times* and the British Broadcasting Corporation's *Listener*), pamphlets, journals, reports and Hansard. There are index cards of quotations culled from wide reading and pocket books of speaking notes regularly revisited and revised. Meticulously selected, marked or transcribed, these materials testify to a sustained program of largely autodidactic synthesis, usually soon turned into some form of speech, radio address or press commentary.

In this commentary, Watt was also exploring new forms of authority. The international as 'news', as a defined category of information, was deeply formed by its media and associated assumptions of audience—ever since Jeremy Bentham first noted the term taking 'root in the language' of 'reviews and newspapers'.[48] By the inter-war years, these media were undergoing rapid change. The Melbourne *Herald* borrowed the promise to 'put a girdle round the earth' in the rapid transmission of international reporting, conveyed in headlines, wireless communication, picture-grams and frequent editions. Radio, in particular, began making an even more direct appeal, bringing a world of voice and sound into the informal spaces of the home. In 1933, on one of his overseas trips, Watt sought particularly to build connections with the British Broadcasting Corporation (BBC). He brought back a report on the power of broadcasting to evoke familiarity over distance that noted, by way of illustration, the impact 'for Australian listeners [when] the first broadcast of an English nightingale seemed to bring them nearer home'.[49] He also brought back an enthusiasm for organising 'listening groups': small collections of interested people who would gather round a radio to listen to a program and then, perhaps with guidance from materials provided, discuss their views.

The League of Nations itself was astutely aware of, and partly a product of, such potentialities in the flow of information. Any interested person, as Watt reminded readers and listeners, could receive the league's 'Radio Nations'. The league's engagement with new media was, however, guarded. Responding to the growth of cinema, the British LNU was prepared to name Charlie Chaplin as Foreign Ambassador to the World in 1925, but argued more generally that it was ill-advised 'to deliberately misrepresent Western culture' by providing through most of the film that was available to people beyond the West 'a succession of facile peeps at the frothy sides of life, and so stir up racial animosity and antagonism'. The league's 1937 convention on broadcasting required nations to 'stop without delay...any transmission which is detrimental to good international understanding'—a policy readily adopted by governments keen to minimise discussion of fascism.[50]

Less cautiously, Watt embraced radio with an almost Wellsian mission of 'world education' through a cultivated persona fastidiously searching through 'the cables' while imaginatively engaged by the material covered. A 1935 talk for nine–twelve year olds began: 'I want to draw a picture for you. Will you close your eyes? Let's imagine Geneva.' A 2GB broadcast on 27 September 1937 began (as the script has it):

> Japan bombs Chinese cities! Civilian cities! The incident means, of course, this!—the thing so much feared has become a FACT...[a city bombed] to terrorise a nation into submission, and children, and women, as well as men, have had to take the shock of military ruthfulness [sic].[51]

Such a presentation would usually end with an appeal for the listener to think about the issue: why did they feel about it as they did? Without the 'oracle' status of the Australian Broadcasting Corporation's (ABC) 'Watchman', Watt was discursive rather than opinionated.[52] If not offering the professionalised analysis Macmahon Ball called for in 1938, when lamenting the quality of information Australians received about international developments (there was 'plenty of spot news', but 'no serious attempt to weave the spots into an intelligible pattern'),[53] Watt sought to bring significance to the 'facts' he accumulated. In this, he insisted, expertise was no solution in itself—particularly given the propensity of ABC programmers to be 'half-mesmerised by [academics'] show of learning' rather than exploring more flexible ways of generating interest.[54]

There was evidence that some officials in government regarded the league and the LNU as pacifist or dangerously left wing (as evident in attempts in 1938 to terminate Constance Duncan's talks on international affairs on ABC women's sessions, and to insist that she not speak as a representative of the union).[55] Watt, however, secured undoubted and enduring popularity. By 1941, engaged by the Commonwealth Department of Information, he could confidently adopt a highly personalised appeal. Prompting listeners to recall him as a delegate to league assemblies, he prepared scripts to be read with a colleague, Arthur Moorhead, in which he played an over-eager aficionado to Moorhead's world-weariness. One broadcast began:

> M: Well, what do you think is the 'most important news' today?

W: Oh, a little item tucked away in just a few words—like so much of the really important news.
M: Oh, stop it—which one?
W: The one about the appointment of the American Ambassador to London.
M: As it happens, I didn't notice it—whom did Roosevelt appoint?
W: Winant—John G. Winant!
M: I never heard of the man—was he one of your colleagues, like Halifax, at Geneva?
W: No, he was after my time there, but I know his views very well.

So the exchange developed, outlining the contribution Winant might make as a former director of the ILO with a keen interest in social security, and effectively positioning the international as a field of interest somewhere between the figures of Watt and Moorhead, both seeking a point of access to a rapidly changing world.[56]

These changing modes of sociability and communication reveal some of the ways in which the world as an object of interest was made accessible in the inter-war years. It is easy to dismiss them as mannered, and of a piece with the 'failure' of the league to prevent the return of world war. Perhaps, however—following Stuart Macintrye—it is more rewarding to see them as 'negotiating a transition'. Before this point, the international was either a social movement or a field defined by roles allocated in a strict social and political hierarchy, often those of 'empire'. Soon it would, under pressure of World War II and then the Cold War, become increasingly compartmentalised into credentialled practice on the one hand and, on the other, a public discourse attuned not so much to the 'morality' of abstract principles ('Peace', 'Goodwill', 'Humanity', as they might be acted out in a pageant) but to the 'moralism' of positions taken in the name of 'democracy' or 'freedom'.[57] Watt was a product of this transition and would himself experience the changes it wrought.

World events in the late 1930s scarcely favoured support for the league. Continuing to search for ways of raising the LNU's profile, Watt led moves to associate it with assistance to Chinese and European refugees, including through the foundation of the Refugees Emergency Council of New South Wales in 1938. In this, the union joined a new diversity of organisations that sought to represent specific cultural and religious affiliations, including the Australian Jewish Welfare Society, the German Emergency Fellowship Committee and the Continental Catholic Migrants Welfare Society. Despite deepening uncertainty among LNU leaders as to whether their mission should be advising government or acting as the 'conscience of the community', Watt hoped to formalise a state-sponsored role for the union in actively leading and assisting resettlement.[58] While he continued to broadcast on the topic—even prompting one listener to offer a portion of his farm in Tumbarumba to the league, if only for the resettlement of 'the peasant type'[59] —the refugee issue itself indicated ways in which the modes of the international were changing. World government was becoming international management, supporting the victimised and persecuted populations of brutal nations and seeking to strengthen and unify others.[60]

With the outbreak of World War II, Watt was restless. Union membership was declining: 'weakest in churches, strongest in schools'. By 1946, it stood at 406 in New South Wales.[61] Older patterns of sociability were difficult to sustain in a fully mobilised society, and international relations resolutely became matters of states. 'Information' itself assumed a new character. In 1940, Watt was one of 'the carefully selected people in key positions in the community' who received a regular bulletin from the Lord Mayor's Committee for Civil Morale, providing talking points to use in conversation, speeches, for publication, 'whenever you can help to inform or inspire'—including statistics on bomb and submarine construction, rationing schedules and the supply of petrol and rubber.[62] Taking leave from the league that year, Watt contested the federal Sydney seat of Martin for the Australian Labor Party; his publicity featured a fulsome endorsement from Dr H. V. Evatt: '[I]n the world of international movements, Raymond Watt has rendered magnificent service in the cause of Labour and Humanity.' He lost but reduced the sitting member's majority from 7000 to 139.[63]

By 1941, Watt was himself mobilised into the short-wave radio division of the Department of Information. In 1942, he moved to a publicity unit established in the Department of War Organisation and Industry, where he drafted lectures and speeches on the necessity of restraint, 'preparing the public mind' for regulation and developing extensive contacts with fellow journalists. Watt had, so the unit's assistant director Creighton Burns allowed, a real challenge: Sydney was judged to be deeply hedonistic and anarchic, and 'clearly the most difficult [city]…in the Commonwealth…to persuade' to comply with sacrifice in the name of victory.[64] Even with this allowance, Watt was less effective in exerting restraint on the press than he had been as a publicist. After losing preselection for Martin in 1943, in 1945, he was placed in charge of the war department's Civilian Requirements Section, overseeing the allocation of resources to toy production. There was no lapse in his association with the league. He continued as national secretary of the LNU and in 1943 became vice-president of the NSW branch. Numbers in his WEA classes on international affairs continued to be rivalled only by those in psychology. Even in the WEA, however, it was clear that a more academic caste was defining the syllabus. Among the tutors listed in New South Wales, only Watt and those taking 'child study' now had no university qualifications.

In an executive meeting on 10 July 1945, the union agreed to support the new United Nations Organisation, effectively acknowledging the end and failure of the League of Nations. Three weeks later, the LNU became the United Nations Association of Australia (UNAA). Watt was confirmed as president of its NSW branch and elected to the national executive. It was soon clear, however, that more than a name change was anticipated. A federal organiser was appointed to assist with the revival of the cause. In rebuilding membership and visibility, stockbroker R. P. Greenish advocated a shift in activities from public meetings and lunch or evening lectures to the screening of films in suburban halls on Sunday evenings, followed by discussion led by 'outstanding people'. The UNAA should, Greenish advised, develop its own film unit, staffed by 'experienced people, preferably ex-servicemen with [the] latest knowledge of 16mm films', who would exhibit documentaries on 'agriculture, public health, industry' and so on, perhaps prefaced by a cartoon 'thrown in for entertainment value' as part of an 'essentially democratic people's program'.[65] Older devotees of the LNU, such as Mildred Muscio—a feminist whose networks spanned the National Council of Women and the Racial Hygiene Association—complained to Watt that she was uncertain whether the new federal organiser was to be 'servant or master'.[66] Clearly, however, a new direction was set. 'Face-to-face' fellowship, the talk or address interspersed with recitation or song, was to be replaced with an 'educative' process, seeking to heighten, as Greenish put it, 'the international exchange of knowledge, skills and the arts'.[67]

In March 1947, Greenish became national secretary of the UNAA; R. J. F. Boyer, recently appointed chairman of the ABC, had already been elected to succeed Watt as NSW president. Establishing 'standing committees' on human rights (canvassing the 'happy assimilation' of Aboriginal Australians) and the status of women (dealing with equal pay), the UNAA moved away from the normative, empirical, social engineering cast of the league—Watt's emphasis on 'regulation by consent'—to a mode more attuned to the universalism of rights proclaimed by the United Nations.[68] 'The UN Story' and 'UN Specialists Talk to You' replaced Watt's radio talks. 'UN Science Magazines' were screened in venues organised in association with Rotary and church clubs.[69] The valiancy of the international began shifting from standards whose basis lay in political economy to values to be upheld in the application of expertise and the pursuit of 'democracy'.[70] No doubt this latter language seems more familiar to us now, more pragmatic if not more credible, but it is worth pausing to consider what was lost as well as gained in this rapid transition in modes and authority.[71]

Conclusion

Having negotiated a career in one mode, Watt now had to find new paths through the 1950s. At each step, it was clear how much had changed in the political and cultural valiancy of the international. He gave lectures for the Henry Lawson Labour College on the future of Palestine, the influence of economic security on the political life of nations and the psychological effects of the atomic bomb.

Narrowly defeated for preselection for the state seat of Lane Cove in 1946, he unsuccessfully contested the federal seat of Bennelong in 1949. Employed briefly to teach English at the Burwood Migrant Hostel, he established a secretariat and library for the emerging South Pacific Commission before securing regular work for the Information Section of the High Commission for Pakistan.[72] Gradually, he built a 'public relations consultancy', providing services for industries seeking to break into emerging overseas markets, whether with opals, condensed milk or poultry feed. In 1961–62, he wrote on commission for the Department of Trade, surveying, for example, the access gained by Victa prefabricated homes or DefENDer snail repellent to buyers in Asia.[73] This was not quite the world of open international exchange he had envisaged through the 1930s, when his mantra had been 'we either fight or trade'.

In the postwar decades, then, Watt found a meagre purchase on new modes prevailing in international engagement. While selling Chamber's Encyclopedia door-to-door in 1951, he was drawn into conversation by an Australian Security Intelligence Organisation (ASIO) officer to whom he was 'known' as once being a 'figure of interest', but who now reported he found nothing of note in Watt's views.[74] When Alan Watt, who had joined a fledging diplomatic corps in 1937, was appointed permanent secretary of the Department of External Affairs in 1950 (returning, it was said, Australia's diplomacy to the safe hands of a career diplomat), the *Daily Telegraph* speculated on the possible influence of his older brother, who had 'spent most of his sixty years as an apostle for international understanding'. It was not a link Alan made himself: Ray does not appear in his memoirs.[75]

What can be made of these contrasts across three decades, symbolised poignantly in the different circumstances of these two brothers: a parable of the talents? If one appeal of transnational history is to enable an appreciation of opportunities that exist when categories predetermined by national themes are suspended, Ray Watt—in his activism if not mobility—gives us one such narrative. Further, his experience prompts questioning of how concepts of the international are shaped. What gains legitimacy in that field and connects it with our sense of ourselves? A meeting with prayers, a radio talk or a pageant at the Trocadero are very distant from the 'conspicuous compassion' of 'Live Aid' and the shock and awe of CNN. Both are, however, performances of a kind, even if the last is managed through a television remote control that regulates for us (in Graeme Turner's words) a world of 'ubiquity that seems to displace geography altogether' and put in its place 'a generic corporate professionalism' in covering the world.[76] Dying of cancer in 1967, Watt gratefully accepted financial support from the Australian Journalists Association, of which he had long been a proud member. In his letter of thanks, he noted that while radio had stimulated open discussion, 'whoever controls television will sooner or later control governments'.[77] For all his archaism, Watt can continue to prompt reflection on what shapes the ways we enact the international, and what these modes enable or deny.

Notes

[1] Iriye, Akira 2002, *Global Community: The role of international organisations in making the contemporary world*, University of California Press, Berkeley.

[2] See Mackinnon, Alison 1997, *Love and Freedom: Professional women and the reshaping of personal life*, Cambridge University Press, Melbourne; Allen, Judith 1984, *Rose Scott: Vision and revision in feminism*, Oxford University Press, Melbourne.

[3] See Ellis, A. D. 1922, *Australia and the League of Nations*, Macmillan, London, p. 6.

[4] Moore, W. Harrison 1935, 'Separate action by the British Dominions in foreign affairs', and Latham, John, 'Some recent international problems', *The Australian and New Zealand Society of International Law: Proceedings*, Melbourne University Press. Melbourne, pp. 1, 19.

[5] Hancock, W. K. 1943, *Argument of Empire*, Penguin, Harmondsworth, p. 102.

[6] Russell, Penny 1990, 'Jessie Street and international feminism', in Heather Radi (ed.), *Jessie Street: Documents and essays*, Women's Redress Press, Marrickville, pp. 181–3.

[7] Moorhouse, Frank 1993, *Grand Days*, Vintage, Sydney, p. 74.

[8] See, in general, Iriye, *Global Community*.

[9] Typescript in R. G. Watt Papers, National Library of Australia (hereafter NLA), Mss 1923, Box 17, unnumbered folder.

[10] See, generally, Wohl, Robert 1980, *The Generation of 1914*, Weidenfeld and Nicolson, London.

[11] Stead, Christina 1965, *The Man Who Loved Children*, Holt, Reinhardt and Winston, New York, p. 49.

[12] *Commonwealth Parliamentary Debates*, vol. 139, 23 May 1933, p. 1634.

[13] Watt, R. G. 1931, 'The League of Nations: some current tendencies', *Morpeth Review*, vol. 11, no. 2, p. 37.

[14] *Sydney Morning Herald*, 17 October 1930, p. 11; Watt to Janet Mitchell, 21 October 1920, Watt Papers, NLA, Mss 1837, Item 31; Iriye, *Global Community*.

[15] See, generally, Birn, Donald S. 1981, *The League of Nations Union*, Oxford.

[16] Moorhouse, *Grand Days*; and Moorhouse, Frank 2000, *Dark Palace*, Picador, London.

[17] Tyrrell, Ian 1991, 'American exceptionalism in an age of international history', *American Historical Review*, vol. 96, no. 4, p. 1031.

[18] Heydon to Eileen Watt, 20 March 1967, Watt Papers, NLA, Mss 1923, Box 7.

[19] Watson, Adam 1992, *The Evolution of International Society: A comparative historical analysis*, Routledge, London.

[20] Transcript of a talk given on 2GB on 18 July 1932, Watt Papers, NLA, Mss 1535, Box 1c.

[21] J. D. B. Miller, interview with Sir Alan Watt, NLA, TRC 306.

[22] *The School Magazine*, Part 4, Class 6, vol. 23, no. 7, p. 2.

[23] Minutes of NSW branch annual meeting and conference, Watt Papers, NLA, Mss 1923, Box 1, Folder 12.

[24] Watt Papers, NLA, Mss 1923, folder of letters headed '2UW', Box 6.

[25] Langmore, Diane 1996, 'Duncan, Constance Ada (1896–1970)', *Australian Dictionary of Biography. Volume 14*, Melbourne University Press, Melbourne, p. 48.

[26] Minutes in folder marked 'Executive Committee: World Peace Congress', Watt Papers, NLA, Mss 1923, Box 13.

[27] League of Nations, NSW Branch, minutes for meeting of November 1931, Minute Book, Watt Papers, NLA, Mss 1923, Box 4.

[28] Mitchell, Janet 1938, *Spoils of Opportunity*, Methuen, London; Mitchell to Watt, 18 October 1930, Watt Papers, NLA, Mss 1837, Item 30.

[29] Foley, Meredith and Radi, Heather 1983, 'Hinder, Eleanor Mary', *Australian Dictionary of Biography. Volume 9*, Melbourne University Press, Melbourne, p. 304.

[30] Hinder to Watt, 23 May 1926, Watt Papers, NLA, Mss 1837, Item 21; 10 September 1926, Item 22.

31 Ada Adams to Watt, n.d., Watt Papers, NLA, MSS 1923, Box 7.

32 Hobsbawm, Eric 2002, *Interesting Times: A twentieth century life*, Allen Lane, London, p. 137; see also Barrow, Logie 1989, 'The environment of fellowship around 1900', in Roy Porter and Sylvana Tomaselli (eds), *The Dialectics of Friendship*, Routledge. London, p. 166.

33 See Howe, Renate 2001, 'The Australian student Christian movement and women's activism in the Asia-Pacific region, 1890s–1920s', *Australian Feminist Studies*, vol. 16, no. 36, pp. 311–23. Persia Campbell and Marie Byles were also Watt's associates, the first eventually working for agricultural and consumer groups in the United States and advising Presidents Kennedy and Johnson, the latter travelling in South Asia and settling in an ashram.

34 Alan Watt to R. G. Watt, 19 November 1923, Watt Papers, NLA, Mss 1837, Item16.

35 Watt to Joyce Beeby, 15 February 1925, Watt Papers, NLA, Mss 1837, Item 18; Anderson, Francis 1935, *Peace or War*, League of Nations Union, Sydney, p. 41.

36 Watt to Joyce Beeby, 15 May 1925, Watt Papers, NLA, Mss 1837, Item 18.

37 See Anderson to Watt, 12 August 1931, Watt Papers, NLA, Mss 1837, Item 42.

38 Watt to Stead and A. H. Garnsey, 1 January 1931; Garnsey to Watt, 2 March 1931, Watt Papers, NLA, Mss 1923, Box 5, unnumbered folder.

39 'BSIA Report for Year Ending December 1930', Copland Papers, NLA, Mss 3008, Box 50, Folder 1; see also Macintyre, Stuart 1994, *A History for a Nation; Ernest Scott and the Making of Australian History*, Melbourne University Press, Melbourne, pp. 125–37.

40 League of Nations Union NSW Branch 1931, *Quarterly Bulletin*, no. 1, p. 1; no. 2, p. 8.

41 A survey of the *Australian Dictionary of Biography* indicates that, among those selected for inclusion in the dictionary and whose association with the LNU figures in their entry, 32 per cent (38 people) were affiliated with the Church of England, 12 per cent (14) were Presbyterian, 8 per cent (nine) were Methodist, 4 per cent (five) were Jewish, 3.5 per cent (four) were Baptist and 2.5 per cent were Catholic (one), Theosophist (one) and Australian Church (one). The percentage of lawyers was 14 per cent (16), academics 12 per cent (14), welfare workers and doctors both 7 per cent (eight) and clergymen 5 per cent. Forty per cent of the dictionary's selection were women.

42 League of Nations Union NSW 1935, *Quarterly Bulletin*, no. 6, pp. 2–3.

43 Notes in Watt Papers, NLA, Mss 1923, Box 18, unnumbered folder; Minute Book of League of Nations Union NSW Branch Council, 30 April 1930, Watt Papers, NLA, Mss 1923, Box 4.

44 Justice Rich, *Give the League A Chance: Appeal to Australia*, League of Nations Union, Sydney, in Copland Papers, NLA, Mss 3800, Box 14, Series 25.

45 Notebook in Copland Papers, NLA, Mss 3800, Box 14, Series 25 (Copland's emphasis).

46 Watt to Anderson, 22 September 1936, Watt Papers, NLA, 1837, Box 13.

47 Alexander to Watt, 23 February 1945, Watt Papers, NLA, Mss 1923, Box 14, Folder 1; Watt to Anderson, 4 November 1936, Box 1, Folder 9.

48 Bentham, Jeremy 1948, *A Fragment on Government and an Introduction to the Principles of Morals and Legislation*, Blackwell, Oxford, pp. 426–7.

49 Typescript summarising visit, Watt Papers, NLA, Mss 1923, Box 3, Folder 2; Hilda Mathieson, Report to the Secretary of the Committee on Intellectual Cooperation, 1931, in Watt Papers, NLA, Mss 1923, Box 11.

50 See Johnson, Lesley 1988, *The Unseen Voice: A cultural study of early Australian radio*, Routledge, London, pp. 181–3.

51 Typescript of broadcast on 2GB, 27 September 1937, Watt Papers, NLA, Mss 1923, Box 3, Folder 34.

52 Inglis, K. S. 1983, *This is the ABC: The Australian Broadcasting Commission 1932–1983*, Melbourne University Press, Melbourne, p. 63.

53 Ball, W. Macmahon 1938, 'Introduction', in W. M. Ball (ed.), *Press, Radio and World Affairs: Australia's outlook*, Melbourne University Press, Melbourne, pp. 17, 20, 23.

54 Watt to Duncan Hall, 14 December 1937, Watt Papers, NLA, 1837, Item 100.

55 Johnson, *The Unseen Voice*, pp. 181–2; League of Nations Union (Victorian Branch) 1938–39, *Annual Report*, p. 14.

56 Typescript of 'Spotlight on Today's Cables', Watt Papers, NLA, Mss 1923, Box 6, unnumbered folder.

[57] Macintyre, *A History for a Nation*, p. 125; see also Brown, Wendy 2001, *Politics Out of History*, Princeton University Press, Princeton, p. 26; Hunt, Lynn 2007, *Inventing Human Rights: A history*, W. W. Norton, New York, p. 212.

[58] Minutes of annual meeting and conference, Australian League of Nations Union, 17 June 1940, Watt Papers, NLA, Mss 1923, Box 1, Folder 12.

[59] David Macleod to Watt, 22 November 1941, Watt Papers, NLA, Mss 1923, Box 9, unmarked folder.

[60] See Iriye, *Global Communities*, p. 32.

[61] Minutes of annual meeting and conference, Australian League of Nations Union, 17 June 1940, Watt Papers, NLA, Mss 1923, Box 1, Folder 13.

[62] Bulletins in Watt Papers, NLA, Mss 1923, Box 11, unnumbered folder.

[63] *Standard*, 10 August 1943.

[64] Burns to Director-General, Department of War Organisation and Industry, 6 May 1943, Watt Papers, NLA, Mss 1923, Box 14, unnumbered folder.

[65] Report from Federal Organiser, 10 July 1947, Watt Papers, NLA, Mss 1923, Box 2, Folder 24B.

[66] Muscio to Watt, 2 December 1946, Watt Papers, NLA, Mss 1923, Box 2, Folder 24A.

[67] Report from Federal Organiser, 10 July 1947.

[68] Minutes of meeting of NSW UNAA Council, 10 February 1949, Watt Papers, NLA, Box 2, Folder 22.

[69] See UNAA NSW Branch 1950–51, *Annual Report*, pp. 3–4.

[70] For a detailed study of a similar transition, see Haraway, Donna J. 1996, 'Universal donors in a vampire culture: it's all in the family: biological kinship categories in the twentieth century United States', in William Cronon (ed.), *Uncommon Ground: Rethinking the human place in nature*, New York, pp. 321–66.

[71] See Anderson, Perry 1992, *A Zone of Engagement*, London, p. 367; and Douzinas, Costas 2000, *The End of Human Rights: Critical legal thought at the turn of the century*, Oxford, pp. 115 ff.

[72] References and testimonials in 'Office of Education, Applications for Positions', National Archives of Australia (hereafter NAA), A1361/1 34/11/4, Part 784; typescript, Watt Papers, NLA, Mss 1923, Box 13, unnumbered folder.

[73] Correspondence and clippings in Watt Papers, NLA, Mss 1923, Box 11, Folder mislabelled 'WEA 1948'.

[74] 'Watt, Raymond Gosford', Miscellaneous Papers, NAA, AA 6119/90.

[75] Watt, Alan 1972, *Australian Diplomat: Memoirs of Sir Alan Watt*, Sydney. Watt does allow, in his interview with Bruce Miller, that Ray 'maintained a deep interest in foreign affairs and under other circumstances would have made some mark, I think, in that field' (NLA, TRC 306, p. 3).

[76] Turner, Graeme 2005, *Ending the Affair: The decline of television current affairs in Australia*, Sydney, pp. 126–7.

[77] Letter to President, NSW Branch of the Australian Journalists Association, 1 March 1967, Watt Papers, NLA, 1535, Box 1c.

Intimacy

Intimacy might seem a curious inclusion in a book on the transnational aspects of life stories, since it evokes the ties that bind individuals to a beloved home, not the impulses that send them roaming across the earth. It is, however, precisely that tension—the yearning towards home of the migrant or wanderer, or the ties that keep the cosmopolitan mind bound to a finite geographical space—that makes intimacy a vital component of this volume.

The essays in this section deal with migration stories. Maggie Mackellar reads the ambiguities of 'Home' in the letters of early Western District squatting families: home as a site of nostalgic yearning, home as emblem of new attachments, homes unthinkingly destroyed in the very act of colonising. Kate Bagnall traces the unhappy story of a marriage between an Anglo-Australian woman and a Chinese–Australian man—a relationship that collapses after the couple visits China, the affection between two people inadequate to combat cultural difference and Australia's discriminatory immigration laws. James Hammerton and Alistair Thomson both focus on the generation of British migrants who formed the postwar 'British diaspora'. Thomson shows how Dorothy Wright's letters home provided her with a 'reflective space' in her 'hectic life': a space in which she could articulate and explore the ups and downs of domestic life, and reach out for the advice, support and sympathy of her mother and sister in Britain. Hammerton shows how the 'lens of migration' takes precedence over any other way of constructing a life story in the narratives that migrants tell of their lives. Drawing on his interviews with British migrants in the second half of the twentieth century, Hammerton shows that there has been a growing trend for migrants to understand their lives as inherently adventurous, mobile and cosmopolitan, to migrate serially and to manage a far-flung family life. Francesco Ricatti tells how postwar Italian migrants in Australia wrote with lyrical intensity of their idealised 'first loves', lost either as a cause or an effect of migration. Here, the 'lens of migration' facilitates the operation of fantasy and nostalgia, producing stories of romantic perfection across a gulf of rupture and loss.

Migration strains intimacy—not only for those divided by migration, but for those fragments of families compelled into propinquity and precarious dependence by their migration to a strange land. In different ways, all these essays show how migrants struggled, using words, images and memories, to shore up those intimate bonds, and to create new ones. A stream of words has issued from the attempts of thousands of migrants to make sense of the experience of displacement, to make and remake connections. As Kate Bagnall shows, however, sometimes the deepest ruptures are papered over with silence. In the essays that follow, intimacy is both a casualty and a product of migration stories.

Chapter 6

Love, loss and 'going Home': the intimate lives of Victorian settlers

Maggie Mackellar

In May 1885, Arbella Winter Cooke received a letter from her son Sam, who was on an extensive honeymoon in Europe. He and his wife, Alice, were having a wonderful time and liking Florence 'very much' but, Sam assured his mother, she need not fear that 'it or any other place will charm us away from Victoria'. With a flourish, he added, 'We are looking forward to our return *Home*.'[1]

Samuel Winter Cooke (1847–1929) had been taught from early childhood that the great European cities on his tour were the centres of civilisation and culture. From the cosmopolitan city of Florence, however, he wrote to reassure his mother that all he longed for was held in the word 'home'. Home was 'Murndal', a cattle and sheep station three days' ride from the flourishing city of Melbourne. In this brief sentence, Samuel poignantly asserted his yearning for the bush life.

In the past year, I have been reading the diaries and correspondence of the Western District squatting families of Victoria, selecting documents for publication. This material, held in the State Library of Victoria, offers some new perspectives on the idea of transnationalism.[2]

As I read through the letters and journals, my knowledge of the famous names of Victorian settlement was fleshed out and, rather than caricatures of dour Scotsmen, Irish gentry and colonial Englishmen made unimaginably wealthy on the golden plains of the Western District, I began to see evidence through the letters of the anxiety, uncertainty and pain of starting a new life on the other side of the world from their homeland. These settlers did not conceive of themselves as crossing the boundary of nations. They wrote, not as new Australians, nor even as Victorians, but simply as Britons, who had travelled a long way from their homeland to establish another home. They packed their culture along with the family silver and, no matter how far they travelled, they maintained their daily rituals: dressing for dinner, observing a Sabbath day of rest, tending their English gardens. They ventured forth into new worlds in hermetically sealed units, resisting change and cultural exchange; and rather than build a new reality, they strove to make the world around them resemble the home they had left behind. Notwithstanding their desires, the new world that had accosted them with its strangeness gradually impinged on them, forcing them to change, forcing them into a new conception of what was home.[3]

In all the correspondence that flowed between the old world and the new, there was no sense of displacement across nations. There was distance, certainly, and there was transformation, but it did not change their ways of cultural interaction, nor did it necessarily change their sense of a national identity. For these settlers, the very idea of 'home' was so assured and fixed, so embedded in the British Empire, that it seems the very reverse of transnationalism, representing instead a monolithic British patriotism.

Paradoxically, it is for this very reason that the colonial experience is important to analyse as one of the more common forms of 'transnationalism' in the nineteenth century. As Patrick Wolfe argues:

> Putting the definitional niceties of the term 'nation' aside for the moment and using it, in a vernacular sense, as something like 'country', both race and colonialism are inherently transnational phenomena…Even in internal-colonial contexts, at least one of the contending parties originally came from somewhere else, a fact that continues to demarcate the relationship.[4]

Figure 6.1: Murndal Homestead. Samuel Cooke inherited it from his uncle Samuel Pratt Winter in 1878.

Photographer unknown. Winter Cooke Family Papers, State Library of Victoria.

Colonialism, on this understanding, is inherently transnational, and the letters I have been reading offer ample evidence of how ideas of home were maintained and transformed in this context. In this chapter, I want to coax out the peculiarities of colonial experience and ask how theories of transnationalism can illuminate the settlers' ways of thinking about home. In particular, I argue that the way settlers wrote about home echoes not only their personal experience of migration; behind their words, we can hear another echo of the trauma suffered by the Aboriginal people they dispossessed. Though settlers recorded this displacement with indifference, their words capture, however incidentally, this other story. For in the shadow of the homes the white settlers built lay the ruins of the Gunditjmara homes they had destroyed.

What is striking about the British colonies is how settlers in their letters and journals are so confident of 'home', even though the making of it is such a fraught process. The breathtaking assurance of colonialism almost precludes a discussion of transnationalism. In the colonists' confident assertions, home could be both England and Australia. One could leave home to travel Home without any need to explain the difference. Taking these articulations of home as self-evident, however, glides over the process and experience of dispossession, on both sides of the frontier. Closer examination reveals that the confidence of these assertions of home came at a cost. As Sara Wills has argued, not all the settlers were so settled.[5]

Reading my way through many of the letters collected from Western District families, I became aware that it was the intimate spaces between people that were stretched by the experience of migration, and it was these spaces they sought to bring back into being in their letters. Their words sought connections across distance as they struggled to make sense of an experience that changed them. In these moments, a more complicated picture emerges of the tangle of allegiances that exists in the colonial world around the concept of home.

Twelve-year-old Arbella Winter (1821–92) had been an orphan for three years when two of her brothers, Samuel and Trevor, left Ireland to seek their fortunes in Van Diemen's Land in 1833. As she grew up, she remained certain that her future lay with them. After convincing her guardian of her commonsense and earnest desire to join her brothers, she left Ireland at the age of eighteen with her oldest brother, George. A whirlwind shipboard romance saw her arrive in Van Diemen's Land an engaged woman, to be married two days after the couple left the ship. In 1839, however, Van Diemen's Land offered few prospects for an ambitious colonist, for the good grazing lands had been taken up long since. With her new husband, Cecil Pybus Cooke (1813–95), Arbella crossed Bass Strait and set off into the relative wilderness of the Wimmera District.[6]

Of Anglo-Irish gentry stock, Arbella must have been a formidable woman. After losing her first baby while living in Portland, she twice gave birth in later years out on the run her husband took up. She cooked for the men, shepherded the sheep when required, drove cattle—and after years of this was forced to give up the run when it did not make a profit.[7] The Cookes returned to the Portland district and, in 1849, took up another run at Lake Condon, not far from 'Murndal', the flourishing station of Arbella's brother Samuel Pratt Winter. In 1854, the family made the decision to take their older two boys, William and Samuel, back to England to be educated. The boys were ten and eight years old. It cannot have been an easy decision. The expense was great, and the pain of parting from these two eldest children must have been intense. Through the next years, Arbella wrote regularly to her sons, but her letters contain only snippets of the loss she felt. There is a glimpse in the letter she wrote to Willie in 1856.[8]

> Lake Condon,
>
> 9th October, 1856
>
> You will be thirteen before you receive this letter growing out of the child into the youth, it is now a whole year since I saw your dear little faces, and you must think how often I long to see you and the only alleviation we could have for the pains of absence is to hear that you are improving in every way and that our pains and expenses are not thrown away. We were very glad to hear that you had risen in Latin, I hope too you are getting on in Arithmetic.[9]

It is loss mixed with the anxiety and guilt of an absent mother. Reading this collection of letters, I was struck by how Arbella struggled to hold on to an image of the boys she had left in England. She repeatedly reminded herself and them of why they were separated, and what they were gaining by being so far away.

It is in a letter from their father, Cecil, however, that we get a glimpse of what the boys were missing while 'bettering' themselves in England. Reading this letter draws more than just a picture of station life; it shows us the intimate relationship the boys have with the station. We see just how involved they were, how well they knew the names of the bullocks, how they had obviously written begging for details of the changes that had occurred since they had left home. After reading this letter, it becomes obvious that the boys thought of home as a very local, specific site in the Western District of Victoria. 'Home' also was where they had been sent, but, between those two worlds, home was a very different place. This letter also gives an insight into just how important Aboriginal labour was to the establishment of infrastructure.[10] Their father wrote:

> The blacks have made me a dam about a quarter of a mile above the first Creek you cross going to the Lake Paddock.—

> The Kangaroos are much more numerous than ever, (I miss poor old 'Oscar' very much) they are in large droves now 40, 50, and sometimes 60 together in a drove.—The wretches are devouring the grass of my cattle.
>
> We have only 'Tinker', 'Smiles' and 'Prince' of the old working bullocks that you know of, the others have been sold or exchanged…[Uncle Sam] was here yesterday on his way to the Bay, he has made a stone addition to his House, it has 2 rooms below and 3 above and [he] wants Mamma very much to go and live with him but she does not like selling Lake Condah[11] and I expect you would miss the old place when you came back. I have written to you my dear boy all the gossip and information you wished for, about the station and I hope it will please you both, but I should not wish you to read it at school to any of your schoolfellows but you can if [you] like show it to any of your relatives, but they of course won't understand the contents of it so well as yourself.—
>
> Try all you can to get on with your studies for recollect that time wasted and idled away is money lost, and be particular not to associate with naughty Boys.[12]

We can sense here how distance tears at the relationship between father and sons. Their mother was similarly moved to demonstrate to the boys that their English education would be vital in the Australian bush. She exhorted them to tell her what books they had read and which ones they preferred, reminding them that though their ambitions for a future might lie in running a station, they would still need an English education. '[Dr Russell] says he knows no place which requires a man to be well educated as the bush as a man's resources must all be within himself.'[13] There was an edge of desperation to her letters as she sought to instil the values she held important in children so far away as to be lost to her, were it not for the frail connections forged by her words. 'We were very sorry to hear from your letter that you had given up all thought of being an engineer, or even studying with that aim. We are afraid you are too easily disheartened.'[14] The letters are a mixture of tones: in turn cajoling, encouraging and admonishing. Within them, however, hangs Arbella's loss of intimacy with her children.

Another letter written by their younger brother Edmund managed to capture what the boys were missing most: the bustle and drama of life on the station. Edmund Cooke was just six years old when he wrote this letter to his brother Samuel in England.

Lake Condah

July 15 1862

My dear Sam,

I would like to see you very much. You have got six horses one of your mares is the finest one on the station, it would fetch fifty pounds in the Melbourne market. We have got some beautiful Kangaroo dogs…I have got one he is a half bred scotch staghound. The baby is a nice little fellow, when he is in bed at night if there is not a candle alight in the room he will scream until there is, and then he will talk himself to sleep in his own language; his name will be Herbert Pybus…he is a great little bounce, but he laughs like I don't know what.[15] Papa has a splendid stockyard he has just sold 250 head of store cattle, The yard is up to your knees in mud there was one cow rushed at a black fellow and only for a tree that was in the yard she would have spiflicated him; we have them jammed between two fences and there we brand them without ropeing them Willie branded some of them. Papa Willie and Cecil went out one day and killed 33 kangaroos besides bringing in some cattle.[16] I went one day and caught a lot of Fish with my hands There is a splendid stream coming down into the Lake and plenty of Fish we had a dish of them this morning they are very nice, Willie went this morning to get them, and while he was getting them he tumbled into the water and was nearly washed away but he held on by a stick. We have herd that the english mail is in…I am just beginning to read Robinson Crusoe, I think it is a stunning book. Trevor read a nice one, Cecil began to read it a good bit ago, but he did not care about it. Cecil and I went into the garden to see if there were any opossums we found one Cecil fired at him and killed him dead and *half the* tree too, and now I must conclude with my love to grandmamma and grandpapa, Encles and Aunts and all friends, they all send there love to everybody

I am your affectionate brother

Edmund Gerald Cooke

Clearly, Arbella was not allowing distance from school to get in the way of Edmund's education. He too, however, was destined for an English school. In this letter, his boyish prose etches with passion the drama and bustle of life on a working station. Caught in the images is an idyllic childhood in which the business of the station is meshed with the valorised pleasures of Victorian boyhood. So we have details of going fishing, work in the cattle yards, descriptions of his new dog and his brother's mare, shooting possums in the garden and the joy of the 'splendid' *Robinson Crusoe* to read. Through this childhood, Edmund and his brothers have formed an attachment to a particular place. Lake Condah in the Western District of Victoria is specifically home—although they have been sent 'Home' to be educated. For the boys, first-generation Australians, home is local, specific, no longer able to be generalised. When Willie and Sam write from England therefore and ask for all the 'gossip' of the station, they are dreaming of the home to which they will both eventually return.

Edmund's story ended more tragically. He was also sent to England to school and would perhaps have been destined to follow his older brother Samuel's success academically and at the Bar. He was never to have this chance. He returned to Victoria before he could finish his education, probably having contracted tuberculosis. He died in 1876.

In their focus on the local, the Cooke letters are typical of much of the material collected from the Western District and held at the State Library of Victoria. Within the creation of this home in the new world, there was, however, very little appreciation of those who had been dispossessed in order that the cattle might be fattened, the wool grown, crops planted, fences put up and houses built. Very few of these pioneering families noticed what they had done: it seemed to take a particular kind of mind, even a sternly Calvinistic conscience, to acknowledge the wrong on which prosperity was built. One potential settler clearly articulated the relationship between his ability to make a success of squatting and the removal of Aborigines from the land he occupied.

Niel Black (1804–80) arrived in Port Phillip District in September 1839 after first rejecting Adelaide and Sydney as suitable locations in which to secure land for his company.[17] He had sailed for Australia on the barque *Ariadne*, setting off on 4 April 1839. He landed in Adelaide in July, but finding the land prices too high he travelled on to Sydney. There, he set about purchasing supplies and organising all he needed to set up a station in the Port Phillip District. Black kept a journal that came to serve as an account of his time, as a confessional and as a link between his new world and the one he had left behind. What makes the journal such fascinating reading is the way Black applies his analytical mind to the new society he sees around him. He constantly noted the price of basic tools (spades, nails, candles), stock (sheep, cattle, horses) and land (in Adelaide, Sydney and Port Phillip). He wrote voluminously of the sort of people he met in his travels and scrupulously recorded his impressions of people, places and potential for profit. Within what has to be seen as one of the most thorough journals of early Australia, he also sought to describe how important the transformative act of writing was to his sense of connection with what he had left behind.[18]

Figure 6.2: Niel Black, who was born in Argyllshire, Scotland, shared a love of Scottish regalia with Prince Alfred, Duke of Edinburgh.

Museum Victoria.

> My thoughts are often of home and at home, and I never begin to scribble in the book but what I am in imagination holding a sort of conversation with the Friends I have left there, and telling them the truth according to my own judgement of all I hear, see and think, and this renders it a pleasure to me in place of a toil.[19]

As part of his analysis of his potential success, Black quickly realised the connection between the productivity of a squatting run and the ruthless eradication of the Aboriginal people. He writes frequently that he has no stomach himself for killing people in the fight for the land, but he has no such compunction in profiting from buying the licence to a run on which the Indigenous people have been decimated. Black is careful to emphasise that although Aborigines do pose a threat to the success of a squatting run, there are plenty of ways around the 'problem' of Aboriginal resistance.

> The way is to go outside and take up a new run, provided the conscience of the party is sufficiently seared to enable him without remorse to slaughter natives right and left. It is universally and distinctly understood that the chances are very small indeed of a person taking up a new run being able to maintain possession of his place and property without having to recourse to such means—sometimes by whole sale—but I do not think that this is by any means common, and it is only outside that they are ever called upon to act in so brutal a manner. It, however, seems to be little thought of here as it is only done in defence of self and property. The natives who have not been brought into subjection have a strange propensity to spearing and stealing sheep and cattle, and the settlers agree that lead is the only antidote that effectively cures them of this propensity. When a few are shot the rest become timid and are easily kept at bay…It is, however, a difficult matter to obtain distinct information respecting the murders committed on the natives. There is nothing but 'bouncing' as in [it] is called (bragging) here, and many persons bounce about their treatment of the natives. This they can only do by hints and slang phrases, as the Protectors of the Aborigines are always on the lookout for information against the whites, and anything plainly said would subject them to a prosecution…I believe, however, that great numbers of the poor creatures have wantonly fallen victims to settlers scarcely less savage tho more enlightened [than] themselves, and that 2/3rds of them does not care a single straw about taking the life of a native, provided they are not taken up by the Protectors. But this need not deter any one from coming here as they may buy a run already occupied.[20]

A month later, Black recorded his purchase of the run that was to be the centre of his operation. He confessed that one of his main considerations in buying this run was how cruelly treated the Aborigines had been by the previous superintendent: consequently, they would give very little trouble. Black had a personal repugnance grounded in his strict Presbyterianism to involving himself in any sort of violence on the land; at the same time, however, he justified and accepted that violence as necessary to the European presence.

> The run is one of the most wonderful in the colony, situated about half way between this and Portland Bay, and this makes it valuable as it will

> be at least 5 or 6 years before it is sold. The blacks have been very troublesome on it and I believe they have been cruelly dealt with. The late superintendent ran off from a fear that he wd be apprehended and tried for murdering the natives. The poor creatures are now terror stricken and will be easily managed. This was my principal reason for fighting so hard for it.[21]

Black's decision to purchase 'Strathdownie' came down to the policy adopted by the previous overseer: this man's ruthless eradication of the Aboriginal people whose lands the run covered ensured that Black would not be faced with stock losses from native raids. Frederick Taylor had been established as overseer for G. McKillop and J. Smith by March 1839. Shortly after his arrival, the Aborigines began stealing sheep from the folds. His reputation spread around the district as a man who would take violent measures against the local people. In early 1840, the newly appointed Protector of Aborigines, George Augustus Robinson, heard that Taylor 'had killed a whole tribe'. According to Robinson's journal, Taylor had set out with a number of men to attack the Aborigines' camp. They were reported to have formed a long line with Taylor at the centre. The camp's occupants were asleep as the line fired on them. Only one person was reported surviving out of a camp of 35 men, women and children.

So extreme were Taylor's actions that he fled the colony, fearing a government inquiry into his role in murdering the Aborigines. Black wrote in his journal that, according to Blackie, the former overseer, 'about thirty-five to forty natives have been dispatched on this establishment and that there is only two men left alive of the tribe'.[22] Jan Critchett, in her book *A Distant Field of Murder*, notes that years later James Dawson was told how Bareetch Churneen, who was also known as Queen Fanny, had swum across Lake Bullen Merri with a child on her back and thus escaped pursuing Europeans, who had murdered nearly all her people.[23]

Black finished his entry on this massacre with an assurance to his financial backers and concerned relatives that the overseer 'is certain we will never be troubled with any of them on this run. I think myself remarkably fortunate in a run as well upon this acct as because I believe it perhaps all in all unequalled in the colony, and the situation, as far as I can judge, is the best possible.'[24]

Black renamed his run 'Glenormiston'.

Black's journal sometimes reveals more than he was comfortable with, for although he wrote with great disapproval of the behaviour of settlers towards Aborigines, he could not entirely separate himself from such behaviour. In another passage a month later, Black wrote of chasing down a group of Aboriginal women on his run.

Figure 6.3: Emu Creek, c. 1880, near where the manager of Glenormiston Station, before Niel Black purchased it, led a massacre of the traditional custodians.

Photographer unknown. La Trobe Picture Collection, State Library of Victoria.

Feby 9th.

Started this morning at 7 o'clock and rode across bleak, barren and inhospitable plains. On one of the plains we spied five lubras (women) gathering roots. We were rather close upon them before they observed us, but when they saw us they fled with the fleetness of a roe. We gave them chase and came up with them. No creatures could be under greater fear [than] they were when they could not escape from us. The more we cryed to them, the faster they fled, but all in vain. Such a cackling as they set up when we pulled our horses before them; I could compare it to nothing else than a whole flock of geese running together and crowding round their young when disturbed too early in the morning. One of them pulled a little female child out of a bag on her back and presented us with it. We gave it a little damper and came away; then they set up the most hideous cackling—I must mount again.

…About 6 o.c. we came to a station distant from Strathdownie (now called Glenormiston) about 10 miles, after riding 50 miles across a barren plain affording neither one mouthful of food nor one drop of water over all its extent, excepting in one place where a brackish creek runs over it, the same that passes Glenormiston house. This was an ill spent Sabbath.[25]

Reading Black's account, I wondered why he chose to write about this clearly distressing incident. Such an encounter partly fulfilled a sense of the exotic and emphasised Black's role in gradually controlling this strange and new world, but Black wrote almost compulsively because of the way his journal had come to serve as a confessional. It was only when Black was stirred deeply by a particular event that he would interrupt his day's activities to write by the side of his horse. He did so on this occasion and also after he witnessed a horrific accident in Collins Street in Melbourne. He turned to his journal to unburden his conscience. His admission to himself that 'this was an ill spent Sabbath' seems an admission that he has been drawn into participating in a terrifying encounter for these women. It was an encounter that might easily have ended in the violence Black so detested. The vision of the woman suddenly thrusting a child at him must surely have stayed with him long after the chase was over. Her action in that moment was possibly an appeal to his humanity. From chasing the women, Black, in sudden compunction, offers the child some damper. Did her action deter a potential rape? The menace of it lies heavy under Black's description, but I do not think it occurs. Whatever the motivation and whatever the real facts of the afternoon's activities (for there seems to be a lot unsaid between the lines of Black's description), it remains a disturbing vignette of frontier contact.

A month later, Black recorded his destruction of an Aboriginal shelter, this time with the manifest intention of forcing the Aboriginal people off their land.

> On Sunday last Donald Black and I fell in with a native Chief's Myoh Myoh (native hut)—from the superior style in which it was built we judged it to be such...We ordered it to be tumbled to the ground, and a piece of paper folded up containing a small quantity of powder put into the end of a split stick or piece of wood and the other end stuck into the ground among the ruins of their hut to show them [the natives] that it was done by whites and that we did not want them near us. I believe that the greatest mercy that can possibly be shown them is to keep them entirely away.[26]

Everywhere in his journal, Black evoked his Scottish homeland. He would draw up its recollection as he looked on a landscape and compare what he saw before him with what he had left behind. There was a strong note of melancholy in his journal, which was at its most vocal when he recalled all he had given up to make a new life or at least some money in the 'new world'. He was a relatively honest and self-reflective correspondent, one of the few who recorded openly how crucial the removal and subjection of Aboriginal people was to the commercial success of squatting. Despite this recognition, he never made the emotional connection between his own sense of loss and his destruction of Aboriginal homes as he built a new home in the image of the old.

Figure 6.4: Glenormiston Homestead in 1868. Niel Black waits in Scottish regalia to greet Prince Alfred, Duke of Edinburgh, during the duke's Australian tour.

Frederick Grosse, *Illustrated Australian News*, 4 February 1868. Print: wood engraving. State Library of Victoria. Image no. mp001275.

If Black was one of the few pioneering settlers to articulate that his future prosperity was built on the violent removal of Aborigines, Arbella Cooke's brother Samuel Pratt Winter was even more in the minority in recognising the symbolic importance of the replacement of one set of cultural institutions with another. Margaret Kiddle wrote of Samuel Pratt Winter as a man of culture more reflective of eighteenth-century Ireland than nineteenth-century commercial Britain. He was tall, charming and exceedingly handsome, though he never married and was a renowned agnostic. Of all the early successful squatters it was Samuel Winter who might perhaps have been expected to return to live out his days in England or Ireland. He had travelled extensively and supervised his pastoral interests from all points of the world, but he returned to spend his elderly years in the Western District.[27]

In the Winter Cooke collection, there are two letters written by an Aboriginal man, John (Jacky) White, to Samuel Pratt Winter. These letters are a powerful articulation of loss and a political statement of Jacky White's right to return home. The letters are written from the new Aboriginal mission[28] at Lake Condah and though the first one starts formally, the English gradually breaks down and the words tumble over each other as the writer gets to the crux of his letter: his desire to return to his country.

Mission Station

Lake Condah

April 14. 1876

Mr Winter,

I feel great pleasure in writing these few lines to you, hoping that they will find you in good health as they leave me at present. Mr Hogan our teacher is going away [in] about two or three weeks time. we are all very sorry for him he has done all he can for us, he has taught us how to read and write, I recollect coming to your home, father said that you used to gather the natives together, and has taught them how to be civilized,

We are all very sorry that poor Doctor Russel is dead, the first day we heard of it we were very sorry, Mr Hogan told us that he died in the ship when he was coming out from England. Father said that you were the last Masters that he ever had, and also he said that he grew up to live with you, and we would all like to come and see our native land, very much, we are living very miserable, without boots and cloth, my friends are all dead, and I am left alone in the wide world, I hope to be down there [?]…next month before the winter comes in, I like to come and see my country whenever I come to your house and ask you to give me something, you always give it to me, I don't like to be here, I like to be in my country where I was brought up. Timothy and his wife and children do not like to come down, they sooner be in there own country. I have no more to say, so good bye,

I remain

Your Aboriginal Friend

John White[29]

There is one other letter from Jacky White in the Winter Cooke collection. Written nine months after the first letter, it is far more desperate in tone. The change reflects White's increasing frustration at his virtual imprisonment, his exile from his country. The lack of polish could also be attributed to the absence of the teacher Mr Hogan, mentioned in the last letter. The absence of the formality evident in the first letter makes the second letter all the more gripping: 'I want to come back to Wannon.' The words shout from the page; there are no polite inquiries after Winter's health, as in the first letter. Instead, White gets straight to the point and begs for Winter's help in removing him from the mission country, where he is a 'stranger'.

There is no evidence of a reply to these letters.[30] Their existence, however, in the midst of the overwhelming correspondence between settlers in the Western District and family and friends in England, reminds us of another story of home—untold among all those letters. Though the country might be described, translated and transformed by the pens and the hands of European settlers into a place they could call home, the pen and the hands of Aboriginal people resisted that transformation and continued to articulate their own understanding of their homeland. Jacky White wrote his helpless appeal therefore and, in doing so, gave us a glimpse of that other story: the flip side to the image of Niel Black destroying an Aboriginal house, piece by piece.

Mission Station

Lake Condah

January 7 1877

Mr Winters,

Dear Sir,

I want to come back to Wannon, I knew you ever since I was a boy you used to keep us live. I recollect about thirteen or fourteen years ago when you used to travel about five or six miles to bring us to your place, so will you be obliged to write to the government to get us off this place, so if you will write to the government for us, and get us off here, I will do work for you and will never leave you so I wish you get us off this place, I always wish to be in my country when I was born, I'm in a mission Station and I do not like to be here, they always grumble and all my friends are dead, I lost my friend Doctor Russel, I recollect him living at Hillgay when Mr and Mrs Russel were young, and now we are old, and I am now miserable, all the Wannon black fellows are all dead and I am left, my poor uncle YellertPerne is dead he was quiet young when he came here when I see his grave I always feel sorry. I can't get away without help from the government. This country don't suit one [me], I am a stranger in this country I like to be in my country. When I used [to go] to places where I aught not to be Mr Russel used to get me out, wherever I used to be on a station I used to work Mr Jackson wanted to give us ground and we did not take it so I am very sorry that we did not take it. This is all I have to say,

I remain you affectionate

friend Jacky White[31]

There is no evidence in the rest of the Winter Cooke papers to suggest Jacky White was ever allowed to return to the Wannon country.[32] Aldo Massola, in his book *Aboriginal Mission Stations in Victoria*, lists the surnames of Aboriginal people who died at the Lake Condah Mission between 1876 and 1912. White is listed under the category 'Pure Black'.[33]

The story of Jacky White's desire to die in his home country has another parallel. On the night of his final illness, Samuel Winter, White's potential rescuer, gave instructions for how his body was to be buried. He asked his brother Trevor to bury him 'in the stones where the blacks are buried...On no [account] to have any tablet inscription or memorial of any kind erected nothing but a large stone cairn.'

His instructions were never carried out; the thought was too outrageous. Instead, he was buried on the hill overlooking the Murndal homestead in the place designated as the family plot. A stone wall was put around the grave and a bronze tablet inserted.[34] It was a long way from Winter's wish to be buried as a native, but it leaves an interesting question as to how we think of home in the context of empire and colonialism. For, in ignoring his brother's instructions, Trevor Winter aptly illustrates the tension between the local and colonial world.

It is in this instruction, and in its being ignored, that we are left with a historical moment that can be interpreted as both recognition *and* suppression of the transnational nature of home in the colonial context. Ultimately, it is a moment of impasse between the local and the colonial world that is overcome by refusal of the local. The colonial home inscribes a transnational conception of home onto landscapes in such a way that the previous occupants are rendered invisible. In this moment, the local is transformed into a place that shifts across the boundaries of nations and in so doing is blind to those deeply embedded cultural boundaries.

Samuel Winter's deathbed request to be buried as an Aborigine was partly an expression of his agnosticism, but it was more than this. In his yearning to be buried as a native, Winter recognises the process of colonisation in which one set of cultural values has displaced another. It is perhaps his cosmopolitanism, his education and reading that leads Winter to a desire to seek his resting place in a way that will express his final acceptance of this new world as his home. Niel Black, who was Winter's contemporary, certainly recognised that the Aboriginal enacting of home had to be destroyed if his own construction of home was to be successful. Black's journal leaves us with evidence that he is at times burdened with the knowledge of the destruction of Aboriginal culture.

Black's patronising dismissal of the future of the Aboriginal people is an interesting contrast with the Cooke children's apparent indifference. If their parents' generation accepted the inevitability of the destruction of an Aboriginal homeland, first-generation Australians, it seemed, were blind to the transnational encounters that were happening all the time. Edmund Cooke could write of an

Aboriginal stockman being nearly 'spiflicated' by a mad cow in the newly constructed stockyards without any sense of the change that had occurred over little more than a decade for this nameless man to be working with cattle. His father, Cecil Pybus Cooke, though a man who had a reputation for treating Aborigines with kindness and respect, likewise would write of the transformation of the land by Aboriginal labour with no recognition of the process of displacement that was occurring. Within this collection of letters and journals, there is evidence of the process whereby 'Home', and the development of a national identity, is homogenised. It is this homogenising of England and Australia—home and Home—that has blinded Western District settlers and often us to the transnational encounters that occurred across the Australian frontier.

Notes

[1] Samuel Winter Cooke to his mother, Arbella Cooke, Florence, 8 May 1885, Winter Cooke Papers, State Library of Victoria (hereafter SLV). Samuel Winter Cooke married Alice Margaret Werge Chambers on 6 January 1883 at All Saints, St Kilda. See Bate, Weston 1981, 'Cooke, Samuel Winter (1847–1929)', *Australian Dictionary of Biography. Volume 8*, Melbourne University Press, pp. 101–2.

[2] Published as MacKellar, Maggie 2008, *Strangers in a Foreign Land: The journal of Niel Black and other voices from the Western District*, Miegunyah, Melbourne.

[3] For a longer discussion on the ways in which the new environment influenced settlers' sense of place, see MacKellar, Maggie 2004, *Core of My Heart My Country, Women's Sense of Place in the New Worlds of Australia and Canada*, Melbourne University Press, Melbourne.

[4] Wolfe, P. 2005, 'Islam, Europe & Indian nationalism: towards a postcolonial transnationalism', in Ann Curthoys and Marilyn Lake (eds), *Connected Worlds: History in transnational perspective*, ANU E Press, Canberra, p. 233.

[5] Wills, Sara 2002, 'Unstitching the lips of a migrant nation', *Australian Historical Studies*, no. 118, pp. 71–89.

[6] For Arbella and Cecil, see Hone, J. Ann 1969, 'Cooke, Cecil Pybus (1813–1895)', *Australian Dictionary of Biography. Volume 3*, Melbourne University Press, p. 450.

[7] Forth, Gordon 1991, *The Winters on the Wannon*, Deakin University Press, Geelong, p. 110.

[8] William Winter Cooke would eventually leave the Western District after being overlooked by his uncle Samuel Pratt Winter in his will. Samuel Pratt Winter chose William's younger brother Samuel as his heir. See Forth, *The Winters on the Wannon*.

[9] Winter Cooke Papers, SLV.

[10] Cecil Pybus Cooke was well known throughout the district as being benevolent towards the Aborigines, offering them employment, food and shelter. See Forth, *The Winters on the Wannon*, pp. 148–9.

[11] Cyril Cooke changed the European name 'Lake Condon' to Lake Condah, which he mistakenly thought was the local Gournditch-jmara term for the black swan that was plentiful on the lake (see http://www.walkabout.com.au/locations/VICLakeCondah.shtml). 'Lake Condah' was sold in 1864, but the buyer could not complete payments and it reverted to Cooke. See Hone, 'Cooke, Cecil Pybus'.

[12] Winter Cooke Papers, 1856–60, SLV.

[13] Winter Cooke Papers, 1857, SLV. For Dr Russell, see Smith, Sydney H. 1967, 'Russell, Francis Thomas Cusack (1823–1876)', *Australian Dictionary of Biography. Volume 2*, Melbourne University Press, pp. 405–6.

[14] Ibid.

[15] Herbert Pybus Cooke took Holy Orders as an adult. See Hone, 'Cooke, Cecil Pybus'.

[16] Cecil Trevor Cooke became a station manager as an adult. See Ibid.

[17] See Kiddle, Margaret (1961, *Men of Yesterday: A social history of the Western District of Victoria 1834–1890*, Melbourne University Press, Melbourne) for Black's role in the development of the Western

District. See also Ward, Russel 1969, 'Black, Niel (1804–1880)', *Australian Dictionary of Biography. Volume 3*, Melbourne University Press, pp. 171–2.

[18] Mackellar, *Strangers in a Foreign Land*.

[19] Niel Black Journal, 8 November 1839, SLV.

[20] Niel Black Journal, 9 December 1839, SLV.

[21] Niel Black Journal, 4 January 1840, SLV. 'Strathdownie' was a 43,520-acre (17,612-hectare) run near Lake Terang. See Ward, 'Black, Niel'.

[22] Niel Black Journal, 21 February 1840, cited in Critchett, Jan 1990, *A 'Distant Field of Murder': Western District frontiers 1834–1894*, Melbourne University Press, pp. 128–9.

[23] Ibid., p. 129.

[24] Niel Black Journal, 21 February 1840, SLV.

[25] Niel Black Journal, 9 February 1840, SLV.

[26] Niel Black Journal, 13 March 1840, SLV.

[27] Kiddle, *Men of Yesterday*. See also Hone, J. Ann 1976, 'Winter, Samuel Pratt (1816–1878)', *Australian Dictionary of Biography. Volume 6*, Melbourne University Press, pp. 424–5.

[28] Lake Condah Mission Station was proposed in 1867 and gazetted in 1869. Cecil Cooke had not been as clever as some of the other squatters during the *Duffy Land Selection Acts* of the 1860s; however, he managed to retain 6000 acres (2400 hectares) of land and continued to hold about 4000 acres (1600 hectares) under licence until most of this poorer-quality land was set aside for the Lake Condah Aboriginal Reserve in 1869. See Forth, *The Winters on the Wannon*, pp. 150–1.

[29] Winter Cooke Papers, SLV.

[30] Though the letters were addressed to Samuel Pratt Winter, he was very ill throughout the final year of his life and no longer lived at 'Murndal'.

[31] Winter Cooke Papers, SLV.

[32] Forth (*The Winters on the Wannon*, p. 161) mentions the letters but also couldn't find any evidence of whether Winter replied. He comments that as there is no other mention of White it would suggest that he did not come to live at 'Murndal'. See also Massaola, Aldo 1970, *Aboriginal Mission Stations in Victoria*, Hawthorn Press, Melbourne. Lake Condah Reserve was returned to the Gunditjmara people in March 2008; see Lake Condah returned to traditional owners, Media release, Victorian Minister for Environment and Climate Change, 30 March 2008, available from http://www.legislation.vic.gov.au/domino/Web_Notes/newmedia.nsf/b0222c68d27626e2ca256c8c001a3d2d/130628a4441c385cca25741c008206f6!OpenDocument

[33] Massola, *Aboriginal Mission Stations in Victoria*, pp. 111–17.

[34] Ibid., p. 166. Samuel Winter Cooke, Arbella's eldest surviving son, inherited 'Murndal'; see Hone, 'Winter, Samuel Pratt'.

Chapter 7

A journey of love: Agnes Breuer's sojourn in 1930s China

Kate Bagnall

In his 1933 book, *White China: An Austral-Asian sensation*, journalist John Sleeman discussed the story of a young Queensland woman that had appeared in Sydney's *World* newspaper the previous year.[1] The sensational article claimed that after marrying a Chinese man in Townsville, the woman had gone with him to China where she was treated badly by her husband and his family. The *World* wrote that a fortnight after having a baby, the woman was 'forced to work in the rice fields like a coolie', that she lived 'under conditions that an Australian would scorn to allot to a diseased dog' and that her child was taken away by her husband's Chinese wife. The story had come to the *World* from a party of Anzac members of the Hong Kong Volunteer Defence Corps who had helped the Salvation Army 'rescue' the woman from China and facilitate her return to Australia.

The *World* article was like something from the pages of a melodrama: a sensationalist tale of slavery, immorality, racial pollution, cruelty, kidnapping and piracy mixed together with tropes of female helplessness and the heroism of the white Australian male. It spoke of a 'thrilling rescue' from a 'Chinese hell', of 'terrible conditions' and 'frightful cruelties'. Its white Australian heroine, identified only by the Chinese name of Low Mun, was nineteen years old and 'very beautiful'—and she was but one of a number of women in similar situations, the article claimed, two of whom were still 'being held captive'. Moralistic as well as sensational, the article ended with a quote from one of the woman's Anzac rescuers. He said, 'Australian women who marry Chinese should heed the perils attached to such, and should on no account accompany their husbands to China.'[2]

In *White China*, Sleeman countered the *World*'s version of the woman's experiences by reproducing a statement she gave to customs officials on returning to Australia. Her statement, as published in the book, itself given a journalistic gloss by Sleeman, highlighted the exaggeration of the newspaper reports and noted that some of her Anzac rescuers were, in fact, press men (in Sleeman's words, 'scandal-mongers intent on falsifying fact to get a thrill out of falsehood'). The statement addressed particular points of exaggeration from the *World*'s account. The woman had not had to live in a hut, nor did she have to work in the rice fields; instead, she had stayed in a flat on the main street of the town and had not even been made to do her own housework! She was certainly not held captive and could have left for Australia at any time, albeit not easily with her infant son.

The real root of her difficulties, she said, came from her father-in-law's objections to her marriage to his eldest son. Her father-in-law had been angry with her and with his son, whom he disowned for marrying against the family's wishes. Picking up on this, Sleeman argued that:

> It is the sort of thing that is happening every day, everywhere. It is the story of a family dispute. The least said, the soonest mended. The girl had a very unhappy experience, the sort of experience that thousands of Australian girls have at home without taking a trip to China to find.[3]

The woman had married her husband of her own free will, and of her own free will had gone with him to China. According to Sleeman's argument, it was a simple example of 'domestic infelicity' and he suggested that this one case should not be made to stand for all, saying: 'Many of our women who have married Chinese have lived happily and have reared children who to-day are playing a big part in the most important stage of world history.'[4]

Sleeman's *White China* was, according to Shirley Fitzgerald, 'perhaps the most widely read work on [the] China–Australia relationship in the '30s'.[5] The book's main argument concerned the state of trade between China and Australia, yet its tone was far from that of a dry work of economic theory. Sleeman, a former publicist for NSW Labor Premier Jack Lang and editor of the short-lived but vivacious weekly magazine *Beckett's Budget*, was an old hand at wrapping politics and idealism in colour and drama. *White China* followed the same formula, ranging widely in its discussions: 'Chapters on Chinese culture and political events were juxtaposed with details of Australian involvement and attitudes, from the heroic to the villainous, in a compilation designed to target the Australian conscience.'[6]

Sleeman placed the Queensland woman's story in a chapter on 'The women of China'—among accounts of some of the Middle Kingdom's great and legendary women, including Madame Sun Yat-sen, the Dowager Empress T'zu Hsi and Yang Kuei-fei—and he gave it as many words as he gave any of them. There was something about the story, or perhaps more particularly about the way it had been told in the press, that was behind Sleeman's decision to include it in the book; it certainly gave him another opportunity to lecture his reader about the foolishness of Australia's attitudes towards Asia and Asians. There was, however, also an untold personal connection between Sleeman and the unnamed woman, through their separate connections to businessman and Chinese community activist William Liu. It is likely that Sleeman was given access to the woman's statement—'duly signed and witnessed, to the Australian Government, through the agency of a Customs officer'—through Liu.

A sensational story

The *World* article appeared on Wednesday, 21 September 1932 and further details about the dramatic events in China were revealed in the next weeks, as the press in Sydney and Queensland pursued the story. On the evening of 21 September, a Brisbane newspaper retold the story from the *World* under the banner 'Young Queensland woman rescued from Chinese—wife in Australia was slave in Orient'.[7] The next day, the *Townsville Evening Star* gave full details of the woman's identity, but it was likely that much of the Townsville population would already have known who she was, had they chanced on the papers of the previous day. The *Evening Star* stated that she was 'originally Agnes Breuer', and that she had married, late in the previous year, 'a cultured young Chinese named William Lum Mow, the son of a well-known Chinese merchant, formerly of North Queensland, but now resident in China'.[8] It outlined how in March that year the young couple left Australia for Shekki in China and how it was there that the Australian wife discovered the presence of a Chinese wife—an event that was only the beginning of her 'sensational story'. On 26 September, the *Daily Mail* published a photograph of the couple and their newborn son—a seemingly happy young family—sent to her parents and just arrived with the Hong Kong mail.[9]

On 27 September, the *Evening Star* reported that Agnes was finally on board the SS *Taiping*, 'bound for home and safety after a succession of terrifying experiences as the wife of a Chinese'. It quoted from a letter from one Harold Brockenshire, 'Australian journalist, resident in China', who had written to a Sydney friend with news of Agnes's plight and plans for the rescue:

> After the marriage the Chinese carried the girl off to his native village. She found on arrival that he already had a Chinese wife and a couple of concubines. She has had a baby, and is in a bad way. To-morrow we catch the boat to Macao [from Hong Kong], dash to the village, and seize the girl.[10]

The press coverage of Agnes's 'rescue' and return to Australia drew on the themes presented first in the *World* article. Headlines included 'Rescue in China—Townsville girl's plight—sensational story of bondage', 'Fled from life of sorrow—rescue of white girl in China' and 'East is East—Australian girl's rescue—married to bigamous Chinese'.[11] Agnes spoke to the press on her arrival in Australia on 4 October, firmly denying the allegations made by the *World* about her time overseas. Nevertheless, her story was an unhappy one and she confessed that during her stay she had lived under 'wretched conditions'. 'I am very pleased and excited to get back home to Australia,' she said.[12]

Her Anzac rescuer's comment in the *World* article—that 'Australian women who marry Chinese should heed the perils attached to such, and should on no account accompany their husbands to China'—echoed sentiments expressed time and again in discussions of Anglo-Chinese intermarriage in previous decades. These discussions, together with that of Agnes's experiences, focused greatly on troubles caused by the fact that women not only chose to marry across racial boundaries, they left Australia (or England or America) and went with their husbands to China. Crossing the racial line in choosing a husband was one thing, but going with him to 'heathen', 'barbarian' China was another. It was thought widely that the chances of a successful marriage between a Chinese man and a white woman were generally very slim, but in China were virtually impossible.[13]

Sleeman was unique among commentators in arguing that Agnes's situation was one common to many Australian women, that it was a personal and familial problem in which race, culture, language and place played little part. Most accounts were generally negative and frequently condescending, and there were very few published accounts by families themselves that could be used to counter the dominant narrative.[14] With the case of Agnes Breuer, however, there is a small but significant collection of personal documents, which together with Sleeman's *White China* and Agnes's statements to the press and correspondence with government officials, reveals a level of detail of her own thoughts and personal experience that makes it possible to go behind the superficial public commentary about her relationship and to consider from a more intimate perspective the particular challenges faced by white wives who chose to accompany their Chinese husbands to China.

In these documents, the challenges to love across racial and cultural boundaries in white Australia become apparent. Nineteenth and early twentieth-century Australia could be ambiguous and contradictory in its reactions to interracial sex and marriage between white women and non-white men.[15] Increasingly, white women who formed intimate relationships with Chinese men and bore their children found that the interracial and sometimes transnational nature of their love and relationships conflicted with the ideologies, policies and mechanisms of the emerging nation-state. Their lives and personal dramas became not simply stories of family trouble, but could be and were drawn into and impacted on by wider narratives of racial and national anxiety.

Figure 7.1: Agnes and William Lum Mow, with baby William, Shekki, August 1932. Agnes Breuer told Australian reporters that William Lum Mow's Chinese wife was 'furiously jealous' of this photograph (*Telegraph*, 4 October 1932). She sent the picture to her parents from China and it was published in the *Daily Mail* on 26 September 1932 under the heading 'A cheerful couple'.

Courtesy: Liz McNamee

Australian wives in China

Agnes Breuer was one of a small number of non-Chinese women who travelled to southern China with their Chinese partners between the 1880s and the 1930s.[16] These women came from diverse cultural, social and religious backgrounds: from Australia, New Zealand, England, Europe, America, Canada, Hawai'i and South America. They had met and formed relationships with Chinese men who themselves had travelled overseas—to work as indentured labourers, to find riches in the colonial goldfields or as part of continuing familial migrations based on business and kinship. In Australia, intimate relationships had formed between white women and Chinese men since the mid 1850s, with numbers increasing as the Chinese population established itself in the colonies with the Victorian and NSW gold rushes.[17] Marriage records show that between the 1850s and the turn of the century, there were about 2000 legal marriages between white women and migrant Chinese men in Australia's eastern colonies, probably with similar numbers involved in de facto relationships of various kinds.[18]

The Chinese men who came to Australia were primarily from the areas in southern China around Canton, inland from Hong Kong, and it was to these same areas that their white wives accompanied them on journeys home. Hong Kong itself, with its British and Eurasian population, was the destination for some;[19] others travelled inland to the ancestral towns and villages in the Pearl River Delta region, as Agnes Breuer did. Agnes travelled to Shekki, the bustling county capital of the district of Zhongshan. Zhongshan and other parts of Guangdong Province such as Taishan, Kaiping, Dongguan and Zengcheng had prospered through the influence of significant overseas migration during numerous decades; by the knowledge, technologies, goods and money transferred from Chinese overseas. Agnes's father-in-law, Lum Mow, the 'well-known Chinese merchant, formerly of North Queensland, but now resident in China', had returned to Shekki in the late 1920s after nearly three decades as a merchant in Townsville.[20] The family was originally from a village called Seung Hang, several kilometres out of the town, but Lum Mow built his family a substantial and modern home in Shekki itself.

With the opening up of Hong Kong and Canton throughout the course of the nineteenth century, it was not only Chinese who were travelling back and forth. Non-Chinese claimed a presence in southern China, and there were numbers of British, Australian, American and European women resident in Hong Kong and Macau and in the Chinese Treaty ports. Most of these women had come to China with their husbands, who were employed in trade, missionary or government services. Other women came independently as missionaries (including some who lived outside the established foreign communities of the larger cities), as travellers and holidaymakers.[21] The differences between the experiences of these women and the wives of Chinese men were, however, significant. They might have shared feelings of homesickness, unfamiliarity with their surroundings and isolation—as well as those of excitement, adventure and discovery—but the experiences of wives were particular. When in China, non-Chinese wives became absorbed into their partners' families and into local cultures and communities in intimate ways that other non-Chinese women did not; theirs was an experience of Chinese domestic and family life usually inaccessible to foreigners. The experiences of wives in travelling to and from China were also shaped by the discriminatory attitudes and exclusionary policies of white expatriate communities and of governments at home.

Figure 7.2: 'Water Front, Shekki, Canton, June 1932', taken during Agnes Breuer's visit to China.

Courtesy: Liz McNamee

Agnes and William

Agnes Breuer was born in 1913, the daughter of a naturalised German father and an English–Australian mother. Her parents had married in Victoria in 1901, but the family moved north and Agnes, the only daughter after two sons, was born in Brisbane. In 1924, the family moved from Brisbane to Townsville, where her father, Adolf, an electrical engineer, took up a position as a teacher at the Townsville Technical College. Agnes was well educated and bright, and is remembered by her family as strong and stubborn; in the early 1930s, when she met her future husband, William Lum Mow, she was a lean, blonde teenager, a young woman with a talent for dancing and fond of dressing herself in the fashions of the day.[22]

William Lum Mow had arrived in Townsville in 1921 under the name of Lum Wie.[23] He had come to Australia on a Chinese student passport to live with his merchant father and attend school.[24] He was fifteen years old at the time and the eldest of four sons. In the following years, William attended Townsville's public school and the local Christian Brothers College. His school reports noted that he was a good student, his head teacher commenting in 1924 that he 'is really a splendid scholar; clean in his dress, thoroughly well behaved, and good at his work'.[25] In 1925, William enrolled in night courses at the technical college (where Adolf Breuer taught) and about the same time took over control of the family business when his ailing father returned to China for medical treatment. The family business, a successful fruit merchants and general importers in Stokes Street, Townsville, was established by William's father. It was one of about 50–60 Chinese stores in the town during the 1920s.[26]

Figure 7.3: Thomas Lum Mow (front) in the Lum Mow family store, Townsville, c. 1931.

Courtesy: Liz McNamee

At the age of twenty-two, William returned to China for nine months—from February to November 1928—and there he married a woman of his family's choosing, Li Yunying. His new wife remained in China and lived as a member of the Lum family in their home.[27] It seems that William disregarded this marriage after he arrived back in Australia, as he returned to the Australian life he was growing increasingly accustomed to. His father remained in China, and

William had control of the family business and care of his younger brothers: Norman, who came to Townsville in 1924, and Thomas, who arrived in 1930.

It is not clear exactly when William and Agnes began their relationship. An annotation in William's hand on the back of a photograph of himself, given to Agnes as a token, reads 'To Miss Agness [sic], Remembrance of Happy Days' and is dated 8 August 1931. Certainly, by late 1931, Agnes and William were planning to be married and William was also beginning to make arrangements for someone to manage the store while he returned to China for 'personal and business reasons' in early 1932—honeymoon plans, perhaps. Photos taken about this time (it seems William was a keen amateur photographer) show the couple carefree and relaxed, playing tennis, picnicking with friends in the countryside, posing in the office at the back of the family store—a young couple clearly much in love.

Figure 7.4: Agnes Breuer (back centre) and William Lum Mow (back left) picnicking with friends in Townsville, c. late 1931.

Courtesy: Liz McNamee

A Chinese holiday

Agnes and William were married on 18 December 1931 at the Townsville Registry Office. Agnes had just turned eighteen and William was twenty-five. Before the marriage, Agnes and her father had paid a visit to the Sub-Collector of Customs in Townsville to inquire about her 'legal position' if she were to marry William. The sub-collector later stated that Adolf Breuer had 'seemed to be against that union but must have consented'; the birth of Agnes's son in early August the next year suggests that the marriage, and her father's consent to it, could have been prompted by a pregnancy. The sub-collector told Agnes that the marriage would not confer any right on William to remain in Australia and that her nationality would change to that of her husband; in the face of these warnings, however, Agnes maintained that she 'had considered all aspects of the matter' and still wanted to be married.[28]

William had made preparations to leave Australia for a honeymoon in China, and his father returned in early January 1932 to care for the family shop while William was away. Lum Mow's visit was cut short, however, and he returned to China three weeks later. Lum Mow was apparently taken ill again, but knowing of the events that were to follow, it is likely that Lum Mow left at least in part in anger at his son's marriage. William and Agnes's Chinese holiday was delayed until March while arrangements for the management of the shop were taken care of. By this stage, it was confirmed that Agnes was pregnant. A medical certificate presented to customs officials before the couple's departure noted that she was about three months' pregnant, 'but is quite fit for travel and is in good health'.[29]

Having married William, Agnes lost her rights as a British subject. In the eyes of the Australian Government, she was now 'Chinese', and her unborn child would not only be ethnically Chinese, it would be born in China. Agnes was given permission to leave Australia and return within two years; her baby could return on 'evidence of its bona fides', providing it returned with Agnes before it was three years old. William's certificate of exemption, which allowed him to remain in Australia first as a student and then as manager of his father's business, was due to expire but as it had been renewed time and again for the previous 11 years it was presumably thought by William to be of no great matter. He would return from their holiday to resume his place as manager of the family store.

Transnational families

Recent scholarship has asserted the transnational nature of Chinese migration to countries such as Australia, New Zealand, Canada and the United States in the nineteenth and twentieth centuries.[30] Transnational connections could be found in many aspects of society and culture in the home counties of Guangdong Province and in Chinese communities overseas, including in family life. Adam McKeown has suggested the idea of the transnational overseas Chinese family as a way of describing the influences that resulted from the significant numbers of Chinese men who travelled overseas for work during this period.[31] The family of Lum Mow was typical in many regards.

When Lum Mow arrived in Australia in about 1896, it was not a one-way migration. He sent money home to China and returned himself on numerous occasions and fathered children. His wife remained in China, their sons were raised there and Lum Mow chose to return to China in his old age, taking a second wife, who bore him a daughter. As his sons grew up, Lum Mow arranged for them to come to Australia to be educated and to work in the family business. His second son, Norman, married in China, where his wife and children lived in the family home in Shekki until they later migrated to Australia. His youngest two sons married in Australia to Australian-born Chinese women, but they too continued the connection with China. The family of Lum Mow in Townsville was part of an extended network of kinsmen that stretched along Australia's east coast.[32]

The transnational nature of these families meant that they developed new patterns and strategies to support the family lineage. Among these were the taking of a younger wife to bear children or the adoption of sons to carry on the family line; coming and going to and from the Chinese home to father children (as Lum Mow did); the establishment of two or more households, and wives and families, in China and overseas; and in some cases, as Adam McKeown has noted, the formation of relationships with non-Chinese women overseas. This intermarriage could be thought of as one strategy through which Chinese men continued their family line where other factors did not allow a Chinese marriage.[33] William's decision to marry Agnes when he already had a wife in China was not without precedent then, nor was it perhaps as unusual an action as might otherwise be thought. Many before him had acted similarly, but in his case particular family dynamics meant that his father objected very strongly to the marriage. The precise reasons for his objections remain uncertain.

Often those writing about Chinese family life in nineteenth and early twentieth-century Australia have taken intermarriage between migrant Chinese men and white Australian women as an indicator of the 'assimilation' of Chinese men. Intermarriage and the formation of Australian families, particularly with white women, has been read as an abandonment of ideas of China as home and as a severance of ties to the extended Chinese family lineage, Chinese culture, customs and language—if not for the men themselves, then certainly for their children. Such a framework does not, however, help explain the actions of particular individuals and families who maintained strong family or business connections with the Chinese communities in Australia or with those in China itself. Thinking of interracial couples and the families they created as part of a transnational family system, however, provides a conceptual space in which to consider and perhaps understand more fully the complex dynamics operating within and around interracial relationships.[34]

Family

After leaving Queensland, Agnes and William travelled to Hong Kong and then inland to Shekki, arriving in mid April 1932. Their reception from William's father was cold. He disapproved of his son's decision to marry Agnes. Three days after arriving in Shekki, in Agnes's words, 'a big family consultation was held as to the attitude to be taken towards us and on its completion we were informed to get out of the house'.[35] William was to be disowned.

Agnes had experienced another shock on her arrival in China. It appears that she had been unaware of William's Chinese wife, Li Yunying, and the place she held within the wider Lum family.[36] Li Yunying had been living with her parents-in-law since her marriage to William four years earlier.

At first, Agnes and William, together with Li Yunying, went to stay at the Shekki home of Thomas Wing Lun, whom they knew from Townsville. After two months, they had to find other accommodation after their hosts were intimidated by the wealthy and influential Lum Mow. They moved to a flat on the main street of the town. Cards and letters sent home by Agnes, and photographs taken during the holiday, show that in spite of these difficulties there was continuing contact between Agnes and William and his family (there is a photograph of Agnes and other young women from the family, for example) and there was the opportunity for day trips, sightseeing and shopping.[37]

Agnes's son was born at the beginning of August, but his birth was the cause of increasing family conflict. William was an eldest son, her son likewise. For the extended Lum family, this child belonged first and foremost to their lineage, not to his natural mother. Agnes felt that Li Yunying was very jealous of the baby and stated that, besides her father-in-law's wrath, 'the only unpleasantness I experienced was from my husband's so-called Chinese wife who was prepared to vent her spite when the opportunity offered more particularly after the birth of my baby'.[38]

Convinced that a family reconciliation was impossible, Agnes became anxious to return to Australia. She wrote to her parents. They contacted the local Salvation Army, who arranged a passage and informed their Hong Kong colleagues. Her situation was, in Agnes's words, 'apparently exaggerated to Hong Kong' and her 'rescue' was effected in the manner described earlier. Agnes stated that she could have left of her own accord, but her main concern was whether she would have been able to take the baby with her if she had. Her father-in-law had promised to pay for her passage home only if she left the baby behind. Agnes also knew that William would oppose the baby's departure; she said that her departure from Shekki went so smoothly only because her husband had been out of the house at the time she and the baby left: '[H]ad my husband been home at the time there would have been trouble.'[39] Their departure shocked William and he wrote that the 'sudden and unexpected taking away—even without a parting word between wife and husband—had broken my heart'.[40] William regretted the way in which Agnes left, but at this point he and Agnes felt that their marriage was not over, that they would be reunited in Australia at a later date.

Agnes waited for 16 days in Hong Kong for the next boat to sail for Australia. She was in communication with her husband, who came to Hong Kong to see her, 'but on hearing of rumours of the treatment held in store for him from the Anzacs he immediately returned to Shekki', without even seeing her.[41] Agnes and the baby stayed with one of the Anzacs, a Mr J. P. Way of the Manufacturers Life Insurance Company, and the Anzacs presented her with a birthday gift of $HK100 before her departure.[42]

White Australia

William wrote to Agnes and to their son from that moment of their departure in 1932 until 1950.[43] After Agnes and the baby left Shekki, however, they never saw William again. It was at this point that national imperatives impacted on the transnational relationship of Agnes and William.

Agnes and the baby were permitted to return to Australia as had been arranged with customs officials in Townsville before they left. Things were different, however, for William. He had been allowed to remain in Australia after his schooling as a substitute for his father as manager of the family store. Soon after Agnes and William's departure, an officer in the Department of Home Affairs was already questioning whether William should be allowed to return at all, specifically citing his marriage to an Australian woman as the reason:

> Lum Wie [William Lum Mow] was here as substitute for his father Lum Mow. We gave authority for him to return to Australia to continue to act in that capacity. During Lum Wie's absence a younger brother is acting as substitute for the father.
>
> In the case of an assistant of H Louey Pang's we refused to allow him to return for some time because of his marriage to an Australian born girl.[44]
>
> In the circumstances it is submitted as to whether Lum Wie shall be allowed to come back as his father's substitute.[45]

While the direction was given in the first instance that William was to be allowed to be readmitted,[46] the same officer was firm on this point after Agnes's return: William should not be allowed back into Australia because there was nothing that recommended his readmission.[47]

Agnes viewed the situation otherwise. The disagreement within William's family meant that he would not be admitted to work in his father's business, but Agnes wrote to the Minister for Home Affairs in December 1932 and again in March 1933 asking if there was some other way that William could be allowed to return. She proposed that he should establish a business with capital brought from China. The sum he could bring was perhaps not large enough to meet the requirements, but she argued that he would soon have it built into a substantial enterprise, saying, 'He was very successful in improving his father's business in Townsville during the time of his management, and was in high esteem of all local and overseas wholesale dealers.'[48] He was, she said, very anxious to return to Australia to support his child and wife.

The department's decision, however, was final. Before he could be admitted as a merchant, William would have to demonstrate that he was representing a reputable importing or exporting house in China and that he would be undertaking a genuine wholesale import–export business. The value of capital and goods he was required to bring was no less than £500—more than double what William could muster. Having been disinherited, William no longer had the support and connections offered by his wealthy father. William and Agnes were stuck.

Australian authorities were unwilling to make allowances for their situation, despite Agnes's polite and thoughtful requests for assistance and despite the power the authorities had to make lenient decisions in cases they felt were deserving. In November 1932, after Agnes Lum Mow's case made the headlines, the Secretary of the Department of the Interior, A. R. Peters, requested that if customs officials were approached by white wives of Chinese for passports or documents for travel to China, his department should be informed and a report provided 'as to the husband's status (i.e. whether domiciled here or merely under exemption), his occupation, the object of the intended visit and proposed length of stay in China'.[49] Officials did not want a repeat of the events; nor were they particularly sympathetic to Agnes's plight. In the margins of one memo from the Customs and Excise Office in Townsville are scribbled the words 'The woman is not worth this trouble'.[50]

Personal journeys and public scrutiny

The public and official discussions of Agnes's experiences in China are typical of those about other non-Chinese wives of Chinese men in China. Missionaries, journalists, charitable bodies and governments focused on the unhappy, the unfortunate and the outright unsuccessful aspects of their journeys and their relationships.[51] They told moralistic tales of marital unhappiness, ill treatment, bigamy, ill health and maladjustment, underscored by a belief that a non-Chinese woman could never be truly happy as the wife of a Chinese man, particularly in China. Most of these discussions are one-sided or very brief and matter-of-fact, which makes the case of Agnes Breuer and William Lum Mow unusual in the comparative richness of source material about the circumstances of their separation. In the surviving documents, letters, photos and press clippings, the tensions between public discourse and private sentiment are evident.

Agnes chose to speak publicly about her experiences in an attempt to counter what the press were saying about her and her family. How far this was her own idea, or that of others, remains unknown. William urged Agnes, in a telegram from China, to tell the truth about what had happened, and to contact William Liu for help.[52] Liu was a businessman and social activist who devoted much of his time to improving the lot of Chinese people in Australia and to promoting greater understanding between Chinese and white Australians.[53] He was on amicable terms with government officials and was their frequent correspondent; he had acted on behalf of the Lum Mow family before, writing formal and personal letters to F. J. Quinlan, Assistant Secretary of the Department of Home Affairs, about their situation.[54] Liu had visited William and Norman Lum Mow in November 1931 in Townsville, as he travelled north from Sydney to China; he knew the Lum Mow family through his business connections with the Mar family of Wing Sang & Company in Sydney.

Liu attempted unsuccessfully to use his official connections to help Agnes and William. He wrote to the Department of the Interior in November 1932 giving some clarification of the circumstances of the case, and raising the issue of William Lum's return to Australia.[55] Sleeman's *White China* also stands as evidence that Liu took steps to clear the name of the Lum Mow family. Sleeman and Liu were friends, and much of *White China* was based on conversations they had about the situation in China and its importance for Australia. It is most likely that it was through Liu that Sleeman obtained a copy of Agnes's statement and heard details of the events. *White China* was widely read and praised by the Australian Chinese community, as well as the wider white community.[56] Although it did not mention the family by name, *White China*'s Chinese Australian audience would have known who the family involved was.

The telegram from William that prompted Agnes to contact Liu came several weeks after she had left him in China. It is one of a handful of their personal letters that remain. Government officials, missionaries and the press dismissed the genuineness of Agnes's feelings and desires, yet the personal correspondence between Agnes and her family while she was overseas and the communication between Agnes and William themselves in the time after their separation suggested a different scenario, in which their relationship was inhabited by love and a desire to be together as a family with their baby son. They also reveal a defensiveness in Agnes against what was said publicly about her treatment in China and a continuing bitterness against her husband's family with whom she continued to interact in Townsville. In her letter to the Minister for Home Affairs in December 1932, Agnes wrote that her father-in-law had 'instructed his sons at Townsville to be very rude to me, and to ridicule me as much as they possibly can'.[57] Stories of the events passed down in the Breuer and Lum Mow families suggest the strong emotions were felt on both sides.

Postscript

Among Agnes Breuer's remaining papers is a small, lined notebook. At one end are rough pencil sketches of ladies' suits and dresses, their style dating them to about the 1930s. Turning the notebook the other way up, in the back one finds pages of text, at first in ink, then in pencil. In this small notebook, Agnes had copied the passages from Sleeman's *White China* (in ink) and then (in pencil) the text of the *World* article from 21 September 1932. It seems unlikely that Sleeman and Agnes ever met through their connection to William Liu, yet Sleeman's words, his explanation, his justification of those dramatic and heartbreaking events in her life could well have provided her with a feeling of reassurance and comfort.

Agnes and her son, William junior, were marked by the events of 1932; the events existed, mostly unacknowledged and unspoken, in the background of their lives. Agnes's efforts to be reunited with her husband, William, continued for almost a year.[58] She went on to have other relationships and, after finally gaining a divorce in 1964, married again. William remained in China and kept in contact with Agnes and their son over the passing years; in 1935, while living in Hong Kong, he had made unsuccessful efforts to gain custody of William junior.[59] Over time, his heartfelt letters to Agnes shifted to cards and photos addressed to his son; the last contact Agnes had from him was in December 1950.[60] Their son never told his own family of his father's Chinese background, and it wasn't until after his death that they began to unravel some of the mysteries of his early life.

Was Sleeman right in saying that Agnes's troubles were nothing more than common 'domestic infelicity'? Reading the sensational press reports, together with Agnes's heartfelt letters to the government, the formal memos and informal comments scribbled in margins of government documents, it is hard to imagine that it was quite as straightforward as that. Agnes Breuer pursued a relationship outside the bounds of what was considered acceptable to white Australia—an imagined community that struggled with the idea and the reality of love that crossed racial and national borders. Her journey to China was made because of her love for her husband, but it was also a journey in which that love was tested by cultural difference and the expectations and prejudices of the two very different communities she and her husband were part of. Exploring her story in detail opens possibilities for considering how and why those who lived interracial and transnational lives could find themselves at odds with the communities and nations they called home.

Notes

[1] Sleeman, John H. C. 1933, *White China: An Austral-Asian sensation*, self-published, Sydney, pp. 126–32.

[2] *World*, 21 September 1932.

[3] Sleeman, *White China*, p. 131.

[4] Ibid., p. 132.

[5] Fitzgerald, Shirley 1996, *Red Tape, Gold Scissors: The story of Sydney's Chinese*, State Library of New South Wales Press, p. 128.

[6] Ibid., p. 129.

[7] Unreferenced newspaper cutting, dated 21 September 1932, National Archives of Australia (hereafter NAA), A433, 1942/2/3297.

[8] *Townsville Evening Star*, 22 September 1932.

[9] *Daily Mail*, 26 September 1932.

[10] *Townsville Evening Star*, 27 September 1932.

[11] *Townsville Evening Star*, 22 and 27 September 1932; *Telegraph*, 4 October 1932.

[12] *Brisbane Courier*, 4 October 1932; *Townsville Daily Bulletin*, 4 October 1932.

[13] See, for instance, Norton-Kyshe, James 1971, *The History of the Laws and Courts of Hong Kong from the Earliest Period to 1898. Volume 2*, Vetch and Lee Ltd, Hong Kong, pp. 520–1. It is interesting to note that Chinese Australian commentators were similarly opposed to the idea of relationships between Chinese men and white women. See, for example, *Tung Wah Times* [*Donghua xinbao*], 26 August 1899, 29 November 1899, 14 and 21 September 1907. An introduction to questions of gender in the nineteenth-century Chinese Australian newspapers can be found in Poon, Yulan 1995, 'The two-way mirror: contemporary issues as seen through the eyes of the Chinese language press, 1901–1911', in Shirley Fitzgerald and Garry Wotherspoon (eds), *Minorities: Cultural diversity in Sydney*, State Library of New South Wales Press, Sydney.

[14] Two examples of detailed and publicly accessible accounts of the experiences of white wives in China are Mae Franking's *My Chinese Marriage*, originally published in 1921 (Porter, Katherine Anne 1991, *Mae Franking's My Chinese Marriage: An annotated edition*, University of Texas Press, Austin), and Yue Henry Jackson, 'My reminiscences 1890–1917', Micro MS 112, Alexander Turnbull Library, National Library of New Zealand.

[15] See, for example, Haskins, Victoria and Maynard, John 2005, 'Sex, race and power: Aboriginal men and white women in Australian history', *Australian Historical Studies*, vol. 37, no. 126, pp. 191–216; Ellinghaus, Katherine 2006, *Taking Assimilation to Heart: Marriages of white women and indigenous men in the United States and Australia, 1887–1937*, University of Nebraska Press, Lincoln and London.

[16] It is difficult to know with any certainty the precise numbers of non-Chinese wives who travelled to China. There are scattered references to them in a range of sources. See Bagnall, Kate 2006, Golden shadows on a white land: an exploration of the lives of white women who partnered Chinese men and their children in southern Australia, 1855–1915, PhD, University of Sydney, Section 5.

[17] On the history of Anglo-Chinese relationships in southern Australia, see ibid.; Hales, Dinah 2004, 'Local histories: Chinese–European families of central western New South Wales, 1850–80', *Journal of Australian Colonial History*, vol. 6, pp. 93–112; Rule, Pauline 2002, 'A tale of three sisters: Australian–Chinese marriages in colonial Victoria', in Kee Pookong et al. (eds), *Chinese in Oceania*, Association for the Study of the Chinese and their Descendants in Australasia and the Pacific Islands, Chinese Museum and Victoria University of Technology Centre for Asia-Pacific Studies, Melbourne; Rule, Pauline 2004, 'The Chinese camps in colonial Victoria: their role as contact zones', in Sophie Couchman, John Fitzgerald and Paul Macgregor (eds), *After the Rush: Regulation, participation, and Chinese communities in Australia 1860–1940. Otherland Literary Journal*, no. 9.

[18] See Bagnall, Golden shadows on a white land, Section 2.

[19] On the interactions between Chinese, Europeans and Eurasians in Hong Kong, see Lethbridge, Henry 1978, *Hong Kong: Stability and change, a collection of essays*, Oxford University Press, Hong Kong, pp. 175–7. On Eurasians in Hong Kong, see Lee, Vicky 2001, Hong Kong Eurasian memoir: identity and voices, PhD, University of Hong Kong.

[20] Certificate of domicile for Lum Mow, 1 March 1904, NAA, J2482, 1904/57.

[21] For discussion of white women in China, see, for example, Hoe, Susanna 1991, *The Private Life of Old Hong Kong: Western women in the British colony, 1841–1941*, Oxford University Press, Hong Kong

and New York; Croll, Elisabeth 1989, *Wise Daughters from Foreign Lands: European women writers in China*, Pandora, London.

[22] Sources for the family of Agnes Breuer include the remaining papers and photographs belonging to Agnes Breuer held by her family (hereafter Agnes Breuer Papers); other information supplied by the Breuer family; and NAA, A435, 1946/4/3678, and A435, 1947/4/3233.

[23] See NAA, A433, 1942/2/3297. This large Department of the Interior file documents William Lum Mow's time in Australia between 1921 and 1932, as well as later correspondence between Agnes Breuer and the Australian Government. Much of the biographical information about William Lum Mow in this article comes from this file, together with information supplied by Lum Mow family members.

[24] On the admittance of Chinese students to Australia on exemption, see Yarwood, A. T. 1967, *Asian Migration to Australia: The background to exclusion 1896–1923*, Melbourne University Press, Melbourne, especially Chapter 6; Palfreeman, A. C. 1967, *The Administration of the White Australia Policy*, Melbourne University Press, Melbourne, especially Chapter 4.

[25] School report on Lum Wie by E. J. Moorhouse, Head Teacher, Central State School, Townsville, 18 March 1924, NAA, A433, 1942/2/3297.

[26] Harvey, Thomas 2001, Missing persons: the Chinese in Townsville, 1864–1940, BSS Honours, James Cook University, pp. 80, 83. In 1929, Lum Mow was the sole proprietor of his business, employing four staff, and the turnover of the business was valued at £15,000 per annum; Minute paper, Sub-Collector of Customs, Townsville to Collector of Customs, Brisbane, 15 March 1929, NAA, A433, 1949/2/7501.

[27] NAA, J2773, 172/1928; *Telegraph*, 4 October 1932.

[28] Sub-Collector of Customs, Townsville, to Collector of Customs, Brisbane, 10 October 1932, NAA, A433, 1942/2/3297. Agnes Breuer later applied to regain her status as a British subject; see NAA, A435, 1946/4/3678.

[29] Copy of medical certificate from Dr H. J. Taylor, Townsville, 22 March 1932, NAA, A433, 1942/2/3297.

[30] See, for example, Fitzgerald, John 2007, *Big White Lie: Chinese Australians in white Australia*, University of New South Wales Press, Sydney; Williams, Michael 2002, Destination *Qiaoxiang*: Pearl River Delta villages and Pacific ports, 1849–1949, PhD Thesis, University of Hong Kong; McKeown, Adam 2001, *Chinese Migrant Networks and Cultural Change: Peru, Chicago and Hawaii 1900–1936*, University of Chicago Press, Chicago; Hsu, Madeline Y. 2000, *Dreaming of Gold, Dreaming of Home: Transnationalism and migration between the United States and South China, 1882–1943*, Stanford University Press, Stanford.

[31] See McKeown, Adam 1999, 'Transnational Chinese families and Chinese exclusion, 1875–1943', *Journal of American Ethnic History*, vol. 18, pp. 73–93, and *Chinese Migrant Networks and Cultural Change*.

[32] This network included merchants Mar Leong Wah and Mar Sun Gee of the Wing Sang Company in Sydney. The Mar and Lum Mow families were from the same district in southern China, Zhongshan, and in time Lum Mow's second son, Norman, would marry a daughter of the Mar family in China. The connection with the Mar family also brought the Lum brothers into contact with businessman and social activist William Liu, who was a director of Wing Sang & Company.

[33] See McKeown, *Chinese Migrant Networks and Cultural Change*, pp. 70–4, and *Journal of American Ethnic History*. Romanzo Adams' work on interracial marriage in Hawai'i supports this thesis. He stated that before 1900, a proportion of Chinese who married Hawaiians 'were not intending to abandon Chinese custom', but rather that 'the marriage was merely a temporary adjustment to the situation in a foreign country'. See Adams, Romanzo 1969, *Interracial Marriage in Hawaii: A study of the mutually conditioned processes of acculturation and amalgamation*, Patterson Smith, Montclair (originally published by The Macmillan Company, 1937), p. 47.

[34] For further exploration of these ideas, see Bagnall, Golden shadows on a white land, Section 5, pp. 246–50.

[35] Statement given by Mrs A. H. Lum Mow, October 1932, NAA, A433, 1942/2/3297.

[36] The presence of a wife and household in China as well as one overseas was not uncommon among overseas Chinese communities; neither was the added complexity this created during visits by foreign wives to China. See, for example, 'Report of the Royal Commission into Chinese Gambling and Immorality', *New South Wales Legislative Assembly Votes & Proceedings 1891–92*, p. 138; Don, Alexander 1898, *Under Six Flags*, Wilkie & Co., Dunedin, p. 116; Ng, James 1995, *Windows on a Chinese Past: How the Cantonese goldseekers and their heirs settled in New Zealand. Volume 2*, Otago Heritage Books, Dunedin; McKeown, *Journal of American Ethnic History*, p. 109, 61n; McKeown, *Chinese Migrant Networks*, p. 72.

37 One newspaper reported that Agnes had 'smuggled out a letter, unfolding her terrifying experiences' (she did write to ask her parents for assistance in returning to Australia), but most of the postcards and photos sent home to her family did not reflect on the difficulties she was going through. *Townsville Evening Star*, 22 September 1932; postcards from Agnes Breuer to family members, April to August 1932, Agnes Breuer Papers.

38 Statement given by Mrs A. H. Lum Mow, October 1932, NAA, A433, 1942/2/3297.

39 *Townsville Daily Bulletin*, 4 October 1932.

40 William Lum Mow to Miss Rains (Salvation Army, Hong Kong), 7 September 1932, Agnes Breuer Papers.

41 Statement made by Mrs A. H. Lum Mow, October 1932, NAA, A433, 1942/2/3297.

42 *Townsville Evening Star*, 20 October 1932.

43 Draft petition for dissolution of marriage between Agnes Hubertine Lum Mow and William Lum Mow, 1963, Agnes Breuer Papers.

44 The mention of an assistant of Louey Pang's refers to David Louey Shue, who arrived to work for his uncle Louey Pang in Melbourne in 1922. After he had been in Australia on exemption for seven years, Louey Shue married a Chinese–Australian woman. Officials in the Department of Home Affairs felt that he had done this as a deliberate attempt to remain permanently in Australia. After the couple and their child went to China for a holiday in 1930, the department had, as a form of chastisement, allowed Louey Shue to return to Australia only if his wife remained overseas. She was subsequently allowed to return in 1932. Louey Shue continued to live in Australia on exemption until the 1950s; NAA, A433, 1948/2/2879.

45 Handwritten note, dated 13 April, at the bottom of memorandum from Collector of Customs, Brisbane, to Secretary, Department of Home Affairs, 4 April 1932, NAA, A433, 1942/2/3297.

46 Handwritten note, undated, at the bottom of memorandum from Collector of Customs, Brisbane, to Secretary, Department of Home Affairs, 4 April 1932, NAA, A433, 1942/2/3297.

47 Handwritten note, dated 21 October, at the bottom of Sub-Collector of Customs, Townsville, to Collector of Customs, Brisbane, 10 October 1932, NAA, A433, 1942/2/3297.

48 Agnes Lum Mow to Secretary, Department of the Interior, 6 March 1933, NAA, A433, 1942/2/3297.

49 Department of the Interior circular memorandum no. 31/2306, 21 November 1932, NAA, A433, 1942/2/3297. See also NAA, B13, 1932/17435.

50 Memorandum, Customs and Excise Office, Townsville, 2 November 1932, NAA, A433, 1942/2/3297.

51 It is typical and indeed not altogether surprising that unhappy or unfortunate cases appear most commonly in the sources. See, for example, *Overland China Mail* [Hong Kong], 12 February 1898; *Hong Kong Telegraph*, 18 January 1898; Hong Kong Benevolent Society 1904, *Report for 1903*, Hong Kong (also reports for 1904–06); Edward S. Little, Australian Trade Commissioner in China, to the Prime Minister, 29 March 1923, NAA, A1, 1924/31745.

52 The telegram reads: 'Correct newspapers Exaggerations save our name. Consult Wm Liu Sydney, Quong Chong, So Gun, Norman. I will return Townsville soon. Money follows.' Telegram from William Lum Mow (Hong Kong) to Agnes Breuer (Townsville), 18 October 1932, Agnes Breuer Papers.

53 William Liu's papers are held by the Mitchell Library, Sydney, as ML MSS 6294. Details of his life and career can be found in, among others, Fitzgerald, *Big White Lie*; Liu, William 1979, 'Australia's Chinese connection', *125th Anniversary of the Battle of the Eureka Stockade: 5th Annual Lalor Address on Community Relations*, Commissioner for Community Relations, Canberra; Liu, William 1978, Conversation with William Liu [sound recording], 17 February 1978, Hazel de Berg Collection, National Library of Australia; Sleeman, *White China*; Walker, David and Ingleson, John 1989, 'The impact of Asia', in Neville Meaney (ed.), *Under New Heavens: Cultural transmission and the making of Australia*, Heinemann Educational Australia, Port Melbourne; Wang Gungwu 1992, 'The life of William Liu: Australian and Chinese perspectives', *Community and Nation: China, Southeast Asia and Australia*, Allen & Unwin, St Leonards; Yong, C. F. 1977, *The New Gold Mountain: The Chinese in Australia 1901–1921*, Raphael Arts Pty Ltd, Richmond, South Australia.

54 See, for example, two letters (one formal, one personal) from William Liu to F. J. Quinlan, Department of Home Affairs, 26 November 1931, NAA, A433, 1942/2/3297.

55 Memorandum, 11 November 1932, NAA, A433, 1942/2/3297.

56 See Society of Chinese Residents in Australia c. 1934, *Relating to Chinese–Australian Trading Relationships and the International Question: An appreciation addresses to J. H. C. Sleeman, Esq., Sydney, Australia, Author of* White China, Sydney, Alert Printing & Publishing.

[57] Agnes Lum Mow to Secretary, Department of Home Affairs, 23 December 1932, NAA, A433, 1942/2/3297.

[58] Agnes wrote in June 1933 that she planned to apply for divorce on the grounds that her husband had not provided sufficient means of support. Agnes Lum Mow to A. Peters, Secretary, Department of the Interior, 28 June 1933, NAA, A433, 1942/2/3297.

[59] In January 1935, William wrote to the Townsville Sub-Collector of Customs about whether it would be possible for him to have custody of his son, subject to Agnes's approval. Investigations revealed that Agnes was seriously ill in hospital and could not comment on the situation, but her father, who 'had the responsibility for caring for the child since his arrival in the Commonwealth', declared that he and Agnes would be opposed to the idea of sending the child to China. William Lum Mow to Sub-Collector of Customs, Townsville, 28 January 1935, NAA, A433, 1942/3297.

[60] Draft petition for dissolution of marriage between Agnes Hubertine Lum Mow and William Lum Mow, 1963, Agnes Breuer Papers.

Chapter 8

Life stories, family relations and the 'lens of migration': postwar British emigration and the new mobility

A. James Hammerton

This chapter offers some reflections on the changing ways in which Western—and more particularly British—emigrants have come to describe and reflect on their lives in the second half of the twentieth century. It arises from a current project on late twentieth-century British emigration to multiple locations, which explores ways in which the post-1960s period of heightened mobility and cheaper transport has brought about shifts in migrant identities while retaining some continuities with traditional modes of migration and migrants' own telling of their stories.[1] It involves scrutiny of ways in which migrants construct their life histories and how that has changed since the period represented in Australia by the 'ten-pound Poms' generation of British migrants from the 1940s to the 1960s, with some particular reference here to marital and family relations.[2] 'How we emigrate now' has undergone profound changes since about the 1960s, and it is timely to begin to undertake the historical task of tracing how one mode of migration, and the expression of the migrant life and identity, has evolved into a different, more transnational, one in the past four decades—albeit with elements of both continuity and change in practice. Given the enormous exodus of the British in the 30 years after 1945, the sustained and newsworthy level of the British diaspora right down to the present, and still with the great benefit of the colonial dividend—which bequeathed half a world of convenient linguistic migrant destinations—the British make an excellent case study in the evolution of the modern mobility among the populations of the West.[3] Their migration stories, in which Australia plays a central but not exclusive role, are quintessentially transnational, and underline the value of viewing even the most intimate accounts of migrant biography through a transnational lens.

Several themes emerge from a qualitative study of the life histories of those modern, often serial migrants to a succession of countries, who left Britain in the years after the late 1960s. First, the old self-improvement ethos in family and individual terms, which, arguably, characterises most British emigration from the early nineteenth century until the 1960s, has been replaced, gradually, by a different set of attitudes to migration, which define it primarily in terms of adventure, the consumption of transnational experience and a sharp eye for expatriate money-making around the globe.[4] Second, from about the 1970s, we can see the emergence of a new definition of the migrant self as inherently mobile and transnational, encapsulated in frequent declarations such as 'I'm a citizen of the world', 'I'm international' and 'I don't belong to any one country'. This is closely related to the tendency for migrants to construct the narrative of their lives through a lens of migration, regardless of the power of other events in their lives. It has competed with and often edged aside more traditional constructions of migrant identity around notions of migration as an epic struggle to succeed and an ultimate vindication of the decision to leave and settle permanently in one country. Third, among a substantial minority there is a tendency for modern migrants' marriages to be transnational. Increasingly, the dynamics of global occupations and multicultural societies have facilitated the incidence of multiracial marriages that are themselves likely to be highly mobile. More commonly, British migrants have first met and married transient Australians, Canadians, New Zealanders or Americans in Britain, and then decided to relocate to their spouse's country. While such migrants are quintessentially modern products of a mobile world, the implications for married life, regardless of the gender of the migrant spouse, tend to be very similar to those we associate with the migrant 'war brides' of the 1940s. The more traditional courtship and marriage of a settled migrant to a native-born partner in the new country carries quite different meanings for both spouses compared with the effective 'importation' of a spouse new to the country; in recent decades the wider choices available to newly married but unsettled partners can lead to more volatile marriages. For such reasons, the implications of migration for marriage and family life are particularly important.

These are the kinds of themes that surface when migrants recollect their life stories, whether in written form or into a microphone with an oral historian, and they will recur in some of the narratives that follow. For the autobiographically minded, the transformative potential of migration has often served as an additional spur to record their experiences and reflections of them. Kate Boyle, who came to Melbourne in 1998 from Staffordshire, noted that her fortieth birthday in 2005 seemed 'an appropriate time to consider the journey here'. She sent us this communication before writing a long life history that placed her migration at its centre:

> I would love to tell my story and hear others, the whole experience is so life changing that it is hard not to tell others some of the stuff you go through in the process of moving home, country, leaving behind relatives and friends, making new friends, getting to know in-laws, encountering new health and education systems.[5]

Figure 8.1: 'Nomads on the Move Again': modern migrants. Since the 1960s migrants have tended to see themselves as inherently mobile and transnational.

Undated news cutting, Portsmouth, 1970.

There is nothing particularly new about the migrant experience driving life writing. While researching personal histories of the immediate postwar British emigrant generation to Australia—the 'ten-pound Poms'—we routinely encountered ageing grandparents, acutely conscious of the enduring impact of their migration, who had already written an autobiography for the benefit of their families. The son of one of these celebrated the fact that his father's 'great knowledge of the last nearly eighty years will not be lost upon his death. We can read it ourselves and hand it to our children to read and they can hand it to their children.'[6] In more recent years, prompted in some ways by a younger, more middle-class, often tertiary-educated migrant generation, at ease with writing, the urge to narrate the migrant life has taken a rather different form. For Boyle in 2005, it focused on how the major differences between English and Australian landscapes, which initially struck her, were diminishing over time: '[M]aybe the differences are becoming less significant the longer I am here and this landscape means "home" to me.'[7] Such reflections can serve a useful purpose in the continuing project of coming to terms with the meaning of migration in a mobile life that might seem to be in constant flux. Life writing in these cases is likely to be undertaken largely as a therapeutic exercise, for the self rather than the family, often to speculate on possible moves still ahead. Caroline Streeter, for example, concluded her long reflections on 30 years of movement between England and Australia with an eye on the future, the certainty that for her and her family the migratory journey was unfinished: 'It seems that our migration story is not over yet, and may take some very interesting twists and turns in the years to come.'[8] All migrants tend to dwell on the reasons that drove them to leave their homeland in the first place, and the reasons invariably owe something to socioeconomic and political contexts; for young migrants of the 1980s, for example, the resort to the explanatory label 'Thatcher refugees' is remarkably common.[9] Emotional factors, too, well beyond strictly economic imperatives, have invariably played some part in migrant motivations; in the immediate postwar years, for example, the opportunity to make a 'new start', perhaps to revive a failing marriage, was occasionally remembered as the crucial motivating factor.[10] As the option of migration became financially easier in the later twentieth century, however, when a decision to relocate across the globe could be made virtually on a whim, such personal stories and explanations have tended to intrude more commonly into autobiography.[11] These can include the quest for a lifelong romantic fulfilment, reaction against a narrow parochial or dysfunctional family life or the traumatic events and complications of a transnational marriage. Such matters are routinely the stuff of autobiographical writing, but can be complicated when blended with a migration narrative, which, in recollection at least, is likely to emerge as the centre and driving force of the life story.[12]

The migration-centred story in life writing is also common in oral testimony. Informants, especially older migrants, for the book I wrote with Alistair Thomson, *Ten Pound Poms*,[13] tended to interpret their life and identity through their 'lens' of migration, the central turning point through which they reflected on their lives before and after the act of migration—an act that coloured evaluation of their life, whether told through stories of family, marriage or career. Informants who had experienced some other life-changing event, such as war service, prisoner-of-war experience, childhood evacuation or the early death of a parent, which might normally be expected to be the critical turning point, shifted priority to migration for their sense of its power to transform their lives. This pivotal transformation was seen most dramatically in terms of domestic, marital and family life. The stories elaborated below illustrate ways in which the self-styled mobile persona, when enmeshed closely with family attachments, can obscure as much about migrant subjectivity as it explains.

Given the conditions of postwar Britain, with the slow pace of reconstruction, shortages and the continuation of rationing until 1954, it should not be surprising to find migrants of the 1940s and 1950s dwelling on their escape from postwar austerity to the greater opportunities of Australia, and this is one of the distinguishing features of the migration stories of that generation. Albert Lougher, who emigrated in 1954, had suffered traumatic experiences as a twice-captured prisoner of war in Tobruk and Italy, and spent time in slave-labour conditions near Dachau building Farben's poison gas factory.[14] He spoke about his feelings on demobilisation, of wishing he was dead, of alienation from what he thought was a re-emerging class-ridden society that had left his father unable to provide for his family, and bitterness about feeling cast adrift. His recovery began when he gained an apprenticeship as a watchmaker and he began to aspire to a more comfortable suburban life together with his new wife, Ann, his 'saviour'. For Albert, however, looking back on his life in retirement in Sydney, his major life transformation came not with this occupational lift, nor even with his beloved saviour wife, but with his migration, which enabled him to live out his belief that in postwar Britain, and then in Australia, he was part of a 'new generation, not like my Dad'. He meant by this his ability to provide for his family in ways his father never could in London, and not being bound to traditional rigid and authoritarian ideas of family and marriage. When asked about the best and most enduring result of his migration, Albert responded with a celebration of his family life:

> Well, I think we've given Australia three good kids and five grandchildren...We've been married now 52 years this year. And we've reaped the benefit of family life. Our children are our companions, we're friends...in fact I've got a daughter coming over this afternoon and she'll bring a bottle and we'll have a wine and a laugh. They always brought their friends in. And I think it's from there...that good life comes.

Albert and Ann, like thousands of postwar British migrants, told their story around that time-honoured password of the migrant—opportunity—but more broadly in terms of what we understand as the self-improvement ethos. Although self-improvement in material terms has always been basic to voluntary migration, we associate the twentieth-century self-improvement ethos powerfully with nineteenth-century movements for respectability and education, which drove migration to the Americas and the Antipodes. In this respect, postwar British migrants could be said to have more in common with their nineteenth-century forebears than with those of their more modern successors from the late 1960s. In both periods, self-improvement has carried a moral as well as an economic meaning, and a powerful belief that a respectable working and family life could be fulfilled more easily through emigration to a new land. Its class connotations were embedded in the alluring propaganda that, for example, promised all the suburban trappings of 'the Australian way of life' to struggling skilled and semi-skilled postwar migrants. It was expressed in all those family stories written for grandchildren by our informants, by men such as Leonard Hedges, who went along with his wife's drive to emigrate for 'something better' and insisted that 'family comes first',[15] and by women such as Margaret Hill, who, after she left a controlling and violent husband in Adelaide, struggled to get her children back and build a life for them alone in Melbourne, and has now written two books telling the story.[16] Their realisation of the eagerly prized opportunity usually bequeathed an undivided loyalty to the new country, so that in these stories the migrant's Australian identity, virtually given as a reward for benefits received (as in Albert Lougher's declaration, 'we've given Australia three good kids and five grandchildren'), is straightforward. These are fairly uncomplicated stories, then, viewed through a framework of loyalty to the nation-state.

Significantly, however, it was during the years of this same postwar migrant generation that seeds of change were sown for a new and more complicated transnational outlook. Until the 1980s, the postwar schemes to all the former colonies of white settlement were so open ended that almost anyone could qualify to use them for whatever long or short-term purpose they chose. The notable beneficiaries of this were young single men and women intent on 'adventure' and the two-year or more working holiday. These, of course, were the precursors of today's backpackers, but also migrants with more flexible plans about their future, more prone to itinerancy, to pre-planned return and to open-ended readiness to be influenced by shifting employment opportunities and seeing more of the world; they can appropriately be labelled 'serial migrants'. Cheaper mass air travel from the 1970s was central to this change, as were newer corporate employment practices that encouraged skilled and managerial employees to relocate as expatriates, more or less temporarily, around the world—practices that frequently encouraged those expatriates to become permanent migrants. In these conditions, the old self-improvement ethos faded as a primary motivation for migration across the class spectrum. Work and family ambitions remained central to migration decisions, but this was now much more likely to be combined with notions of adventure, which rapidly became the new catch-all motivation, leading to the modern notion of continuing migration and travel as consumerism rather than the traditional self-improvement ethos. In practical terms, however, modern migrants continued to face all the traditional challenges of managing in a new country. Among the most persistent and vexing of these challenges were those to marriage and family.

An example from a woman who began her travels as a single adventuring sojourner to South Africa and who later re-emigrated to Australia should illustrate some of the challenges. Among the popular postwar choices of migrant destinations for the British, apartheid South Africa rapidly became the most problematic, with racial issues commonly cited among primary reasons for choosing other alternatives. By the 1970s, many British South Africans were reconsidering their settlement decision and either returning to Britain or moving on to third countries, with Australia one of the most popular destinations.

Initially, this was stimulated for the British by racial issues, including the flight from apartheid and the associated instability; subsequently, it was more often driven by security fears. None of these fears concerned Ros Smith when she emigrated, single, to Cape Town in 1972, in company with a young woman friend.[17] At this stage, Ros was the classic sojourner emphatically seeking 'adventure' and a good time, with plans to move on to Australia after two years; she had made earlier plans to travel with a South African boyfriend, but when he decided he needed to travel alone instead—and to South America—she resolved to embark on her adventure without him. Despite the fact that she refused to answer his letters, in 1973, several months after he returned to South Africa, they married. Her wedding illustrated her ambiguous status as a migrant wife. 'I knew seven people at my wedding, including my husband,' Ros recalled, 'his parents actually lived in Zambia at the time and they drove down from Zambia to South Africa and, they just had two cars loaded with presents from people I didn't even know, I've never met them.'

The isolated English wife's marriage to a South African journalist known for his opposition to the apartheid regime made for a testing social life, and much of Ros's story of this time struggles to express her distress at her isolation and sense of insecurity. 'We would have dinner parties...in South Africa...they used to get very heated and there was table-thumping and I would usually end up in the kitchen sobbing over the dishes.' This was compounded by security fears and the ever-present threat that her husband, Chris, like some of his left-leaning colleagues on the *Rand Daily Mail*, might be incarcerated by the government; after the birth of her son, Ros feared that if she was to stay in South Africa he would be conscripted into the army to do the regime's dirty work. Political matters thus intruded into family life, and Ros, the migrant wife with few sources of emotional support, recalls a sense of powerlessness and alienation. In response, she struggled to find sympathetic friends and a place in what seemed to be a hostile and threatening society. It took years, first in Cape Town, later in Johannesburg, for her to create a close network of women friends to balance her relative powerlessness. While feeling no religious commitment, she joined the Methodist Church:

> I wasn't religious in England...but then in South Africa I joined the Methodist Church...I went to all sorts of Bible readings, I became friends with my minister and his wife, they came for dinner with us...all the time, I just needed support...I needed a...crutch, I couldn't deal with it. The politics were too big for me.

Ros also had to negotiate her recurrent homesickness, which threatened her marriage with Chris, her South African husband, who was quite unable to understand his wife's emotions, but with a surprise revelation in store for him when they ultimately moved on to Melbourne in 1982:

> [I]t wasn't until we came here that Chris understood how *I* felt. Chris is, was, never tolerant of homesickness because he thinks my home is wherever *he* is. Which is not true…you're not home—homesickness is a very strange thing…it's not for *people*, and it's not for place, it's for a real mixture and it's for emotions, it's for smells, it's for familiarity, it's just a whole network of things we miss.

Ros's reflections on how things changed when they fled South Africa and migrated to Australia provide some insight into her condition as a migrant wife in South Africa, in contrast with the advantage she enjoyed during their brief period in England, and the more equal footing she shared with Chris in Melbourne, when both of them carried a migrant identity.

> Well, one of the good things…for me, a personal thing, is that [Australia] was neither of our homes. Okay, when I went to South Africa it was Chris's home, and his friends, and they became my friends, I have no quarrel with that, but somehow, because he is a very dominating person I find here, okay we're [on a] level playing field…Yes, it's up to both of us now.

Recalling that when they had resolved to leave South Africa they canvassed several alternative destinations, especially Canada, and return to England, Ros described Chris's aversion to the English weather, how she deferred to him on that issue, but then reflected on how her identity as a woman had evolved along with her migrant identity and personal growth.

> So the reason not to go back to England was the weather, he *hated* the weather…I was torn, I think is probably the honest answer, but I had to consider him. Chris is not easy to live with if he isn't happy, and I have had years of him being unhappy politically and I thought if I got him somewhere where he's happy he'll be easier to live with…I can say that now because I've come to terms with all of this now, if you'd asked me ten years ago I don't know that I could have answered that, because now I've reached a stage in my life, I'm nearly 60, and if Chris is unhappy and it's not me causing the unhappiness, it's his problem and he must sort it out, I'll help him, but I don't take it on any more as my problem. Whereas I was taking England's weather and being responsible for it making him unhappy, that's what would happen. I've moved, I've grown…I still value my marriage very much but women nowadays are much stronger, as I'm sure you know, and I am an independent woman now and I'll do things and discuss things with Chris and I would never deliberately upset him but if he doesn't like it, like he doesn't like me going back to England without him to see my mother, well he's revolting before I go, he sulks when I get back, I still go, whereas I wouldn't have done in those days.

Ros's narration of her life history here is certainly driven by her lens of migration; it recurs when she recounts persistently what a success the move to Melbourne became for Chris, herself and her children. It is magnified each time she embarks on her nearly annual family visits to England, and occasionally to South Africa—an experience that sets her generation far apart from that of the early postwar years, and keeps alive her subjective perception of herself as routinely mobile. Ros is, however, conscious here too of a different kind of journey in her reference to her growth as a person, a woman and a wife as well as a migrant. 'I've moved, I've grown' is a powerful motif of personal and literal movement. Ultimately, while Ros is conscious of her migrant identity, it remains unresolved, and perhaps unresolvable, whether her personal journey towards greater confidence and autonomy has been more central to her than her geographical mobility and Australian attachment. Her story underlines the complex, and not necessarily simply causative, relationship between migration and personal change.

On first contact with us, Ros described herself as a 'research project waiting to be discovered', hinting at the importance she attached to her magpie-like accumulation of documents from her migrant past and trying to make sense of her life history. For Ros, as for others, this has translated into the writing of a detailed migration-centred autobiography. Another woman who sent us her initial 50-page draft—apologising: 'I've worried at times that it's too much like a soap opera'—wrote at length about her marriage in England to an Australian and the steep learning curve she experienced on the ship voyage to Australia in the late 1960s when, quite suddenly, she saw a new, and unwelcome, side of her husband. She shared the experience with a woman in a similar situation: 'Our stories have many parallels; we had married men we didn't really know, who could keep up a pretence away from home and we were both very naive about the decision to emigrate.'[18] The parallels here with earlier war-bride experiences are striking: a reminder that among the huge changes in Western migration between the 1950s and 1990s, there remains an interplay of change and continuity. Among the continuities, the strongest is a preoccupation with the influence of migration on marriage and family and, conversely, the power of marriage and family to shape migration.

The ubiquitous family emphasis can be seen in a wide variety of migration experiences. Maurice Bassindale, like Ros Smith, was a serial migrant and, like her, his marital and family history was bound up deeply with his migration, but his mobile trajectory could not have been more different.[19] Maurice, who began working life in 1956 in his native Lincolnshire as a trained motor mechanic, soon graduated to the management of the maintenance and operation of large vehicle fleets and seemed set for a successful career at home. By 1960, he was married with two children and had a prosperous future ahead, although most of his work involved frequent travel around Britain, so he was often away from home. By

1977, after several moves, buying and selling houses, and with the children in private schools, life was comfortable but constrained by mortgage debts, and the offer of twice the salary for a contract position in Saudi Arabia seemed to Maurice an opportunity too good to refuse. After earnest family conferences, Maurice left for Riyadh, alone, and his wife, Maureen, joined him in 1980. The strain of separation and expatriate compound living, however, took its toll, and Maureen returned to England in 1982, and the couple divorced in 1984. By then, Maurice had transferred to Houston, Texas, in 1983, with the same employer.

Throughout this period, Maurice never considered himself to be a migrant, rather simply a transient worker temporarily away from home. From the 1950s, the temporary employment of British skilled workers such as Maurice in developing countries, especially those of the Middle East such as Saudi Arabia, opened up new possibilities for continuing mobility among a much wider cross-section of British society. In effect, this promised the democratisation of the expatriate experience well beyond the upper and middle-class foot soldiers of the old empire, bringing the abbreviated 'expat' label into much more common currency. For many, it was defined by living in compounds and sharp separation from the local community, and this is largely what Maurice experienced in Saudi Arabia. He remembered his single quarters and conditions:

> We all each had a room in…like a guest-house and with a communal dining room, you had your own bathroom toilet facilities, no social life really…you got up in the morning and went to work…We didn't have a swimming pool, or anything like that, so we had virtually no recreation at all.

When Maurice transferred to Houston in 1983, the compound living ceased and he experienced something of American life, but he continued to regard himself as an expatriate, with frequent visits back to Britain. During those visits, he formed a new relationship, with an English woman, who eventually joined him in Houston, and when the company offered a further transfer to Sydney, Maurice took it up with enthusiasm, she joined him, and they married in Sydney in 1986. The second marriage was, however, unstable, and Maurice's regular work travel around Australia meant that although they enjoyed numerous world holidays together there was little home life to nurture the relationship, and in 2001 they divorced. As Maurice remembers it, he also came to miss what he had enjoyed of his family life with his first wife.

> I did miss the family life that Maureen and I had had…And bearing in mind that Maureen and I, we knew each other two or three years before we married and then we…were married for 26 years, and when you've…been that close to someone for that long, you do miss a lot of little intimate things about your partner.

While his second marriage was fragile, it did, in the early years, exercise for Maurice a critical influence on his identity. Soon after marrying his second wife, Maurice's company offered him yet another transfer back to Saudi Arabia, initially, at least, alone on what was called 'bachelor status'. Not willing to leave his new wife, he declined, and with other plentiful Australian job offers to consider and an application for Australian permanent residency nearing approval, he left his employer and soon obtained other attractive work. In Maurice's narrative, this was the crucial moment when he moved from being an impermanent expatriate to a settled migrant, under the impetus of marriage in the new country, an interest in citizenship and a sense he had begun to feel since arrival that Australia was a country he could call home.

> I settled in Australia by choice…I felt very comfortable there…I remember the day I arrived from…Houston and we were collected at the airport and driven into…North Sydney where I was staying, and…immediately I felt very comfortable, I felt as though: 'This is like home'. It was very green, and little shops, rather than the big…shopping malls that I'd got used to in Houston, and none of the concrete and glass that existed in Houston. And…the longer I stayed the more I felt this was home. I enjoyed the…warmth and…the sort of semi-outdoor life.

The settled migrant, however, remained highly mobile, with regular trips back to England, where he maintained close contact with his two adult children. Family and mobility again changed Maurice's story. His daughter, Susan, had, he thought, inherited his own penchant for travel and adventure, and developed a promising career working in cruise ship casinos; she eventually married a business partner and they managed the casinos together, regularly travelling around the world. By 1987, they had decided to settle on shore, in Vancouver, where their first child was born. In 2001, they moved to Victoria, British Columbia, and since Maurice had recently retired he offered to help with the move. After a return visit to Sydney and an offer from Susan to stay with them, the move ultimately changed to permanent settlement in Canada. More changes, however, lay ahead. His first wife, like Maurice in the throes of ending a second marriage in England, made a visit coinciding with Maurice's in Victoria, they renewed regular contact after many years being out of touch and, by 2002, Maureen had emigrated to Victoria, where they again lived together. As Maurice wrote, this was 'a very large bonus': Maureen was now 'enjoying being with me and close to our daughter and her family. We hope to live happily ever after! Is that a happy ending or what!?'

As is common, however, a mobile past leads to an open-ended and potentially unfinished mobile future. At the time of the interview, Maurice had been living in Canada for only three years, and while he was gradually coming to feel settled he still missed many aspects of Australia, where he had assumed he would settle permanently. After reading the transcript of our interview, he wrote an addendum to stress his continuing attachment.

> I feel very patriotic towards Australia, returning as frequently as possible, and would live there permanently if my family were prepared to relocate there. Some of my best friends are Australians and we keep in touch regularly by e-mail and occasional phone calls. I certainly miss them and am always pleased to hear from them.[20]

As his crucial qualifier insists, however, he is happy for family to dictate the future. A similar response governed his attitude to living in Britain, where there was little doubt about his priorities: 'I go back to Britain, and I don't particularly want to go back and live in Britain, but…I wouldn't say never, but if the family were there I'd go tomorrow…I don't see anything wrong with Britain.' So while Maurice has come to take a mobile persona for granted, he is content for its direction to be shaped by family dynamics, which have progressively loomed larger in his own narration of his life story. Ultimately, the intense geographical mobility that has sculpted his identity has been eclipsed by his primary role as a family man, albeit a man whose later migrations have been driven by the migrations of his own family. In his autobiographical reflections, he is emphatic that his first national loyalty belongs to Australia, but it is a contingent loyalty that ultimately gives way to the transnational ties of family.

In their different ways, the stories told by Ros Smith and Maurice Bassindale provide vivid illustrations of the power of the lens of migration to shape autobiographical narratives. In the past generation, this has come to be defined increasingly by the migrant's perception of the self as a well-travelled mobile personality. One of the stimulants of change in the late twentieth century was the shift from a colonial to a global context for migration in the British world, and these migrants illustrated that shift in their internalisation of a sense of themselves as inherently mobile personalities, more or less settled in one country while not exclusively tied to any; it was symbolised by some migrants' declarations that they wished to have their ashes scattered in more than one country, when the bonds of family finally loosened.[21] At the same time, however, in their family centredness, these transients continue to shape their lives and tell their stories in deeply traditional ways, albeit with varying notions of family and contrasting experiences that might be explained, as with Ros and Maurice, by gender difference. Both carry an awareness of the powerful ways in which mobility has shaped their sense of identity, but both of them also place equal weight on dynamics such as family attachment and personal growth in telling their life stories. Their narratives therefore struggle to balance shifts in personal family belonging with a world that allows geographical mobility on an unprecedented scale. These migration stories might point the way to closer understanding of the effects of intense global mobility. Modern migration has affected the most intimate details of migrant lives and created a dizzying web of transnational ties, and now it has gradually come to redefine how people see themselves. At the same time, the traditional bonds of family have continued to drive the course of migration and to shape the identities people construct when they strive to make sense of their past.

Notes

[1] The project draws on migrant testimony in written and oral history form from more than 180 British migrants—123 interviewed—mainly to Australia, Canada and New Zealand, including returnees and 'serial migrants' to more than one country. A monograph, tentatively titled *The Modern British Diaspora*, is scheduled for publication in 2010.

[2] On the postwar British migrant generation to Australia, see Hammerton, A. James and Thomson, Alistair 2005, *Ten Pound Poms: Australia's invisible migrants*, Manchester University Press, Manchester.

[3] For the most recent exploration of the extensive British diaspora, describing it in 2006 as the world's third largest (p. viii), see Sriskandarajah, Dhananjayan and Drew, Catherine 2006, *Brits Abroad: Mapping the scale and nature of British emigration*, Institute for Public Policy Research, London.

[4] Self-improvement can be shown to motivate virtually all migrations of austerity or of rising expectations, but I refer here to the more explicit movement, setting in from the early nineteenth century, associated with the striving of workers for not just economic welfare but for respectability and intellectual and social improvement, at home by, for example, joining mechanics' institutes and friendly societies and participating in chapel activities, and abroad through emigration. A similar drive for migrants' respectability in the postwar years linked advanced economic conditions with opportunities for improved educational prospects for children. See Harrison, J. F. C. 1961, *Learning and Living, 1790–1960: A study in the history of the English adult education movement*, Routledge and Kegan Paul, London.

[5] Correspondence, Kate Boyle to A. J. Hammerton, 26 June 2005, and Written account, La Trobe University Archive in British Migration (hereafter LU), DB50. Alistair Thomson's use of women migrants' letters alongside interview testimony in Chapter 9 of this volume offers a variation on the same theme.

[6] Baines, John Edward n.d. [c. 1998], *Life Wasn't Meant to be Easy*, Bet Saleter and Eileen McKechnie, Geelong, Victoria.

[7] Kate Boyle, Written account, June 2005, LU DB50.

[8] Caroline Streeter, Written account, February 2006, LU DS120.

[9] For example, Viviane King, Interview, Sydney, 23 March 2007, LU DK20.

[10] For example, Joanna White, Interview, South Melbourne, Victoria, 24 June 1998, LU 0991; Hammerton and Thomson, *Ten Pound Poms*, p. 80.

[11] Financial capacity is of course highly variable, but relates here to the tendency for British migration since about the 1970s to take on a more middle-class profile statistically; see Sriskandarajah and Drew, *Brits Abroad*, pp. 22–5.

[12] Collections of contemporary migrant letters can serve a similar function, illustrated by Alistair Thomson's use of postwar women migrants' letters alongside their interview testimony in Chapter 9 of this volume.

[13] Hammerton and Thomson, *Ten Pound Poms*, pp. 17–18, 62.

[14] Albert and Anne Lougher, Interview, Balgowlah, New South Wales, 22 June 1999, LU 0544; Hammerton and Thomson, *Ten Pound Poms*, pp. 57–62.

[15] Leonard Hedges, Interview, Claremont, Tasmania, 25 September 1999, LU 0410.

[16] Margaret Hill, Interview, Chelsea, Victoria, 11 September 1998, LU 0423; Hill, Margaret 1999, *Corrugated Castles*, Cromwell, Melbourne, and 2003, *Water Under the Bridge*, published privately; Hammerton and Thomson, *Ten Pound Poms*, pp. 78–9, 234–6.

[17] Ros Smith, Interview, Melbourne, 28 October 2005, LU DS50.

[18] Amanda Stuart, Written account, March 2006, LU DS125

[19] Maurice Bassindale, Interview, Victoria, British Columbia, Canada, 13 April 2006, LU DB35.

[20] Maurice Bassindale, Addendum to transcript, 28 July 2006, LU DB35.

[21] See Susan Charles-Jones, Interview, Yackandandah, Victoria, May 2005, LU DC30.

Chapter 9

'I'm not a good mother': gender expectations and tensions in a migrant woman's life story

Alistair Thomson

> I'm not a good mother—not what Dr Spock calls a 'slow mother' who leaves her chores to make sure junior gets the right treatment. In fact, tho' I love my 2 children, I just loathe the continual 'hampered' feeling.
>
> — Dorothy Wright, letter to 'Mummy', 16 March 1961

Dorothy Wright was a perfectly 'good' mother. When her two children were growing up in the late 1950s and 1960s, in Britain and Australia, Dorothy was a full-time housewife and mother. She cooked her children's meals and cleaned up after them; she sewed and knitted their clothes; she read stories, organised birthday parties and took them swimming. Like most mothers, however, Dorothy struggled to be good enough as a mother and as a housewife and, despite what Dr Spock had to say, it was not easy to do both jobs well at the same time (in fact, for mothers such as Dorothy, the prescriptions of childcare experts such as Dr Spock sometimes made the job harder and the feeling of failure greater). Although Dorothy loved her children, being a mother was not an entirely satisfying role and it 'hampered' aspirations for her own life apart from the family.

Dorothy Wright's years as a young mother coincided with the family's move to Australia. The letters she wrote home to her mother and sister back in England, and the stories she now tells of a memorable chapter in her life, evoke in rich detail the experience of motherhood in the 1960s and the challenge of meeting the competing expectations of society, family and self. A transnational perspective enriches our understanding of the lives of migrant women such as Dorothy Wright. We know about her experiences because she was impelled to write letters to bridge the emotional distance between Australia and home and sustain intimate relationships with her British family (and because she preserved her letters and photos as a keepsake of a memorable episode). Letter writing was perhaps the most significant reflective space in Dorothy's hectic life and, in her letters, Dorothy articulated and explored her experiences as a migrant mother. In return, Dorothy's mother and sister wrote back with advice and encouragement, and occasional admonishment, about mothering. In Australia, Dorothy had to make her own way as a mother and housewife, but her maternal path was shaped powerfully by transnational lessons from family and society, from Britain and Australia, and from past and present.[1]

Figure 9.1: 'The end of a perfect birthday' (caption in photograph album). Dorothy Wright reading to her children, Nicholas and Bridget, at home in Hornsby Heights, Sydney, on Bridget's first birthday, 25 March 1961.

Born in 1928, Dorothy Bailey was the second of three sisters in a middle-class English family. The Baileys lived in a village on the rural outskirts of the Surrey town of Guildford and, as a girl, Dorothy relished outdoor life and adventures in the open fields beyond the home, away from the strict domestic routine and stuffy moral codes of elderly parents who had grown up during Queen Victoria's reign. Dorothy left Guildford County School for Girls at age fifteen to follow her dream of a farming life, but opportunities for a fulfilling career on the land were limited for a young woman in the late 1940s, and Dorothy soon took a more typical though less satisfying path into secretarial work. In 1955, at the age of twenty-six, she married Mike Wright, an engineer who had also grown up in Guildford, and three years later she had her first child, a son, Nicholas.

Marriage and motherhood was a conventional pathway for young British women in the 1950s. Dorothy, however, had an adventurous spirit and a lifelong enthusiasm for Australia that had been inspired by school geography lessons that 'entranced' her with 'all that sunshine, those enormous areas of waving corn, sheep by the million, open spaces, horse riding and so on…as an 11 year old I was in a very romantic phase and saw myself as a "tough guy" living the great free outdoor life'. Images and ideas about another country and another life had a resonant place in Dorothy's imagination and now unsettled conventional domestic expectations. A few months after Nick was born, 'itchy feet set in'. Mike's best friend's sister-in-law, June, 'had gone to Australia and was sending back glowing reports' from Sydney, including news of plentiful employment. Mike wanted to get head-office experience to further his engineering career and Sydney was more appealing than London, Birmingham or Manchester. The 'ten-pound' assisted passage scheme would pay their way and June agreed to sponsor the Wrights and find them accommodation in Sydney. This would not be an outback adventure, but Dorothy knew from June that the outer suburbs of Sydney were 'far less densely developed than, say, Wimbledon', and promised a sunny climate for outdoor living. 'We would have sufficient money to put down on a house, and we had bags of optimism that we would do well.'[2]

The Wrights arrived in Sydney on 23 December 1959. For the first few months they rented accommodation until, in April 1960, they moved into their own fibro bungalow in Hornsby Heights on the edge of bush and suburbs in north-western Sydney. Mike secured a well-paid engineering job with Nestlé Australia that required daily commuting into the city office and regular stints away refitting factories around the state. Dorothy managed the practicalities and economics of buying and creating a new home in Australia, mostly by herself, with impressive skill and confidence. Managing two young children was much more difficult, and Dorothy's first year in Australia was shadowed by exhaustion and emotional pain as she struggled to cope as mother and housewife in a new country and without the support networks of family and home. Dorothy was five months' pregnant on arrival and, with an active and demanding toddler who was just about to walk, motherhood in Australia was never going to be easy.

Though the baby she was carrying was 'fit as a flea', in her autobiographical writing Dorothy recalls a miserable period as she came to full term in the heat of an Australian summer.

> I was very lonely during the daytime, homesick, increasingly uncomfortable with grossly swollen ankles, and Nicholas suffered from prickly heat all round the folds of his chubby neck. The heat was dreadful, as the flat faced north—I'd never realised that in Australia that is where the sun is. Shops were in walking distance, but there was no shade on the way, and at that time opening hours were only 9 am to 5 pm, so I had to go shopping through the heat of the day.

Bridget was born on 25 March 1960. While Nick was boarded out at a nursery, Dorothy and Bridget spent a fortnight in Hornsby Hospital while Dorothy rested and recovered from stitches.[3]

When Nick was born in England in 1958, Dorothy had been 'just *clueless*, it was *Mike* who sort of knew how to change nappies and things'. She explains that 'Mother wasn't terribly maternal and having children round her all the time like some mothers are' and that, as a tomboy, Dorothy had no girlish interest in babies. As a first time mother, she had 'soon caught on' to the hard work of washing terry-towelling nappies in a bucket of cold water. She had learnt the lesson of routine from her mother and from Phyl, a 'mother's help' who lived with the Bailey family for more than a decade and who was 'the real Mary Poppins' in Dorothy's childhood. 'We were routine-ised as children. You know, you feed every four hours and you bath at the same time every day and go for walks in the afternoon and do all this sort of thing.' In Dorothy's own upbringing, Phyl had performed much of this routine child care (for example, Mrs Bailey often had a rest in the afternoon when Phyl took the girls out for a walk in the pram). Dorothy could not, however, afford a 'mother's help', and assumed the prevailing postwar attitude that the mother should be the primary child-carer, and, perhaps in response to her own mother's maternal limitations, she wanted to raise her own children. 'The very *thought* of somebody else going through the stages of Biddy being weaned and starting on solid food and seeing her walk for the first time and all that, I just couldn't…[I thought] "I can't do that, don't think I want to do that".'[4]

As a young mother in Sydney, Dorothy was guided, apart from the lesson of routine, by *The Good Housekeeping Baby Book*, a gift from her mother, and the English magazine *Parents*. Dorothy was particularly impressed by *Parents*, which Mrs Bailey posted to her.

> Whenever you get a problem with the children, and the *Parents* comes, then, the answer is always there in an article by them, it seems most extraordinary…I do enjoy it, and you can get all the other English women's books out here—but not that. Funny, only one Aussie mag. offers anything similar & that's a Dr. Spock sponsored thing—& he & I don't agree.

Dr Spock's modern, scientific recommendations about the 'placid' mother who should follow the natural rhythms of the child and prioritise the child above all else, did not match up with Dorothy's more traditional preference for routine, in child care and housework.[5]

Feeding routines were particularly important for Dorothy, not least so that she could cope with two small children and her other domestic responsibilities. She wrote to her mother about following feeding advice from their sponsor, June, who was an experienced nurse and mother of three sons.

> I'm doing some rather unorthodox things with her, but with Nick to cope with too, it does make life easier. Of all the awful things, I prop

little Biddy's bottle up beside her & leave her to feed herself! Last night also I ignored her cries for food at 2am, she went into the farthest corner of the house & just waited till 6am. It was nice to get 7 hours sleep straight off & Bridget seems none the worse.

A few weeks later, Dorothy reassured an anxious Mrs Bailey that 'I haven't choked Biddy yet!! Don't worry I keep a careful eye on her & keep popping in to look at her while she's feeding.'

By July, Dorothy proudly reported that Biddy was regularly sleeping through the night, though Dorothy sometimes woke her in the morning. 'Have to do that or the routine is all to blazes & I get muddled & can't get breakfast ready in time.' In December, Dorothy wrote to Barbara about another mother who seemed to manage without routine: '[H]ow I wish I could happily be as chaotic as she is!! You can set the clock by the times I feed my kids.'[6]

Bottle-feeding helped with routine. Bridget had fed well at the breast from the start, but was doing complementary feeds from the bottle within a fortnight. Much later, Dorothy recalled that her sickness on the voyage to Australia had been so traumatic that she was able to breast-feed Bridget only for a few weeks. At the time, she was advised about bottle-feeding by a nurse from the Nestlé Feeding Service (a connection made through Mike's work, and a sign that Dorothy's approach to child care was informed by ideas from Australia as well as England, and by the powerful influence of domestic science and consumerism that prevailed in both countries). Dorothy wanted Bridget to sleep through the night after a big feed (she also wanted a decent night's sleep herself) and was keen 'to put her completely on the bottle then I shall *know* what she is getting'. Within a month, Dorothy had established

> a revolutionary routine for dealing with two babes…It goes like this 6 a.m. (and one has to keep rigidly to time) give B. her bottle, leave her to go and wash and dress myself, return to burp, top and tail her, put on her day clothes. 6.45 a.m. Wash and dress Nick. 7 a.m. Breakfast, and in the evening 5 p.m. Feed Nick, then return to B. and burp and change her. 6.15. Baby in cot asleep (?). 6.30 Nick in cot. In between whiles Nick has to go in his playpen and he is very good about this…It all works very smoothly although nighttime is a bit breathless for an hour or so.[7]

Dorothy's reassuring letters to her mother at this time convey the impression that she is busy but coping. Just occasionally, a glimpse of exhaustion and misery sneaks through. The worst that she can write about her pregnancy is that she is uncomfortable and impatient (though two days before the birth 'Mike is beginning to feel the strain & says to me every morning rather pathetically "Have a baby to-day, Dossie".') When Bridget is about two months old and Mike has just returned from a week working away up country, Dorothy admits to her mother that 'I'm glad he's home, gets a bit boring on my own', and that she feels 'fine but get tired at the end of the day which isn't to be wondered at when I start at 6a.m. & finish at 10.45 p.m. However, it won't last forever.' Two weeks later, writing on a 'miserable dull, windy & cold day…to the tune of Bridget "exercising her lungs"' and 'Nicholas…in his playpen beating hell out of one of my baking tins', Dorothy confides, 'I always think you will understand with two babies life is hectic & somewhat tiring.' In August, she writes of another English mother with two small children: '[S]he is indeed feeling very lonely & I can sympathise—we are only just coming out of the state ourselves.' The careful language and third-person pronoun soften the impact of an admission that can be shared only once the worst is almost over.

In November, with Dorothy 'nearing screaming point', she and Mike agree to use the £9 quarterly child allowance to pay for both children to stay with a child-minder so they can have their first weekend away together since arrival in Australia 11 months earlier: a Peter Sellers' movie, a picnic drive in the Blue Mountains, dinner and star-gazing with friends from Mike's work, and 'my first bathe in the Australian surf…most exhilarating and exciting'. To her sister, Barbara—who often received letters that were more frank about domestic life than those to her mother, but who had heard nothing of her sister's difficulties to this point—Dorothy now explained that 'I feel as if I've just emerged from a rather bad dream, I look back over the last 7 mths & feel with relief (& some pride) "well, alone I done it"!! Tho' not alone, Mike's been wonderful.'[8]

Many years later, Dorothy found it easier to articulate this immensely difficult period of her life and to explain it in terms that were not available to her in 1960. In 2000, she wrote that

> things were not right for me. I was still so lonely, especially as winter and short daylight hours drew on. I was homesick, I was over-tired, nights were disturbed by the children—Bridget cried a lot in the first six months, and I always went, Mike never heard. Did I suffer from culture-shock? Always I had a terrible feeling in the pit of my stomach. I cried often, sometimes when I was on my own with the children, and I remember Nicholas at 2 years old trying so hard to comfort me. Perhaps all these things contributed, but it was not until years later when Bridget was expecting her first baby and had all the latest books about pregnancy etc that I suspected the real cause. Post-natal depression. I read to Mike the symptoms from her book, and said 'Does that remind you of anyone?' 'Yes', he immediately knew that had been my problem, when such conditions were not spoken of—at least to me. But I battled on.[9]

Figure 9.2: Caption in Wright photo album, 1960: 'Under our gum tree. 13 weeks old (not the gum tree or Dossie).' Dorothy wanted to show off her new baby in this photo, which she sent to family in England, but the look on her face hints that all was not well.

Hormonal changes caused by pregnancy and childbirth could well have contributed to the cluster of physiological and psychological effects that could now be labelled as 'postnatal depression'. The severity of Dorothy's depression was, however, almost certainly exacerbated by other factors in her life as an isolated suburban mother in the early 1960s. In her migration memoir, Dorothy wonders whether she suffered from 'culture shock', but there is not much evidence in her contemporary or retrospective accounts that she struggled to deal with a new culture and society; indeed, this was an aspect of her life that she seemed to manage very effectively. A letter in April 1961 suggested that the success of her family's migration was challenging but also positive and affirming for Dorothy. 'One is busy, there is a new and completely different life, and it may sound odd, but one seems to change—perhaps in my case "grow-up" or "mature" may be better words than "change".' Though Dorothy missed her family, she also relished the adventure of making a new life in Australia and took pride in her independence and success.[10]

Dorothy was, however, as she recalls, 'over worked…lonely and homesick', and the loss of support of close family and friends was especially difficult—as it was for many migrant mothers and, indeed, for any Australian mother who had moved to a new suburb and away from extended family networks. In September

1961, and then again in March 1962, Dorothy wrote to Barbara to squash family rumours that she might be expecting a third child.

> Between you & me I don't feel I've recovered my breath since Biddy yet, but I expect that's partly due to the fact of our being here & having no relations to dump the kids on even for an evening of relaxation…I'd like a third sometimes—2 doesn't seem a complete family (is that because we were 3?)—but can't contemplate an addition while we're here—in simple Bernard Shaw language it's B_ not having anyone to go to who really *will* think your kids are sweet & won't mind the hell they raise in the house.

One elderly aunt by marriage who lived at Wyong on the north coast was a particular solace, and her daughter, Mildred, served as godmother at Bridget's christening, but they lived 50 miles away and could not offer practical everyday support. In her letters, Dorothy emphasised that Mike did his best to help. Before Bridget's birth, he was 'very helpful with Nick—getting him up before he leaves & foregoing [sic] his evening pint of beer (or "schooner" as it's called here) to get home & help bath & bed him', and after the birth he cleaned the house and prepared a roast chicken for Dorothy's return from hospital. During the working week, however, Mike had little time for the children. He had a busy and demanding city job and was often working away from Sydney for days at a time. Just occasionally, Dorothy's letters expressed her frustration at doing the child care mostly on her own, and in our interview she recalled one particular tension.

> Just after seven the bus would come round and off he'd go. He didn't get home till about eight. And I couldn't make this out for a long time, and *then* I found out [laughs] that he'd go down the 'Rubbity' [the pub], wouldn't he, with the others! And come on a later train.[11]

Managing a baby and a toddler was a particular difficulty for Dorothy—she wrote to Barbara, 'Isn't it awful with only 18 months difference'—and Nick was a particularly challenging toddler. Teething and tantrums were a constant refrain in letters. 'Nick reduces me to a quivering lump of jelly by the time Mike gets home most nights…Wish I knew how to cope.' Barbara, who also had young children, was attending a psychology class in England and Dorothy wondered what that had to say about what 'one does about "the stage of development to be expected between 2 & 3"'. She bought herself a book on child psychology that explained 'a lot of things but doesn't tell you what to do about them'. Eventually, Dorothy made her own sense of the problem, in a painfully frank letter to Barbara.

> Nick is dreadful sometimes, rude, cheeky, difficult & just plain 'ornery', in fact sometimes I actually dislike him—get quite a guilt complex over it! Then he can be quite sweet. I think several things make N. like he is.

1. I had so little time for him when Biddy was a baby & so little experience with children & no-one to ask (like mothers or sisters you know) 2. Biddy is such an easily managed child that seeing her do the right thing makes him dig his toes in & be even more obstinate 3. He is 'sensitive' (a phrase I always connect with soppy mothers with unruly kids) 4. He adores Mike & Mike doesn't have enough time to spend with him & when he is home he's tired & very 'cranky' with the children. 5. He really needs his relations to spoil him a bit & show him love whatever he does 6. He's over-ready for school. Adding it all up I feel a bit of a failure with him!

At the time, Dorothy probably could not articulate another possible cause of Nick's behaviour: that he too had been affected by his mother's depression and from trying, as a two-year-old, 'so hard to comfort' his depressed parent. In retrospect, Dorothy still feels that 'perhaps it was my fault as much as his, you know, I wasn't placid, and he was always into everything. He was a typical boy, I expect, and I didn't know about typical boys, 'cause we didn't have boys in our family! [laughs]'[12]

Dorothy's determination to be a good housewife as well as a good mother also contributed to her depression. Throughout these first difficult years in Australia, Dorothy worked hard to maintain the domestic cooking, cleaning, washing, shopping and clothes-making routine that she had learned from her mother in England and that was expected of a modern suburban housewife. Her letters are packed with details of domestic work and the challenge of combining child care and housework. As she wrote to Barbara, 'I never seem to have the time to get on with things.' Of course, the routine that she inherited from her mother was almost impossible without a mother's help, as Dorothy came to realise.

Oh, I couldn't keep pace, 'cause you see there it was my upbringing, my mother had one day for doing the washing, one day for doing the downstairs and one day for doing the upstairs and another day she went shopping and it was all very organised. Well, she had somebody to look after us in between whiles!

At the time, however, Dorothy internalised failure as a mother and housewife as her own fault. In March 1961, she wrote to her mother about enrolling Nick to start kindergarten later in the year.

I find him very difficult to entertain, especially in the mornings when I'm busy, & I'm sure he's bored. So thought school would be the answer. I'm not a good mother—not what Dr. Spock calls a 'slow mother' who leaves her chores to make sure junior gets the right treatment. In fact, tho' I love my 2 children, I just loathe the continual 'hampered' feeling. I'm afraid I'm apt to scream at him to get out & let me get on—which as

Mike points out does neither of us any good. How does Barb. manage? I've a feeling she has a lot more patience than I.[13]

In Dorothy's eyes, she was 'not a good mother' because she was distracted by her chores, but also because she loathed 'the continual "hampered" feeling'. Dorothy did not get a break from the children until she reached 'screaming point' almost a year after her arrival in Australia, and in that first year she had very little time for herself or for activities outside the home that might affirm her own sense of self-worth. Even letter writing, one of her only personal pleasures at this time, and an opportunity for quiet reflection, was often interrupted and delayed by other demands. In our interview, asked about her domestic and maternal role in the first years in Australia, Dorothy exclaimed,

> Hated it! I really hated it. Did my best, I always did my best but they didn't seem as if they wanted to respond!...I didn't like doing it. I suppose I wanted to sit and read or write or do my own thing or something, you know.[14]

Dorothy began to emerge from her postnatal depression after about eight months. The weekend away from the children in November 1960 was an important turning point, and other more gradual changes had a positive impact. As Dorothy got used to coping with two small children, she eased her load through 'a bit of rearranging of the children's routine', as she explained to her mother in September 1961:

> We now all have supper to-gether at 6 p.m. and only a light lunch at mid-day. I'm sure you will have qualms about the advisability of giving the children a big meal just before they go to bed, but they don't seem to come to any harm, and it is certainly easier for me, than preparing vegetables and a sweet twice a day.

Household economies such as this were more feasible as the children grew older and Bridget became a toddler. Dorothy recalls that 'the children were easier to manage at the toddler stage', especially after Nick started one morning a week at nursery in July 1961. Nick 'loved it', and Dorothy relished 'a bit of peace!!' and the chance to leave Bridget with a neighbour and do the grocery shopping on her own. School holidays, and illnesses that kept the children home from nursery or school, now became the most frequently noted stress points in Dorothy's letters.[15]

Dorothy slowly developed a vital support network of neighbours and friends. Among her new friends were an English migrant mother she had met in the maternity ward, another Nestlé family that had just moved to Sydney and lived 10 minutes' walk away, and neighbours of Phyl's in England who were on a two-year posting and lived in an inner Sydney suburb. Phyl's friend, Pat, was also 'feeling very lonely...Pat and I just got on like a house on fire. She was like

Phyl and she giggled and giggled and I giggled and giggled and we all giggled and giggled and we had a *lovely* time!' From August 1960, Dorothy's letters began to fill with accounts of daytime visits with the women in these three families, all of whom were at home with young children, and occasional evenings out with Mike and the other couples or weekend excursions to the beach or bush. These friendships—and the new car that made them possible—were a lifeline. Neighbours in Hornsby Heights provided more practical support, minding Bridget when Dorothy was shopping, or babysitting when Mike and Dorothy went out for an evening. Dorothy, however, still felt the awkward alienation of a foreigner and found it 'difficult to know the women round here', as she wrote to her mother in November 1961.

> The Aussies seem very 'sticky' to me—seems like they have a defensive wall around them as if they have an inferiority complex. Julie (English as you know) is fine but the 2 miles between us are awkward when there's kids to think of. Even now I can't really call [next-door neighbour] Shirley a bosom pal. I just can't seem to find anyone close by to click with! perhaps I'm rather aggressively Pommie![16]

By the end of 1961, social and recreational life with Mike was also much improved. Until that point, Dorothy's letters had often detailed Mike's recreations away from home—drinking with workmates at the end of the day, a weekend of bushwalking and dinner functions at work—and, just occasionally, Dorothy's envy was apparent.

> I suppose Daddy used to go out a lot to dinners, did it make you mad? No I don't suppose so, you aren't the type! I just feel I'll *never* have any unencumbered social life again. I suppose I'm selfish! anyway can't help feeling a little jealous when Mike comes rolling in full of conviviality and about 4 doz. oysters (they are about 2/- a doz. here)! Oh, well...

In September 1960, Dorothy and Mike had their first night out together since Bridget was born—a meal with friends—and, after that, with friends and neighbours willing to babysit, they began to enjoy more frequent dinner parties, trips to the theatre (in June 1961, Mike bought *My Fair Lady* tickets as a wedding anniversary gift) and Nestlé social events ('[V]ery pleasant, I seem to know Mike's mates & their wives now'). They also began to make their own home entertainment. In July 1961, Mike built a table-tennis table 'to get our figures in trim, & get my circulation going' during evening workouts, and, in December, a new television supplanted the radio as a dominant presence in the evenings. By March 1962, Dorothy was blaming a reduction in her letter writing—and the loss of her quiet reflective space—on 'the T.V., a complete menace, I'd turn it off many times but Mike finds it relaxing (& I do think his job makes him need relaxation & time to unwind...), anyway evenings go like a flash & no letters written'. When the television eventually went back to the rental company in May 1963 (while Mike was away setting up the family's move to Victoria), Dorothy mused, 'I don't know which I miss most my husband or my T.V.!!' On a more serious note, during the worst of her depression, Dorothy had not wanted sexual intimacy with Mike, but now, as her spirits and social life improved, so too did their sexual relationship, as 'we learnt things to help us'.[17]

Perhaps most important for Dorothy's re-emerging self-esteem were new activities just for herself. As well as writing letters, Dorothy had always been a keen reader. In July 1960, she joined the Reader's Digest Book Club, which delivered four condensed novels a quarter, and, in September, she joined the Hornsby Library (she was annoyed that you had to pay to use a library in Australia), though three months later she reported that it had closed. Her letters list an eclectic, international assortment of reading: French novels, Australian history, *The World of Suzie Wong* (Dorothy told her mother 'it might shock you'), the new English Bible ('you can read it like a novel, makes everything much clearer, tho' I don't say it completely replaces the Authorised version, one misses the old well known phrases that are poetry') and Maurice Nicole's 'enlightening' religious book, *The Mark*. From February 1961, Mike babysat one night a week when Dorothy joined an art class at Hornsby Evening Institute. 'I went last night for the first time. The teacher just said "To-night do a landscape"!!! I felt really flummoxed, however managed to produce something.' Within a few weeks, she was 'really enjoying' the class. 'I do find the colour and freedom of expression very relaxing.'[18]

Meditation was not mentioned in letters home, but it played a significant role in Dorothy's recovery. A friend in Guildford had introduced Dorothy to Subud, a spiritual movement that had its origins in Indonesia. In Sydney, Dorothy joined a Subud meeting that helped her overcome the depression.

> Initially you were supposed to go twice a week and I used to go on Tuesdays and Thursdays or something like that. Mike used to come home in time to be with the children and then I'd get a train, I suppose, about half past seven, and go in and then get back…You just stood there [laughs]. It sounds ever so silly…it's not something one talks about very much and I don't *like* to talk about something, but it had a great influence on helping me through. And someone said, 'Begin' and you closed your eyes and sort of waited and you might dance or laugh or sing or cry or anything. And then, after half an hour they'd say 'Finish' and you'd stop. That's all. It sounds *silly*, doesn't it?…It helped, yes, tremendously…I improved, I wasn't so utterly depressed and, and…upset all the time. So, it just helped.[19]

The reflective and expressive social opportunities of the art and Subud classes were matched by the physical pleasure and exuberance that Dorothy experienced through swimming. On Dorothy's first weekend away from the children, she enjoyed an 'exhilarating and exciting' initiation in the Australian surf. Because of the wartime closure of English public swimming pools, Dorothy had never learnt to swim properly.

Figure 9.3: 'Dorothy on beach by the surf' (caption from family photograph album), Hawks Nest, March 1963.

As the Wright family began to visit beaches around Sydney most weekends, Dorothy decided that she needed to learn to swim so that she could save her children if they got into difficulties in the water. In February 1962, she started swimming lessons at a local pool and within a few weeks her letters reported that 'I've enjoyed every minute'. A year later, after swimming 50 metres out to sea on a 'wonderful' family day at Narrabeen Beach, Dorothy declared that 'I count my last year's swimming lessons among the "best-things-I've-done" and they've paid off in opening up new fields of enjoyment—or rather "oceans" of enjoyment!' With both children now at kindergarten and three mornings a week for herself, Dorothy enrolled in advanced swimming and diving lessons. Years later, and after a career as a swimming instructor, Dorothy wrote about her discovery of swimming in Australia: 'I can't begin to say how this changed my life. I never would have had such opportunities in England, nothing would have induced me into our cool (or cold) waters. But there in the warmth I blossomed.'[20]

The outdoor lifestyle of Dorothy's adopted country enabled and symbolised a personal transformation, a 'blossoming'. The pleasure and skill of swimming in pool and ocean was an energising and affirming alternative to Dorothy's more 'hampered' life at home. The outdoor physicality of swimming recaptured the exhilarating sense of freedom and adventure that had been so important in Dorothy's semi-rural youth, which was vital for her sense of self but had been missing in her life as a housewife. Most importantly, swimming, along with new friendships and socialising, and Subud meetings and art classes, enabled Dorothy to enjoy herself and to feel good about herself, not just as a mother and housewife, but in her own right, and it helped lift the depression that had marked her first year in Australia.

This account of one episode within the life of a migrant woman illuminates a number of historical themes. Dorothy Wright's experience matched that of many migrants who struggled as mothers, housewives or workers in a new country, who had lost family support networks and had to create new ways for everyday living. Dorothy's experience, however, also matched that of other postwar women—migrant and otherwise—who were 'hampered' or unfulfilled in the role of suburban housewife, and who Betty Friedan identified in her 1963 best-selling critique of *The Feminine Mystique*. Eventually, as her children grew older and more independent, Dorothy's life began to 'open up' again. Dorothy Wright's life story is a journey to herself, as she negotiated changing social circumstances and expectations for women, and an inner conflict between the domestic role model—inherited in England and reinforced in postwar Australia—and her own interests and needs.[21]

The letters through which we know of Dorothy's early years in Australia are also evidence of the significance and value of letter writing within transnational family relationships. Dorothy wrote home to maintain intimate relationships, to reassure and seek assurance and advice, to describe and explain her new life and, occasionally, to conceal and protect. Letter writing was emotional work with significant practical benefits, but it also sustained some of the tensions and difficulties of family relationships. Dorothy was justly proud of her independent success as she made a new home and life for her immediate family in Australia. Through letters, however, Dorothy's mother communicated advice and expectations—from 19,000 kilometres away—about how a 'good mother' should perform. These were expectations that Dorothy had learned in childhood, which she struggled to maintain as an adult, and which she sometimes resisted and subverted: by adopting new childcare routines; by expecting Mike to take a more active role in family life than had her own father; by eventually developing her career as a swimming instructor. Dorothy Wright 'blossomed' in outdoor Australia, but perhaps also because, away from her English family, it was easier to assert her independent self. Transnational family relationships required—and were sustained by—regular correspondence, yet the tyranny of distance and separation also created an opportunity for practical and emotional independence. a transnational perspective opens new and unexpected windows into the intimate detail of migrant family life.

If the maternal bonds of this life story—between Mrs Bailey and her daughter, and between Dorothy and her son—carried deep psychic and social significance, there was another arena of psychic tension that was forged in Dorothy's childhood and played out within the social and material circumstances of her adult life. The responsibility and routine of the housewife and mother was internalised in Dorothy's Surrey childhood and from cultural expectations for postwar women in Britain and Australia. From her childhood, however, Dorothy had a competing passion for outdoor life and adventure, for physical activity and freedom that could not be satisfied in the kitchen. The Wright family's Australian sojourn offered an adventure alongside motherhood, but in Australia Dorothy suffered a depression that was, in part, caused by the difficulty of reconciling the maternal and domestic roles and her personal need for affirmation and fulfilment beyond the home. On the beach and in the surf, Dorothy found a way to link her maternal responsibilities and her adventurous self, and a way forward to being more than just a good mother.

Notes

[1] The letters, photographs, memoir and oral history interview that comprise the evidence for this essay were donated by Dorothy Wright and will be archived with the British Australian Migration Research Project collection (Wright Papers, W16) at the Mass Observation Archive, University of Sussex, England. Dorothy Wright commented on and approved a longer version of this essay, which will be part of a forthcoming book by Alistair Thomson (with Phyl Cave, Gwen Good, Joan Pickett and Dorothy Wright) to be published in 2009: *Moving Stories, Women's Lives: British women and the postwar Australian dream*, Manchester University Press. In this essay, Dorothy's words—from letters, memoir and interview—signify and highlight her significant contribution to our writing. Punctuation of letters is reproduced as in the original.

[2] Wright, Dorothy 2000, I was a £10 Pom, Unpublished memoir.

[3] Ibid.

[4] Dorothy Wright interviewed by Alistair Thomson, 6 June 2006; letters to Alistair Thomson, 22 June 2006 and 8 August 2007.

[5] Wright interview, 2006; audio letter to 'Mummy', c. Easter 1964; letter to Mummy, 4 October 1963.

[6] Letters to Mummy, 26 April 1960, 19 May 1960, 22 July 1960, 6 December 1960.

[7] Letters to Mummy, 10 April 1960 and 15 April 1960; Wright interview, 2006; letter to Mummy, 1 May 1960.

[8] Letters to Mummy, 3 March 1960, 23 March 1960, 19 May 1960, 3 June 1960, 5 August 1960, 1 November 1960; letter to Barbara, 15 November 1960.

[9] Wright, I was a £10 Pom.

[10] Letter to Mummy, 3 April 1961.

[11] Wright, I was a £10 Pom; letters to Barbara, 28 January 1962 and 21 September 1961; letters to Mummy, 23 March 1960, 10 April 1960; Wright interview, 2006.

[12] Letters to Barbara, 21 September 1961, 12 April 1961, 6 December 1963; letter to Mummy, 26 March 1961, 26 April 1961; Wright interview, 2006.

[13] Letter to Barbara, 6 December 1960; Wright interview, 2006; letter to Mummy, 2 March 1961.

[14] Wright interview, 2006.

[15] Letters to Mummy, 7 September 1961, 11 August 1962; Wright, I was a £10 Pom; Wright interview, 2006.

[16] Letter to Mummy, 5 August 1960; Wright interview, 2006.

[17] Letters to Mummy, 10 November 1961, 29 June 1961, 9 December 1962, 20 July 1961, 28 May 1963; letter to Barbara, 18 March 1962; Wright interview, 2006; letter to Alistair Thomson, 8 August 2007.

[18] Letters to Mummy, 10 May 1961, 15 September 1961, 10 November 1961, 8 February 1961, 16 March 1961.

[19] Wright interview, 2006. See http://www.subud.org/english/faq.html, accessed 20 June 2007.

[20] Letters to Mummy, 1 November 1960, 12 March 1962, 28 January 1963; Wright, I was a £10 Pom.

[21] Wright interview, 2006.

Chapter 10

First love and Italian postwar migration stories

Francesco Ricatti

This chapter considers written memories and fantasies of first love as retold by Italian migrants in Australia in the late 1950s. These stories of first love were written in letters sent between 1957 and 1961 to *Il Salotto di Lena*, a weekly column of the Italian-language newspaper in Australia *La Fiamma*. In this column, readers were asked to tell a true story from their past. After strong editing, the best stories were published and their authors received a prize of £10. In this chapter, however, I will consider the original, unedited letters written by migrants, which are kept at the Mitchell Library at the State Library of New South Wales.[1]

It is possible that by selecting, reading and analysing memories and stories written by migrants about their lives before migrating, one loses the perception of the transnational character of these lives and memories. On a historiographical level, this also implies the risk of locating these (hi)stories exclusively within the national boundaries of Italy. These risks are inherent in this chapter, despite my intention to write migration history from a transnational perspective. In fact, migrants' memories of ideal loves in the autobiographical stories that I consider here were often situated in a nostalgic geographical and temporal dimension, corresponding with migrants' youth and their life before migrating to Australia. Migrants usually wrote about love as a past experience, which was often idealised, set in their small town of origin in Italy, and permeated with literary resonances.

Despite these characteristics, it is only by acknowledging that these letters were written in Australia, usually a few years after migrating, that we can really understand migrants' emphasis on an idealised past in Italy. Migration history does not have to be a history of migration in a strictly literal sense. A strong focus on migrants' (hi)stories of their lives before migration is essential in order to understand the reasons why people migrate and the way past experiences in the country of origin are re-elaborated by migrants in the light of their experiences of migration and settlement. From this perspective, the migratory lens to which Hammerton refers in his chapter is at work not only when migrants tell their experiences of migration, but when they remember and tell how their lives were before they even thought about migrating.

Figure 10.1: Italian migrants at Broken Hill mines, 1953.

National Archives of Australia: 2004/00287481, A12111,1/1953/16/16.

Drawing on Paolo Bartoloni's reflections on memory and translation,[2] I consider memory—in this case, memory of first love—not as a passive recollection of the past, but as an 'active recollection' that migrants use to 'remember forward'.[3] I argue that migrants play with memories not simply to remember, but to forget. They reinvent their past in order to live their present, to give it meaning and to imagine and build their future. Therefore, while the stories that I consider in this chapter are set exclusively in Italy and are constructed mainly through references to Italian culture and traditions, they can be understood only from a transnational perspective.

In the introduction to this volume, the importance of researching and writing a transnational history of Australia has been emphasised. This means going beyond the boundaries of the Australian nation and challenging 'a comfortable frame for a historical inquiry'. Furthermore, it means taking into consideration those lives of migrants who were framed by the strict scrutiny, particularly of women, by an often hostile Australian society, as well as by close and conservative ethnic communities. As Thomson's chapter demonstrates, transnational lives can be paradoxically constrained. When studying the lives of migrants from a non-English background, it becomes even more apparent how strict boundaries are imposed on migrants by their family, their community of origin, their ethnic group and by the host society. This is why it becomes essential for historians to consider, as Thomson brilliantly does, those spaces in which migrants are really able to transcend the restricted and imposed limits of their respectable lives. My chapter demonstrates how one way to do so is for migrants to recreate idealised memories. When considering migrants' intimacy, there are no doubts that one of the most intimate, protected and vital spaces for them is that of their own fantasies, imaginations and memories; these are safe shelters in which the limits of their lives can be extended, challenged and sometimes even surpassed. Stories of migration are always stories of intimacy, in which love, memory and imagination bridge physical and cultural distances.

Figure 10.2: *Il Salotto di Lena*.

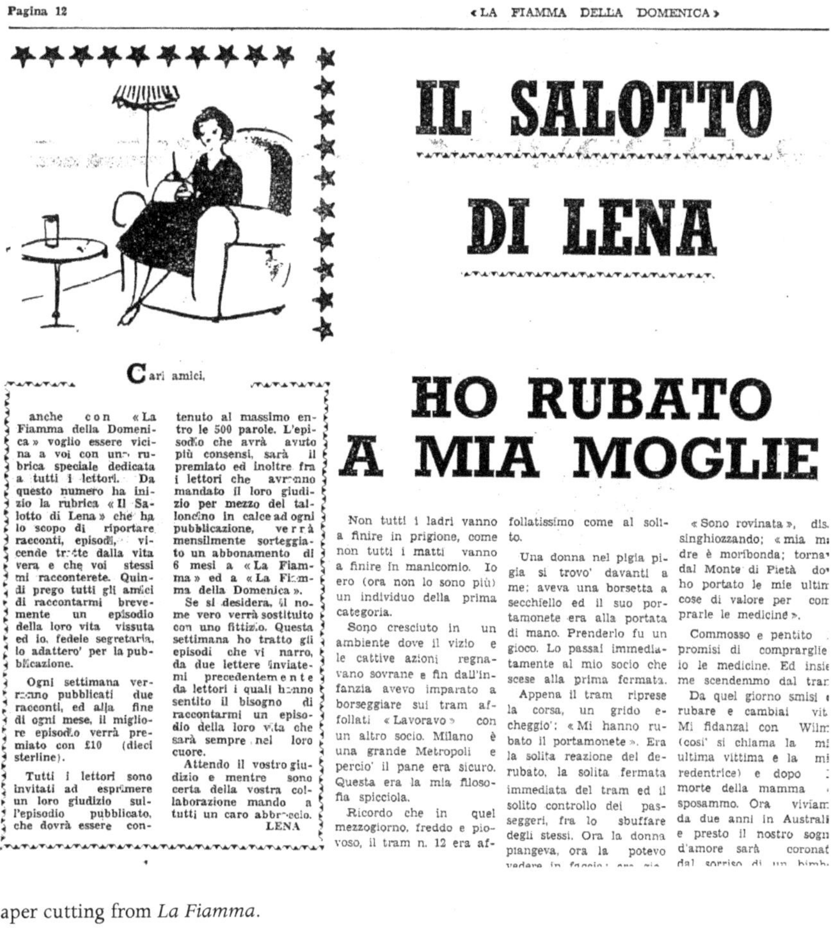

Pagina 12 «LA FIAMMA DELLA DOMENICA»

IL SALOTTO DI LENA

Cari amici,

anche con «La Fiamma della Domenica» voglio essere vicina a voi con una rubrica speciale dedicata a tutti i lettori. Da questo numero ha inizio la rubrica «Il Salotto di Lena» che ha lo scopo di riportare racconti, episodi, vicende tratte dalla vita vera e che voi stessi mi racconterete. Quindi prego tutti gli amici di raccontarmi brevemente un episodio della loro vita vissuta ed io, fedele segretaria, lo adattero' per la pubblicazione.

Ogni settimana verranno pubblicati due racconti, ed alla fine di ogni mese, il migliore episodio verrà premiato con £10 (dieci sterline).

Tutti i lettori sono invitati ad esprimere un loro giudizio sull'episodio pubblicato, che dovrà essere contenuto al massimo entro le 500 parole. L'episodio che avrà avuto più consensi, sarà il premiato ed inoltre fra i lettori che avranno mandato il loro giudizio per mezzo del talloncino in calce ad ogni pubblicazione, verrà mensilmente sorteggiato un abbonamento di 6 mesi a «La Fiamma» ed a «La Fiamma della Domenica».

Se si desidera, il nome vero verrà sostituito con uno fittizio. Questa settimana ho tratto gli episodi che vi narro, da due lettere inviatemi precedentemente da lettori i quali hanno sentito il bisogno di raccontarmi un episodio della loro vita che sarà sempre nel loro cuore.

Attendo il vostro giudizio e mentre sono certa della vostra collaborazione mando a tutti un caro abbraccio.

LENA

HO RUBATO A MIA MOGLIE

Non tutti i ladri vanno a finire in prigione, come non tutti i matti vanno a finire in manicomio. Io ero (ora non lo sono più) un individuo della prima categoria.

Sono cresciuto in un ambiente dove il vizio e le cattive azioni regnavano sovrane e fin dall'infanzia avevo imparato a borseggiare sui tram affollati «Lavoravo» con un altro socio. Milano è una grande Metropoli e percio' il pane era sicuro. Questa era la mia filosofia spicciola.

Ricordo che in quel mezzogiorno, freddo e piovoso, il tram n. 12 era affollatissimo come al solito.

Una donna nel pigia pigia si trovo' davanti a me; aveva una borsetta a secchiello ed il suo portamonete era alla portata di mano. Prenderlo fu un gioco. Lo passai immediatamente al mio socio che scese alla prima fermata.

Appena il tram riprese la corsa, un grido echeggio': «Mi hanno rubato il portamonete». Era la solita reazione del derubato, la solita fermata immediata del tram ed il solito controllo dei passeggeri, fra lo sbuffare degli stessi. Ora la donna piangeva, ora la potevo vedere in faccia: ...

«Sono rovinata», dis... singhiozzando; «mia m... dre è moribonda; torna... dal Monte di Pietà do... ho portato le mie ultim... cose di valore per com... prarle le medicine».

Commosso e pentito ... promisi di comprarglie... io le medicine. Ed insie... me scendemmo dal tra...

Da quel giorno smisi ... rubare e cambiai vit... Mi fidanzai con Wilm... (cosi' si chiama la mi... ultima vittima e la mi... redentrice) e dopo ... morte della mamma ... sposammo. Ora viviam... da due anni in Australi... e presto il nostro sogn... d'amore sarà coronat... dal sorriso di un bimb...

Newspaper cutting from *La Fiamma*.

As I will demonstrate in this chapter, many Italian migrants' memories were constructed out of a national repertoire of rhetorical tools, narratives and *topoi* that were imposed on them through school, religion and popular culture, and travelled with them around the world. The history they contribute to creating is therefore much more a transnational history than a migration history. In other words, my chapter does not attempt to answer the question of what it means to be Australian, or Italian in Australia. This question in fact reaffirms the centrality of the nation at the exact moment in which it seems to challenge it. Rather, I am interested in understanding how cultural tools imposed by the nation can be employed when living, remembering and (re)creating a transnational life.

Homi Bhabha has argued that individuals do not have multiple identities to choose from; instead, they have to fight every moment of their lives in order to construct one individual self that is really less, not more, than one.[4] This does not mean that identity is unchangeable. On the contrary, it is essential to consider the 'doubleness, and ambivalence, and contradictoriness of the subject'.[5] In this sense, the concept of multiple identity should be replaced with an interpretation of identity as a continuous 'repetition with a difference',[6] which determines changes, relocations, reinterpretations and renegotiations.

For migrants playing and displaying these 'repetitions with a difference', the interaction between memory, tradition and fantasy was fundamental. This could be seen most pertinently in letters written by migrant women. The mnemonic and imaginative repetitions of their experiences of first love were based on the repetition of idiomatic expressions, common sayings and rhetorical discourses. These repetitions, however, also present elements of difference that need to be brought to light, emphasised and analysed, as they contain the core of Italian migrant women's agency and freedom in remembering their past, living their present and building their future.

It is from this perspective that I consider, in particular, the migrants' use of the heart and the eyes in discourses about love. For instance, the repetition, particularly by migrant women, of idiomatic expressions, banal metaphors and common metonyms about heart and love, *cuore e amore*—two words that in Italian also rhyme—really opened a space for defining their identity, their personality and their relationship with the world around them. Moreover, these corporeal parts, which we might assume were made innocuous by their stereotypical, metonymical and metaphorical use, could signify an attempt by the writers to (dis)cover themselves—that is, to discover and express their subjectivity under the protection of traditional and often conservative literary models and idiomatic expressions. This ambiguous use of certain corporeal metaphors, metonyms and *topoi* related to the sentiment of love was possible because of the origins of this use, which needed to be identified in the materiality and corporeality of love. As Roland Barthes argues, '[W]e use this metaphor [of the heart] in a dull and slightly cowardly way, while in reality I believe that "heart" refers to an extremely strong emotiveness, which is full of sexuality.'[7]

The appropriation of traditional stories and *topoi* by Italian migrant women in their memories and fantasies of first love is particularly important when considering the social environment in which they were living in Australia. For instance, between 1947 and 1960, 90.4 per cent of Italian women in Australia married Italian men.[8] This statistic seems to suggest a very strong link between gender and ethnicity, in particular women's role in preserving ethnic and religious identities and values. Ellie Vasta[9] and Franca Iacovetta[10] have rightly emphasised that Italian migrant women were cultural custodians, playing a vital role in cultural maintenance. Together with the repetitions of traditions, stories and memories, however, we need also to emphasise the small but significant differences in their discourses—differences that came to constitute the core of their stories and their lives.

In the body of letters that I considered, first love—*il primo amore*—was usually represented by migrants as that moment of life when for the first time one was in love with a person who returned this love, and when everything seemed to be perfect. Nevertheless, this wonderful moment of love always ends for various reasons: the protagonist might discover an unspeakable or unacceptable secret; the beloved person dies; love is impeded or prohibited by parents, relatives, envious enemies or poor socioeconomic conditions. A common love story often told by migrants is the kind interrupted by the experience of migration. The perfect love usually ends, despite lovers' promises. Sometimes the story told was the one of a man who left his first love to migrate. Sometimes writers declared that their decision to migrate was in fact determined by the end of their relationship. In other cases, the fact that migration was the real reason for the end of a relationship was hidden behind improbable narrative explanations. This was the case with a man who, despite the fact that '*il mio cuore ardeva sempre perciò non c'era ragione che io potevo lasciare il mio amore*'[11] [my heart always burnt so there were no reasons to leave my love]', he decided to migrate to Australia. The girlfriend was supposed to have joined and married him, but, unfortunately, she was killed by a lightning strike: '[L]*a saetta di fulmene malvagio e crudele a stroncato la tenera vita di Maria*'[12] [The flash of lightning of the cruel and wicked thunderbolt ended Maria's young life].'

In these stories of ideal love as retold by migrants, the love is perfect precisely because it is already impossible. Indeed, this perfection is contingent on the absence of the beloved person from the narrator's present life. In other words, the ideal love can be described and retold only when it has already ended, usually for a reason that is external and independent from the two people in love. It exists only as a memory of a sentiment that ended before it could be spoilt by the protagonists themselves. What makes love impossible also makes it perfect, unchangeable and incorruptible, moving it from the dimension of reality to the dimension of memory, fantasy and imagination.

While this representation of perfect, impossible love is typical of popular culture,[13] it is also constructed out of a large cultural tradition that runs from biblical texts, liturgical formulas and classical Italian literature to contemporary literature and cinema. In autobiographical letters about first love, a literary tone is typically expressed through what Abruzzese calls *'ricordo di feuilleton'* (memory of feuilleton).[14] That is, the tone of these stories is informed by memories and fragments of stories, characters, situations and expressions typical of mass literature and broadly related to European literary tradition.

Two important characteristics of this memory of feuilleton need to be pointed out. First of all, popular culture makes use of many different models of tradition: religious and liturgical texts, poetry, famous novels and artistic and religious icons. Moreover, popular culture recycles all these materials through many different artefacts, discourses and media, such as film, popular literature, proverbs and everyday life discourses. These memories of feuilleton are therefore available even to those people who have never read mass literature. For instance, religious references frequently used in the letters—such as comparing a girl with a blonde Madonna or with an angel, or expressing the desire to spend life in a convent (usually after being disappointed in love)—are drawn from religious stories and religious iconographies, as well as popular and high literature. The representation of the pure and beautiful girl as blonde or angelic probably came from classical Italian literature (Petrarch and the *dolce stil novo*, respectively) and religious iconography.

The second and even more relevant point regarding the use of feuilleton was the fact that, while references to models of mass literature and popular culture were motivated in general by a literary intention, for migrants they also represented, using the definition of Abruzzese, a *'strumento di organizzazione emotiva della memoria'*[15] (a means of emotive organisation of memory). In other words, literary models gave the writers a plot and a repertoire of situations and expressions through which they could organise and retell their own life experiences, and elaborate and express the emotions related to such memories. Sometimes the fictional character of the narrative was taken from a typical plot of popular literature and erased the direct experience of the writer. In the following example, a man explains that he wanted to marry his girlfriend but suddenly discovered she was his sister:

> [*Mio padre*] *mi abbracciò piangendo, mi strinse più volte a sé dicendomi ripetutamente 'Perdonami, perdonami figlio mio' e, ad un tratto, con una voce che non aveva più niente di umano mi gridò…'è tua sorella.' Credetti che sarei impazzito.*[16]

[My father embraced me while he was crying, he pulled me close many times saying to me continuously: 'Son, forgive me, forgive me,' and, all of a sudden, in a voice that didn't seem human, he screamed at me...'She is your sister.' I thought I would go crazy.]

While this story is clearly fictional, it is important to note that the author uses it in order to motivate his decision to migrate to Australia. He also wrote that he continued to write hundreds of letters to this girl, without being able to forget her. While it is impossible to know the facts behind this story, it is clear that a popular plot is often the medium through which a real sentiment of detachment and unacceptable suffering, related to the experience of migration, is expressed. A complex interplay between memory and tradition, and between absence and presence, is evident here, as well as in many other letters in which this appropriation and reinvention of models is clearly related to real biographical events, and helps writers to elaborate their emotional memories. As already anticipated, this is particularly evident in the rhetorical reduction of the body to heart and eyes, which were considered not as corporeal organs, but as literary tools for describing the experience of love.

The relationship between heart and love has a great tradition in European culture. The heart and the eyes are the two parts of the body that have also been used traditionally in describing love in Italian literature since its origins. The rhetorical use of the heart in speaking and writing about love is obviously related to physical sensations, particularly to rising heart rates in emotional situations and during sexual activity. In relation to love, however, the heart is rarely described as a natural organ that strongly and physically influences our relationship with the loved person. Rather, its use is abstract and rhetorical. One of the rare references to the heart as a physical organ in the corpus I have analysed appears in a woman's letter retelling the first encounter with the man she loved:

Non riuscivo proprio a spiegarmi perché dovessi sentirmi il cuore battermi così forte e le ginocchia farsi così deboli al solo vederlo.[17]

[I couldn't understand why I should feel my heart beat so strongly and my knees become so weak just from looking at him.]

Even in this case, however, the heart is also treated metaphorically: '*Il cuore mi cantava dentro* [18] [My heart was singing inside me].'

Pure love is typically expressed through reference to the heart, in implicit but substantial contraposition to genitals and orifices. As such, the heart is used as a metonym for love and it implies the exclusion of the body and corporeal sensations from the sentiment of love. It is therefore not surprising to find in this corpus a sentence such as '*L'amore non conosce età...come il cuore non invecchia*[19] [Love does not know age...like the heart, it does not grow old]'. In this sentence, the reference is clearly not to the heart as an organ but as a rhetorical *topos* expressing love. This does not, however, necessarily mean that references to the heart are always purely romantic and immaterial. While the heart often takes a paradoxically incorporeal connotation in relation to love, it also signifies the involvement of the person who is in love and, as such, leaves writers a certain space in which to express their subjectivity. References to the heart are therefore important not only because they represent perfect love, but because they represent this love through the exclusion of the world and the people around the two protagonists. It is precisely in this imaginary and suspended space—accessible only to the lovers—that writers and readers, above all women, can find a way of (dis)covering themselves.

A similar process can be identified in the role played by the romantic gaze into each other's eyes—a *topos* as common as that of the heart. The essential difference between the rhetorical use of heart and eyes is in the fact that the heart expresses the individuality of the loving subject, while the romantic gaze expresses the isolation of the loving couple from the world. For this reason, while women often use the heart to emphasise their subjectivity in relation to the family or the loved person, men and women often use references to eyes (and in particular the romantic gaze) in order to portray the couple as one entity, clearly distinct from (if not opposed to) the social environment. Not surprisingly, this gaze is usually specular—that is, he looks at her as she looks at him. Due to these specific characteristics, the romantic gaze is often used in order to describe a happy love that is over or that is opposed by people and/or situations external to the couple, particularly by the act of migrating—in this context, often retold as unavoidable—and by the opposition of the woman's parents (especially the father).

Through the analysis of a series of excerpts from the corpus of letters to *Il Salotto di Lena*, it is my intention to better illustrate the elements of migrants' love stories that I have pointed out. After a first example through which the general elements will be demonstrated, I will focus on some of the numerous letters that insist on the metonymy of the heart/love, and then on the most significant letters that represent love through the references to eyes and the romantic gaze.

In the first example, the woman who retold her story was just 15 years old when she met the man who '*doveva legarmi a sé col suo amore per tutta la vita*[20] [was going to bind me to him with his love for all of my life]'. He was handsome and three years older than her. This is how she describes their first encounter:

> *Ci guardammo e ci leggemmo negli occhi tutto ciò che contenevamo nei cuori, ma purtroppo non sapevamo ciò che il destino ci aveva riservato...Io ero felice del mio bellissimo principe azzurro.*[21]
>
> [We looked at each other and we read in each other's eyes all that was contained in our hearts, but unfortunately we didn't know what destiny had in store for us...I was happy with my handsome Prince Charming.]

In this excerpt, the influence of popular culture is evident in the description of the beloved as 'Prince Charming' and in the expression 'we didn't know what destiny had in store for us'—a typical narrative device that makes the reader sympathetic with the two main characters and, at the same time, curious to discover the end of the story. It is also possible to note the clear references to the eyes and heart, which represent the reciprocal understanding and feeling of the two lovers. The letter then retells how the writer's parents forced her to marry another man. In the conclusion of the letter, she addresses her beloved directly, and she writes:

> *Amor mio…sappi che il primo posto nel mio cuore è stato occupato da te, e così sarà per sempre finché i miei occhi si chiuderanno.*[22]
>
> [My love…you must know that the first place in my heart has been for you, and so it will be forever until my eyes close upon this world.]

Her love for him was eternal precisely because their relationship was interrupted forever by external factors—in this case, her parents. The dimension of love constituted the space in which this woman could affirm her (relative) independence from her parents. The heart is the place that is inaccessible to everybody but the lover, where not only love, but independence can be affirmed. The final sentence of the story is particularly emblematic:

> *E dall'aldilà aspetterò con ansia che quel Dio che abbiamo sempre chiamato in nostro aiuto mi darà la grazia di tenerti il posto vicino a me così si unirà in cielo ciò che in terra gli uomini hanno voluto separare.*[23]
>
> [And from the next world I will wait with longing that the God we always called to for help will give me the grace to keep a place close by me so that what men wanted to rend asunder can be joined together in the sky.]

Here the writer inverts the same liturgical formula of the Catholic wedding ceremony that trapped her in an unwanted marriage.

In a second example, it is possible to identify another typical plot from popular literature. A young woman's boyfriend dies in a car accident, so she marries his brother. In this case, however, the story was probably related to the real experience of the writer. In a short note attached to the letter, she affirmed that what she wrote was '*realmente realtà*'[24] [really reality]'. Moreover, to judge from the woman's other letters to *Il Salotto di Lena*, it appears probable that she did indeed marry the brother of her deceased boyfriend. Even if the story did correspond with the facts, however, this does not mean that it had to be retold through realistic features. In the first part of the story, she describes falling in love with the boyfriend through an opposition of heat and cold that recalls the tone and language of a romance:

> *Ed il mio viso vampò di rossore...di sfuggita accoglievo i suoi sguardi brucianti...ogni suo sguardo dava una scintilla al mio cuore facendolo palpitare che fino all'ora era stato di gelo. Con le sue calde parole piano piano, squagliava i miei freddi sentimenti.*[25]
>
> [My face went bright red...I fleetingly welcomed his burning looks...every look sent a spark to my heart and made that which had been ice, until that moment, beat. With his warm words, little by little he melted my cold sentiments.]

In the second part of the story, she tells how, after the boyfriend died, his brother went to see her at the psychiatric hospital and declared his love:

> *Vedendo in me tanta sofferenza con una mano alzo il mio viso ancora disfatto dalla sofferenza, e vidi nei suoi occhi tanta speranza...'sappi che c'è ancora qualcuno che ti vuole bene...e da molto che il mio cuore ti aspetta' Ma la mia anima parlava ancora in silenzio...la ferita e ancora aperta il mio cuore sanguina ancora...Il destino mi donò in cambio suo fratello che pazientemente aspettava che il mio cuore gli dasse un po' di affetto.*[26]
>
> [Seeing so much grief in me, he lifted up my face, still wasted by grief, with his hand, and I saw much hope in his eyes...'know that there is still somebody who loves you...my heart has been waiting for you for a long time.' But my soul still spoke silently...my wound is still open, my heart still bleeds...Destiny gave me his brother in exchange, who was patiently waiting for my heart to give him some affection.]

As is evident in these two excerpts, references to popular literature—what the writer herself calls '*le storielle*[27] [silly little stories]'—gives a literary tone to the story and, at the same, represents a means of structuring and organising past memories, which are characterised by a strong emotional involvement. The image of the injured and bleeding heart is certainly inspired by the religious iconography of the Madonna of the Sacred Heart. What seems to be more relevant is that the heart is cited four times in the few lines I have quoted from a very long letter, and it clearly expresses the difference between her love for her boyfriend and her love for her boyfriend's brother. In the first part, her heart is passive and cold and is eventually warmed by the boyfriend: the boyfriend is clearly acting on her and determining her sentiments. In the second part, the heart of her boyfriend's brother takes on a passive behaviour: it is waiting for her. The female protagonist's heart now becomes active: instead of being warmed, it bleeds; instead of receiving the vital sparks of the loved man's gaze, it gives some affection to her future husband. The different ways in which hearts are represented express the woman's feelings, but also the difference between the ideal love—already impossible as the boyfriend has died—and the affection for the person she marries, linked to her everyday life.

While there are good reasons to suppose that this story has some links with reality, what is more important is that through this story the protagonist/writer expresses herself as a woman. The metaphorical and metonymical use of the heart, even if influenced strongly by given models, is neither abstract nor immaterial, as it refers to implicit and explicit corporeal sensations. Such use gives once again to the female writer the possibility of covering and discovering herself simultaneously, precisely because it is so stereotypical but at the same time finds its origins in corporeal sensations.

The importance of such ambiguous rhetorical use of the heart becomes explicit in another woman's letter. After discovering that the man she loves is already married, she convinces him to go back to his wife. In this letter, in which she retells her sacrifice, the heart is used three times, each time expressing a very different emotion:

> *La felicità che esisteva fra loro* [the man and his wife] *fu come un balsamo soave che scendeva nel mio cuore ferito...però un leggero velo di malinconia si stese sul mio cuore...Cara Lena, non so se il fatto successomi possa valere di esser scritto ma sapesse come mi sento il cuore più leggero ora che mi sono in un certo senso sfogata.*[28]
>
> [The happiness that existed between them (the man and his wife) was like a delicate soothing balm for my wounded heart...but a subtle film of melancholy extended over my heart...Dear Lena, I don't know if what happened to me is worth writing but if only you could know how my heart feels so much lighter now that I have shared my pain.]

The first use of 'heart' supports the moralistic tone of the letter: her injured heart recovers when she sees that the man she loves and his legitimate partner are happy together again. In the second instance, she expresses her sense of melancholy for losing the man she loves. In the third, she makes the importance of writing to Lena explicit in order to share her pain.

The importance for women of using *topoi* and stereotypical phrases related to the heart in order to (dis)cover themselves within and beyond given boundaries makes an interesting contrast with the frequent but substantially different use of the heart in men's letters about love. In these letters, the use of the heart seems not to have any strong meaning. It would be possible to quote many purely rhetorical sentences written by men, such as: '[F]*arei di essa la regina del mio Cuore!!?*'[29] (I would make her the queen of my heart!!?); '[*I*]*o quelle parole ce lo scritte nel cuore*'[30] (I have those words written in my heart); '[*T*]*i amo, ti amo con tutto il cuore*'[31] (I love you, I love you with all my heart); '[*I*] *nostri piccoli cuori battevano di un sincero affetto*'[32] (Our little hearts beat with sincere affection).

These sentences suggest that men use common expressions related to the heart as empty formulas, behind which it is impossible to uncover any real attempt to express their feelings and their subjectivity. This rhetorical emptiness was consistent with the cultural habits preventing men from expressing emotions. Once appropriated by women, however, it often became a tool for expression, while also protecting them with the apparently harmless but implicitly corporeal metonymy of heart/love.

The gendered difference in the rhetorical use of a metonymy is not typical of all the letters about memories of love. In particular, narrators' insistence on the romantic gaze characterises in similar ways women's and men's letters. Such insistence is often strong, as in the following passages, taken from two different letters, the first written by a woman, the second by a man:

> *In quello istante meraviglioso in cui i miei occhi fissarono i suoi compresi che il mio timore e la mia speranza erano veri, c'era solo lui nella mia vita...I nostri occhi esprimevano solo quello che due occhi innamorati possono dirsi.*[33]
>
> [In that wonderful moment when my eyes looked into his I understood that my worry and my hope were true, there was only him in my life...Our eyes expressed what only two eyes in love can say to each other.]
>
> *Ti vidi, mi vedesti, ci guardammo e furono sguardi d'amore quei primi sguardi che ci scambiammo.*[34]
>
> [I saw you, you saw me, we looked at each other and they were looks of love those looks that we exchanged.]

In another letter, recounting a love story that ended after the man migrated to Australia and the father of his girlfriend forced her to marry another man, all the most relevant passages in the story were emphasised by references to the romantic gaze and the lovers' eyes: 1) the moment in which they fell in love ('[C]*i guardammo negli occhi e ci fu tanto da notare in quello sguardo*'[35] [We looked into each other's eyes and there was so much to see in that look]); 2) the first kiss ('[C]*i guardammo negli occhi ancora una volta ma questa volta ben differente*'[36] [We looked into each other's eyes once more but this time in a different way]); 3) their life while they were in love ('*Se mi prometti che vieni allora mi metto a cantar. Ed io con un cenno d'occhi le facevo accettativa e lei di nuovo riprendeva a cantare*'[37] [If you promise me that you will come, I will start to sing. And I with a wink accepted and she again started to sing]); 4) the separation ('[F]*ra le lacrime degli ultimi appuntamenti ci abbiamo promesso tutto quello che poi svani*'[38] [Between the tears of the last dates we promised each other all that which later vanished]); and 5) the present moment, in which he was remembering and retelling his story ('[T]*utto mi appare innanzi agli occhi in questi momenti*'[39] [Everything appears before my eyes in these moments]).

First love and Italian postwar migration stories

The opposition between the couple and the world is expressed through two narrative strategies, often complementary. The first consists of emphasising the moment in which for the first time the two lovers meet each other and look into each other's eyes. This representation, focusing on the reciprocal lovers' gaze and on its importance to the first time they meet, clearly defines the unity of the couple and the importance of their love, in contrast with the following obstacles that make (or made) that love impossible. The second stratagem consists of describing the moment in which this romantic gaze is broken, the moment in which the two lovers are forced to break off their relationship. This moment is frequently emphasised by tears, which metaphorically mark the breaking of the gaze and physically mark the pain of separation. Here, I wish to quote two very similar passages from two different letters, the first written by a man and the second by a woman:

> *Si dammo l'ultimo bacio si facciamo le ultime promesse e poi fissandoci nelli occhi in lacrime con il fazzoletto nella mano si dammo l'ultimo addio.*[40]

> [We kissed each other for the last time, we made the last promises and then staring into each other's eyes, in tears, with handkerchiefs in our hands we waved our last farewell.]

> *Vidi che piangeva e fra le lacrime mormorò: 'Non partire.'...Lo vidi allontanarsi curvo, io lo seguii con lo sguardo fino a vedere una piccola ombra lontana...L'urlo della nave mi fece colmare gli occhi di lacrime.*[41]

> [I saw he was crying, and, in tears, he whispered: 'Don't leave.'...I watched him leave hunched over, I followed him with my eyes until I could see just a small, far shadow...The cry (toot) of the ship made my eyes fill with tears.]

In both these examples, the moment described is that of separation because of the man's migration to Australia. This moment takes a definitive relevance as in both cases the father of the woman has forced her to become engaged to and/or to marry another man. At the same time, it also gives the writers the possibility to express in very emphatic terms the tragic moment when migration begins, as a separation from the beloved person.

It is essential to note how the *topos* of the romantic gaze has a rhetorical meaning elaborated from the physical experience of human beings. For this reason, its use in narrative discourse can vary from a purely literary resonance to the strong expression of a memory of love and/or a sentiment of rebellion.

In concluding my analysis of the role played by the romantic gaze in migrants' memories of first love and migration, it is important to specify that in other kinds of migrants' discourses this romantic reciprocal gaze becomes a strong and unidirectional gaze of men on women's bodies. In other words, while men and women in love stories look into each other's eyes, women are regularly prevented from moving their gaze from the man's eyes to the man's body. In romantic stories, the gaze is reciprocal and is fixed mainly on the beloved person's eyes; in other discourses, it becomes an exclusive male gaze on the feminine body.

It is for this reason that I consider my final example particularly noteworthy. It suggests a different possibility from the romantic reciprocal gaze in love stories and the unidirectional gaze of men on women's bodies in sexist and misogynist discourses. It suggests the possibility of women gazing at men. A woman retells her first encounter with the man she subsequently married. They were on a bus, seated beside each other. She described the scene in these words:

> *Noi donne vediamo anche senza guardare e continuando a sfogliare il giornale vidi che il giovane era biondo e aveva dei meravigliosi occhi Verdi.*[42]
>
> [We women can see even without looking and while still reading through the newspaper I saw that the guy was blond and had wonderful Green eyes.]

In this sentence, the fantasy seems to be coherent with social norms that prevented women from gazing at men, particularly at strangers. The writer avoids and at the same time respects this prohibition, through her ability, as a woman, to see without looking. Such a fantasy, however, should not be considered simply a rhetorical trick. The sentence 'we women can see even without looking' sounds like a popular adage and implies a fundamental reflection on the ability of women to secretly control their environment and, in particular, their men. What she is essentially affirming is not the ability of women to see without looking, but the ability to look at men without being discovered. In fact, she pretends to read a newspaper while she is really looking at him.

The few examples I have proposed throughout this chapter have illustrated the importance of memories, fantasies and stories of first love for Italian migrants, particularly but not exclusively women. Recounting memories of first love gave migrants the opportunity of coping with complex feelings, which were related not simply to the love for a person, but to the experience of migration, cultural displacement, loneliness and nostalgia. At the same time, migrants' stories of first love also show how migrant women appropriated and re-elaborated models of popular culture and literature in order to express their desires and their relative independence. Memory and tradition, in their interplay between presence and absence, constituted a possibility for migrants, particularly migrant women, to construct in autobiographical stories their provisional and incomplete identity, out of discursive practices that could certainly be described as repetitions with a difference. While those repetitions were at the core of women's role as guardian angels of the house and traditional values, that difference allowed them to express the secret core of their stories and their transnational lives.

Notes

[1] Lena and Dino Gustin Papers, 1909–92, Readers' correspondence, 1956–64, ML MSS 5288 Add-on 1982/6–10(70), Mitchell Library, State Library of New South Wales.

[2] Bartoloni, Paolo 2005, 'Memory, translation and the urban space', *Literature & Aesthetics*, vol. 15, n. 2, pp. 109–18; and 2006, 'Face-to-face with tradition', *International Yearbook of Aesthetics*, vol. 10, pp. 40–7.

[3] Bartoloni, 'Memory, translation and the urban space', p. 109. Bartoloni took the term 'active recollection' from Husserl, Edmund 1970, *The Crisis of European Sciences and Transcendental Phenomenology*, Northwestern University Press, Evanston, p. 360.

[4] Bhabha, Homi 1994, 'Between identities', in R. Benmajor and A. Skotnes (eds), *Migration and Identity. International yearbook of oral history and life stories 3*, Oxford University Press, Oxford and New York, pp. 183–99.

[5] Ibid., p. 197.

[6] Ibid., p. 198.

[7] Barthes, Roland 1981 [2001], 'L'ultima solitudine', in R. Barthes, *Frammenti di un discorso amoroso*, Einaudi, Turin, p. 247 (my translation).

[8] Favero, Luigi and Tassello, Graziano 1983, 'Caratteristiche demografiche e sociali della comunità italiana in Australia e della seconda generazione', *Studi emigrazione*, no. 69, pp. 58–80.

[9] Vasta, Ellie 1992, 'Italian migrant women', in Stephen Castles et al. (eds), *Australia's Italians*, Allen & Unwin, Sydney, pp. 140–54.

[10] Iacovetta, Franca 1993, 'Scrivere le donne nella storia dell'emigrazione: il caso italo-canadese', *Altreitalie*, no. 9, pp. 5–47.

[11] *Avevo diciassette anni*, 2 October 1960, Lena and Dino Gustin Papers, 1909–92, Readers' correspondence, 1960, ML MSS 5288 Add-on 1982/8(70), Mitchell Library. Original migrants' letters have been reproduced without editing, therefore grammatical mistakes have not been corrected. In referring to migrants' original letters, it was my intention to protect the privacy of the migrants and to facilitate the search for specific letters, which were stored uncatalogued in large labelled boxes in the Mitchell Library, State Library of New South Wales. I have therefore substituted the name of the author with a title in italics and the date of the letter. This title contains the original title of the story told by the writers. When a title is not present in the original letters, I have given the title as the first few words in the letters, with the exclusion of typical openings such as 'Cara Lena', 'Cara mamma Lena', 'Gentile Lena', and so on. When an original letter has been cited more than once, I have inserted the full reference for the first quotation and only the title for the following quotations. In translating the excerpts from migrants' original letters, I have tried to respect as much as possible the original contents and forms. The resulting translation could therefore sometimes seem strange and/or grammatically incorrect, however, I have also tried to make the English version immediately intelligible to readers even when translating excerpts that were scarcely intelligible in Italian due to the limited literacy of the writers. It is only by reading the original excerpts in Italian that it is really possible to grasp the textual characteristics of the excerpts.

[12] *Avevo diciassette anni*.

[13] A good example of this is in the film *Titanic*, directed by James Cameron. The love of the two protagonists can be remembered by the main female character (and can be perceived by the audience) as a perfect love precisely because of the death of the main male character, played by Leonardo Di Caprio.

[14] Abruzzese, Alberto 1983, 'Antagonismo e subalternità nella produzione di scrittura', in Alberto Asor Rosa (ed.), *Letteratura italiana. Volume VII. Produzione e consumo*, Einaudi, Turin, p. 482.

[15] Abruzzese, 'Antagonismo e subalternità', p. 482.

[16] *Atroce dilemma*, n.d., Lena and Dino Gustin Papers, 1909–92, Readers' correspondence, 1957–59, ML MSS 5288 Add-on 1982/6(70), Mitchell Library.

[17] *Lui: una scoperta*, n.d., Lena and Dino Gustin Papers, 1909–92, Readers' correspondence, 1957–59, ML MSS 5288 Add-on 1982/6(70), Mitchell Library.

[18] Ibid.

[19] *Spero che sarò compreso*, 13 August 1963, Lena and Dino Gustin Papers, 1909–92, Readers' correspondence, 1963–64, ML MSS 5288 Add-on 1982/10(70), Mitchell Library.

[20] *Espiazione*, n.d., Lena and Dino Gustin Papers, 1909–92, Readers' correspondence, 1958–59, ML MSS 5288 Add-on 1982/7(70), Mitchell Library.
[21] Ibid.
[22] Ibid.
[23] Ibid.
[24] *Ti ho perduta*, 27 March 1958, Lena and Dino Gustin Papers, 1909–92, Readers' correspondence, 1958–59, ML MSS 5288 Add-on 1982/7(70), Mitchell Library.
[25] Ibid.
[26] Ibid.
[27] Ibid.
[28] *Cuore ferito*, 16 February 1959, Lena and Dino Gustin Papers, 1909–92, Readers' correspondence, 1958–59, ML MSS 5288 Add-on 1982/7(70), Mitchell Library.
[29] *Anchio, come tanti altri Italiani*, 28 August 1958, Lena and Dino Gustin Papers, 1909–92, Readers' correspondence, 1957–59, ML MSS 5288 Add-on 1982/6(70), Mitchell Library.
[30] *Prega per me*, 12 September 1958, Lena and Dino Gustin Papers, 1909–92, Readers' correspondence, 1957–59, ML MSS 5288 Add-on 1982/6(70), Mitchell Library.
[31] *Sogno di gioventù*, n.d., Lena and Dino Gustin Papers, 1909–92, *Il Salotto di Lena/Vicende vissute da pubblicare*, 1957–61, ML MSS 5288 Add-on 1982/6(70), Mitchell Library.
[32] *Un fiore che non colsi*, n.d., Lena and Dino Gustin Papers, 1909–92, Readers' correspondence, 1958–59, ML MSS 5288 Add-on 1982/7(70), Mitchell Library.
[33] *Il giovane dagli occhi verdi*, n.d., Lena and Dino Gustin Papers, 1909–92, Readers' correspondence, 1960, ML MSS 5288 Add-on 1982/8(70), Mitchell Library.
[34] *Cosa farò*, n.d., Lena and Dino Gustin Papers, 1909–92, Readers' correspondence, 1957–59, ML MSS 5288 Add-on 1982/6(70), Mitchell Library.
[35] *Il primo amor non si può scordar*, n.d., Lena and Dino Gustin Papers, 1909–92, Readers' correspondence, 1957–59, ML MSS 5288 Add-on 1982/6(70), Mitchell Library.
[36] Ibid.
[37] Ibid.
[38] Ibid.
[39] Ibid.
[40] *Questa è la mia vicenda*, 30 April 1960, Lena and Dino Gustin Papers, 1909–92, *Il Salotto di Lena/Vicende vissute da pubblicare*, 1957–61, ML MSS 5288 Add-on 1982/6(70), Mitchell Library.
[41] *Il diario dell'infanzia che mi portò fortuna*, n.d., Lena and Dino Gustin Papers, 1909–92, Readers' correspondence, 1957–59, ML MSS 5288 Add-on 1982/6(70), Mitchell Library.
[42] *Il giovane dagli occhi verdi*.

Intellect

Imagination, curiosity, ambition, acquisitiveness and intellectual activity have all served as impetuses for transnational lives. Historical subjects' diverse stories show how some have travelled the globe in the pursuit of intellectual and commercial enterprises, while others have crossed linguistic and cultural boundaries without travelling abroad. Ann Lane's intriguing story of the imperial entrepreneur Henry Wickham shows the interconnections between imperialism, scientific curiosity and commercial ambition. The British Empire of the late nineteenth and early twentieth centuries spawned Wickham's experiments in botanical transplantation, which ranged from complete failures to spectacular success. Wickham showed that Enlightenment-inspired taxonomy was integrally linked with individual and imperial adventuring. Australia's second Prime Minister, Alfred Deakin, exemplifies how an avid reader can 'look out' on the world while staying put. Mark Hearn catalogues and discusses Deakin's astonishingly extensive and varied reading lists of a late stage of his life. His intellectual tastes for French literature, idealism, spiritualism and theosophy, the philosophy of Henri Bergson and William James, the works of Rudyard Kipling and Olive Schreiner, among many others, show the extent to which this founder of the Australian nation saw himself as a citizen of the world. Intellectual engagement enabled such a reader to be at once an introvert and a cosmopolitan.

Chapter 11

The Pacific as rhizome: the case of Sir Henry Alexander Wickham, planter, and his transnational plants

Ann Lane

> Isn't there in the East, notably in Oceania, a kind of rhizomatic[1] model that contrasts in every respect with the Western model of the tree?
>
> — Deleuze & Guattari 1983[2]

Sir Henry Alexander Wickham (1846–1928), pioneer planter and adventurer, is remembered for his role in the founding of the hugely lucrative imperial British rubber industry.[3] He was knighted in 1920 for his services 44 years earlier, when he collected and took 70,000 seeds of the Pará rubber tree, *Hevea brasiliensis*, out of the Amazon rainforest and across the world by boat to deliver to the Royal Botanical Gardens at Kew. Although fewer than 4000 of the 70,000 seeds germinated, those 4000 were enough to become the basis of thriving plantations in the British colonies, and the eventual result some decades later was of enormous economic benefit to Britain. At that time, the demand from the emergent American motor-car industry for rubber—for tyres in particular—was increasing exponentially and the market for plantation rubber was assured.[4] Previously, the rubber for European and American industry had to be bought from South America, where it was not in plantations but 'hunted' in the wild, supplied and sold at prices and with availability not under the control of Britain or the United States. After the successful British colonial planting of the stock of Kew seedlings in Ceylon and Malaya, there were, by the time of Wickham's death in 1928, 80 million rubber trees growing in British territories where none had grown before.

Wickham's name is most associated with rubber—'my rubber', as he would fondly refer to *Hevea brasiliensis*. In his long career, however, he promoted and grew many other plants, developing firm ideas for their best cultivation and inventing machinery for processing. He also promoted useful economic plants for other planters to grow, plants he claimed to have 'discovered' during his time in America, and specimens of which he periodically sent to Kew. He hoped that Kew would propagate and distribute these economic plants to planters (exclusively of British countries and dependencies) via its network of botanical gardens. In his own planting years, he grew a great range of plants himself in diverse places. In Santarem on the Amazon River, he planted sugar, tobacco, manioc and other crops. In North Queensland, he tried his luck for 10 years with tobacco and coffee. Later, in British Honduras (now Belize), he grew bananas, cacao, oranges, lemons and mangoes, while trying to establish a small number of *Castilloa* rubber trees. In New Guinea, at the age of nearly fifty, he took out a 25-year lease on the Conflict Islands east of Samarai. He tried to develop sponge growing and the scientific cultivation of pearl oysters, and a plantation of coconuts for copra. A decade later, on yet another lease, in Mombiri, in north-eastern Papua, he tried for the first time in his career to grow *Hevea brasiliensis*, planting his trees along the lines he had long been advocating, with the trees spaced much more widely than in the Malayan plantations.

Amid all this variety of activity and location, however, the part of his life that has attracted attention is only the South American phase with rubber—a success story with high dramatic appeal, the tale of a 'seed snatch'. Wickham first exploited the popular appeal of this story in a book he wrote and illustrated himself. *On the Plantation, Cultivation, and Curing of Para Indian Rubber* [5] narrates the story of a race against time, begun in February 1876, when he started to collect the *Hevea* trees' just-ripening seeds in the wild and, at the same time, had to find a means to transport these oily seeds, which, even if he could gather enough in the time available, would soon grow rancid or dry out on the long boat journey to England. Wickham gave an account of smuggling and dodging the Brazilian customs service, though in fact there was no Brazilian regulation to prevent the exportation of seed. He also played up the element of chance, although the ship *Amazonas* was really on a scheduled voyage to Liverpool when Wickham commissioned it in the name of His Majesty's Royal Botanical Gardens at Kew. In Wickham's story, a threatening Brazilian gunboat added a further element of danger.[6]

Some of this story was used as movie material first in a classic 1938 German film *Kautschuk*, which was filmed partly in South America. In one scene, Wickham wrestles an anaconda. Today, the South American adventure is again being proposed for a film. Joe Jackson, author of a 2008 biography of Wickham, is advertising his story, *The Thief at the End of the World*, on a web site of film properties. It is a larger-than-life tale of bio-piracy:

> A riveting narrative of the true story of Henry Wickham, a reckless Victorian adventurer who went deep into the malaria-filled jungles of the Amazon and risked disease, death, and the loss of his entire family to grow rich in that contemporary El Dorado, the rubber trade. He failed, but in his despair agreed with the powers in London to raid the Amazon's most treasured possession—its supply of *Hevea brasiliensis*, the valued source of 'India-rubber' which grew nowhere else in the world. His

unlikely success of smuggling 70,000 seeds to London changed the world economy, bankrupting Brazil, handing the world monopoly in rubber to the British Empire, and turning the US against the UK just as the American automobile revolution envisioned a world dominion of its own.[7]

Figure 11.1: Henry Alexander Wickham.

http://www.bouncing-balls.com/serendipity/images/photo_gallery/henry_wickham.jpg

In fact, towards the end of Wickham's life, it was a member of the Rubber Manufacturers Association of America who sought to secure him an American pension, and on Wickham's eightieth birthday, the American founder and manager of the US rubber plantations in Sumatra and Malaya sent him £5000, accompanied by a further £1000 contributed by the American oil kings.[8]

When Wickham died, his obituary in the *Times* eulogised him as 'every inch the pioneer, broad-shouldered and heavily-built with an extraordinarily long wavy moustache, his physical strength…as great as his resolution'.[9] The entry in the current British *Oxford Dictionary of National Biography* concludes that '[h]is shortcomings aside, he remains a paradigm of the nineteenth-century British adventurer and individualist'.[10] He is a representative figure at once typical and outstanding. The largely forgotten larger story of Henry Wickham, however, reveals the chronological and spatial deficiencies of a success-driven narrative. If his failed plant ventures are included rather than set aside, his activities are of more considerable historical interest. The failures are typical of the times too, but what is special about Wickham is the grand scale for a single individual and the vigorous proliferation of his ventures. In nationality, he was a proud citizen of empire rather than a Briton simply, and he was at different times an equally strong proponent of British investment in Brazil and in New Guinea, which he regarded as a country of great promise. Though he farmed for more than 35 years, he was not an emigrant-settler. Though he farmed in four different countries, he was not an itinerant contract worker. Transnational comparisons from the point of view of a settler-farmer are striking when focused by this single-minded man's activities as planter and plant entrepreneur in widely diverse global locations. His experiences usefully show that problems of labour and the availability of capital investment or land concessions had common extra-national elements, sometimes simultaneously, in diverse parts of the late nineteenth-century world. As for the plants themselves, the lucrative successes of certain major British plant transfers during the eighteenth and nineteenth centuries—of tea, anti-malarial cinchona, as well as rubber—are well known. Extrapolating from Wickham's various endeavours, it becomes clear that a fairer representation of the activities of imperial transfers would include many attempts that did not meet with success. His various failed attempts are graphic reminders of how the fate of a plant transfer is determined by much more than just agricultural conditions. Indeed, timing and chronology in Wickham's theatre of activity—the 'New-New World' of the nineteenth-century Pacific—become subjects for reconsideration. Here is a tale that shows coincidences that are not entirely matters of chance, initiatives that come just before the time is ripe and a life that crosses imperial and commercial modes of plant transfers.

One striking feature of Wickham's life, if considered as a whole, is how extremely 'transnational' his activities were.[11] The historian of New Guinea plantations, D. C. Lewis, was surprised to find a figure as noteworthy as Wickham appear in New Guinea in 1896, 'almost as if from nowhere'.[12] This rhizome-like behaviour of popping up in a new location, after 'underground' undetected transits, was typical of the man. In Wickham's case, the emergences were in globally separate locations, and the pathways were cross-oceanic voyages. He was in this way a case comparable with the London Missionary Society missionary John Williams in Polynesia: 'one of those nineteenth century figures who kept turning up on the edges of the world's maps.'[13] Williams, in an exemplary instance of the ethos of self-help celebrated in Samuel Smiles' 1859 book, hand-built his own boat, *The Messenger of Peace*, even manufacturing the smith's bellows, to take the gospel to every island along a 2000-mile (3200-kilometre) line in the Polynesian South Pacific. Williams built churches in Rarotonga (one of the Cook Islands) and in the Samoan Islands, reaching finally as far as the New Hebrides, where he was killed. In the latter part of the century, Henry Wickham pursued his secular form of idealism with imperial plant transfers across larger oceanic distances. Like Williams, Wickham wrote books to publicise his activities, and made frequent trips back to London to raise investment capital for his enterprises. The irony of such a mobile life for a planter underscores an important fact about the Pacific area at this stage. At a time when the voyages Wickham was making by ship lasted months in duration, the far-flung locations of Brazil, Queensland, British Honduras and New Guinea were nonetheless unusually integrated—all available to a planter such as Wickham. Each of these places offered opportunities and incentives in the form of land concessions to planters and cheap labour, and they were connected as a global area through new commerce-enabling technologies such as coal-powered shipping and underwater telegraph cables, as well as through international investment.

Henry Wickham does not figure in the *Australian Dictionary of Biography*, despite his more than 25 years in Queensland and New Guinea. The period spent in New Guinea, from 1895 to 1911, covered the time when Eastern New Guinea became an Australian colony, after very public confrontations of imperial and colonial authority. Queensland claimed New Guinea in 1883 in the name of Queen Victoria; the British Government then rejected the claim. Germany capitalised on the spat and 'Kaiser-Wilhelmsland' was annexed in the north-east. In response, Britain reversed its decision and New Guinea was made a protectorate in 1884. In 1906, administration of New Guinea was transferred to Australia. As a result, it was a governor answerable to Australia, Sir William Macgregor, who approved Wickham's application for a lease of the Conflict Islands Group, visiting the next year and reporting favourably on the progress with sponge farming and the planting of thousands of coconut trees. The omission of Wickham from the *Australian Dictionary of Biography* is therefore revealing of the conditions for becoming part of the national biographical record. This paradigm of a British adventurer is, from a historical point of view in Australia, a non-entity. Between 1877 and 1886, however, after delivering the rubber seeds to Kew, Wickham was an Australian colonial planter near the lower Herbert River in North Queensland, his entrepreneurial drive—evident in his exercises in public self-promotion and in his attempts to draw investment for his big-scale projects—undiminished. He presented himself in the press as a tobacco expert, and published a pamphlet on tobacco growing and curing through the Government Stationers Office. He became a member of the Queensland Acclimatisation Society, a chief source of new plants for farmers, and in one of his first letters to them he claimed to be successfully growing the much sought-after Liberian coffee. This was a modestly presented case of a planter's boast, since at this time the Acclimatisation Society was eagerly trying to obtain seedlings and seeds of the coffee from Kew Gardens, but they were not surviving the voyage out to Australia.[14] Finally, after his tobacco plantation failed, Wickham, far from being cowed by the failure, sold the property for subdivisions for a new town that never eventuated.[15] In the years from 1895 to 1912 spent in eastern New Guinea, at a time when it was effectively being administered from Australia, Wickham pursued even larger, diverse planting, trading and investment schemes, while challenging certain legalities of his lease. He regarded New Guinea as a land of great promise for the cultivation of rubber, sugar cane, tobacco, cotton and other produce, a country that would certainly reward large-scale British investment.

Though not a personality to go unnoticed at the time, Wickham's South Seas phase is now mostly forgotten. At the time, his way of suddenly emerging in different locations worked to his advantage, contributing to his success in promoting his confident image of himself, his plant discoveries, his ideas for cultivation and his manufacturing inventions—a confidence little supported by reality. For example, the tobacco 'expertise' he claimed when he arrived in Queensland was based on his few years' struggles to establish a plantation at Santarem on the Amazon. In his first book, *Rough Notes on a Journey Through the Wilderness from Trinidad to Para, Brazil, by Way of the Great Cataracts of the Orinoco, Atabapo and Rio Negro*, he had 'come to the conclusion that the valley of the Amazon is the great and best field for any of my countrymen who have energy and a spirit of enterprise as well as a desire for independence'.[16] By the time Kew approached him about collecting the rubber seeds, however, this interruption to his farming was a saving windfall and he never returned to his South American plantation after delivering the seeds. Twenty years later, when he was trying to raise money for his schemes in the Conflict Islands, he estimated profits for the pearl shell and copra alone as being £9400 in the first year, rising to £26,100 in the third year. He justified his optimism to prospective investors by claiming that the ideal conditions for mother-of-pearl production in the Conflicts were unparalleled in the world—a belief that an associate who knew him well described as 'nonsense. It is not a locality where anyone would, or could, work MOP [mother-of-pearl] for the reason that the tides or currents are too strong there; and what few shells are to be found are very inferior.'[17] At the time of his knighthood, Wickham was advisor to a syndicate planting in Malaya. Shareholders, who knew him only as father of the rubber industry, were assured by the Arghan Company that 'there is no other man living with whom we would have embarked our reputation and capital', a person with 'simply amazing' knowledge of tropical agriculture and forestry. Elsewhere, others had formed opposite assessments of Wickham's abilities. Sir Henry Ridley, director of the Singapore Botanical Gardens and the person who, more than any other, had persuaded farmers to develop rubber plantations in Malaya, said:

> I looked on him as a failed planter who was lucky in that for merely traveling home with a lot of seeds had received a knighthood and enough money to live comfortably in his old age...He ordered natives to bring him in the seeds and to pack them in crates and put them on board ship. One cannot help feeling he was jolly well paid for a little job. He was no agriculturalist. He knew nothing about rubber...As for his abilities in planting I should say he had none.[18]

When a chief value in recovering the life of Henry Wickham is to bring into single focus diverse and far-reaching dynamics of plant economics in the trans-Pacific area, Wickham's failed enterprises are of importance. One venture that was typical of the long time scales involved, the high expectations and the disappointing results obtained, was with another of the South American trees he had promoted to Kew at the same time as the *Hevea*. This was the timber tree *Piqui-á*, whose nuts produced an oil that could provide an alternative in times of butter shortage. The high aim in this case was to introduce a new food staple. More than 40 years after his original proposal, Wickham succeeded in having *Piqui-á* planted, on Birkhall Estate in Kedah. By the time of his death, the *Piqui-á* trees had reached a height of 12 metres and were producing abundant fruits. The nuts produced by the Malayan trees did not, however, have the anticipated fat yields, and the cost of preparation proved very high. The Irai Company growing the *Piqui-á* was wound up in 1929.[19]

Even to divide Wickham's enterprises into successes or failures in a clear-cut way is, however, misleading. In a time of great ferment of investments in new locations, new crops and new technologies, Wickham was trying projects that might have succeeded if the location, or date, or his personality had been a bit different. For example, when, in closing up his Queensland enterprise, Wickham tried to sell his plantation for a new town site, all the buyers of his Mount Maragan property were absentee landlords, and no town eventuated, though in an apparently identical case, the nearby town of Halifax, initiated in the same way from scratch through the sale of land subdivisions, was successfully started in the same year.[20] In New Guinea, there was another property mishap. In 1895, the Governor of British New Guinea, Sir William Macgregor, had granted Wickham the lease of the Conflict Group for 25 years, with a clause inserted in the lease instrument that reserved for the lessee the option to purchase the freehold title during the period of the lease. Unluckily for Wickham, however, under the *1905 Papua Act*, crown lands could now be granted on leasehold tenure only, and Wickham failed in his several applications for the freehold purchase of the Conflict Islands. In 1920, however, the freehold title was granted to Anglo-Papuan Plantations Limited. In the Conflicts, Wickham was ahead of his time in adding to the usual trade items sea sponges, which he was the first to treat and export. He was even more strikingly ahead of his time when, in 1899, he invited an expert to come to see whether pearl culturing might be viable in the Conflict Islands lagoon.[21] These were very early experimental days in the cultured-pearl industry: William Saville Kent, the most eminent naturalist of the period, at this time Commissioner of Fisheries in Western Australia, developed his pearl-sac theory and produced the first genuine spherical cultured pearl in the 1890s, and formed a company to culture pearls at Somerset in the Torres Strait in 1906. In 1904, Japanese cultured-pearl researchers patented the Mise-Nishikawa Method. Wickham's plans for cultured pearls were therefore very far-sighted. This has, however, to be put cheek-by-jowl with clear errors of judgment, stemming from an excess of optimism common in his circles and his time that could readily lead to loss of money—especially other people's money—on a large scale.

If one of Wickham's plants could be taken as an emblem for the life and times of this planter, that plant would not be the *Hevea* rubber tree but one of the other American plants he promoted: the arghan.

Figure 11.2: (Andre) C. H. Wright, bromeliaceae *Bromelia magdalenae*, 1923.

Kew Centre for Economic Botany.

The enterprise with arghan was a latter-day commercial, stock market-funded variant of the earlier, scientific-economic, imperial, Kew-coordinated transfers of South American trees such as *Hevea brasiliensis* and, earlier, the anti-malarial drug producer, cinchona. While in British Honduras, Wickham had become interested in a plant that produced silky fibre of exceptional strength, used by indigenous peoples for rope, fishing nets and lines, bags, fans, sandals, sewing thread and strings for musical instruments. Wickham was convinced of the commercial potential of this fibre for British industry. Nothing came of his suggestion to transfer it until some decades later, when in 1919 a company was floated on the London stock market to develop the plant, newly renamed as arghan. At this time, American manufacturers were increasingly taking up cotton supplies and problems in Russia were causing a 70 per cent shortage in flax. Speculators therefore predicted that British manufacturers would gladly prefer the new fibre of the mystery plant arghan for their finest products. Trials on arghan had shown it to have remarkable salt-resisting power and 'tensile strength three times that of silk, and weight for weight as strong as steel'.[22] Furthermore, arghan could apparently be grown in British colonies and dependencies by companies exclusively British owned.

In 1919, the newly incorporated Arghan Company, advised by seventy-three-year-old Wickham, sent an expedition to British Honduras. After 15 months of labour, the plants were transported to the Federated Malay States. By 1922, the company director reported to shareholders that he had secured a valuable land concession of 30,000 acres (12,000 hectares) free of all premium, and there were plans for further plantations in India and Ceylon (Sri Lanka). He told the extraordinary general meeting—the purpose of which was to increase the capital of the company to £100,000—that no less a figure than the Secretary of State for the Colonies, Winston Churchill, had communicated his support for the company by telegraph to the Governor of Ceylon.[23]

The story of arghan presented to the public during the heady days when it was being 'boomed' in the media had melodramatic elements reminiscent of the story of Wickham and *Hevea brasiliensis*. It was a story fit for the optimistic large-scale commercial dreams of the times. One 1922 newspaper columnist even saw film potential in the arghan story:

> Met a man yesterday who was telling me things about this new fibre 'arghan,' which seemed to me like extracts from a thrilling American film. It seems that one of our Empire builders found the plant abroad, and was struck with the strength of the fibre of the leaves. He gathered every plant he could find and had the lot transferred to British territory in Malaya. Most of the plants died, but several survivors found their new surroundings so agreeable that they passed the convalescent stage and formed the beginning of this new Empire product. The plants are

still grown in considerable secrecy, and foreign countries are very anxious to obtain specimens by various means. Representatives of one great nation have tried to get specimens of the plant, but have been suavely refused, while another interested country has tried to obtain specimens and information by less straightforward methods. Apparently 'arghan' is being as carefully guarded as an Oriental potentate's treasures, or as a child millionaire in danger of abduction. Both similes, I suppose, are near the mark.[24]

Off the public stage, too, there were elements of high drama in plenty. The chairman of the Arghan Company was himself a centre of controversy. The credibility of this Jewish financier and businessman, Abraham Montefiore (previously Abraham Rosenthal, who had taken his wife's name), was much questioned by the various government officials and botanists discussing the company's applications for land in the Federated Malay States and in British North Borneo, as well as the merits of the mystery plant itself. Was the venture speculative or honest? Was Montefiore himself 'a slippery Jew', attempting a gigantic stock-selling swindle? Was the Arghan Company merely a promotion company, wanting 'to get hold of a large concession which they can hawk round for sale'? And what relation, if any, was the Arghan Company to Eastern Cultivation Limited, operating from the same London Pinners Hall address, but making separate bids for land in Malaya to cultivate arghan? Was Montefiore dishonest and conniving, or just venial but infuriating? He was perhaps rather an 'irrepressible optimist', impossible to deal with in a business-like way, who undermined his colleagues' confidence to such an extent that a committee of shareholders formed in December 1923 to investigate the company's affairs recommended the formation of a new board.[25]

The outcome of the arghan story was the opposite to that of the rubber transfer: the venture came to nothing. The arghan plants did not thrive in their new locations in Malaya and no satisfactory machine was invented that could decorticate the leaves economically. As the company collapsed with the loss of its entire capital in 1924, some months after Montefiore died,[26] the plants in the field were dead, the European estate manager and his assistants in Malaya had been left for months without their salaries and the Chinese labour force had to be taken off by the local authorities and fed from the police station in Kuala Lipis.[27]

The management of arghan's transfer was poor, but even if it had been well administered, even if the plants had flourished in the Malay plantations and even if the machinery had been developed to mechanise the fibre's extraction, it probably could not have become the fibre equivalent of Pará rubber on the London market. There was no problem with the quality of the fibre itself, which was genuinely extraordinary. According to the report of the two scientists,

Messrs Cross and Bevan, commissioned by the Federated Malay States Government to conduct thorough tests: '[O]f all the innumerable fibres submitted to us during our long professional practice, of potential industrial importance, Arghan stands out pre-eminent.'[28] The timing, however, was against it. The development of human-made textiles, after centuries of experiment, made swift strides under pressure of pre-wartime shortages of natural fibre. Soon the market had no need of another natural fibre such as arghan. In a striking example of how closely one development could impinge on another, the same Cross and Bevan who conducted the tests on arghan were also the discoverers and patentors of the two great new processes for making artificial fibre: the viscose process, patented in 1892, and the cellulose acetate process, patented in 1894.

Furthermore, as the botanical identity of arghan was investigated, it was found that, though new to British investment, and at first not properly distinguished botanically from other plants in the same family, the plant newly named 'arghan' was far from being a plant 'discovered and pioneered' by Henry Wickham. It was in fact a South American plant known as pita or ixtle, whose fibre had been known and sold in Europe since at least the 1800s. Because of its extreme salt-resistant powers, it had been used for rope for rigging sailing ships crossing the Atlantic.[29] 'Arghan' was an even newer name for the plant identified rather belatedly by botanical classification in the nineteenth century as *Aechmea* (or *Bromelia*) *magdalenae*. It is a larger-than-life member of the pineapple family, the bromeliaceae. It has leaves up to 2.5 metres long. As the plant is a rhizome reproducing from suckers rather than seeds, the strange result is that it sometimes grows in large mono-specific clusters, along streams, in swampy areas and on hillsides in lowland tropical rainforests from Mexico to Ecuador. These large clusters were called '*pitales*' (plantations), an anachronistic marvel of nature imitating European civilisation's horticultural art of plantations.[30] Already with its own history of trans-Atlantic travel as rope on ships, and with its familial relationship to a more famous earlier traveller, the pineapple (brought to Europe from the West Indies by Columbus in 1493), *Aechmea magdalenae* failed to make its early twentieth-century Wickham-prompted transit to Malaya.

With arghan/pita, as with Henry Wickham, a biography with wide extra-national geographical range and chronological elasticity works best. And, as an image for Wickham's larger-than-life activities, large-scale ambitions and failures, and his sudden personal emergences in different parts of the British tropical empire, the rhizome *Aechmea magdalenae* is a good choice.

Notes

[1] I gratefully acknowledge the generous help of Dr Robert Cribb, Department of Asia-Pacific History, The Australian National University; Dr John Loadman, author of *Tears of the Tree* (2005, Oxford University Press, Oxford); and Dr Mark Nesbitt, Centre for Economic Botany, Royal Botanical Gardens at Kew.

A familiar example of a rhizome is the potato. Its pathway of growth is via a horizontal stem that lies flat underground, emitting adventitious roots at intervals below and leaves above ground or buds that develop into new plants. The visible parts of a rhizome are not discreet plants, but are interconnected underground.

[2] Deleuze, Gilles and Guattari, Félix 1983, 'Rhizome', *On the Line*, Translated by John Johnston, Semiotext(e), New York.

[3] The fullest source of information about Wickham's life is a set of articles by Lane, Edward V. 1953, 'Sir Henry Wickham: British pioneer. A brief summary of the life story of the British pioneer including an account of the inception of plantation rubber', *Rubber Age*, August, pp. 649–56; and 1953–54, 'The life and work of Henry Wickham', *The India-Rubber Journal*, December 1953 – January 1954, I —'Ancestry and early years', II — 'A journey through the wilderness', III — 'Santarem', IV — 'Kew', V — 'Pioneering in North Queensland', VI — 'Pioneering in British Honduras', VII — 'The Conflict Islands and New Guinea', VIII — 'Piqui-á and arghan', IX — 'The closing years'.

[4] In 1907, Henry Ford introduced the assembly line into the manufacture of cars; sales rose from 44,000 in 1907 to 65,000 in 1908 and to 187,000 in 1910.

[5] Wickham, Henry 1908, *On the Plantation, Cultivation, and Curing of Para Indian Rubber*, Kegan Paul, Trench, Trübner & Co. Ltd, London.

[6] Lane, 'Life and work of Henry Wickham', III — 'Santarem', p. 20. See also Loadman, John 2005, *Tears of the Tree*, Oxford University Press, Oxford; and 'Sir Henry Alexander Wickham', available from http://www.bouncing-balls.com/timeline/people/nr_wickham1.htm (accessed 20 August 2007).

[7] Jackson, Joe 2008, *The Thief at the End of the World: Rubber, power, and the seeds of empire*, Viking, New York. For film rights, see http://www.lukeman.com/film--rights--list.htm (accessed 20 August 2007).

[8] Quincy Tucker's commentary on Lane, 'Sir Henry Wickham: British pioneer', p. 653. See also a 1928 American journal's obituary notice cited by Lane.

[9] Cited in entry on Sir Henry Alexander Wickham in *Oxford Dictionary of National Biography* (electronic publication), Oxford University Press, 2004–06.

[10] Ibid.

[11] I am using 'transnational' loosely here, since while Brazil was independent in 1822, Australia was pre-national during Wickham's years there, and New Guinea (independent in 1974) and British Honduras/Belize (independent in 1981) were not even pre-national.

[12] Lewis, D. C. 1996, 'The plantation dream: developing British New Guinea and Papua 1884–1942', *The Journal of Pacific History*, Canberra, p. 26.

[13] Daws, Gavin 1980, *A Dream of Islands: Voyages of self-discovery in the South Seas*, W. W. Norton & Co., New York, p. 45.

[14] Queensland Acclimatisation Society Records, Reports of monthly meetings 1876–78, Heritage Collections, State Library of Queensland. The Liberian coffee plants were from 175 seedlings presented to Wickham by Kew in a Wardian case for their sea journey. See Lane, 'Life and work of Henry Wickham', V — 'Pioneering in North Queensland', p. 17.

[15] Barrie, Douglas R. 2003, *Minding My Business: The history of Bemerside and the lower Herbert River district of North Queensland Australia*, S. & D. Barrie, Brisbane, pp. 133–5.

[16] Wickham, H. A. 1872, *Rough Notes...*, W. H. J. Carter, London, cited in Loadman, *Tears of the Tree*, p. 86.

[17] Lane, 'The life and work of Henry Wickham', VII — 'The Conflict Islands and New Guinea', p. 9. Wickham did not get the additional £20,000 capital he sought from London investors to develop the Conflicts, to build a steamer for cargo and passengers and a smaller steamer for collecting produce from neighbouring islands, and to hire 100 native workers and European overseers, clerical staff, sailors and scientific experts. He had to settle for selling his enterprise and remaining on as manager until the owners paid him to keep away from the islands.

[18] Lane, 'Life and work of Henry Wickham', IX — 'The closing years', pp. 7–8.

[19] Lane, 'Life and work of Henry Wickham', VIII — 'Piqui-á and arghan', p. 8.

[20] Barrie, *Minding My Business*, p. 135.

[21] Lewis, *The Plantation Dream*, p. 27.

[22] Arghan Company Limited, Report of Extraordinary General Meeting, 3 April 1922.

[23] Arghan Company Report.

[24] Unidentified newspaper clipping, 22 October 1922, File on arghan fibre, UK National Archives (hereafter UKNA). This 1919–26 archive (CO874/950) is not listed in the *Oxford Dictionary of National Biography* entry on Wickham. For secrecy, see Wickham, *On the Plantation, Cultivation, and Curing of Para Indian Rubber*, quoted in Lane, 'Life and Work of Henry Wickham', IX — 'Closing years', p. 5; for identification, see *Bulletin of the Imperial Institute* XVI (1918) and XVIII (1920); Dawe, M. T. 1920–21, *Tropical Life*, December 1920 – January 1921; and Stockdale, F. A. 1923, 'Fibres: Colombian pita', *The Tropical Agriculturist*, vol. LX, pp. 337–45.

[25] UKNA.

[26] 'Wills and Bequests', *The Times* (London), 12 May 1924, p. 20.

[27] Clipping from the *Truth* newspaper, 9 April 1924, UKNA.

[28] Lane, 'Life and Work of Henry Wickham', VIII — 'Piqui-á and arghan', p. 9.

[29] Tickin, Tamara 2002, 'The history of *ixtle* in Mexico', *Economic Botany*, vol. 56, no. 1, p. 92.

[30] Dawe, cited in Stockdale, 'Fibres: Colombian pita', p. 337.

Chapter 12

A transnational imagination: Alfred Deakin's reading lists

Mark Hearn

Between 1906 and 1914, Alfred Deakin (1856–1919) kept an annual record of his reading. In those nine years, in either the front or back pages of his rough diary (and sometimes in both front and back), he documented a total of 864 books—on average, 96 books a year, at a rate of nearly two a week.[1] While he read these books, Deakin served variously as Prime Minister of Australia and opposition leader, finally retiring from politics in 1913. The period 1906–09 was perhaps the busiest and certainly among the most politically productive of his career. As Prime Minister of a Liberal protectionist government, Deakin entrenched his vision of the post-Federation Australian settlement through the New Protection Program, fulfilling the ideal of limited government intervention in the lives of the people, within a federal system that itself upheld the principle of limited governance—a system Deakin had helped shape as a leading federal convention delegate in the 1890s.[2]

Deakin's papers include inventories of some of the 1500 books crammed into his Melbourne home at the time of his death in 1919 at the age of sixty-three, revealing the extraordinary variety of his interests in philosophy, spiritualism, literature (particularly French), biography, history, health, essays and literary criticism, poetry and agriculture.[3] This chapter focuses on those works recorded in his rough pocket diaries to explore some sense of Deakin self-consciously recording his reading at a specific period, and how this reading might reflect a public life at a critical moment of influence and transition towards its conclusion. Deakin's reading and his extensive papers allow us to follow the spiritual and existential crisis that approaching retirement and failing health summoned in him in the period 1910–13.

Historians and biographers have observed the depth and range of Deakin's reading, but some significant aspects remain unexplored, including Deakin's reflections on the French philosopher Henri Bergson, who was an inspiration for him at a time of personal crisis.[4] Deakin's notebook reflections on Bergson's works, in an intense burst of creativity in 1911–12, were perhaps his last embrace of a new source of self-transformation before his final decline. Deakin's engagement with Bergson's ideas dramatically drew together the entangled intellectual, emotional and spiritual needs that had impelled Deakin's obsessive reading and private writings throughout his life. In temperament and in intellectual and spiritual interests, Deakin powerfully reflected fin de siècle preoccupations with the exploration of new ideas in philosophy, politics and social and moral conventions and alternative belief systems such as theosophy and mystical speculation. In his reading, Deakin drew eagerly on fin de siècle ideas, seeking intellectual stimulation and spiritual comfort.[5]

Figure 12.1: Alfred Deakin with book in hand.

National Library of Australia: nla-pic-an23302838.

Deakin had made a half-hearted attempt in 1903 to record his reading in his diary, but it was only in 1906, at the age of forty-nine, that he began a dedicated process of numbering and listing. The project was that of a middle-aged man, renewing the quest for self-improvement. The lists also reflected the gathering crisis of a man who believed he was slowly losing control of his memory—that vital tool of political skill and self-mastery. For nine years, Deakin dedicated himself to the discipline of reading and recording until, at the end of 1914, he apparently felt compelled to surrender the quest, defeated by the debilitating illness that overwhelmed him in the years before his death.

For much of the period 1906–14, Deakin commented anonymously on Australian politics in a weekly article to the London *Morning Post*, and each day he corresponded with a wide range of friends and politicians.[6] Every day, he briefly recorded his activities in his diary. He was also a husband and father and, for Deakin, home was a refuge and his diaries reflected how he cultivated a meaningful family life.[7] Contemporaries in government observed Deakin's capacity for hard work.[8] They were not aware that in his private notebooks Deakin maintained a demanding routine of hours of intense spiritual and philosophical reflection, often writing into the early hours of the morning. Reading was not a punishment; it reflected Deakin's essentially solitary nature. He found happiness, as he observed in 1910, in the immersion in books, and 'the inner life of speculation…my only true being…this is my "self"…This is my real life, and joy—far more real than the other.'[9]

An almost obsessive sense of self-improvement characterises Deakin's reading. Deakin told his friend and son-in-law, Herbert Brooks, that 'certain books are to be read as discipline whether you like them or not'.[10] That self-disciplinary principle compelled Deakin's reading, his private reflections and his liberal politics, which sought to create self-governing subjects guided by restrained state intervention.[11] Self-discipline was reflected in the steady, careful order of the lists, unfailingly numbered and identified by author and title and usually spanning about three pages of each year's diary. The entries reflect Zygmunt Bauman's 'geometry of order', a grid of 'classification, inventory [or] catalogue' to create order and eliminate ambivalence, to identify phenomena and exert control over the world.[12] Few leading Australian figures sought to master such self-control as Deakin strove to achieve, even in an age that produced such determined self-improvers as Deakin's contemporaries (and avid readers) Henry Bournes Higgins, William Jethro Brown and Deakin's friend and intellectual role model Charles Pearson.[13]

Deakin's correspondence with Walter Murdoch represented a rare commentary on his reading shared with a contemporary. Murdoch felt that Deakin was 'too susceptible to the latest idea…the newest theory'. This was a habit that left Deakin receptive to unusual and stimulating points of view—a useful susceptibility in a period characterised by such a diversity of ideas. In 1906, Deakin confessed to Murdoch that 'Nietzsche I found very valuable for though to me he acts as "advocatus diaboli" he pricks so many conventional bubbles & sounds the shallows of masquerading "morality" so well that he helps to drive one to deeper foundations & more sincere inspiration'.[14] Unconventional thinking was an inspirational trigger for Deakin, found in the interrogation of the latest idea.

Ann Curthoys argues that a transnational history 'places heavier emphasis on the notion of diaspora...the formation of a diaspora of people who maintain a sense of identity...across national boundaries'.[15] As an idea that might be applied to Deakin, a transnational interpretation could be developed in terms of Deakin's cultural affinity with Britain or in relation to French literature and philosophy, which were certainly evident in his reading. Deakin's reading lists, however, reveal not so much a transnational pattern of familiarity as an imagined diaspora of difference, an outsider's search for moral reassurance and spiritual comfort, a search that seemed to grow more difficult with advancing years and despite ever-accumulating knowledge. Deakin looked on the world through Australian eyes and, in the fin de siècle, Deakin's reading reflected the search of a people looking to secure their place in the world. Deakin's ability to link the ideal of nation building with the desire to construct a secure Australian identity facilitated his emergence as a national leader, although Deakin's reading also suggests that being an Australian in the fin de siècle was complicated by the possibilities available to the formation of that identity. Deakin's reading reveals what he could not necessarily reconcile with a nation-building cause: an imagination sensitive to an extraordinary range of insights, whether expressed in the subtle personal forms of fiction or in the more abstract reflections of philosophy. In his search for meaning, Deakin explored deeply the transnational domain of the Western imagination, receptive to a wide range of ideas that might help clarify identity, although in the final decade of his career Deakin's quest was driven by two impulses: to face the ethical challenges posed by life, and the inescapable reality of personal decline and death.

A fin de siècle imagination

Few better records exist of a hungry, relentlessly curious fin de siècle imagination in Australia than Alfred Deakin's reading lists, ranging across harsh satire and dreamy mysticism, tough social critiques and gentle literary elegies, and a determined interrogation of the turbulent welter of ideas and tensions circulating across the planet in the decade before World War I. Among Deakin's favourites was the mordant futurist and social critic H. G. Wells. Deakin read Wells' works as they were published: his social satires *Tono Bungay*, in 1909, and *The Kingdom [Country] of the Blind*, in 1911; *The War in the Air*, in 1908, Wells' prophetic fictionalisation of new technology intensifying global conflict; the novel *The*

New Machiavelli, about the moral struggles of a British Liberal MP, in 1910; and *First and Last Things* in 1909, a self-styled 'metaphysical' work that outlined Wells' moral beliefs and in which Deakin perhaps recognised a kindred spirit. It was the work, Wells said, of an 'amateur philosopher', and he described himself as 'an ingenuous enquirer with, I think, some capacity for religious feeling, but neither a prophet nor a saint'.[16]

Deakin's immersion in the works of George Bernard Shaw illustrated his intense commitment to a preferred author. Like Wells, Shaw seemed to attract Deakin for his vivid skill in provocatively mixing philosophy, sharp social critique and satire in essays, fiction and, in Shaw's case, drama. Deakin re-read *Man and Superman* in 1912 (it was Deakin's habit to note his return to a work). *Man and Superman* was a long, philosophical comedy that pitted a male desire for creative freedom against a female nurturing instinct. Celebrating the 'life force', Shaw borrowed French philosopher Henri Bergson's *élan vital* to champion 'the man of action'.[17] Deakin recommended the two volumes of Shaw's *Dramatic Opinions and Essays* to Walter Murdoch, and recorded reading them in 1907, 1909 and 1910.[18] Deakin also read *John Bull's Other Island*, Shaw's analysis of the 'Irish Question', and *The Quintessence of Ibsen* in 1907 (and Ibsen's *The Pillar of Society*, an attack on moral hypocrisy and suffocating social conventions, in the same year); *The Sanity of Art* in 1910; *Press Cuttings*, *The Doctor's Dilemma* and Archibald Henderson's biography of Shaw in 1911; and *Misalliance* and *Dark Lady of the Sonnets* in 1914.[19] In 1907 and 1911, Deakin read Joseph Conrad's new novels *The Secret Agent* and *Under Western Eyes*, among the first fiction to probe the psychology and politics of alienation that fed the disturbing modern phenomena of terrorism and espionage. *Under Western Eyes* was Conrad's 'bleak' account of a young Russian student caught up in the aftermath of a terrorist bombing, and of the problematic nature of Western attempts to understand an alien Russian consciousness—at once mystical and cynical.[20]

For a pillar of Australian society, Deakin was remarkably susceptible to reading works that were subversive of moral and social codes, if not political or class structures. It was a way of distinguishing himself from others, a private awareness of a more acute and sensitive perception, and a way of striving for a more authentic existence, as he observed in his notebook in November 1910:

> [R]eading does open doors which remain open all one's life making an essential contrast to those who to judge by appearances live not so much in accordance with themselves as with the 'living pictures' supplied by their associations with & observations of others, by the particular environment in which they live & by the march of events affecting them or around them.

The energies of 'most' people were dissipated in the 'struggle to adapt themselves' to the daily circumstances of earning a living, their opinions 'mostly those of the street & newspapers casually picked up & imperfectly understood'. In contrast, 'even as a lad solitary, introspective, shrinking, timid & fascinated by literature more or less instinctive, made me while a lively boy a dreamer & a reader beyond all cure'.[21]

Charles Pearson encouraged Deakin to read French literature in the 1880s, and it was a task the young member of the Victorian Parliament embraced with intense dedication: more than 230 French titles were listed in Deakin's household inventory, and it was not complete.[22] Dreaming in another language opened up a whole new and private realm: Deakin read novels by Honoré de Balzac, Maurice Maeterlinck, Emile Zola and Alexandre Dumas, and Guy de Maupassant's stories; he read the Goncourt brothers' journal and works by Jean Baptiste Racine, Moliere and Anatole France. The literary critics Sainte Beuve and Emile Faguet were favourites. Deakin read several works by Romain Rolland, including *Les Amies* and Rolland's biography of *Michelangelo*. In 1911, he read *L'Aube*, a volume of the 10-part novel *Jean Christophe* that won Rolland the Nobel Prize for Literature in 1915.[23] Deakin seems to have read most, if not all, of the instalments. Rolland was inclined to a mystical idealism and wrote his novel as an expression of French–German rapprochement. *Jean Christophe* is the epic story of a German musical genius, based partly on the life of Beethoven. Rolland portrayed his protagonist as a heroic figure and a fighter for social justice. In the end, when Jean Christophe dies, his soul mystically rejoins 'the River of Life'.[24] In Murdoch, Deakin found a sympathetic correspondent for the exotic pleasures of French literature and criticism: 'What demons at exposition these Frenchmen are!' Deakin enthused in a 1907 letter. 'I shall always be grateful to you for putting me on to Faguet and the *Revue* [*Latine*]. There is always something luminous in it.'[25] In private, Deakin was willing to explore perspectives that he felt must be denied an impressionable public: as Victorian Chief Secretary in the late 1880s, he sought to ban translations of Zola's work.[26]

The imagined diaspora of difference that Deakin searched for inspiration had an unworldly and spiritual quality, and it was these elements perhaps that drew him to Edith Wharton's stories. Deakin read *The Hermit and Wild Woman* in 1909.[27] A somewhat overheated fin de siècle religious parable, the story describes, in a medieval setting, the encounter between a mystical Catholic hermit and a wild woman he meets as he struggles alone with nature, having abandoned his community. 'His longing was to live hidden from life' and escape the tormenting moral choices that confronted him: 'There seemed to be so many pitfalls to avoid—so many things were wicked which one might have supposed to be harmless. How could a child of his age tell?' In order to be 'perfectly good', he had to flee from his fellow men. The wild woman became his 'penitent', while remaining essentially untamed, declining to reconcile herself with traditional faith or to 'confess her fault and receive the Sacrament with him', although they finally find release in a transcendental death. *The Hermit and Wild Woman* reflects, as Carol Singley suggests, Wharton's intense spiritual longing and a sense of 'spiritual homelessness'. An American who sought imaginative and spiritual inspiration in Europe, Wharton struggled with a crisis of belief stirred by the clash of traditional and alternative faiths and scientific rationality at the turn of the century.[28] Deakin's spiritual notebooks also reflect this crisis, and although he seemed to embrace the world energetically, there was also a withheld identity, a part of Deakin that imagined that only by fleeing the world could he find how to be perfectly good.

Deakin's restless search for goodness and spiritual comfort had, since early adulthood in the 1870s, drawn him to an interest in spiritualism and alternative religions.[29] In 1903, he read Charles Leadbeater's *The Other Side of Death*, a study of the afterlife by the leading theoretician of theosophy: 'Scientifically Examined by Clairvoyant Observation and Carefully Described.' Deakin was drawn to occult and theosophical writings that blended speculations on a transcendent afterlife with the apparent credibility of quasi-scientific language—and Leadbeater was skilled in concocting that blend.[30] In 1911, Deakin read *Some Mystical Adventures*, a 'revelation' of the mystical adventures of the theosophist G. R. S. Mead. Chapters included: 'The elasticity of a permanent body', 'Guesses at what to expect', 'Mystic reality', 'The deathless race' and 'Some elementary speculations'.[31] In his spiritual notebook, Deakin expressed his disappointment with a first reading, finding it 'superficial'; but having, as he conceded, 'read it at a gallop', he returned to *Some Mystical Adventures* in 1912 and found that 'I had missed most of its meaning…it is the most practically helpful of all the philosophies of mysticism & has determined me to continue my perusals'.[32]

Deakin was preoccupied with reconciling a morality of life and public duty with his search for spiritual meaning. Idealist philosophy, the belief that reality reflected the workings of the mind, seemed to offer the potential for such an integration, particularly as many of idealism's leading adherents such as Sir Henry Jones, the professor of Moral Philosophy at Glasgow University, encouraged a strong sense of moral and civic duty, including support for New Liberalism's program of state intervention in the causes of social and educational reform.[33] In 1910, Deakin re-read Jones's *Idealism* (having read it only the previous year), a classic statement on the subject.[34] Deakin heard Jones speak on 'The individual and the State' during the philosopher's Australian lecture tour in 1908, and met with him, although Deakin was unimpressed with his fellow Melburnians' response: he told Murdoch that he was 'disgusted to hear of local apathy considering the rarity of men like Jones'.[35] Deakin was also attracted to the work of German philosopher Rudolf Eucken, the 1908 Nobel Laureate and another of idealism's leading exponents in the period. In *Christianity and the New Idealism*, which Deakin read twice in 1912, Eucken argued that as 'modern civilization...fills us with insatiable ambition', it is necessary that 'an independent Spiritual Life should dominate the storm and stress of the conflict, test the world's work, and so separate the pure ore of truth from its alloy of human error'.[36] Such was the project that Deakin had undertaken in his notebooks. Just how seriously he took his quest for spiritual and philosophical understanding is illustrated by a virtually self-constructed course of study he undertook on Eucken in 1912, as he continued to grapple with his decision to quit politics and 'turn in' towards himself, and his restless inquiry into the soul of the 'dimly lit' self.[37] Deakin read five of Eucken's works and re-read two of them in that same year, while also reading about 85 other books (and serving as Leader of the Opposition): *Life's Basis and Life's Ideal* (also twice), *The Problem of Human Life*, *Meaning and Value of Life*, *The Truth of Religion* and *Christianity and the New Idealism*.[38]

Deakin re-read William James' highly influential *Varieties of Religious Experience* in 1912, having first read the American philosopher and psychologist's Gifford Lectures on their publication in 1903. He also read James' *Pragmatism* in 1907 and re-read *Memories and Studies* in 1912.[39] Deakin was a natural student of James, who brought a sensitive perception to the linkage of religion, psychology and mysticism, stressing the importance of personal mystical experience over religious institutions or doctrines, and an acceptance of a pluralist conception of existence and the pragmatic and relative nature of truth.[40] In March 1912, Deakin described James in his notebook as one of the leaders, along with Eucken and Bergson, of 'a new exodus towards sundry "promised lands" of the mind and the soul', breaking away from 'philosophic dogmas and assumptions'. James was a model of intellectual action, 'the dashing cavalry leader...cutting off the forces of the orthodoxies of metaphysics...His contributions to psychology are invaluable—a fascinating man.' Like Bergson, James was 'engaged in the same fight for freedom, conducting it with the same freshness & an "elan vital"'.[41] Bergson's vitalism made a profound impact in the period, not least, as Michael Roe has argued, in Australia.[42] As a man of political if not philosophical action, Deakin perhaps identified with the vital spirit exhibited by James and Bergson, as much as with the content of their ideas.

Marilyn Lake has argued that Deakin looked to the United States, and not only to Britain and Europe, for a sense of identity and for intellectual and imaginative stimulation. Describing Deakin as a 'desiring subject', Lake focused on Deakin's relationship with Josiah Royce, the idealist philosopher and close friend of William James, and issues of white manhood and self-respect acquired through power. Deakin's desire was also focused intensely on his spiritual quest, as suggested by his relationship with Royce, who, typically of the thinkers who appealed to Deakin, mixed his philosophy with a strong religious influence.

Deakin was adept at identifying political rationales in his reading, drawing on Royce's *The Philosophy of Loyalty* to welcome the Great White Fleet of the United States Navy on its Australian visit in 1908.[43]

Deakin selected books to develop the scope of his Liberal politics and the cultural values and anxieties that nurtured those politics. He had read John Robert Seeley's *Expansion of England*, a ringing endorsement of the imperialist mission, and had been troubled by his friend Pearson's *National Life and Character*, and its fearful prophecy of the threat to the white race and its diaspora, swamped by the populous hordes of Asia.[44] In 1911, Deakin read the British Commander-in-Chief Lord Roberts' *Fallacies and Facts*, which advocated compulsory military training—a cause that Deakin had strongly supported in Australia, and a policy designed in part as a form of racial defence for a nation concerned about its vulnerability in the Asia-Pacific region.[45] Having lost the prime ministership to Labor's Andrew Fisher in 1910, Deakin took solace in being unable to attend the 1911 Imperial Conference in London by reading Richard Jebb's *Imperial Conference*, a two-volume 'history and study' of this unique imperial institution, and John Findley's *The Imperial Conference of 1911 from Within*.[46]

Lake argued that Deakin exhibited a 'profound ambivalence about the British connection'.[47] Deakin described himself as 'an independent Australian Briton' and embraced the cause of imperial federation, striving to build closer ties of empire between Britain and the Dominions. It is true that he delighted in challenging British authority, but he also drew willingly on Britain for the pragmatic ties of defence and the appeal of cultural identity; he felt British politicians and Colonial Office public servants insufficiently understood the empire's needs. Attending the Imperial Conference in London in 1907, Deakin took time from his demanding schedule to meet Rudyard Kipling, Wells and the Webbs, representatives of the dynamic current of new ideas emanating from the metropole.[48] As an avid reader of Kipling, Deakin identified with the imagined diaspora of empire and its ancient heritage. Between 1906 and 1912, he read Kipling's children's book *Puck of Pook's Hill*, which allowed readers to transcend time in imaginary connection with heroic figures who had shaped Britain's history. He also read Kipling's science-fiction adventure *Actions and Reactions*, and re-read *Kim* and the *Second Jungle Book*.[49]

A passionate sense of Australian identity was reflected in Deakin's enthusiasm for Australian literature. As a young man in the 1870s, Deakin had written poetry and verse dramas, often with a setting in Australian nature, but eventually felt he lacked the necessary skill to pursue a literary career; he remained a reader receptive to new work by Australian writers and willing to champion it.[50] In 1896, Deakin lavished praise on Henry Lawson, whose stories spoke for 'the workman, the tramp, the shearer…the inner Australian beyond civic or imported influences—the most Australian Australia'. Lawson and the poet Banjo Paterson were 'racy of the soil'; he also praised Ada Cambridge, Tom Collins (Joseph Furphy) and Miles Franklin in a 1905 address: '[W]e have good reason, when in patriotic mood, to be proud of the promise of Australian literature.'[51] That promise is not strongly reflected in Deakin's reading lists in the period 1906–14, where relatively few Australian titles appear, although this could be due, as John La Nauze suggests, to Deakin's increasing immersion in philosophical and spiritual speculation.[52] He read Henry Handel Richardson's novel *The Getting of Wisdom* in 1911, and E. J. Brady's *River Rovers* in 1912, which described a trip down the Murray River in an open boat. He read two books by Charles Bean, *On the Wool Track* in 1910 and *The Dreadnought of the Darling* in 1912, the accounts of what a city journalist found when he ventured into the nation's bush wool sheds and down the Darling River.[53] These works reflected a romanticised exploration of Australia, familiarising the Australian experience and the land for an urban readership. Bean's books cultivated a narrative of bush mateship and Australia's place within the empire, at once loyal to Britain but distinctive and inclined to a sense of independence, reflecting 'the quality of sticking…to an old mate'—a careful if ambiguous construction that Deakin would have identified with.[54]

Just as Deakin might have been inclined to read books that reinforced his political and cultural values, he also read works that challenged them. In 1911, he read Olive Schreiner's *Woman and Labour*. A South African feminist, novelist and political activist, Schreiner argued that women's labour, especially domestic labour, was 'wearisome and unending', and neither adequately recognised nor recompensed. Schreiner championed equal pay for women, equality in marriage and a belief that 'sex and the sexual relation between man and woman have distinct aesthetic, intellectual, and spiritual functions and ends, apart entirely from physical reproduction'. Sex was a physical union that contained 'in it latent, other, and even higher forms, of creative energy and life-dispensing power, and that its history on earth has only begun'.[55] There is little doubt that this transcendent idealism would have appealed to Deakin. It is less clear that Deakin was receptive to Schreiner's arguments about the value of women's paid and unpaid labour. A year after Deakin read *Woman and Labour*, the Commonwealth Arbitration Court began the process of discriminating against women in the payment of wages, eventually deciding to pay women only 54 per cent of the male wage. The arbitration system that Deakin had championed in parliament did more than any other legislative instrument to make women second-class citizens of the Commonwealth of Australia.[56]

The more subtle, rarefied ideas that Deakin pondered in his private readings might not have often infiltrated his construction of public policy, although it is possible to detect some influence. In the 1903 debate on the *Conciliation and*

Arbitration Act, which Deakin led as Attorney-General, he provided a typically detailed and elegantly argued presentation of the key elements of the legislation. These benefits were not based merely in the pragmatic nature of the employment relationship or the principle of the intervention of the liberal state to create the 'people's peace', a harmonious civil and liberal society; it was a policy, Deakin told parliament, which apparently also reflected that

> [w]e realise now-a-days that society is a living organism in every sense of the term. In all its capacities of adaptation, in its changefulness, and in its varieties of action, it partakes of the nature of the living beings who compose it. They, too, are under the influence of various motives, inspirations and aims, passions, interests, and prejudices, and, although human history may be said to repeat itself, we find that it repeats itself with infinite variety, and never twice in quite the same fashion.[57]

Deakin's remarks reflected Bergson's ideal of organic creativity, of a vital impetus at work in nature and human experience, blossoming in variegated forms, an idea that provided Deakin with a powerful metaphor of transcendence in his spiritual notebooks.

Bergson had achieved international fame by the early 1900s with works such as *Time and Free Will*, published in 1889, and *Creative Evolution*, published in 1907.[58] From October 1911 to January 1912, Deakin read a range of Bergson's work, just as it became available to the Australian reading public and generated interest in journals such as *Bookfellow* and *Salon*.[59] Deakin also typically read works that either discussed or were influenced by Bergson. In 1911, Deakin read Bergson's *Matter and Memory* and *Laughter*, A. D. Lindsay's *Philosophy of Bergson* and John McKellar Stewart's *A Critical Exposition of Bergson's Philosophy*. He also read and re-read L. P. Jacks' *Alchemy of Thought*, which attempted to reconcile religion and science and reflected Bergson's influence.[60] Jacks was the editor of *The Hibbert Journal*, the leading international journal of philosophy and religion. Deakin was drawn particularly to the October 1911 edition, containing Bergson's lecture 'Life and consciousness'. Bergson addressed 'the essential and vital questions': 'What are we? What are we doing here? Whence do we come and whither do we go?' These were questions with which Deakin had struggled throughout his life. Bergson doubted that the evolution of life could be explained solely by 'mechanical forces': 'Obviously there is a vital impulse…something which ever seeks to transcend itself…in a word, to create.' Man might ultimately transcend his own limits: 'Perhaps in man alone,' Bergson speculated, 'consciousness pursues its path beyond this earthly life.'[61] In his notebook reflections on Bergson, Deakin was inspired by this 'master…of thought & style' to conceive of his own creative ideal of transcendence:

> Each of us will at last learn that in his or her own spirit lies another world as well as a world redeemer; that the eternal process of the suns is forever

multiplying spheres...Hence from the heart of the Deity there flows into infinity & eternity never ceasing streams of embodied aspirations, souls which in innumbered [sic] and ever new phases, enlarging (as we would phrase it) the bounds of being & ever multiplying the children of the highest who in constantly varying modes & inexhaustible forms express the ever deepening & ever heightening creativeness of the all in each, of the One in all, of the all in all.

This is why, Deakin explained, he read Bergson, Jacks and James and brought them from the world into his imagination:

[T]hose most important to me since they break the fetters of thought, exhibit the relativity of science & all doctrines orthodox or heterodox that have hitherto tied us & our minds down to the empirical interpretations of the universe that leaves us hopelessly distraught...they help to set us free.[62]

This awareness of living in a relative universe of transcendent science and faith, offering some hope of consciousness beyond this earthly life, represented a powerful way in which fin de siècle ideas sought to break the fetters of nineteenth-century thought and belief. At the end of his life, as Deakin struggled with personal and professional decline, he embraced the relativity and the freedom that this hope opened in his mind and that led him into the passionate outburst that the very page strained to contain, with the rushing, scored and redrafted text spilling from page to page.

Conclusion

Lake observes that 'a trans-national analytic frame that connects the global to the local also serves to illuminate the subjective self-constitution of key individuals in the story'.[63] While drawn from the world, Deakin's reading fed an intensified, inward-looking subjectivity—and fed an awareness that, as he observed in 1904, 'I act alone, live alone and think alone'.[64] It was this emphatic solitude that stood in such contrast with his rapturous longing that humanity would achieve, as he hoped in 1911, a holistic empathy and unity, in all its various and inexhaustible creativeness 'of the all in each, of the One in all, of the all in all'.

Bauman argues that fin de siècle modernism confronted modernity and its quest for holistic order and knowledge with its own impossibility.[65] Deakin tried to find in the diaspora of his imagination what he could not find in Australia. His struggles reflect the idea of mastery and certainty represented by liberal modernity and placed as a demand on the nation and on the self. Such a demanding self-discipline, and such a powerful transcendence, was not available in human experience, and in Deakin's case was increasingly undermined by

1911 by ill health and failing memory, the clamouring demands of public duty and an intimidating accumulation of knowledge that defied comprehensive assimilation or analysis.

By October 1911, all the carefully accumulated wisdom that Deakin had stored in his mind and recorded in his reading lists was dissipating even as it seemed to him to open up 'vast regions of liberties, possibilities and promise':

> Unhappily my whole memory…of the work of theosophists…and their resurrection of ancient texts and of the various gospels, all of which even the Koran have their mystical implications, has vanished except in results, inchoate indistinguishable as to source, & more or less transmuted by being heaped together in that loose bag which represents my mind. This very inapposite break away from my purpose when commencing to write tells its own story of my meandering fidelity.[66]

This meandering fidelity provided its own compelling story. On 15 October 1911, Deakin tried to recall some lines of poetry:

> This morning waking in the peace of a Sunday it took me some time before I could recollect to whom I was indebted for the exquisite and apposite fragment of verse that floated into my consciousness 'The peace that man did not make and cannot mar'—that was all I could recover even when I remembered Arnold's 'In Kensington Gardens' as the source. Such a hopeless wreck is my immediately effective memory.[67]

Alfred Deakin could achieve peace, if only in fragments. Remembering Matthew Arnold, Deakin cast his mind back to a moment of imaginative familiarity, an Australian-born child of the British diaspora who identified with the poet strolling in London's Kensington Gardens. Deakin and Arnold did not really have 'place' in common: they shared, as Arnold concluded the poem, the quest to live and to achieve peace before they died.

Notes

[1] Alfred Deakin Papers, MS1540, Diaries Series 2, 1884–1916, National Library of Australia (hereafter NLA). For Deakin's life, see Norris, R. 1981, 'Deakin, Alfred (1856–1919)', *Australian Dictionary of Biography. Volume 8*, Melbourne University Press, pp. 248–56.

[2] Nethercote, J. R. (ed.) 2001, *Liberalism and the Australian Federation*, The Federation Press, Sydney; Roe, Jill (ed.) 1976, *Social Policy in Australia*, Cassell Australia, Sydney.

[3] 'List of Deakin's books before distribution', Deakin Papers, MS1540/4/692–721; La Nauze, John 1965, *Alfred Deakin, A Biography*, Melbourne University Press, Melbourne, p. 259.

[4] 'List of Deakin's books before distribution'; Gabay, Al 1992, *The Mystic Life of Alfred Deakin*, Cambridge University Press, Melbourne.

[5] 'List of Deakin's books before distribution'; Teich, Mikulas and Porter, Roy (eds) 1990, *Fin de siècle and its Legacy*, Cambridge University Press, Cambridge; Jay, Mike and Neve, Michael (eds) 1999, *1900: A fin de siècle reader*, Penguin, Harmondsworth.

[6] La Nauze, John 1968, *Alfred Deakin, Federated Australia, Selections from Letters to the Morning Post 1900–1910*, Melbourne University Press, Melbourne.

[7] Rickard, John 1996, *A Family Romance, The Deakins at Home*, Melbourne University Press, Melbourne.

[8] La Nauze, *Deakin, A Biography*, pp. 271–4.
[9] Ibid., pp. 640–1.
[10] Gabay, *The Mystic Life of Alfred Deakin*, p. 139.
[11] Hearn, Mark 2005, 'Examined suspiciously: Alfred Deakin, Eleanor Cameron and Australian liberal discourse in the 1911 referendum', *History Australia*, vol. 2, no. 3.
[12] Bauman, Zygmunt 1991, *Modernity and Ambivalence*, Polity Press, Cambridge, p. 15.
[13] Rickard, John 1984, *H. B. Higgins, The Rebel as Judge*, Allen & Unwin; Roe, Michael 1984, *Nine Australian Progressives*, University of Queensland Press, St Lucia; Macintyre, Stuart 1991, *A Colonial Liberalism*, Oxford University Press, Melbourne.
[14] La Nauze, John and Nurser, Elizabeth (eds) 1974, *Walter Murdoch and Alfred Deakin on Books and Men, Letters and Comments 1900–1918*, Melbourne University Press, Melbourne, pp. 9, 24, 27.
[15] Curthoys, Ann 2003, 'We've just started making national histories, and you want us to stop already?', in Antoinette Burton (ed.), *After the Imperial Turn: Thinking with and through the nation*, Duke University Press, Durham, p. 86.
[16] Deakin Diaries, MS1540, Items 2/29 1909, 2/30 1910, 2/31 1911; http://wells.classicauthors.net/FirstandLastThings/
[17] Deakin Diaries, MS1540, Items 2/32 1912; Holroyd, Michael 1989, *Bernard Shaw. Volume II. The Pursuit of Power, 1898–1918*, Chatto & Windus, London, pp. 72–80.
[18] La Nauze and Nurser, *Walter Murdoch*, pp. 29–30; Deakin Diaries, MS1540, Items 2/27 1907, 2/29 1909, 2/30 1910.
[19] Deakin Diaries, MS1540, Items 2/27 1907, 2/30 1910, 2/31 1911, 2/34, 1914.
[20] Deakin Diaries, MS1540, Items 2/27 1907, 2/31 1911; Carabine, Keith 1996, 'Under Western eyes', in J. H. Stape (ed.), *The Cambridge Companion to Joseph Conrad*, Cambridge University Press, Cambridge.
[21] Deakin Papers, MSS1540/3/281, A5 red-spine notebook, 5 November 1910, NLA, p. 70.
[22] 'List of Deakin's books before distribution'; La Nauze and Nurser, *Walter Murdoch*, p. 6.
[23] Deakin Diaries, MS1540, Item 2/31 1911.
[24] Cronin, Vincent 1989, *Paris on the Eve, 1900–1914*, Collins, London, pp. 375–6.
[25] La Nauze and Nurser, *Walter Murdoch*, p. 31.
[26] Heath, Deana 2001, 'Literary censorship, imperialism and the White Australia Policy', in Martyn Lyons and John Arnold (eds), *A History of the Book in Australia 1891–1945*, University of Queensland Press, St Lucia, p. 73.
[27] Deakin Diaries, MS1540, Item 2/29 1909.
[28] Singley, Carol J. 1995, *Edith Wharton, Matters of Mind and Spirit*, Cambridge University Press, Cambridge, pp. 10, 24–5.
[29] Gabay, *The Mystic Life of Alfred Deakin*, p. 11.
[30] Deakin Diaries, MS1540, Item 2/23 1903; Taylor, Anne 1992, *Annie Besant*, Oxford University Press, Oxford, pp. 281–2.
[31] Deakin Diaries, MS1540, Item 2/31 1911.
[32] Deakin Diaries, MS1540, Item 2/32 1912; Deakin Papers, MSS1540/3/281, A5 red-spine notebook, 7 October 1911, NLA, p. 151.
[33] Gabay, *The Mystic Life of Alfred Deakin*, p. 182; Boucher, David 1990, 'Practical hegelianism: Henry Jones's lecture tour of Australia', *Journal of the History of Ideas*, vol. 51, no. 3, pp. 424–5.
[34] Deakin Diaries, MS1540, Items 2/29 1909, 2/30 1910.
[35] La Nauze and Nurser, *Walter Murdoch*, p. 36; Boucher, 'Practical hegelianism', p. 434.
[36] Eucken, Rudolf 1912, *Christianity and the New Idealism*, Harper and Brothers, London, p. 134.
[37] Deakin Papers, MSS1540/3/281, A5 red-spine notebook, 15 October 1911, NLA, pp. 151, 163.
[38] Deakin Diaries, MS1540, Item 2/32 1912.
[39] Deakin Diaries, MS1540, Items 2/27 1907, 2/32 1912.
[40] Richardson, Robert D. 2006, *William James, In the Maelstrom of American Modernism*, Houghton Mifflin, New York, pp. 412, 485, 499; Gabay, *The Mystic Life of Alfred Deakin*, pp. 183–4.
[41] Deakin Papers, MSS1540/3/281, A5 red-spine notebook, 23 March 1912, NLA, pp. 202–3.
[42] Roe, *Nine Australian Progressives*.

[43] Lake, Marilyn 2007, '"The brightness of eyes and quiet assurance which seem to say American", Alfred Deakin's identification with Republican manhood', *Australian Historical Studies*, no. 129, April, pp. 34–6.
[44] Gabay, *The Mystic Life of Alfred Deakin*, p. 90.
[45] Deakin Diaries, MS1540, Item 2/31 1911.
[46] Ibid.
[47] Lake, 'The brightness of eyes', p. 50.
[48] La Nauze, *Deakin, A Biography*, pp. 483–4, 511.
[49] Deakin Diaries, MS1540, Items 2/26, 2/29 1909, 2/30 1910, 2/32 1912.
[50] La Nauze, *Deakin, A Biography*, pp. 26–7.
[51] La Nauze and Nurser, *Walter Murdoch*, pp. 92–8.
[52] La Nauze, *Deakin, A Biography*, p. 259.
[53] Ibid.; Deakin Diaries, MS1540, Items 2/30 1910, 2/31 1911, 2/32 1912.
[54] Inglis, K. S. 1979, 'Bean, Charles Edwin Woodrow (1879–1968)', *Australian Dictionary of Biography. Volume 7*, Melbourne University Press, pp. 226–9.
[55] Deakin Diaries, MS1540, Item 2/31 1911; Schreiner, Olive 1911, *Woman and Labour*, T. Fisher Unwin Ltd, London, pp. 26–7.
[56] Hearn, Mark 2006, 'Securing the man: narratives of gender and nation in the verdicts of Henry Bournes Higgins', *Australian Historical Studies*, no. 127, April.
[57] *Commonwealth Parliamentary Debates*, 30 July 1903, p. 2863.
[58] Cronin, *Paris on the Eve*, pp. 43–7.
[59] *Bookfellow*, 1 May 1912; *Salon*, July–August 1912, p. 18.
[60] Deakin Diaries, MS1540, Item 2/31 1911.
[61] Bergson, Henri 1911, 'Life and consciousness', *The Hibbert Journal*, vol. X, no.1, October, pp. 24, 40, 43.
[62] Deakin Papers, MSS1540/3/281, A5 red-spine notebook, 7–8 October 1911, NLA, p. 160; 18 November 1911, pp. 167–9.
[63] Lake, Marilyn 2003, 'White man's country: the trans-national history of a national project', *Australian Historical Studies*, no. 122, October, p. 360.
[64] Gabay, *The Mystic Life of Alfred Deakin*, p. 66.
[65] Bauman, *Modernity and Ambivalence*, ft. 1, p. 4.
[66] Deakin Papers, MSS1540/3/281, A5 red-spine notebook, 7 October 1911, NLA, p. 152.
[67] Ibid., p. 161.

Imagination

For the political philosopher Hannah Arendt, imagination was the essential element in the making of what she, along with Kant, called 'the world citizen'. Without imagination, it was impossible to develop that 'enormously enlarged empathy through which I could know what actually goes on in the mind of all others'—an enlarged empathy that underpinned judging or critical thinking. 'Critical thinking is possible only where the standpoint of all others are open to inspection,' she wrote in her *Lectures on Kant's Philosophy*.

> Hence, critical thinking while still a solitary business has not cut itself off from 'all others'...[By] force of imagination it makes the others present and thus moves potentially in a space which is public, open to all sides; in other words, it adopts the position of Kant's world citizen. To think with the enlarged mentality—that means you train your imagination to go visiting.[1]

Arendt saw the storyteller as the most potent stimulant of the imagination. By providing vivid pictures of the lives of others, the storyteller transported the reader into other worlds—in other words, the writer (or artist) 'train[ed] your imagination to go visiting'.

The writers and artists whose lives are discussed in this section all explore ways in which the imagination can go visiting, whether from 'home', as in the case of Eleanor Dark, or from 'away', as in the cases of Jean Devanny, Christina Stead and the gay artist David McDiarmid. Because these are real lives, however, or representations of real lives, this process of imaginative visiting is not simple, as Mary Besemeres shows us in her discussion of three English-speaking autobiographical writers who struggle with the problems of making a life in a non-English-speaking country.

Nancy Paxton explores the effects of travel, migration and ideas of internationalism derived from the communist movement in the 1930s on New Zealand novelist Jean Devanny. She traces her development from a somewhat superficial 'cosmopolitan' writer for the international imperial romance market to a serious, gendered 'transnational' subject, who conveyed in her 1935 novel, *The Virtuous Courtesan*, the complexity of colonial, imperial and national identities and of sexual, racial and class relationships. *The Virtuous Courtesan* does not merely exoticise the world of 1930s Sydney; instead, it takes us into a former colonial city whose quiet world is shattered by the outside world. 'Jews! Gentiles! Foreign words,' Devanny writes. 'Suddenly a gusty hate for the strange new forces pulsed and festered in the gigantic web of the world's social fabric surged up in Faith and was expelled in a gush of tears.'[2]

Susan Carson looks at the responses of two Australian writers, Christina Stead and Eleanor Dark, to that same period of world upheaval. Stead, the endless traveller, whose only 'home' is her lover, Bill Blake, and Eleanor Dark, who lived all her adult life in the Blue Mountains west of Sydney, have been characterised respectively as the transnational and the regional writer. Carson demonstrates, however, that both were responding in their work to the national and global pressures of a world approaching war. Stead, in her near-ethnography of international finance set in Paris, *House of All Nations*, and Dark, in her picture of settled and smug Sydney, *Waterway*, critique financial exploitation at the global and national levels and, like Jean Devanny, at the private level of gender relations. Imagination, in both cases, takes them from their local location into the larger world and then home again with a greater understanding of the complex relationship between 'home' and 'away'.

Mary Besemeres points to the fact that most travel writing is about looking rather than listening: Mary Louise Pratt's 'Imperial Eyes' or Paul Theroux's 'seeing-man'. Travelling, in the meaning Arendt gives it, is much more difficult and the power dynamics are more complex, she argues, when it comes to 'language travel'. Examining Gillian Bouras's *A Foreign Wife*, Sarah Turnbull's *Almost French* and John Mateer's *Semar's Cave*, Besemeres demonstrates the difficulties of communication, not just of words, but more importantly of feelings, that inhibit the traveller's ability to 'go visiting'.

The gay artist David McDiarmid, whose creative response to his chosen life in New York is examined by Sally Gray, had no such problems when he visited New York in 1977 and later moved there permanently. He shared not only a language with his fellow New Yorkers; he had already inhabited the city in his imagination, from the advertisements of his childhood to the accounts of gay life in American gay liberationist publications he read as a teenager. 'New York' allowed him to make a life and develop an art that was both 'mobile and located', neither 'Australian' nor 'American'.

Notes

[1] Arendt, Hannah 1978, 'Appendix/judging: excerpts from lectures on Kant's political philosophy', *The Life of the Mind*, edited by Mary McCarthy, Harcourt, New York, pp. 255–72, esp. 257.
[2] Devanny, Jean 1935, *The Virtuous Courtesan*, Macaulay, New York, pp. 143–4.

Chapter 13

From cosmopolitan romance to transnational fiction: re-reading Jean Devanny's Australian novels

Nancy L. Paxton

> For that was how she had thought of Australia; that was how she had read of it; the land of the free. And freedom was the whole body of romance, its seed, its breath, its growth and its fulfillment.
>
> — Jean Devanny, *Out of Such Fires* [1]

When Jean Devanny (1894–1962) left New Zealand in 1929 bound for Sydney, she considered Australia 'merely a transit point' and planned to travel on to England, believing it to be 'a more favourable location for a novelist'. Devanny gradually came to accept Australia as her home, as Carole Ferrier argues, because of her 'double commitment' to the Communist Party of Australia and to her development as a writer.[2] While Ferrier's pioneering scholarship and definitive biography offer invaluable insights into Devanny's life and writing, I will suggest another perspective on both by exploring how her experiences in Australia transformed her into a 'transnational' subject. Many scholars who have surveyed Devanny's fiction, including Ferrier, Drusilla Modjeska, Susan Sheridan and Nicole Moore, have accepted her assertion that *Sugar Heaven* (1936) marked a turning point in her career. By comparing Devanny's fourth novel, *Riven* (1929), a romance describing modern urban life in Wellington, with *The Virtuous Courtesan*, published in New York in 1935 though banned in Australia until 1958, I will show that the process of transformation began at least two years earlier, but the suppression of this notorious novel has partially blocked our view. By recognising that Devanny was a writer who struggled to understand her own hybridity and transnational ties, we can more fully appreciate her formal innovations and daring treatment of female sexuality, marriage, reproduction, art and urban and rural culture in *The Virtuous Courtesan* and later works.

Figure 13.1: Jean Devanny, 1920s.

James Cook University Library, courtesy Jean Hurd.

Most of Devanny's novels about New Zealand seem to conform to the conventions of popular romance, but they also illustrate what I propose to call her 'cosmopolitan' strategy as a writer. In these romances, Devanny attempts to create and address an international audience of sophisticated English-language readers by frequently alluding to well-known English texts. While this strategy apparently convinced her English editors that her novels could be commercially viable, it forced her to reinscribe British imperial values, often in spite of herself. In *The Virtuous Courtesan* and the novels about Australia that followed it, in contrast, Devanny abandoned this strategy and refashioned the conventions of romance in order to represent her more complex transnational perspective on the country she began to consider her home.

Riven invites comparison with *The Virtuous Courtesan* because both novels include characters who illustrate the mobility, cultural sophistication and psychological ambivalence of the transnational subjects described, for example, by Homi K. Bhabha in *The Location of Culture*.[3] By the time Devanny wrote *The Virtuous Courtesan*, she had achieved her long-deferred dream of international travel. After joining the Communist Party of Australia in 1930, she was selected by the leadership as their envoy to the first International Women's Conference of the Workers International Relief Organisations held in conjunction with the Eighth World Congress of Workers in Berlin in 1931. Having found her voice during these years as a powerful public speaker, Devanny was hailed at the conference as the representative of Australian women by well-known feminists such as Charlotte Despard and Clara Zetkin. After the congress, Devanny visited her daughter in Moscow, and travelled to Leningrad, Samarkand and other locations in the Soviet Union, where she witnessed the emergence of a revolutionary culture in which women were extended 'equal property rights', in which mothers had rights to claim their children, in which divorce was 'very easy, and where abortion was legal'.[4] In December 1932, she made a brief visit to London, but her travels ultimately prompted her to conclude that neither Moscow nor London could be her 'home'. She wrote, for example, 'Had Russia been Paradise, I should still, I felt, want to return to my own land and my own people.'[5] After her return to Sydney in January 1932, however, Devanny recognised that she was deeply estranged from her husband and hardly understood her own ambivalent desires. At this point in her career, then, Devanny had created a life that corresponded with the definition of the 'transnational' subject that Desley Deacon, Penny Russell and Angela Woollacott describe in the introduction to this volume, as her life was 'lived in motion...crossed oceans and borders...drew emotional energy, ideological conviction or practical understanding from eclectic, transnational experience'.[6]

Considered in this context, *The Virtuous Courtesan* marks a 'point of change' in Devanny's fiction, illustrating how she began to write more self-consciously, not only as a communist writer who accepted the conventions of 1930s socialist realism but as a gendered, passionate and psychologically divided transnational subject. More specifically, this truly extraordinary novel tests the universalising abstractions of Marxist class analysis by particularising the local conditions of a wide range of men and women living in Sydney during the early 1930s. By juxtaposing the domestic arrangements of gay and straight, as well as bourgeois and working-class, couples in bohemian art circles of Sydney, Devanny demonstrates that her Australian characters, like the rest of us, live in what Paul Rabinow calls the 'in-between'.[7] This novel reveals therefore not only the 'divided loyalties' that Woollacott identifies in the Australian and New Zealand women writers who recognise that 'colonial, imperial, and national identities' are less congruent than they once assumed,[8] it represents men and women who experience themselves as the hybrid and deeply divided transnational subjects that Bhabha has described more generally.

Duckworth, the progressive, London-based press, published *Riven*, the fourth of Devanny's novels, and the book reveals several signs of her efforts to address a cosmopolitan readership. Like many ambitious writers of her generation based in New Zealand, Devanny initially sought publication in England, and, by lucky accident, Duckworth accepted *The Butcher Shop* for publication in 1925. Undeterred when Devanny's first novel was banned in New Zealand in 1926, Duckworth subsequently published her interracial romance, *Lenore Divine* (1926), and her more autobiographical *Dawn Beloved* (1929), before *Riven* appeared under its imprint in 1929.[9]

Like several of the novels that Devanny herself later dismissed as 'petty-bourgeois twaddle',[10] *Riven* seems to present itself as a simple escapist imperial romance. It begins with a dreamy generalised description of 'a flowery town on the edge of a Southern Sea', though it is soon clear that Devanny is describing life in Wellington after the Great War.[11] To be sure, *Riven* conforms in several ways to the class-based formula fiction marketed in the 1920s to a mostly female domestic and international English-speaking audience, which Hsu-Ming Teo, John McAleer and others have characterised.[12] *Riven* also suggests, however, especially in its frank treatment of modern female sexuality and abortion, that Devanny hoped to engage a more progressive cosmopolitan audience. One sign of her success was that Duckworth was able to sell the rights to distribute *Riven* in the United States to Macaulay, a New York-based publisher that catered to the new youth market, a shift neatly encapsulated when they changed the title of this novel to *Unchastened Youth*.[13]

Riven focuses on the attractive, mature middle-class mother, Marigold Jerring, and describes her vague unease as she watches her three adult children prepare to leave their natal home. Initially, Marigold seems to be a modern advertiser's dream: she is an ideal consumer who is busy acting on the advice given by Marie

Stopes, among others, that women can enhance their sex life by increasing their consumption of luxury goods. Married to a prosperous business man, Marigold has inherited enough money of her own so that she can afford to buy elegant clothes for her daughters and subsidise her son's education at an art school in England. Initially, she has neither the language nor the inclination to recognise the emptiness of her marriage, though her children all know that their father is sexually involved with an attractive younger woman.

Unlike the apolitical heroines in most mass-market imperial romances, however, Devanny's Marigold ponders questions raised decades later by feminists such as Betty Friedan, when she wonders, for example, 'What possibilities life offered for the club women, for the lost sheep from domesticity's fold, for the middle-aged unmarried and the mothers like herself, whose young had grown up and refused any longer to be scolded and slapped and put to bed.' She even begins to contemplate 'what a force they could be' for progressive social change in the world.[14] Likewise, because *Riven* ends with the dissolution of Marigold's marriage, it departs significantly from the imperial romances produced by Mills and Boon and other British presses specialising in this genre.

In contrast with more conventional imperial romances, *Riven*, like all of Devanny's New Zealand novels, highlights the dramatic and widespread changes in sexual mores in the postwar urban consumer economy of the 1920s. *Riven* shows how younger women were able to elect a new relationship with the reproductive order and with the capitalist system by reorienting themselves with the ethics of possessive individualism that propelled it. Devanny invited her readers to compare her heroine with the 'New Woman' who appeared in British novels of this period by her frequent allusions to Galsworthy's best-selling *Forsyte Saga* (1906–22). While Devanny clearly uses these references to establish a more familiar literary terrain for her English readers, they also highlight the generational differences between Marigold's more Edwardian, class-specific and myopic view of the 'woman's position under the marriage system' and her daughters' more modern emancipated views.[15] Indeed, Lilith and Fay Jerring, like their aunt Justine, resemble the 'spectacular modern women' that Liz Conor has described in popular Australian and American novels and films of the 1920s rather than British models of the New Woman of the prewar era.[16]

Lilith, for example, is well educated, teaches in a multiracial kindergarten in Wellington and has the skills and disposition that will allow her to live a life of self-sufficient independence. With her dangerous name, Lilith 'firmly declares she will never marry' and is 'so outspokenly grave-mannered, so composedly alert, compact and direct...so unobtrusively studious and brave' that readers are advised to accept her at her word.[17] By the end of the novel, Lilith announces her plans to leave New Zealand in order to study for an advanced degree in the United States. Ironically, by the time *Riven* was published, Lilith's ambiguous asexuality was perhaps even more legible to her readers because of the spotlight cast on lesbian sexuality by Radclyffe Hall's notorious censorship trial in England in 1928 and by the successful appeal in a New York appellate court in 1929 that legalised the circulation of *The Well of Loneliness* in the United States.[18]

Lilith's younger sister, Fay, is a beautiful, cool, 'jazz' girl who enjoys life in the cinemas and cabarets of Wellington and takes for granted 'her mother's caresses as she took her meals—and also her constant service'.[19] Her father's favourite, Fay feels no particular desire to support herself and, like Galsworthy's Irene, she plans to gamble on the marriage market rather than pursue a career like her sister's. In contrast with Irene's ostensible success, Fay's calculating efforts to use her sex appeal to engineer a marriage to the dissolute gambler Martin Slurrick fail when he abruptly leaves town.

It is the transnational character, Justine, Marigold's worldly, sophisticated sister-in-law, who perhaps most clearly reveals the originality and cosmopolitan subversiveness that, no doubt, helped *Riven* earn a place on Duckworth's list. Justine became a transnational subject when she was banished from her brother's home nearly 20 years earlier for some unmentionable sexual sin; she then moved to Australia where she developed a successful line of beauty shops. On her unexpected return to New Zealand, Justine displays herself as a 'product' of her own parlours;[20] she wears skilfully applied make-up, marcels her hair and has preserved a youthful appearance that belies her age of thirty-six. In this respect, Justine resembles the 'spent and slightly soiled flapper' that, according to Liz Conor, expressed some of the ambivalence towards the youth culture of the 1920s.[21]

Most of all, *Riven* differs from imperial romances because it includes a detailed description of Fay's home abortion and dramatises what happens when modern sexually active women refuse the melodramatic role of sexual victim. Devanny's novel contrasts in this regard not only with many Australian romances but with American novels such as, for example, Theodore Dreiser's controversial *An American Tragedy*, published in 1926 in New York by Donald Friede.[22] Because Dreiser suggested that his heroine had premarital sex, because he described her failed effort to obtain an abortion and dramatised her subsequent murder, his novel was banned in Boston and many other localities in the United States, where abortion was outlawed and where literature about it was suppressed under the *Comstock Law* of 1873. Since Devanny's novel unapologetically describes Fay Jerring's successful home abortion in painful detail but allows her to survive relatively unscathed, her publishers in England and in the United States risked similar suppressions. *Riven*, however, cleverly skirts at least three issues that made *An American Tragedy* so provocative: it focuses on a wealthy upper-class family in the exotic world of New Zealand, which was relatively unfamiliar to most of her readers, it avoids the melodramatic consequences of a failed abortion that in Dreiser's novel results in Roberta Alden's murder and her lover's trial, and, perhaps most of all, it omits any reference to organised religion. Because of these strategies, *Riven* was able to pass as an escapist romance; it circulated freely in the United States, the United Kingdom, New Zealand and Australia, where it won a honourable mention for a literary prize.[23]

Devanny's *The Virtuous Courtesan*, her ninth novel, published nearly six years later in New York by Macaulay, showed the marks of her break from the fundamentally individualist paradigm of the romances and mysteries she had been writing to supplement her income and support her family. Duckworth declined to publish *The Virtuous Courtesan*, and Macaulay marketed it in the United States to appeal to a new niche market for sexy popular fiction that it began to develop successfully in the 1930s.[24] With its deliberately provocative title, *The Virtuous Courtesan* included the following advertising copy in the front matter:

> Jean Devanny, the Australian iconoclast, has a sharp disturbing way of stripping character to the buff without sparing or retouching the deformities. Her new novel pitilessly exposes a group of people representing all classes of life in Sydney. In a photographic drama she investigates the elemental sources of their misbehavior and the manner in which passion, greed and circumstances kick the stuffing out of all the ostensible moral values. Incidentally, the plight of unemployed men dependent on women with jobs or the means of support is a part of the theme of the story. The main theme is the cumulating dilemma of Sharon, a successful dancer and artist's model. Married to a worthless sot whom she despises and supports, but is afraid to divorce, she reluctantly is falling in love with an unemployed laborer, Jack Powell. Jack's handsome physique and dynamic qualities are a fatal jolt to Sharon's assumption that men are mere incidents in her life to satisfy a normal hunger. The jobless Apollo, however, has his own ideas and expectations concerning a woman evidently in love. And since the woman has no inclination to assume the discomfort of what passes for virtue, a dark and heavy predicament is brewing.[25]

Readers of this novel argued that Devanny abandoned some of the conventions of romance in order to conform more closely with the social realism endorsed by the Communist Party.[26] While I agree that the reportage style is undoubtedly a strong influence, I will show that *The Virtuous Courtesan* not only presents a more layered, systematic and transnational view of labour practices in Sydney than is represented in her earlier fiction, it defies a straight Marxist analysis by showing how gender, sexuality and 'race' contest class identity and related notions of sexual 'freedom' and pleasure. As the title suggests, Devanny's main focus in this novel is on female spectacularisation, marriage and divorce, and prostitution in the metropolitan world of Sydney in the aftermath of the global economic collapse in 1929.

Abortion is mentioned in *The Virtuous Courtesan*, but it is neither a central theme, as it is in *Riven*, nor a significant element in the plot, as it is in several of Devanny's other New Zealand novels. The couples included in *The Virtuous Courtesan* come not only from the ranks of the petty bourgeoisie—characters who are the main players in most of Devanny's New Zealand novels—they come from Sydney's nouveau riche, from the working classes, the unemployed and the underclass. Sharon Armand, the 'virtuous courtesan' of the title, is a transnational subject like Justine, but with a wider international experience. Like many other performers in the 1920s and 1930s, she established a successful career as a self-supporting professional dancer by performing for various international audiences in London, Paris and New York. In detailing the transnational arc of Sharon's career and describing her performances as a young dancer in London, Devanny describes how Sharon learned to exploit her physical beauty and display her nearly naked body to her mostly male audiences. In other words, Sharon became very successful in presenting herself as a 'spectacle' in the newly commodified spaces that became available for the 'spectacular modern women' in the 1920s, as Liz Conor described:

> In effect this visually intensified scene provided new conditions for the feminine subject. To appear within it was to literally make a spectacle of oneself, to configure oneself as spectacle, to apprehend oneself and be apprehended as image. Some types of the Modern Woman which emerged at this time—the Screen star, Beauty Contestant, and Flapper—were manifestly, though not solely constructed around their visibility.[27]

Moreover, in describing how Sharon self-consciously refashions herself to appeal to international audiences, Devanny invites parallels between performers and writers such as herself who sell their fiction in international markets. As a result of her exposure and mobility, Sharon met and married her relatively wealthy husband, Roy Armand, and thus gained access to a more respectable and comfortable middle-class life in Sydney, though their marriage was unhappy and she stayed with her husband ostensibly for her daughter's sake. Devanny reinforces the parallels between performers and other artists by comparing the Armands' stormy marriage with the equally volatile marriage of the forty-eight-year-old assimilated Jewish sculptor, Foyer, and his much younger, jealous, fashion-obsessed and hard-drinking wife, Inez.

Devanny departs radically from the conventions of imperial romance in this novel not only by detailing how the global economic crisis determines the working conditions of a range of 'culture workers', but by demonstrating how homosexuality and race complicate class identity. *The Virtuous Courtesan* was unique in Australian fiction at the time because it included a gay male and a lesbian couple, reflecting, in part, Devanny's exposure to a bohemian urban culture in her Sydney neighbourhood near King's Cross as well as her efforts to organise the artists and writers associated with Sydney's Workers' Art Club in the three years before the novel's publication. Louis Ransome is the handsome, cross-dressing son of a wealthy department-store entrepreneur, who lives in a well-appointed bachelor flat with Rich Loveday, an amateur boxer with a growing reputation. To this mix of Sydney's rich and famous, Devanny adds a lesbian couple: Rosa Burnham, a wealthy divorcee and Mae-West look-alike, who lives in the 'pretentious Hollywood-like environ of Elizabeth Bay' with Faith Selsey, a beautiful professional cellist, who once reciprocated her patron's affections but now finds her partner's 'unwanted affection' to be 'detestable', though she is reluctant to resume her less-comfortable life as a self-supporting musician and teacher.[28] The social and psychological issues raised by these hybrid characters elude a straight class-based Marxist analysis.

Devanny compares the domestic arrangements of all these couples with the sexual arrangements contemplated by Rosa's working-class maid, Edith, and her unemployed lover, Bill, who lives as a squatter in an abandoned building with his friend Jack Powell. Jack recognises explicitly how class determines marriage practices when he tells Sharon:

> I haven't been long among your set but I've found out that marriage is only a game with you. It's not a game in our world but it's on the bust, all the same. The women are keeping the men. Nearly all the youngsters are just pairing, can't settle down because there's no work. They marry, under rotten conditions, only when the girl is in trouble and they don't know how to procure an abortion.[29]

Jack nonetheless shrugs off any obligation to share his knowledge about birth control, apart from advising his friend not to marry in haste. When Bill subsequently marries Edith, overcoming his reluctance to being supported by her hard work as a maid, Devanny makes it clear that his choice is prompted by his sexual desire rather than an unplanned pregnancy since Rosa has explained birth control to Edith and has referred her to a doctor who supplied it. By the end of the novel, Jack ironically follows Bill's example when he marries Sharon after her divorce from Roy is finalised, though he knows, as he ruefully observes, that he, too, will live 'on the surplus of a woman of another class'.[30]

Devanny moves beyond the conventions of imperial romance in a third way in this novel by exposing the material base of Australian marriage practices through her inclusion of two prostitutes who work entirely outside the marriage and property system, showing how difficult their lives become after the passage of the *Consorting Act* in Sydney.[31] Poppy Laughlin is a thirty-year-old prostitute who has two 'steadies': the man who fathered her son and the priest who eventually agrees to support her so she can retire from her profession. Poppy has given shelter to Jo Fallon, who, at sixteen years of age, is able to support herself by successfully exploiting her johns' preference for young women. Jo's life becomes complicated when she meets the handsome Jack Powell after she stops him on the street and asks him to 'buy her'; after he pays for some food for her and they have sex, she promptly falls in love with him, though he doesn't even consider her as a potential marriage partner, showing that, for women such as her, romantic love and marriage are luxuries they can't afford. Poppy's example, like Sharon's, ultimately challenges the heterosexual norms of much Marxist analysis, since, as Poppy explains, for instance, heterosexual desire does not come naturally to her: 'It was the hate, mixed up with the sex. I hated every man I had even while I had him.'[32]

Indeed, *The Virtuous Courtesan* draws explicit parallels between marriage and prostitution, on one hand, and marriage and the patronage system supporting the arts, on the other, showing how both are undermined by the worldwide economic crisis. Even the well-established and widely respected sculptor, Foyer, recognises that 'the cultural monopoly of the upper classes was a thing of the past',[33] though he protests, nonetheless, when he feels compelled to prostitute his talents in order to make a living. He observes, for example, 'It is the accursed showmanship, this prostitution of a man's finest instincts, the working on order at the command of the commercial riff-raff…that ruins a man.'[34] While Foyer wishfully proclaims that in artistic circles '[t]here are no wives',[35] Devanny reveals Foyer's self-deluding fantasies for what they are by describing the double binds of Australian divorce law in the 1930s when he tries to escape from his failed marriage with Inez. At the same time, Devanny demonstrates how women are disadvantaged as a group by the sexual double standards of divorce laws when Sharon tries to establish grounds for a divorce from her womanising, alcoholic husband, Roy Armand.

While Devanny explores the parallels between art production and prostitution throughout the novel, she insists at the same time that the spectacularisation of women in the 1930s narrowed the gap between female artists such as Sharon and prostitutes such as Poppy and Jo. Sharon recognises the artificial separation between the public and private sexual economy when, during a visit to Jo and Poppy, she insists, 'We're all professionals.'[36] Likewise, by exposing the ugly economic inequalities and personal exploitation disguised by the conventions of romance, Devanny insists that marriage and divorce laws simply cover over the naked prostitution of many legally sanctioned sexual relationships. In fact, she shows that marriages such as Foyer's and Armand's harbour the same potential for sexual exploitation and emotional or physical abuse that might be found in the informal domestic arrangements of Rosa and Faith or Louis and Rich.

Finally, *The Virtuous Courtesan* displays Devanny's transnational perspective not only on art, gender and marriage, but on homosexuality and race, when she describes how several of her characters recognise and respond to the fascist turn in politics at home and abroad in the 1930s. Early in the novel, Rosa Burnham identifies her contested class position when she remarks, 'What's this claptrap about class? I'm waiting for someone to tell me what class I belong to.'[37] By the end of the novel, Devanny has shown that it is not only Rosa's sexuality that complicates her class identity and national affiliation, it is her Jewish heritage, which Rosa equates with race.[38] Rosa signals her political awakening as a Jew in a world on the eve of the Holocaust when she announces that she plans to leave Sydney to learn more about her people. Faith, pushed into a panic by Rosa's newfound identity, privately considers her options:

> Surely Rosa would never take an interest in politics...Might not this side to Rosa be outside her sphere of influence? It foreboded power, a deep well of inner consciousness which might rise up between her comforts and herself. Jews! Gentiles! Foreign words. Suddenly a gusty hate for the strange new forces pulsing and festering in the gigantic web of the world's social fabric surged up in Faith and was expelled in a gush of tears.[39]

Afraid of 'foreign words' such as 'Jew' and 'gentile', Faith is unwilling to leave Sydney with Rosa and, as a result, she faces a return to comparative 'poverty again' as a self-supporting professional musician.[40]

By the final episode of the novel, then, Rosa has recognised herself as a transnational subject and has pledged to act on this knowledge, even if it means the dissolution of her partnership with Faith. Moreover, as Louis sadly notes, there are a lot of 'migrations' in Sharon's social circle at this point.[41] The recently divorced Inez is on her way from Cairo to Palestine, and Rich is soon to depart for the United States to promote his boxing career. By describing the dissolution of all of the bourgeois marriages and homosexual partnerships that she has described, Devanny provides further evidence of her effort to transform the genre conventions of romance. Moreover, the long-term prognosis for the two new marriages that mark the end of this novel is hardly promising. Edith, who is now married to Bill, is about to lose her job as Rosa's maid, and Jack Powell has begun to suspect that Sharon will soon be unfaithful to him. Although the final scenes of the novel demonstrate that Jack, too, has become a transnational subject as a result of his marriage and the capital it offers, he is far from comfortable in his cross-class marriage. As Faith tells Sharon, 'You're a funny pair. Jack grows grimmer every day and you get more contented. What's the secret?'[42] *The Virtuous Courtesan* therefore concludes by showing that although Rosa and Jack have recognised their hybrid identity and achieved a sophisticated international perspective on their lives, their work and their freedoms, they also experience the political and psychological ambivalence that Sharon Armand Powell embodies and exhibits as a transnational subject. Even after Devanny turns her attention next to the working-class Australians who populate her best-known novel, *Sugar Heaven*, she continues to demonstrate how the class identity of her characters is 'riven' by their gender, sexuality and ethnicity.

In conclusion, the radically different fortunes of *Riven* and *The Virtuous Courtesan* remind us that the products of the 'romance industry' do not always flow freely across national frontiers. Devanny's *Riven* remained unchallenged probably because it resembled a mass-marketed romance even though a closer reading shows that it addressed a more sophisticated and politically liberal cosmopolitan audience. Because *The Virtuous Courtesan* explicitly advocated sexual as well as political and economic liberation and critiqued the racism that was central to the escapist imperial romances that pleased and titillated their mainly white readership, it was refused publication in England and recognised as dangerous contraband as soon as it landed on Australian shores, where it was promptly banned from 1935 until 1958. Instructed by her second experience with book banning, Devanny subsequently elected to participate in an alternative to the capitalist culture economy in 1935 when she began to write *Sugar Heaven*; she contracted to publish it not with Duckworth or Macaulay but with the Sydney-based Modern Publishers, a press that produced local editions of banned communist works and other texts. Devanny's later novels about Australia therefore reveal her legacy as a writer who is vividly aware of the psychological ambiguity, material embodiment and idealist promise that expresses her embattled stance as a woman, communist, transnational subject and internationally recognised novelist.

Notes

[1] Devanny, Jean 1934, *Out of Such Fires*, Macaulay, New York, p. 29.

[2] Ferrier, Carole 1998, 'Fiction in transition', in Bruce Bennett and Jennifer Strauss (eds), *The Oxford Literary History of Australia*, Oxford University Press, Melbourne, p. 195. In *Jean Devanny: Romantic revolutionary* (1999, Melbourne University Press, Melbourne), Carole Ferrier documents the Devanny family's financial struggles, Jean's embattled marriage, her children's and her own increasing involvement with the Communist Party of Australia, her work for the party as speaker and organiser, her sexual liaisons with several party members, her trip to Germany and Russia in 1931, her separation from her husband and her deepening appreciation for the workers in rural Queensland. See also Store, Ron 1981, 'Devanny, Jane (Jean) (1894–1962)', *Australian Dictionary of Biography. Volume 8*, Melbourne University Press, pp. 295–6; Ferres, Kay 1994, 'Written on the body: Jean Devanny, sexuality and censorship', *Hecate*, vol. 20, no. 1, May, pp. 123–31; and Moore, Nicole 2002, 'Interrupting maternal citizenship: birth control in mid-wave women's writing', *Australian Feminist Studies*, vol. 17, no. 38, pp. 151–64.

[3] Bhabha, Homi K. 1994, *The Location of Culture*, Routledge, London and New York, p. 5. I have also benefited from studies including Walkowitz, Rebecca 2006, *Cosmopolitan Style: Modernism beyond the nation*, Columbia University Press, New York; and Cheah, Pheng and Robbins, Bruce (eds) 1998, *Cosmopolitics: Thinking and feeling beyond the nation*, University of Minnesota Press, Minneapolis—which define 'cosmopolitan' in interesting new ways. Devanny, of course, knew of Marx's critique of cosmopolitanism in *The Manifesto of the Communist Party* by the time she wrote this novel.

[4] Ferrier, *Jean Devanny*, p. 88.

[5] Ibid., p. 83.

[6] I thank Desley Deacon, Penny Russell and Angela Woollacott for sharing their introduction to *Transnational Ties* with me. My essay is part of a larger study that considers how Jean Devanny, D. H. Lawrence and Radclyffe Hall re-imagined authorship and international readerships in response to government censorship.

[7] Rabinow, Paul 1986, 'Representations are social facts: modernity and post-modernity in anthropology', in James Clifford and George E. Marcus (eds), *Writing Culture: The poetics and politics of ethnography*, University of California Press, Berkeley, p. 258.

[8] Woollacott, Angela 2001, *To Try Her Fortunes in London: Australian women, colonialism and modernity*, Oxford University Press, Oxford, pp. 141–3.

[9] For details on the banning of this novel, see the introduction and afterword by editor Heather Roberts in the 1981 edition of Devanny's *The Butcher Shop* ([1925], Oxford University Press, Auckland and Oxford).

[10] Ferrier, *Jean Devanny*, p. 115.

[11] Devanny, Jean 1930, *Riven*, Duckworth, London.

[12] For discussions about the international readership for colonial romances, see Teo, Hsu-Ming 2003, 'The romance of white nations: imperialism, popular culture, and national histories', in Antoinette Burton (ed.), *After the Imperial Turn: Thinking with and through the nation*, Duke University Press, Durham, pp. 279–92. On British publishers' successful class and gender-based niche marketing of formula romances, see McAleer, Joseph 1992, *Popular Reading and Publishing in Britain, 1914–1950*, Clarendon, Oxford; and Dixon, Jay 1999, *The Romance Fiction of Mills and Boon, 1909–1990s*, UCL Press, London.

[13] On the youth market in the 1920s in the United States, see Morrison, Mark 2001, *The Public Face of Modernism: Little magazines, audiences, and reception, 1905–1920*, University of Wisconsin Press, Madison, pp. 133–56.

[14] Devanny, *Riven*, p. 282.

[15] Ibid., p. 142.

[16] Conor, Liz 2004, *The Spectacular Modern Woman: Feminine visibility in the 1920s*, Indiana University Press, Bloomington, p. 7. On the 'New Woman' in British fiction, see Ardis, Ann 1990, *New Women, New Novels: Feminism and early modernism*, Rutgers University Press, New Brunswick.

[17] Devanny, *Riven*, pp. 9, 12.

[18] On Hall's trial, see, for example, Doan, Laura and Prosser, Jay (eds) 2001, *Palatable Poison: Critical perspectives on* The Well of Loneliness, Columbia University Press, New York. On the trial in the United States, see Emery, Kim 2002, *The Lesbian Index: Pragmatism and lesbian subjectivity in the twentieth-century United States*, SUNY Press, Albany.

[19] Devanny, *Riven*, p. 65.

[20] Ibid., p. 131.

[21] Conor, *The Spectacular Modern Woman*, p. 223.

[22] Boyer, Paul S. 1968, *Purity in Print: The Vice-Society Movement and book censorship in America*, Scribner's, New York, pp. 192–5.

[23] Devanny, Jean 1986, *Point of Departure: The autobiography of Jean Devanny*, Edited by Carole Ferrier, University of Queensland Press, St Lucia, pp. 94–5.

[24] Gertzman, Jay A. 1999, *Bookleggers and Smuthounds: The trade in erotica, 1920–1940*, University of Pennsylvania at Philadelphia, Philadelphia, pp. 70–1.

[25] Devanny, Jean 1935, *The Virtuous Courtesan*, Macaulay, New York.

[26] Ferrier, *Jean Devanny*, p. 71; and Ferrier, Carole 1998, 'Jean Devanny and the romance of the revolution', in Carole Ferrier and Rebecca Phelan (eds), *The Point of Change: Marxism/Australia/history/theory*, University of Queensland, Brisbane, pp. 125–33. See also Nicole Moore's brilliant analysis of abortion in Australian realist fiction (2001, 'Politics of cliché: sex, class, and abortion in Australian realism', *Modern Fiction Studies*, vol. 47, no. 1, Spring, pp. 69–91).

[27] Conor, *The Spectacular Modern Woman*, p. 7.

[28] Devanny, *The Virtuous Courtesan*, p. 192.

[29] Ibid., p. 239.

[30] Ibid., p. 269.

[31] Sheridan (*Along the Faultlines*, pp. 51–68) usefully discusses the symbolic importance of references to prostitution in other Australian women's writing of this period. See also Dixon, Robert 1998, 'Literature

and melodrama', in Bruce Bennett and Jennifer Strauss (eds), *The Oxford Literary History of Australia*, Oxford University Press, Melbourne, pp. 66–88.
[32] Devanny, *The Virtuous Courtesan*, p. 149.
[33] Ibid., p. 98.
[34] Ibid., p. 98.
[35] Ibid., p. 43.
[36] Ibid., p. 69.
[37] Ibid., p. 19.
[38] Ibid., p. 141.
[39] Ibid., pp. 143–4.
[40] Ibid., p. 282.
[41] Ibid., p. 281.
[42] Ibid., p. 279.

Chapter 14

Paris and beyond: the transnational/national in the writing of Christina Stead and Eleanor Dark

Susan Carson

In July 1937, two Australian writers left their respective homes and steamed across the Pacific and Indian Oceans to opposite coasts of the United States. Sailing west from Europe, Christina Stead (1902–83) and her partner, Bill Blake, reached New York on the *SS Aquitania*, while on the *Niagara*, Eleanor Dark (1901–85), with husband, Eric, crossed the Pacific to the west coast and made their way east to New York. Both women were in the great metropolis, the eternal city of the New World, but they did not meet. They had, in fact, lived in adjoining suburbs on Sydney Harbour a decade earlier, and there, as in New York, their paths did not cross. For a time in the 1930s, however, they shared an imaginative space that was informed by their Sydney adolescence and stimulated by inter-war global political and social change.

In the following discussion, I examine ways in which the writers conceptualised transnational experience in their fiction and negotiated the complexities of their own relationships with 'home'. The transnational functions as a barometer of their encounters with aspects of modernity and indicates that their lives, and those of their readers, were increasingly complicated by the transmission of new cultural, political and social convictions that swirled around the world in the 1930s. Dark and Stead represented and influenced this transnational experience (albeit in different ways) and this focus provides a way of tracing imaginative connections between major Australian writers whose work is often discussed in quite different literary contexts. My examination of Dark's *Waterway* and Stead's *House of All Nations* indicates that the tensions of the transnational/national are important emotional, political and thematic dimensions of their fiction and an emphasis on the transnational opens a space for making connections between seemingly diverse Australian writing.

Although the women never met, their imaginative intersections resulted in narratives that intersected on questions of race, class and gender. Later in their careers, their lives would touch—but at arm's length: Stead was a manuscript reader in the United States for Dark's *The Timeless Land* (she imagined Dark as an 'old girl'),[1] while Dark was asked, in 1952, to supply a reference for Stead's application for a Commonwealth Literary Fund award (which she did).[2] Points of connection, however, keep surfacing, especially in the context of the fraught geopolitics of the 1930s, when both writers understood that war might eventuate.

Figure 14.1: Christina Stead, 1940s.

National Library of Australia: nla.pic-an24717059.

Figure 14.2: Eleanor Dark, ca 1945.

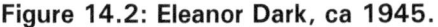

Max Dupain, photographer, Mitchell Library, State Library of New South Wales.

History records that in early 1937 Stead was uncertain as to her next move after nearly a decade away from Australia. She wrote from the cold of a London January that she was back in Britain and had completed a novel 'about banking and full of crooks'.[3] She wondered just where she would live next: revolution had forced an early exit from Spain, a return to Paris was unlikely and although there was work in Moscow and Manhattan she preferred England, despite the climate. A few months later, life changed again and she moved to New York, where, in 1938, her virtuoso critique of international finance was published, the Paris-inspired *House of All Nations*. In Australia, Dark also had completed a novel, *Waterway*, a homage to Sydney, also published in 1938. Dark's two-month visit to the United States in 1937 was to be the only time she left the Australian continent. She returned, eagerly, to Katoomba and the large mountain home that became her base for the rest of her life, with the exception of winter retreats to a farm in Montville, in south-east Queensland.

In future accounts of their lives, the women would be ascribed very different positions in Australian literary history. Stead is confirmed as the most transnational of novelists: a contender for a Nobel Prize, who roamed the northern hemisphere for most of her life. Dark was one of Drusilla Modjeska's 'exiles' at home and a writer of historical fiction who focused on representations of Australian landscape and nation-building. The development of a gap between those who write 'at home' and 'away', however, tends to gloss over the ways in which the writers meet imaginatively, and travel through literature, in turn representing and influencing how Australians think about their world. In investigating the interstices of their work, I have employed Marc Augé's discussion of the spectator–traveller to help describe the extent to which these writers appear to conceive of and write transnationally while producing a location-based narrative.

Challenge

Dark and Stead were born a year apart (Dark in 1901, Stead in 1902) and they shared a beachside adolescence in wartime Sydney. Their mothers died when they were young: Stead's mother when Christina was two and Dark's when Eleanor was eight. They attended academically oriented high schools where their literary pursuits were encouraged. Dark published poetry and short stories in her twenties and her first novel, *Slow Dawning*, in 1932, and Stead's first publication, *The Salzburg Tales*, appeared in 1934. By the time these works were published, the authors were living on different continents and involved in relationships with men that extended their early interest in socialism. Stead's partner, Bill Blake, was a writer on Marxist economic theory and a sometime member of the Communist Party. Dark's husband, Eric, was likewise interested in Marxist politics and he and Eleanor supported a range of left-wing causes. It is not surprising, then, that the novels of the late 1930s, *House of All Nations* and *Waterway*, each critique the exploitative global and local financial structures of mid twentieth-century capitalism. It is interesting to note, however, that this repudiation of capitalism reaches into the private realm via an assault on the economics of marriage.

In *Waterway*, Dark investigates the impact of global economic change on a settled and smug Sydney. Modern transport and communication systems meant that Sydney was a technologically advanced city at the centre of burgeoning international trade. Dark chooses, however, to depict the parochialism of the city and its somnolent ruling class as turning away from international affairs. Dark is fearful of the turmoil of Europe and she is especially nervous about fascism, but she insists that Australia must look out to the world and be part of an intellectual resistance to rampant nationalism. Her novel resonates with the tensions of this ambivalence as the class-stratified characters carefully pick their way in and across Sydney Harbour, almost in slow motion, as preparations for war intensify in Europe. Stead, alternatively, in *House of All Nations*, appears to embrace the growing chaos of Europe as she rushes the reader through the world of bull and bear financial markets driven by fabulous and bizarre characters who meet in Paris in the mid 1930s.

The authors therefore react to the conceptual double-act of early twentieth-century modernity, in which time and space simultaneously shrink and expand, in quite different ways. In his discussion of the relationship between place and space, Augé[4] argues that the spectator–traveller experiences disorientation when passing through a landscape. This disorientation opens a gap that prevents the spectator from perceiving what he views as a place, or from 'being fully present in it'.[5] Stead, as a confessed wanderer—a spectator–traveller, in other words—never seems to be quite present in the European 'place' and this sense of dislocation is transferred to the fictional Paris of *House of All Nations*, where it induces a restlessness and intensity that frames the narrative action. Freed from national and regional boundaries, her narrative captures a cosmopolitan urgency that most fully articulates the transnational impulse. Like Stead, the characters are unsettled and mobile, so that national boundaries become nonsense. Such spectator–travellers inhabit a space that is a 'rhetorical territory',[6] to continue Augé's line of thinking, rather than a 'place'—that is, the cast of *House of All Nations* shares an imaginative transnational space that is characterised by the discourse of finance.

In Dark's work, however, there is an allegiance to place that seemingly overrides the activities of the assembled cast. Sydney, the city, is an eloquent voice in Dark's writing and the harbour and its environs inform every aspect of the novel. At first glance, there appears to be no dislocation at work: the lengthy descriptions of the sea and landscape and the entanglement of character and site privilege a sense of place. At the same time, however, the characters continually engage in an intellectual debate, either with themselves or with other characters, that ranges across international politics, labour conditions, class divisions and Australia's position as a modern nation, as they travel across the water or walk the foreshores of Sydney Harbour. The space they inhabit is almost disembodied but it is through this rhetorical territory that the characters become part of an international community of ideas.

A shared past

Sydney Harbour is at the centre of this imaginative process. Stead grew up in Watson's Bay and Dark lived, for a time, in Vaucluse, the next (and wealthier) suburb. Stead, like Dark's fictional children in *Waterway*, swam in the natural pools along the harbour's edge. At night, she listened to stories of Australia and far away places told by her naturalist father, David Stead. 'I was born into an ocean of story, or on its shores,' she says in writing about the way stories jump time and borders, 'the same thing could have happened anywhere; and anywhere it does.'[7] She writes in *A Waker and a Dreamer* of David Stead's genius for verbiage so that on seeing one of his books, she says:

> I am at home again...the whole landscape of childhood rises up, a marvellous real world, not bounded by our time, fragrant, colored by the books he liked...that landscape rising and depressing coasts, the deeps, the desert; the landscape had no time limits—it had 'giants and pygmies of the deep'.[8]

This sense of being in a marvellous other time, of the transfer of story from place to place, of the insubstantiality of the material world, describes Stead's own life as well as many of her narratives. Her father remarried when she was four years old and she became stepsister and carer for her siblings in an unconventional existence in which there was never enough money. David Stead's stories of his travels and his scientific pursuits further stimulated Christina's thriving imaginative life. It was living by the water, however, in full view of international shipping lanes, that made boarding a ship for England, when she was twenty-seven, 'so natural, because these ships were always in and out, in and out'.[9]

Dark, like Stead, was in the care of a father who was well known in intellectual and political circles. Dowell O'Reilly, a poet, novelist and teacher, married a distant relative when Eleanor was sixteen. Although Dark attended boarding school on Sydney's North Shore, she spent time with Dowell at his various lodgings, where household visitors included the poet Christopher Brennan. O'Reilly, like David Stead, often relied on a daughter to bring order to his home. Both girls became office workers for a time in the city area but when they reached their twenties their life patterns diverged dramatically. Stead decided that although she loved Sydney and that she was 'full of Australian culture', she wanted to go abroad.[10] Eleanor married Eric Dark in 1922 and she was living in Katoomba and settled as a doctor's wife when Stead left Australia in 1928. Dark was content to remain in the Blue Mountains, where she could have a settled home and walk and climb in the Australian bush. Her letters written during a tour of the United States in 1937 reveal her admiration of American open spaces, especially Yosemite National Park, but her reaction to New York is typical of her suspicion of the cosmopolitan crush:

> The really revolting thing about it is, I think, the feeling one has about it is its *packed* population, and that of course is because being on an island it has not been able to spread outward at all and has had to go into the air and down into the bowels of the earth, so that when one is walking the streets one is conscious of sardine-like humanity not only all round one, but up above and below.[11]

Dark's evident distaste for the compression of modernity resonates with the sense of physical freedom she so often associates with life in Australia. This ambivalence about modern life would find its way into her interrogation of 'modern' Australia in *Waterway*, when she celebrated the benefits of a modern attractive city in a peaceful landscape but critiqued the corrosive effects of parochialism and unchecked nationalism. If New York was to be *the* future, it would not be *her* future, and, after publication of *Waterway*, she spent more than a decade focusing on a historical trilogy of Australia, in which she would interrogate the 'idea of Australia', as she told her publisher.[12] Whereas Stead's interests were taken up with European politics and international writers in the 1940s, Dark promoted writing in Australia about Australia, if not a national literature. She told Jean Devanny in 1945:

> Personally, I don't care if the rest of the world is interested in Australian literature or no...What concerns me is that Australian writers should contribute something of value to the literature of their country. This does not mean that I am advocating a narrow nationalism. Australia should be realised as part of the world. The writer's business is to interpret and record Australian conditions in a manner that will lead and guide with its implicit significance.[13]

Dark would always find it difficult to negotiate this realisation. Sydney in the 1930s, however, provided a brilliant location for an investigation of a national rhetoric of modernity and progress. In the white and monocultural space of *Waterway*, characters make their way around the harbour's edges to the city centre, as they ruminate on the difficulties of their lives. Their decision-making processes inevitably involve some form of interaction with harbour water or ocean, which becomes a device for the meeting of the old world and the new.

Ian Harnet, for example, revels in watching ships from afar reach Sydney and he looks at them 'with the eye of the landsman as things haloed with glamour and romance!'.[14] This pleasure in adventure is, however, restrained and he is content to maintain the gap between land and sea, between place and space. The ships bring the imaginary of the wider world across the Pacific to Sydney but neither Harnet, nor any of the characters in the novel, feel the urge to leave Australia. In fact, Winifred Sellman, the only traveller in the novel, tells Harnet how glad she is to be back in Australia, almost echoing Dark's refrain during her American tour.

City spaces

Despite Dark's description of Sydney in *Waterway* as a 'quiet grey city',[15] the outside world intrudes. Professor Channon reads of the failure of peace talks in Europe in the morning paper and understands that the 'greyish patch' in the newspaper (Europe) will soon burst into smoke and flame,[16] and the inference is that Australia will be drawn into the conflict. As a progressive thinker who advocated the benefits of science and technology, Dark was nevertheless uncomfortable with the shrinking of time and space, made material in the development of the city skyline, and she wrote of this in an unpublished note:

> When I was seventeen and saw Kingsford Smith arriving in Sydney after the first flight from England to Australia I felt that nations could never again be separate as they had been before, and this feeling became a conviction as the years passed. Now the mind puts a shadowy question mark after every thought of the future.[17]

How then to act in a time of war? Dark was a socialist and, while her political beliefs were not especially problematic in Katoomba in the 1930s, she seemed to suspect that her loyalty to Australia would be questioned at some point—and she was right. In 1938, however, she could allow her characters to become transnational subjects and express their support for international socialism and to relate to new ideas about environmentalism, workers' rights and gender equality. The growing international interest in conservation fitted well with Dark's preference for an outdoors life in which to be Australian was to hike, climb, drive, walk or swim through the landscape. At this point, the rhetorical territory of transnationalism could be fostered without endangering her sense of place.

Stead was also taken up with thinking about place at this time but, unlike Dark, she celebrated this unease: she was philosophical about her role as a wanderer, saying, '[I]t is like the uneasiness and loneliness felt by Russians, US Americans, Brazilians, who with, at their backs, the spaces and untamed land, seek Paris, the Riviera and New York?'[18] Cities attracted wanderers (which perhaps explains Dark's discomfort in New York) and there are many such characters in *A House of All Nations*. The novel tells the story of the downfall of a private bank, Banque Mercure, 'a sort of cosmopolite club for the idle rich and speculators of Paris, Madrid, Rio, Buenos Aires, New York, London and points farther east and west'.[19] The bank is led by the fabulous Jules Bertillon, a wealthy playboy-banker whose international risk taking knows no bounds: it is entirely appropriate that the name 'Mercure' connotes Mercury, the classical god of merchants and messengers. The book's title refers not just to the bank itself but to a famous Parisian brothel of the period, neatly linking the worlds of prostitution and banking. The bank is, however, the geographical focus of the narrative: richly, if conservatively, appointed, its luxury creates an atmosphere of an illusory financial solidity. This is a novel in which interiors—of the bank, restaurants, bars, dining rooms and the occasional farmhouse—provide the structure against which the transnational game of finance is played. The bank's interconnecting secret passages throughout the Parisian quarter provide the scaffold for the movement of money around Europe and the United States, including drug running and white-slave operations between Africa and South America. None of this, of course, is a concern to the operators of the bank. As Jules Bertillion reminds his employee Aristede Raccamond, 'whoever heard of clean money?'.[20]

Their money flows out of communist Russia and into international markets as Germany, France and Russia take market positions on the British pound sterling. This money has the power to cross race and class boundaries and produce subjects who inhabit a temporary hybrid nationality. Stead populates the work with close descriptions of racial and national stereotypes that are followed by accounts of the ways in which perceptions can lead one astray. Bertillion's trusted advisor, Michel Alphendéry, is a French Jew of German (Alsatian) parentage, and Brigid Rooney argues that Alphendéry is 'a familiar revolutionary—the deracinated, déclassé intellectual of the generation that, after the Dreyfus affair, defined the political activism of modernity's cultural intelligentsia'.[21] Alphendéry certainly attempts to balance being both inside and outside the system and it is this mobility that makes him such an asset to Jules—and, one could say, such an attractive figure for Stead. He finds a perverse pleasure in lecturing working men at night while keeping the bank afloat during the day. He sees capitalism as a form of social organisation and he asks himself why he should wear his life away 'grubbing for rich men'.[22] When the bank collapses, however, he immediately takes a position with another finance house. Alphendéry moves location but not occupation, much as did Stead and Blake when one of their banking colleagues was arrested in the United States.

Like Stead, Alphendéry is a wanderer who, like the money he moves, can disappear across borders. A liberal socialist of Jewish heritage, his cultural background is contrasted with other Jews, such as the grain merchant Henri

Léon, who 'knew no Yiddish. Coming from the Balkans, he spoke various Eastern tongues and the Ladino of the Jews exiled from Spain';[23] and the bankers Franz Rosenkrantz and Franz Guildenstern, who claim: 'We in international business, are never in a foreign country. The market place, the exchange booth is our home...France is just a foothold to do business in. What is there in it to hold the soul of man?'[24] The transnational cosmopolitanism of financial exchange becomes a rhetorical territory in which hybrid languages signify the displacement and time is marked by the opening and closing of the major stock exchanges of the world.

It is obvious that Stead does not unilaterally condemn the amoral world of Banque Mercure, despite the opening credo in which she frames the cynicism and corruption of the novel's main characters. There is a fondness for the charming and desperate characters who stride across the bank's foyer and a humour that lightens the economic wrangling between Jules and Michel or many of the bank's clients or friends. This, of course, could have been a strategic move on Stead's part. She and Blake worked for some years at the Travelers' Bank in Paris, on which Banque Mercure's activities were based. Blake was deeply implicated in the financial dealings of the bank and he resigned only three months before the collapse of the business in 1935. Many years later, Stead said that *House of All Nations* was not 'an attack on the system, it's a picture of the system...there's a certain amount of amusement and love in a way, of the system. I'm not a polemic writer.'[25] Hazel Rowley, however, points out that the American-owned bank had operated for some time on a legal and illegal basis, noting that 'it is plain that she [Stead] was perfectly aware of the illegality of the proceedings'.[26]

By this time, Stead had travelled a long way from her youth in Watson's Bay, but the community of international finance offered her a stimulating framework for social critique. As a citizen of the world who mixed in intellectual circles, she could bring to Australian readers a singular perspective on the financial and political movements that were in turn shaping events at 'home'. Her life became one of continual movement across borders and the fictional accounts of this transnational experience found their way onto the bookshelves in libraries from London to Sydney under the title of 'Australian Literature'.

In Sydney, the financial space that Dark examines is a far more circumscribed and ordered structure in which wealth is derived from trade or property rather than speculation on a gold standard. It is, however, similarly gendered, class based and powerful. The narrative deals chiefly with relations between the upper and lower middle class, with occasional guest appearances from the professions, the politically committed and the unemployed. The two wealthy families of *Waterway* represent this division: Sellman's and Hegarty's share the retail economy in which 'Hegarty's was vast and cheap and amorphous—the Mecca of the lower middle class, but Sellman's stood for quality, distinction, good taste, the last word in modernity'.[27] Dark, unlike Stead, is not troubled by polemics, and the character of Arthur Sellman represents quite literally the ugly face of capitalism. Whereas Stead showcases Bertillon as sophisticated and erudite, Dark's Sellman is overfed, cruel and ignorant. Sellman is opposed by those in the narrative who hold socialist sympathies, including his wife, and he has little understanding of the working class, who, however, have his measure. Dark's working men might have 'tall, loose-knit bones in shabby clothes', but they have 'intelligent' eyes that lack 'utterly any suggestion of deference'.[28] Her narrative sympathy is firmly on the side of the socialists, while worldly sophisticates are treated with disdain. The young man about Sydney, Sim Hegarty, is an air-ace (as is Jules Bertillon), but unlike Jules, Sim does not theorise about the source of his wealth. His only qualms about his future are momentary and personal. With the well-travelled local beauty Lorna Sellman (who has rejected an active modernity by turning down a role in a Hollywood film), Sim represents a passivity that stands in stark contrast with the politically engaged (and Australian-focused) characters, Roger Blair and Lesley Channon. Roger and Lesley are united by left-wing philosophy rather than class or money, which is denounced as 'that false and arbitrary substitute for the real wealth of the soil, of man-power, of brain-power'.[29] These lovers have the interest of their country at heart, but this is couched in the discourse of international socialism.

In an interview, Stead admitted that *House of All Nations* was 'badly received in Wall Street, because it was so true'.[30] She said she liked her work at the bank and found the bankers 'very friendly fellows',[31] who revealed all their business to her, knowing that she was a writer. This is the 'old world' that Blair calls unclean in *Waterway*, a world that has the potential to pollute Australia. He argues, '[I]t's all very well to talk about being international—who wants to rush forward and embrace his brother, the leper?'[32] Dark's answer, in the words of Professor Channon, is that one must look beyond the national to a strong intellectual 'sense of brotherhood'[33] led by scientists and artists. In this emphasis on an international intellectualism, Dark was countering nationalist sentiments of the day: in general, her works of the 1930s offered a stronger contestation of what it meant to be an Australian in that period of modernity than was generally accepted.

Stead and Dark display, therefore, a common distrust of capitalism, but their work provokes different responses to the situation. Stead is content to show the personal and political wreckage caused by the bank, but she stops short of the advocacy of a Professor Channon or Roger Blair. One further way in which the writers do connect, however, is in their discussion of marriage as an economic institution and a form of prostitution—a preoccupation that travels through time and space. The wedding scenes in *Waterway* and *House of All Nations* show with disarming frankness the institutional relationship of sex, marriage and money.

Two weddings and a proletariat

In *House of All Nations*, Jules and his wife, the elegant and perpetually youthful Claire-Josèphe, attend the wedding of new multimillionaire Toots Legris and the son of 'old' money, Duc-Adam Lhermite. Stead's wedding guest list runs for a page of the novel, including:

> It was a garland of youthful vanity and superannuated cunning, hoary rank and young money, famous beggars, notorious debtors, unsuccessful rakes, lordly borrowers, impenitent usurers, princely automobile salesmen and brokers' runners of Bourbon blood, shady viscounts, distinguished pillars of cafés, illustrious readers of the *Journal des Débats*…All of them were news items, and a certain number had money themselves.[34]

The most revealing commentary on the marriage takes place, appropriately, in the bank's plush offices after the ceremony. Toot's father says that he told his future son-in-law, 'Take her, my boy, you been sleeping with her two years anyhow. The sooner she marries you the sooner she'll get tired of you…she's not my daughter: what rot you talking Jules? She's the daughter of seventy million guilders.'[35]

Jules refuses to condemn the amorality of his friends, telling Alphendéry, 'I sleep with my own wife, true; but I sleep with other people's money. And raped money gets people much wilder than raped wives.'[36] The triangulation of money, sex and marriage (the 'recurrent cash–flesh nexus' described by Don Anderson)[37] is made clear by Jules when he tells Raccamond that 'every woman is a whore, but the whores are the ones who never learned the game…What is a whore? A poor girl who never had a chance to go into business with a man and set up a little house of her own.'[38] For Jules, women must use sex as a pathway to financial power both inside and outside of marriage, as do many of the notable women characters in the novel: Claire-Josèphe, Marianne Raccamond and Margaret Weyman are interested primarily in manipulating relationships with men because their feminine status denies them an alternative. The situation is little better for the novel's female intellectuals, who attend Communist Party meetings that are racked by internal dissension and who seem, as much as their wealthy counterparts, to be subject to masculine control. As Rooney notes, the masculinity of the novel is disrupted momentarily in a scene in which three women, Judith (Jean Frère's wife), Henrietta Achitophelos and Suzanne Constant (Adam's wife), arrive at Adam's workshop-flat[39]; but none of these women, despite their powerful disruption of the brotherly proceedings, can ultimately challenge the institutional order.

Waterway's society wedding of Veronica Stewart and George Hegarty will, like its Paris counterpart, make news. The melee of newspapermen and bystanders gathers to watch guests arrive at the city church that has been the site, also, of a demonstration by the unemployed. As the guests arrive, they comment on the 'proletariat' outside the church, while inside Sim Hegarty speculates on the marriage of money and privilege that will secure Veronica and George's future. The institutional and stifling power of the accumulated wealth in the Sydney church is the driving force of a ceremony that is described by way of the heady mix of flowers and summer heat:

> It is not to be trifled with, this power which has filled the church with silent, beautifully mannered people, faintly rustling like trees, giving out perfume like flowers...It is a power to be reckoned with. It is shackling the group of men outside with their notebooks and their pencils and their observant, disillusioned eyes.[40]

Lorna Sellman, conscious that her beauty is her stock-in-trade, manipulates her attendance to her advantage and by the time the ceremony is over she has been able to secure a future with Sim Hegarty. Lorna's credo—'Blessed are they that have anything over five thousand a year...And thrice blessed are they that have titles, no matter how they got them'[41] —preserves her position as one of the rich and beautiful in this 'familiar, material, recognisable city'.[42] Although she has not preserved her virginity, she has been smart enough to be selective in her affairs so that her name has market value. Both writers are keen to promote a view of marriage as a financial transaction, unless, as in Dark's case, politics can smooth the way. For these Australian writers, marriage provokes questions about sexual and class relationships that cross international boundaries.

Dark is, of course, aware that events in Europe will displace the familiar and the recognisable and the novel develops an elegiac tone for a city that will shortly change either by virtue of war or class revolution. Likewise, Stead's bankers have underestimated the rise of fascism in Europe, but the political disruption provides an excellent cover for Jules' disappearance at the end of *House of all Nations*. Stead's narrator speculates on the new rhetorical territory this spectator–traveller will inhabit: 'Adventurers are flying every day and rising again under new governments and speaking new languages.'[43] The dance that Jules led the financiers will be replicated in another time and another place in Stead's transnational world.

Conclusion

Given that both writers were published overseas by internationally based firms, the reviews of these works offered an appropriate closing comment on the relationship between the national and the global before World War II. New York reviews of *House of All Nations*, published a few months before *Waterway* in

1938, commented on the bizarre brilliance of the book and the heightened fantasy elements. Hazel Rowley said that Stead was undoubtedly influenced by the mid 1930s European emphasis on documentary form, but many felt the book was too long and too crowded (there were more than 100 characters in the novel).[44] Sales were not what Stead had expected, although this was due partly to poor marketing. Stead was doubly disappointed as she had wanted to use the income from this most transnational of novels to fund a visit to Sydney. In Sydney, however, reviews were mixed and tended to focus on Stead's style rather than on content.

American critics praised *Waterway* and Australian reviews were generally positive, although the 24-hour time frame and plot devices were a sticking point. Although it was hard to buy the novel in Sydney, it was available in London, where Dark's friends Mary Alice and Bert Evatt saw it on a bookstall at Victoria Station.[45] Dark had similar marketing problems to Stead: publishers complained of disappointing sales, but the books were difficult to obtain in Australia or were subjected to small print runs. Like *Waterway*, *House of All Nations* was not reprinted for many years.

After these works were published, the gap between the authors' writing widened, although they were each subject to the traumas of Cold War politics. Stead continued to live in Europe and America after World War II, writing continually and consolidating an international literary reputation that would see her described, finally, as a major writer in English in the twentieth century. Dark changed literary mode and wrote a historical trilogy, the first volume of which, *The Timeless Land*, was sent to Australian troops. Barbara Brooks wrote that a copy of *Waterway* was held in Changi Prison and, for the Australians, '[n]o-one else brought Sydney home to us as she did'.[46] Dark moved between Katoomba and Montville in Queensland and her longest period of travel was a trip around Australia in 1948.

The women's writing continued to circulate around the world but in Australia they became part of quite different literary traditions. Dark is grouped, usually, with her inter-war network of Australian women authors and precedence is given to her representations of national ideas and a particular geographical sense of place, while Stead's literary stature is configured around the transnational. The points of contact in the imaginative journey that began around Sydney Harbour, however, show how complex and interdependent is the relationship between the national and the global. Stead died in Sydney in 1983 and Dark in Katoomba in 1985. Their respective funerals were attended by a small group of family and close friends but their stories continued to interest successive waves of readers, at home and abroad, in different ways of looking out at the world.

Notes

1. Harris, Margaret (ed.) 2005, *Dearest Munx: The letters of Christina Stead and William J. Blake*, The Miegunyah Press, Carlton, Victoria, p. 16.
2. Rowley, Hazel 1993, *Christina Stead: A biography*, William Heinemann, Sydney, p. 389.
3. Christina Stead to Gilbert Stead, quoted in Rowley, *Christina Stead*, p. 234.
4. Augé, Marc 1995, *Non-Places: Introduction to an anthropology of supermodernity*, Translated by John Howe, Verso, London, p. 84.
5. Ibid., p. 84.
6. Ibid., p. 77.
7. Stead, Christina 1985, *Ocean of Story: The uncollected stories of Christina Stead*, Penguin, Ringwood, Victoria, pp. 9–10.
8. Ibid., p. 493.
9. Wetherell, Rodney 1980, 'Interview with Christina Stead', *Australian Literary Studies*, vol. 9, no. 4, p. 437.
10. Ibid.
11. Eleanor Dark to Molly O'Reilly, 4 September 1937, Mitchell Library, MSS 4545, Box 15, 16.
12. Eleanor Dark to William Collins, 26 November 1937, Mitchell Library, MSS 4545, Box 22.
13. Devanny, Jean 1945, *Bird of Paradise*, Johnston, Sydney, p. 251.
14. Dark, Eleanor 1938, *Waterway*, London, Collins, p. 37.
15. Ibid., p. xii.
16. Ibid., p. 120.
17. Eleanor Dark Papers, Mitchell Library, MLMSS 4545.
18. Stead, Christina 1985, 'Another view of the homestead', in *Ocean of Story*, p. 519.
19. Stead, Christina 1938 [1966], *House of All Nations*, Angus and Robertson, Sydney, p. 19.
20. Ibid., p. 309.
21. Rooney, Brigid 2003, '"Those boys told me everything": the politics of the secretary in Christina Stead's 1930s fiction', *Antipodes*, June, p. 29.
22. Stead, *House of All Nations*, p. 673.
23. Ibid., p. 216.
24. Ibid., p. 168.
25. Wetherell, 'Interview with Christina Stead', p. 441.
26. Rowley, *Christina Stead*, p. 149.
27. Dark, *Waterway*, p. 263.
28. Ibid., p. 264.
29. Ibid., p. 77.
30. Wetherell, 'Interview with Christina Stead', p. 441.
31. Ibid., p. 440.
32. Dark, *Waterway*, p. 80.
33. Ibid., p. 79.
34. Stead, *House of All Nations*, p. 346.
35. Ibid., p. 349.
36. Ibid., p. 351.
37. Anderson, Don 1979, 'Christina Stead's unforgettable dinner-parties', *Southerly*, vol. 1, p. 42.
38. Stead, *House of All Nations*, p. 309.
39. Rooney, '"Those boys told me everything"', pp. 33–4.
40. Dark, *Waterway*, p. 232.
41. Ibid., p. 179.
42. Ibid., p. 181.
43. Stead, *House of All Nations*, p. 787.
44. Rowley, *Christina Stead*, p. 213.

[45] Brooks, Barbara with Clark, Judith 1998, *Eleanor Dark: A writer's life*, Macmillan, Sydney, p. 202.
[46] Ibid., p. 244.

Chapter 15

Australian 'immersion' narratives: memoirs of contemporary language travel

Mary Besemeres

By definition, travel narratives invoke an experience of moving between cultural worlds. Only a fraction of travel books in English, however, emphasise the language borders that are crossed in much international travel, and deal in a sustained way with the question of how language impinges on the self. This question is central to a range of memoirs by migrants *into* English: texts such as *Lost in Translation: A life in a new language* (1989) by the Polish-born Canadian Eva Hoffman, *Polite Lies: On being a woman caught between cultures* (1997) by Japanese-born American Kyoko Mori, or Chilean exile to the United States Ariel Dorfman's *Heading South, Looking North: A bilingual journey* (1998).[1] Migrants into anglophone cultures are increasingly drawing our attention to what is involved in migrating into a new language, but this isn't the case for people travelling in the opposite direction. The issue of language is also absent from major critical studies of travel writing, such as those by Dennis Porter (1991), Caren Kaplan (1996), Inderpal Grewal (1996), Patrick Holland and Graham Huggan (1998), and is only touched on in Mary Louise Pratt's influential study *Imperial Eyes* (1992).[2] Unlike 'landscape', 'language' isn't featured in any of the indexes of these otherwise wide-ranging books.

The lack of interest in language in popular travel writing in English is no doubt connected with the global reach of English, and the fact that many anglophone travel writers are monolingual or envisage a readership with no other language. It is symptomatic of the global dominance of English that questions about language and identity are largely invisible in anglophone travel writing. This chapter explores some atypical travel books in this context—'immersion' narratives that explicitly foreground what might be called 'language travel'—and reads them in relation to a wider critical debate about the representation of self and other in travel literature. I examine three Australian texts—Gillian Bouras's *A Foreign Wife* (1986), Sarah Turnbull's *Almost French: A new life in Paris* (2002) and John Mateer's *Semar's Cave: An Indonesian journal* (2004)—drawing attention to what appear to be some common cultural assumptions in the authors' accounts of their interactions with speakers of languages other than English.[3]

This chapter draws on research for a larger project on the phenomenon of language travel: 'Anglos abroad: narratives of immersion into a foreign language and culture'. One of the aims of the project is to explore the degree to which a metaphorical colonising of 'cultural others' is inevitable in Western travel writing, as Pratt, among other critics, has argued.[4] The prevailing trope that Pratt identifies in Western travel writing, from the French explorer La Condamine to American writer Paul Theroux, is that of the 'seeing-man', a traveller given to a 'monarch-of-all-I-survey' view of the cultural landscape. Pratt presents American critic Joan Didion's 1983 book *Salvador* as an exception to the 'imperial eye' mode: an exception that proves the rule. For Pratt, Didion rightly renounces any claim to insightful comment on El Salvadoran realities: 'Didion identifies her subject matter as inaccessible to her [W]estern...self...her book aggressively and lucidly sought to abdicate the authority of the seeing-man.' Pratt contends that only authors of *testimonio*, such as the Bolivian activist Domitila Barrios de Chungara, can claim to write with authority about Latin America, and that Western travel writing about non-Western places has effectively reached a dead end.[5]

Pratt is concerned primarily with the power differential operating between writers travelling from colonising or neo-colonial powers and the people they write about in colonised or post-colonial countries. This asymmetry of power is not obviously relevant to Sarah Turnbull and Gillian Bouras, who write about their expatriate lives in Europe, although Bouras moves from a middle-class metropolitan context, Melbourne, to a Peloponnesian village. It is clearly present in *Semar's Cave*. Mateer expresses discomfort with his privileged position as a Western traveller who can choose cheap methods of transport such as the *sudako* (or minibus) for the thrill of adventure, while Indonesians would go by cab if they had his money.[6] The question of whether Western travel writing offers alternatives to the 'seeing-man' mode of cultural representation is, however, as applicable to the texts by Bouras and Turnbull as to Mateer's.

Bouras, A Foreign Wife

As an Australian narrative of language travel, Gillian Bouras's *A Foreign Wife* is unusual in being written from the viewpoint of a migrant rather than a temporary traveller. While many well-known Australians have been expatriates based in anglophone countries, until recently few Australian authors have written as long-term migrants to non-English-speaking countries. Bouras (born in 1945) moved to Greece with her Greek-born husband and two Australian-born children in 1980; a third son was born in Greece. *A Foreign Wife* is the first of several books about her experiences in Greece. It was followed by memoirs *A*

Fair Exchange (1991) and *Aphrodite and the Others* (1994), the novel *A Stranger Here* (1996) and memoir *Starting Again* (1999).[7] Settling in her husband's village near the southern city of Kalamata, Bouras was plunged into an exclusively Greek-speaking environment. Although on arrival she could speak and read simple Greek, after-dinner conversation was at first 'a strange staccato rattle'.[8] She evokes from an Anglo-Australian viewpoint the sense of marginality that comes with not speaking the dominant language and, as a parent, the loss of authority that such a lack of cultural literacy and linguistic fluency brings:

> At dinner-time, speaking Greek, I make a grammatical error. Dimitrios and Nikolaos hoot, and then the former crushes me with a look, a practice he has down to a fine art. 'You'll never speak it well,' he announces, firmly, for the umpteenth time, 'not like Sandra, Ken and Teresa. Why can't you be like them?' Why indeed? I feel sick, as I usually do, over any breakdown or error in communication, but make an effort to stand up for myself.[9]

Bouras writes poignantly of the impact on herself and her children of the 'reversal of the child–parent relationship' in which the child becomes the one who 'knows all about language, communication and protocol'. One of the consequences of her loss of status in her oldest son's eyes was his new preference for his grandmother's company in public: 'It was a devastating moment for me when Dimitri announced he would walk through the main streets of the village with *Yiayia*, but not with me. *Yiayia* became the authority on everything from dietary law to bus timetables.' Bouras comments, 'The migrant mother almost inevitably finds herself involved in a power struggle which she is bound to lose.'[10]

Bouras's perspective on her children's induction into Greek compares interestingly with British expatriate author Tim Parks' memoir of his bicultural family life in Italy, *An Italian Education* (1996). Parks writes about two concepts that he sees as key notions in Italian culture: '*spettacolo*' and '*fare festa*' (literally, 'making a party' for someone—an expression that, Parks says, 'combines the ideas of welcoming [someone] and smothering them with physical affection'). He illustrates the centrality of these concepts with an account of a visit by his parents-in-law and its effect on his Italian children, Michele and Stefi.

> It would truly be hard to exaggerate the cooing and crying and sighing and kissing and nose-tweaking and exclamations and tears and tickles and cuddles that now have to take place…Nonna lifts up Michele and dances round and round with him and '*O che bel bambino! O che ometto splendido! O che spettacolo!*'[11]

Parks' children are caught up in a dramatic excitement when their *nonni* arrive, a kind of performance they are drawn into. Parks suggests that there is a strongly visual element to expressing one's feelings in Italian, and it is this that makes

Italian behaviour seem theatrical to an 'Anglo' observer. Although he highlights the cultural basis for this perception, however, he is clearly uncomfortable with his Italian family's expressiveness, and calls its sincerity into question.

> [M]other and father, sons and daughters, all criticise each other endlessly...[Y]et when...the Baldassarres are actually face to face, the gestures of affection, the extravagant *fare festa*...could not be more voluble or enthusiastic.

> My wife embraces her mother rapturously. And her father. Michele watches them. Everybody does seem perfectly...delighted to see each other. The *nonni* are here! *Evviva*! Yet Michele is surely aware, even at five, that we complain a great deal about these [visits]...no doubt the children take all this in, this wonderful *spettacolo* of affection, this carefully choreographed *festa*.

In *A Foreign Wife*, Bouras writes similarly of the theatricality and flamboyance of her sons when they are speaking Greek and their relative quietness when speaking English. Like Parks, she emphasises the connectedness of speech and body language:

> The boys are completely different people when they speak Greek. It's not just the sound of the language, but the sense of drama, the marked emphases, the sweeping gestures and body language which inevitably accompany it. When speaking English, they are quieter, less flamboyant and, Greeks would say, duller.[12]

Just as Parks casts his Italian in-laws' behaviour in theatrical terms ('choreographed', 'show'), so Bouras is struck by the 'sense of drama' that characterises her boys' Greek-speaking selves. Where Parks is sceptical, tending to valorise his own cultural reflexes for all that he is aware of them, Bouras is more sympathetic to this other emotional style. Describing a return visit to Melbourne, she writes, '[T]he boys are too noisy and exuberant for understated Australia, and people here have firm ideas about...the place of children';[13] she identifies more closely here with her children than with the expectations of Australian relatives. Later, she recalls her frustration with what seemed initially to be her sons' 'Greek over-reaction to everything': '"Tone it down," I would say through clenched teeth as they yelled, gesticulated, smote their foreheads and thoroughly indulged themselves. "You're not on stage".'[14] Now, she writes, she no longer thinks they 'exaggerate or over-emphasize'; even so, the phrase 'thoroughly indulged themselves' expresses something of her earlier Anglo-Australian cultural perspective.

As much as any resemblance between Greek and Italian emotional idioms, the use of the metaphor of drama by Bouras and Parks to mark what looks and feels (familiarly) foreign to them suggests a close parallel between British and

Australian cultural attitudes towards expressing feelings. What seems common to both is wariness towards the open expression of feeling, a tendency to see it as self-indulgent and exaggerated. Bouras's writing, however, shows how she has partly incorporated a different cultural take on emotions from the one she grew up with, and has made an inward shift towards a Greek-speaking perspective.

Turnbull, Almost French

Like Bouras, Sarah Turnbull, the author of *Almost French*, writes as the resident of another country. Formerly an SBS television reporter, Turnbull moved to Europe as a freelance journalist in the early 1990s. She went to France initially to visit a Frenchman whom she had met in Bucharest, and eventually made her home with him in Paris. In writing about her life there, Turnbull sometimes resorts to generalisations about 'the French', commenting for example on a national tendency for sober self-criticism alongside a 'glaringly Gallic' quality.[15] Her writing shares something of the spirit of satirical travel guidebooks such as the 'Xenophobe' series, which, unlike much contemporary academic scholarship in the humanities, are not concerned with avoiding essentialism. Turnbull's memoir, however, reflects tellingly on aspects of the relationship between self, language and culture brought to the fore by her experience of living as a foreigner in France. Her most effective writing probes and dramatises differences in expected ways of thinking and behaving that emerge from her conversations with French speakers.

A memorable encounter occurs at a cocktail party in Paris. It strikes Turnbull that the other guests are 'hanging back', none willing 'to break the ice'. She portrays herself trying to 'bridge' the 'cool distance' by introducing herself:

'Hello, my name is Sarah.'

Surprise scuds across the faces of a crisp couple, who step back involuntarily before accepting my outstretched hand…For the next ten minutes I practise my best 'people skills', chit-chatting in the friendly interested sort of way which can always be relied on to start conversation. What do you do? How do you know so-and-so? These people are proving to be much harder work than I imagined, though. While they answer politely enough they don't initiate any questions of their own. Unnerved, I try even harder, filling the silences with embarrassingly inane remarks. *Quel beau salon! Regardez les belles peintures!* Two heads nod impassively at me. It isn't working, I realize…they seem to be shrinking away from me. God, don't they know the golden rule (show interest in others and they'll show interest in you)? Don't they know they're supposed to make an effort? A sudden wave of doubt rushes over me. Could the rules be so different in France? But then how else are you supposed to get the ball rolling if not with preliminary questions…

> Back at the apartment, we carry out a post-mortem of the evening. To me, spending an entire evening talking to your partner is antisocial but Frédéric says this happens all the time at parties in France. As for my bold introduction, to the couple it would have seemed like an intrusion; my clumsy questions cluttering up each comfortable silence. Far from building a rapport, my efforts only seemed to diminish me in their eyes, as though by showing interest in them I had revealed the depths of my own dullness. Enthusiastically admiring the paintings…was inappropriate too. 'In our culture it implies you don't have those sort of things at home and makes you seem a bit *paysan,*' Frédéric says. A bit of a peasant.[16]

This comically one-sided conversation reveals not only that 'the rules' for conversation might be different in the new context, but that getting to know others at a party is not, for the couple Turnbull approaches, the self-evident good that it is for her. One of the strengths of Turnbull's portrayal of French society is the way she captures the diversity of social worlds—not all French gatherings are like this—yet also how styles of interaction that she has grown up with in Sydney don't easily find a purchase in any of the varied social spaces into which she ventures in France.

As Barbara Hanna and Juliana de Nooy point out in a recent paper, Turnbull inverts a convention of anglophone travel writing about France where the spotlight is on the strange or amusing habits of the French, emphasising rather the comic qualities of the figure she cuts herself in French society.[17] Through the medium of Turnbull and Frédéric's post-mortem discussions about what went wrong in her social encounters, the memoir creates a symbolic bridging of the gap between the Australian interloper and her wary, deprecating French audience. We see Frédéric becoming aware that behaviour that seems natural could be culturally inflected, a parallel development to the one that Turnbull herself undergoes.

While she presents her struggles to communicate in a comic light, Turnbull also brings out her frustrated feeling of invisibility in the new language and culture. This is partly a matter of limited vocabulary, but her dislocation is linguistic in a deeper sense, in that cultural expectations about behaviour make themselves felt through underlying scripts for what can or cannot be said, scripts that are largely lost on her. At a reunion lunch for university friends of Frédéric, the hosts seem to ignore her. When another couple greet her warmly—'*Enfin, le kangarou!*'—she feels she could weep with gratitude. Their friendliness, however, which she experiences as a reviving touch of normality, turns out in this cultural context to be an idiosyncratic response. None of Frédéric's other friends at the lunch feel bound to come up with it. Marie, a stylish woman with whom Turnbull has been trying to chat in French, turns suddenly to Frédéric and asks: '"*Et ta petite copine, comment va son français?*" Her words ring across the table, loud and patronising. ("How's your little girlfriend's French coming along?")' Frédéric, embarrassed, tries to include Turnbull: 'Er, I think she can probably answer that herself.' Faced with what seems like a gratuitous insult and unable to formulate a retort in French, Turnbull takes refuge in the bathroom, crying with mortification.[18]

From the retrospective vantage point of several more years in France, Turnbull reads the incident differently. She suggests that in French, Marie's comment, while hardly kindly meant, would not necessarily have been calculated to wound; that in the middle-class, urban French milieu of the lunch, there was no particular expectation of friendliness towards newcomers. Two years later, Turnbull is on good terms with Marie. The hosts of the lunch who appeared so cold ultimately turn out to be 'fun and gregarious'. Asked about their initial unfriendliness, they observe: 'The problem is the French aren't very comfortable meeting new people…For us, friendships form over years, at school or university. And after that, we're not interested, we're no longer curious. We think we've got enough friends already.' For Turnbull, this explanation is 'somehow healing' because, as she writes, 'even though that lunch was more than two years ago now, the cool reception, those unreciprocated what-do-you-do's, my anger, the hurt, had all accumulated in a knot which needed untangling'.[19]

Mateer, *Semar's Cave*

Semar's Cave: An Indonesian journal (2004) by Australian poet John Mateer (born in 1971) gives an account of his time as writer-in-residence in Medan in Northern Sumatra, and later in Java. Unlike the cases of Bouras and Turnbull, Mateer's transnational life predates the travel that is the subject of his book. He was born in Roodenport, South Africa, and migrated to Australia in his late teens, in 1989.[20] When Indonesians and Australian expatriates ask him why he is visiting Indonesia, he explains that he hopes to learn about the origins of Cape Malay, one of the languages spoken in the Cape Colony of Southern Africa in the eighteenth century among slaves from the Dutch East Indies, and the language of poetry he found inspiring as a child. Moments in the narrative in which an Indonesian experience triggers a memory of South Africa often have a particularly strong emotional resonance, as when Mateer's housekeeper in Medan takes him shopping: 'Squeezed together, with Ibu Enim's fleshy arm pressing against mine, I feel as though I have slipped back into my childhood: an African nanny taking care of me.'[21]

Figure 15.1: Cover, John Mateer, *Semar's Cave: an Indonesian Journal*.

Courtesy Fremantle Arts Centre Press.

Mateer conveys sensations and images memorably: the gurgling of drains at night, the sight and sounds of *becaks* (bike-taxis), motorbikes and yellow *sudakos* in the street, the feeling of being a passenger on all of these. The starkly evocative poems he embeds in the text are especially forceful engagements with place, often creating a productive discomfort in the reader. From a transnational perspective, the most striking aspect of the country portrayed in *Semar's Cave* is its precarious status as a nation, where distinct regional worlds have been forcibly yoked together, a status epitomised in a Chinese Indonesian's saying: '[T]here is nothing else holding Indonesia together—only the army and this language, Bahasa Indonesia.'[22] Perhaps Mateer's own transnational trajectory makes him more receptive to such angles of vision than Australians who write of Indonesia in more straightforwardly national terms, against a background sense of their own country as a unified nation.[23]

Mateer is interested in the issue of translation as it relates to poetry and cultural assumptions about the role of poets. He presents himself as frustrated by problems of translation at a poetry reading in Medan at which he has to read out his own poems. A Sumatran poet has chosen the poems Mateer will have to read, and they are not ones he thinks are likely to engage his listeners, whose English he suspects is limited. He is bemused at the lack of fit between what the audience expects a poet to be—someone with a claim to national status—and who he happens to be. Someone asks him why he is not mentioned in a history of Australian literature. Mateer is unwilling to take on the role of cultural representative that he feels is being thrust on him by Indonesians in the audience and Australian officials alike.

Considering his reasons for writing the memoir, Mateer reflects: 'I don't write to present an objective account or a truth but to interrupt the norms of storytelling, travel-writing or even history by giving more detail than opinion; real images instead of my thoughts.'[24] The implication is that the reader, presented with these concrete details, can come to his or her own conclusions about the Indonesia portrayed in the book. The idea, however, that one could convey 'real images' without also conveying thoughts about them seems problematic. The book's privileging of images appears to confirm Michael Cronin's observation that 'engaging with the external signs of alterity may…involve less personal risk (signs seen from a distance) than the direct dialogical encounter of language'.[25] Mateer's descriptions of his interactions with Indonesians include very little explicit comment; they are almost as pared down as transcripts of a tape recording, a method that could be read as privileging Indonesian voices and giving up any claim to authoritative comment. The attitude that comes through in his reported conversations is, however, generally sceptical and critical, not to say aloof.[26]

A typical exchange occurs when Mateer is on his way out of Medan, travelling to the town of Berastagi. A man helps him to find a less cramped position at the front of a crowded bus. They talk as they travel:

> He's getting married tomorrow to a Batak Karo girl. He works and studies computer science in Medan. He doesn't like Medan. He wants to be a farmer in the mountains. His plan is to work hard, earn a lot of money and then return to his kampong to be a farmer.
>
> 'Where is your village?' I ask.
>
> 'Ten kilometres from Berastagi. But I stay in Berastagi tonight. You want to come to my wedding tomorrow?'

> 'Maybe,' I say. I feel odd being invited to the wedding of someone I don't know.
>
> 'You have a place for tonight?'
>
> I don't. I wait for his recommendation.
>
> 'You stay with my friend. Losmen Sibayak. Like the mountain Sibayak.'[27]

What is interesting about this dialogue is that Mateer doesn't contextualise either the wedding invitation or his own response to it. There is no acknowledgment that a wedding in Sumatra might be a different kind of event from one in Perth, not necessarily a private occasion. As a result, despite his helpfulness, the man appears intrusive. Mateer seems to transpose his expectations wholesale, making no allowance for cultural difference, as though to do so would be to exoticise.

A particularly pronounced example of this one-sidedness is found in his representation of his Bahasa Indonesia teacher, Harkiman, who is of Chinese descent. We learn that Harkiman studied in New Zealand, where he did a thesis on the poet James Baxter. We later learn that he becomes an important source of knowledge of Indonesian literature for Mateer. Harkiman writes poetry himself and is evidently drawn to Mateer, as a poet and an Australian, someone who provides an indirect link with the world of his studies. The attraction does not seem to be mutual:

> He is questioning me. He wants to know why I'm here, how I became published, how I manage to make a living...From his urgency I can tell that he has written poems. 'Tell me,' he asks, 'how do you *become* a poet?'
>
> I evade the question. Its tone was almost aggressive.

As with the man on the bus, Mateer responds to Harkiman's questions as though they were rude, rather than expressive of a different cultural style of interaction, one that does not necessarily assume that there are 'personal' questions that are off-limits. Harkiman asks Mateer what his religion is and 'beams' on learning that it is Buddhism, as he himself is a Buddhist. 'According to him,' writes Mateer, 'this is a wonderful coincidence.' He tells Mateer that he looks forward to their classes. Mateer writes: 'I'm a bit taken aback by his enthusiasm. His forcefulness makes me uncomfortable. I'm relieved when...he rises to go and talk with some other people.'[28] The effect of the dialogue is to expose Harkiman as pushy and foolish for imagining a connection with Mateer when there is none. Mateer's discomfort with him is presented as being the natural response to this kind of behaviour. As in the quotations from the memoirs by Bouras and Parks, here there is a resistance to a way of speaking that displays the person's strong feelings, what Mateer calls Harkiman's 'enthusiasm'. This resistance likely has a cultural, as well as a personal, inflection.

During their first class, Harkiman digresses from the language exercises and gives Mateer a 'crash course in Indonesian literature'. He is enthusiastic about Chairil Anwar, Indonesia's first modern poet. Of a major modern poet before Anwar, Amir Hamza, we're told, 'Harkiman has a criticism…an anecdote…and a moral'.[29] There's something reductive in the way Mateer classifies what Harkiman says into these three types of utterance. In her searching review of *Semar's Cave*, Amanda Johnson has drawn attention to Mateer's 'remote narratorial stance' that, eschewing 'other people's accounts' as unreliable, 'can only lead to generalised judgements'.[30] The narrator's interaction with Harkiman seems to me a prime example of this distanced quality. Mateer goes on:

> It is Harkiman's habit to say a lot and then become aware of his impropriety and fall silent for a moment before remembering why we are both here. 'We are supposed to be studying,' he says in frustration. Harkiman, like most people who enjoy poetry, starts talking about it as soon as he meets a like-minded soul. I am sure that my friendship with him will be as it is with all my other poet-friends: a rapid, excited, unending discussion.[31]

The reference to excited discussion comes as a surprise because Mateer's side of the exchange is missing. By not revealing anything potentially vulnerable in his own behaviour, Mateer gives his negative impression of Harkiman an aura of impartiality. We are left wondering if Harkiman's apparent 'sense of impropriety' is really confusion at having failed to elicit much response from his listener.

Conclusion

Mateer's memoir connects in part with the nuanced thinking about nationality proposed by *Transnational Ties*. My chapter, however, aims to complicate the question of what it means to be Australian (or Indonesian) further by bringing in the additional, critical term of 'linguaculture'.[32] Nationality, as this book argues, is a complex, shifting phenomenon, but the cultural assumptions travellers bring with them are often the more persistent for being unexamined, embedded as they are in widely shared concepts—such as 'privacy' or 'friendliness'—that are taken for granted by speakers of the same language.

Whereas Turnbull refers confidently to 'national characteristics' of the French, Mateer attempts to steer clear of cultural generalisations while conveying often haunting impressions of place and personal encounter. I would argue, however, that Turnbull's narrative, despite her unsophisticated recourse to the discourse of 'national types', probes more deeply into the cultural dimension of the self than Mateer's. In choosing to present his encounters with a minimum of overt interpretation, Mateer tends to leave his own cultural perceptions intact, showing us how elements of Pratt's 'seeing-man' might be present even in narratives that are committed to a decolonising vision. Bouras's and Turnbull's greater openness to different styles of emotional expression and interaction, on the other hand, suggests how travel writing in English might go beyond the limitations presented by Pratt, to engage with, and not merely distantly observe, 'cultural others'.

Notes

[1] Dorfman, Ariel 1998, *Heading South, Looking North: A bilingual journey*, Farrar Straus & Giroux, New York; Hoffman, Eva 1989, *Lost in Translation: A life in a new language*, Heinemann, London; Mori, Kyoko 1997, *Polite Lies: On being a woman caught between cultures*, Henry Holt, New York.

[2] Grewal, Inderpal 1996, *Home and Harem: Nation, gender, empire and the cultures of travel*, Duke University Press, Durham, NC; Holland, Patrick and Huggan, Graham 1998, *Tourists with Typewriters: Critical reflections on contemporary travel writing*, University of Michigan Press, Ann Arbor; Kaplan, Caren 1996, *Questions of Travel: Postmodern discourses of displacement*, Duke University Press, Durham, NC; Porter, Dennis 1991, *Haunted Journeys: Desire and transgression in European travel writing*, Princeton University Press, Princeton; Pratt, Mary Louise 1992, *Imperial Eyes: Travel writing and transculturation*, Routledge, London, p. 218. Michael Cronin's excellent *Across the Lines: Travel, language, translation* (2000, Cork University Press, Cork) is an exception to this rule.

[3] Bouras, Gillian 1986, *A Foreign Wife*, McPhee Gribble/Penguin, Fitzroy, Victoria; Turnbull, Sarah 2002, *Almost French: A new life in Paris*, Bantam Books, Milsons Point, NSW; Mateer, John 2004, *Semar's Cave: An Indonesian journal*, Fremantle Arts Centre Press, Fremantle, WA.

[4] See also Kaplan, *Questions of Travel*; and Holland and Huggan, *Tourists with Typewriters*.

[5] Pratt, *Imperial Eyes*, p. 226.

[6] Mateer, *Semar's Cave*, p. 69.

[7] Bouras, Gillian 1991, *A Fair Exchange*, McPhee Gribble/Penguin, Ringwood, Victoria; 1994, *Aphrodite and the Others*, McPheeGribble/Penguin, Ringwood, Victoria; 1996, *A Stranger Here*, Penguin, Ringwood, Victoria; 1999, *Starting Again*, Penguin, Ringwood, Victoria. See McLaren, John 2001, *States of Imagination: Nationalism, citizenship and multiculturalism in writings from Australia and southern Asia* Australian Scholarly Publishing, Melbourne, for a detailed and illuminating discussion of four of these texts.

[8] Bouras, *Foreign Wife*, p. 123.

[9] Ibid., pp. 121–2.

[10] Ibid., p. 146.

[11] Parks, Tim 1996 [2001], *An Italian Education*, Vintage, London, p. 142.

[12] Bouras, *Foreign Wife*, p. 124.

[13] Ibid., p. 15.

[14] Ibid., p. 147.

[15] Turnbull, *Almost French*, pp. 79, 134, 143.

[16] Ibid., pp. 63–5.

[17] Hanna, Barbara and de Nooy, Juliana 2003, Travel memoirs and intercultural learning, 'The Intercultural Narrative', International Association for Language and Intercultural Communication Conference, University of Lancaster, 14–16 December 2003.

[18] Turnbull, *Almost French*, pp. 68–9.

[19] Ibid., pp. 171–2.

[20] *Arts, Ethics and Literature*, The Thylazine Foundation Pty Ltd, available from http://www.thylazine.org/directory/directm/

[21] Mateer, *Semar's Cave*, p. 59.

[22] Ibid., p. 239.

[23] Such as Duncan Graham in his nonetheless insightful *The People Next Door: Understanding Indonesia* (2004, University of Western Australia Press, Nedlands, WA). For a perspective closer to Mateer's, see Hoon, Chang-Yau 2006, 'Defining (multiple) selves: reflections on fieldwork in Jakarta', *Life Writing*, vol. 3, no. 1, pp. 81–102.

[24] Mateer, *Semar's Cave*, p. 274.

[25] Cronin, *Across the Lines*, p. 83.

[26] Australian expatriates in particular come in for a degree of suspicion; they are seen as more or less complicit with neo-colonial power structures. The book conveys Mateer's unease with his own position as the beneficiary of a government-funded cultural exchange program between Australia and Indonesia.

[27] Mateer, *Semar's Cave*, p. 170.

[28] Ibid., p. 50.

[29] Ibid., p. 55.

[30] Ibid., p. 67; Johnson, Amanda 2005, 'Passage to Indonesia, Review of John Mateer, *Semar's Cave*', *Meanjin. Tongues: Special issue on translation*, vol. 64, no. 4, pp. 60–9. Mateer published a critical response on the *Meanjin* web site, but as this page of *Meanjin* is updated and features new material now, it is no longer available.

[31] *Semar's Cave*, p. 56.

[32] See Attinasi, John and Friedrich, Paul 1995, 'Dialogic breakthrough: catalysis and synthesis in life-changing dialogue', in Bruce Mannheim and Dennis Tedlock (eds), *The Dialogic Emergence of Culture*, University of Illinois Press, Urbana, pp. 33–53.

Chapter 16

America and the queer diaspora: the case of artist David McDiarmid

Sally Gray

[New York] felt like home as soon as I went there. It felt comfortable. It felt like a place you could grow. I felt that I'd done everything that I could in Sydney for the moment. It was like going to school on a very high level: on an art level, a sex level—the two most important things. It was like a playground. There was such a lot happening. It was not that frantic, it suited me, the pace. So why not live there? It was a really easy choice.[1]

The life and work of Australian artist David McDiarmid were impacted on strongly by his long-term interest in North American literary, visual and popular culture—an interest that was consolidated during his period of travel and residence in the United States between 1977 and 1987. McDiarmid's art, produced between 1976 and 1995 and which he designated from the beginning 'gay art', might be seen as both 'mobile and located', to borrow a term from Marsha Meskimmon,[2] in the sense that it was neither 'Australian' nor 'American' but an eclectic, multivalent attempt at a gay male art of his time. McDiarmid's diverse art practice was inflected by his evident commitment to the idea of a mobile, 'becoming' sexual, political and creative subjectivity. It was this commitment that was the principal driver of McDiarmid's 1977 decision to live in New York. Before, during and after his American period, he created a body of work that existed across geographical and cultural boundaries and across the interstitial sexual and gender categories explored in recent decades by queer theory.[3]

Nomadic subjectivity and the city

This interstitial character of McDiarmid's art practice involved a play across geography, time and diverse realms of cultural experience. He had a postmodern lack of respect for modernist and Eurocentric hierarchies of culture and his art practice employed a 'maverick orientalism' of cultural appropriation.[4]

Listing books he might one day write, Roland Barthes suggested he might write 'The discourse of homosexuality' or 'The discourses of homosexuality' or, again, 'The discourse of homosexualities', referring to the instability of sexual identity.[5] McDiarmid's art is an evocation of such a notion: of multiple, polysemous discourses of sexuality and multiple possible homosexualities. In the course of his career, and in his pioneering enactment of 'gay artist', McDiarmid chose to place himself in liminal cultural zones relating to geography, sexuality, gender, race, culture, history and aesthetics. This gives his work a multivalent complexity and rewards a viewing of it as more than the simple politics of fixed gay identity. His placement of himself in New York, the then metropolitan centre of international gay male life, gave him the freedom and complexity he sought in order to explore a multifaceted identity in his art and his life, as evidenced in his own account:

> Yeah. Felt very hemmed in by conservative art scene queens who didn't feel that politics was part of art and didn't feel that you can include any kind of confrontational aspect into your work and I never saw art as being a safe thing. I know that exists but that's not something that involves me. My references were always edgy feminist stuff, or whatever, and that was always seen as being marginal [but] I never thought of it in that way. I thought they [feminists] were actually right on the edge concerning my life, my sexual identity, the whole notion of how people are labelled, why we're marginalised.[6]

Art, sex, politics and America

It is not difficult to imagine the pull of American culture, particularly the space and time landscape of New York in the late 1970s, for an artist such as McDiarmid. His visual and sociopolitical sense was already attuned to American artistic, commercial and popular culture and, most importantly, to the gay identity politics that had emerged there, with the aftermath of the Stonewall events of 1969 building on the cultural politics of the civil rights and women's liberation movements. In addition to his engagement with dissenting American cultures, McDiarmid was interested in the big, bold and outrageous qualities offered by American wealth and cultural promiscuity.

From the point of view of more adventurous Australian artists, by the mid 1960s, the United States was beginning to supplant Europe as the mythical centre of the Western avant-garde culture. Australian contemporary art curator John Stringer, who spent several years in the United States, wrote:

> Due to colonial legacies and cultural allegiances, most [Australian] artists up until [the] mid [twentieth] century were inclined to seek their artistic nemesis [sic] in Europe—which for most Australians meant London—but with the 1960s this monopoly was broken, and...adventurous souls [drifted] to the renowned centre of New York.[7]

Moreover, by the late 1970s, the Australia Council for the Arts was funding Australian artists to take up residencies in its supported studios at PSI in Long Island City and Greene Street in Soho.[8] For McDiarmid, however, a few months supported by an Australia Council grant, followed by return to Australia to exhibit the work produced and write up a grant acquittal report, was not what he was seeking. As a politically aware gay man, McDiarmid saw himself as an international or diasporic gay male subject rather than as an 'Australian' artist. He was, as evidenced in his recorded views and his personal and creative decisions, more interested in immersing himself in a sexually dissident American urban culture, which resonated with his embrace of a mobile 'becoming' subjectivity. He was convinced that his art, his life and his sexuality all needed to be developed in New York and he needed to make himself 'American' in some way for this to happen. The city provided an opportunity to release his subjectivity and his creative identity from 'fixed referents', to use Nigel Thrift's term, and to form and reform personal subjectivity in, as Thrift said, a 'hybrid and dialogic' context in which identity was being constantly 'copied, revised, enunciated and performed'.[9] While McDiarmid continued to exhibit in Australia throughout his period of residence in New York, which ended in 1987, he was, in taking up what was intended to be permanent residence in New York, moving his centre from Australia to America. 'Why not live there?' he recalls in the 1992 interview quoted at the beginning of this chapter.

America as fantasy

No doubt it was the idea and the fantasy of New York that drew McDiarmid, like so many other artists and immigrants, to the city. 'A city named in certain ways also becomes that city through the practices of people in response to the labels', and they 'perform the labels', argue urban theorists Ash Amin and Nigel Thrift.[10] Hal Foster also makes the observation in his catalogue essay for the 1982 exhibition *Brand New York*, at the Institute of Contemporary Art in London, that 'New York is a projection as well as a place'.[11] While that observation is true of many cities, New York holds a special place, especially for artists, as the ultimate modern city of the twentieth century. The idea of 'America', as I have said, was part of McDiarmid's mobile sexual and creative identity formation. America represented the new, the culturally and sexually radical, the artistically innovative and avant-garde, the profligate, excessive and rich, the hip and the cool.

Richard Sennett, in his essay 'Civic bodies: multi-cultural New York', writes that before he came to New York for the first time in the 1970s, he had, as he puts it, 'read his way into' Greenwich Village, in the pages of Jane Jacobs' influential book *The Death and Life of Great American Cities*.[12] McDiarmid also 'read his way into' New York but in his case it was through the *Village Voice*, Andy Warhol's *Interview*, gay periodicals such as *Christopher Street*, the work of the Beat writers William Burroughs and Allen Ginsberg and other gay male writers including James Baldwin, Edmund White, Gore Vidal and Samuel Delany.

McDiarmid's 'America' and gay liberation

In 1972, at the age of twenty, five years before his first visit to the United States, and before he identified himself publicly as an artist, McDiarmid wrote an essay for the *Sydney Gay Liberation Newsletter*, a journal that he, as an early member of Gay Liberation, had helped found, edit and illustrate. Entitled 'Memoirs of an oppressed teenager', the essay noted that it was the reading of American gay liberationist publications that had convinced him that embracing same-sex desire, rather than hiding it—regarded as a sensible self-protective option in early 1970s Melbourne—might help him open opportunities for personal and creative growth.[13] His friend and co-resident of New York, the Australian artist Sam Schönbaum, later recalled the Melbourne in which both men had grown up as 'a closet of protestant mediocrity'.[14] Instead of the repressive tolerance that McDiarmid's essay suggests he thought he might expect from his friends, family and the broader world, there was a world—and he saw it as America—in which a new kind of utopian gay male sociality, and the promise of an ecstatic sexuality, was there for exploration. In this, he was not alone. Mark Turner, writing about gay male street cruising in New York and London, states:

> [T]here are many gay stories, but the story that touches my subject is the one about urban migration, the move of the marginalised from the country to the cities and capitals of America and Europe, many of which represented a New Gay Jerusalem or Mecca by the end of the twentieth century. San Francisco. New York. London. These cities had long established and thriving queer cultures and cultures of sexual dissidence, which have become the subject of academic and popular studies seeking to put gay urban history on the map.[15]

McDiarmid was part of this diasporic global movement of gay men into New York and other major American cities that accelerated from the late 1960s and early 1970s. These cities had their own gay male subcultural networks and underground maps of important locales that were a magnet for the oppressed and the daring until the beginning of the AIDS epidemic began to be felt in the early 1980s.

The imagined city

The materiality of McDiarmid's art, its content, ideas and technique, are all influenced by the experience and the idea of 'America'. *Alphabet City* (Figure 16.1), a work created in New York in 1983–84 and exhibited in *David McDiarmid: New work* at Roslyn Oxley Gallery, Sydney, in October 1984, refers not just to a geographical place—the zone around Avenues A, B, C and D east of First Avenue on the Lower East Side of Manhattan, close to where McDiarmid then lived—but to a condition of being in that space.

America and the queer diaspora: the case of artist David McDiarmid

Figure 16.1: David McDiarmid, *Alphabet City*, 1983–84.

Acrylic on cotton bed sheet, 228 cm x 251 cm. Private Collection. Reproduced with permission of the McDiarmid Estate.

The making of this work coincided with the growth of the East Village and the Lower East Side generally as the radical edge of the New York art world, challenging Soho as the locale of the newest, most interesting and youthful art. The small shopfront galleries of the East Village showed work that, among other things, embraced the excitement and abjection of street life.

This painting forms part of a series of works by McDiarmid, known as the 'bed-sheet paintings' because they are executed on cotton sheets. The series adopts the style and iconography of subway graffiti of the 1970s and 1980s and the New York street memorials of the 1980s.[16] The work intersects with that of other artists working with graffiti-derived techniques at this time, such as Keith Haring and Jean Michel Basquiat.[17] McDiarmid's work, however, is celebratory of the city in a way that the work of the American-born artists is not. McDiarmid's *Alphabet City* is a celebration, by an insider who is also an outsider, of the diversity and cultural promiscuity of New York, encompassing as it does the idea of an excessive 'everything' from A to Z. The employment of the visual trope of a familiar yet fictitious New York skyline—with the then iconic twin towers of the World Trade Centre, Philip Johnson's AT&T (now Sony) Building and the Empire State Building placed in a line—reveals a telescoped viewing position that is not in itself *of* New York. This work is a fictional postcard of a self-invented nomadic world located in downtown Manhattan and viewed from the vantage point of an insider–outsider member of a diasporic gay male community.

Art and sex

McDiarmid's attraction to New York was first and foremost to the homosocial and sexual possibilities in a city that had a high population density, broad racial and cultural diversity and was inscribed with a subcultural map of gay male places of significance, some of which had been gay meeting places for decades and others of which had sprung into prominence post Stonewall. As George Chauncey showed, New York, as one of the major port cities of the world, had been a magnet for thousands of homosexual men from the armed services who had declined to go home to their provincial towns and farms after World War II demobilisation.[18] Stonewall—the events in and around the Stonewall Inn in Lower Manhattan in 1969—was subsequently a trigger for the burgeoning of an urban gay male scene that was reproduced and emulated by other large Western cities, including San Francisco, London and Sydney.

By the time McDiarmid finally moved to New York to take up settled residence there, in June of 1979, at the age of twenty-seven, he was a self-identified gay political artist. His first one-person show, *Secret Love*, had explored gay male sexuality and sociality inside and outside of the closet. The drawings and collage works of this exhibition asserted a centrality for homosexual desire and made political claims for social and legal equality. He also exhibited in, and designed the poster for, the first self-identified exhibition of Australian gay and lesbian artists at Watters Gallery, Sydney, in July 1978. Entitled *Homosexual and Lesbian Artists*, this exhibition was associated with the Fourth National Homosexual Conference held at Paddington Town Hall in August of that year. By the time of McDiarmid's first visit to the United States, three months after the *Secret Love* exhibition, the enduring interconnection between his art practice, his political consciousness and his sexuality was established.

The work for the 1976 *Secret Love* exhibition was already inflected by ideas of 'America'. McDiarmid used aspects of American popular culture, including

Hollywood films and literature, in works with titles such as *A Straight-Stud Named Desire* (a collaged image of Marlon Brando from *A Street Car Named Desire*), *Myra Lives* (referencing Gore Vidal's *Myra Breckinridge*) and *Plato's End* (with collaged images of film star Sal Mineo in his role as the closeted gay love interest in *Rebel Without A Cause*). The title of the exhibition, *Secret Love*, quoted the words of the song, famously sung by Doris Day in the film *Calamity Jane*, about a 'secret [in this case gay] love', which need be 'secret no more'. This camp appropriation of American popular culture was interspersed with other works that referenced more Australian concerns.

Influenced by America Pop Art collage in its content, method and politics, McDiarmid's 1976 work expressed a personal idiolect, which was neither wholly Australian nor wholly American. By this I mean that his visual language and artistic conceptual concerns were refracted through the embrace of American culture in such a way as to form the kind of 'hybrid' and 'dialogic'[19] language that arises from a nomadic 'becoming' subjectivity. After his first trip to the United States in 1977, McDiarmid's work adopted an even more American visual and conceptual language in response to his intoxication with urban New York.

> Firstly, every street is a beat!! If you walk around for an hour or so, just looking in shop windows, soon enough some number will look, and then look again, and then look again, and then say 'Hi! How ya doin'? Wanna get it on?' Honey it's unbelievable. I went to Bloomingdale's last week (the ultimate dept store…ultimate, ultimate) and was just wandering around, and sure enough, in 10 mins, there's 2 sets of eyes following!! Found out yesterday it *is* a notorious beat, but at the time I was stunned.[20]

McDiarmid's one-person show *Trade Enquiries*, held at Hogarth Galleries, Sydney, in 1978, explored the visuality and coded communication of gay male bars and street cruising in New York and San Francisco. Exhibited the year after his first visit to the United States, this work references the performative dress and image typologies of gay men in urban America. Materials for this series of collaged and offset printed works included graphics and text from the American gay press and hyper-masculine images of gay male visual identity: 'clones', lumberjacks, studs and cowboys.[21] The collaged appropriated fragments that made up the 1978 *Trade Enquiries* artworks included sexually coded ads from the 'personal' columns of gay newspapers, romantic popular song titles, published pornography and fetish imagery, portions of colour-coded bandanas denoting coded sexual practices and images of well-groomed moustached 'clones'—'juicy fruits', who look identical but are given by the artist interchangeable names: Ralph, Joe, Frank, Jack, Tom, Steve, Rick and Charlie (Figure 16.2). These works, produced out of the beats, bars, backrooms and clubs of San Francisco and New York, embody pleasurable engagement and ironic detachment.

Figure 16.2: David McDiarmid, *Juicy fruits: Ralph, Joe, Frank...*, 1978.

Offset lithograph from *Trade Enquiries*, series of nine prints with cover, 37.1 cm x 28.2 cm. Private Collection. Reproduced with permission of the McDiarmid Estate.

On his first visit to the United States from March to October of 1977, McDiarmid travelled extensively on the east and west coasts, focusing on the gay male urban communities of the Castro in San Francisco and the zones surrounding Christopher Street in Lower Manhattan. The America that McDiarmid was attracted to was not the world of official or dominant American culture but that of 'America's own rebellion', as Janet Wolff put it[22] —not the world of what became known as Reaganomics, conservative family and religious values and what Wolff called America's 'institutionalised and pervasive racism', but the world of sexual permissiveness, interracial mingling and urban cultural innovation and daring.[23] For a young man from the geographical and cultural periphery, the bright lights and cultural complexities of New York, the metropolitan centre, along with its abjections, provided a compelling magnetism that animated McDiarmid's personal and creative life for the remainder of his career.

> This city is breath-taking. I thought California was great but this is *it*! I never want to leave! The air is electric, the sidewalks are magic and the people are crazy crazy crazy.[24]

McDiarmid's early interest in gay liberation politics and the idea of a potential 'gay art' were intensified by the experience of being in New York, the home of admired gay male artists Andy Warhol, Keith Haring, Robert Mapplethorpe and David Wojnorowicz. This gay male art of the 1970s and 1980s, which Emmanuel Cooper called 'virtually a new art', was based on a 'new homosexual eroticism'[25] that McDiarmid had explored since his earliest exhibited work, the *Secret Love* show in December 1976 just before his first trip to the United States.

Before Mayor Giuliani's 'zero-tolerance' New York

A poetics of sensuality through drugs, music and sex was uniquely available in New York in the late 1970s, before the inner boroughs underwent gentrification-related transformation from the mid 1980s.[26] It was still possible for artists and the culturally radical or marginal to afford to live in metropolitan New York, and McDiarmid was attuned to the relative cultural freedom that the streets of the city offered at this time, before 'zero-tolerance' policing of street misdemeanours changed the cultural character of inner city New York.[27] McDiarmid had been interested by the more dissident traditions in American intellectual and cultural life, as evidenced in his 1972 essay and in subsequent interviews.

In spite of conservative political regimes such as those of Ronald Reagan (US President from 1981–89) and Margaret Thatcher (British Prime Minister from 1979–90), the 1970s and early 1980s in the urban West were a period of paradoxical cultural and social radicalism. The idea of 'politics' had been extended beyond the traditional parameters of the liberal and Marxist left to include personal and private life, sexuality, gender and race and to incorporate hitherto incompatible cultural themes and political methodologies. Andrew Ross describes this post-1960s politics, largely of the Western middle class, as generating 'a vocabulary of dissent and anti-authoritarianism', wielded against an establishment that was 'struggling to resolve, through consumerism, its long crisis of over production'. In this struggle,

> [t]he discourses of hedonism began to outstrip the limits of the controlled structures of consumer society, and soon a wholesale ideology of disaffiliation from the institutions of establishment culture was in place, complete with its own structures (in the areas of the family, education, labour, media, taste, lifestyle, and morality), founded on utopian premises.[28]

McDiarmid's personal and creative practice—the kind of art he made and the kind of sociality he engaged in—fell firmly on the hedonistic side of the hedonism–consumption tension mentioned by Ross. His oeuvre as a whole, while remaining intensely political, engages the hedonistic politics of pleasure and excess extending to the utopian and the ecstatic.

'America' and cultural excess

As an artist, McDiarmid was attracted to the popular, the glamorous and the commercial, as well as to the critical and political, and his work engaged the visually pleasurable, perverse, camp and ironic interfaces between commercial popular culture and the high-art world, which had also animated American Pop Art. America was perhaps an inevitable destination for an artist for whom the eroticism in advertising and commercial graphic design was an enduring trope of his own sexuality and his creative imagination, as he recounted in a 1992 interview:

> I constructed sexual fantasies around advertising, which was around when I was a kid. I was 11 years old when I saw a newspaper ad for Jantzen swimwear. It was 1963, and the look was American collegiate and blonde. I can still remember the pattern of chest hair on the model's washboard and the shape of his thighs. The image stayed with me for days and weeks, until its power drove me to spend an afternoon searching through a stack of old newspapers in our garage, looking for that picture.[29]

Ecstasy and utopia in McDiarmid's New York work

America was the exciting, 'excessive', 'overloaded' option for McDiarmid;[30] Europe was merely the redundantly authoritative and stuffy one. In the last quarter of the twentieth century, when McDiarmid was coming to political and cultural awareness in Melbourne and Sydney, and when it came to making cultural choices, he chose 'excessive' and 'overloaded' over authoritative. In this context of pleasurable excess and utopian sensuality, African-American dance music and underground dance clubbing would also become an important influence on McDiarmid's life and art.[31]

All of the themes of cultural excess and sensuality to be found in 1970s New York came together in the 1979–81 suite of work to which McDiarmid gave the title *Disco Kwilts*—making reference to the black and Hispanic, gay underground dance club Paradise Garage. Located in a disused trucking garage at 84 King Street in Lower Manhattan, and operating between 1977 and 1987, Paradise Garage was known for its groundbreaking DJ Larry Levan, one of the originators of house music. The club's state-of-the-art lighting and sound systems were unsurpassed in the years of its operation, and the club's dedication to making each night a huge private party for its mixed-race clientele was legendary.[32] Reflective shining surfaces and a camp glamour were hallmarks of disco music and dancing and the underground house-music club scene that grew out of disco. Gloss, glamour, glitz and an underground idea of 'celebrity'—gained by being a stunning dancer or dresser—were an implicit part of the experience and the imagined idea of the Paradise Garage. The house-music dance club is, as Brian Currid writes, 'a site in which the performance of "self", the spectacle of the "other", and one's reception as a spectacle of "otherness" provides a complex site for identity formation, and the fabrication of communal histories'.[33]

McDiarmid's *Disco Kwilt* series of work was created as what could be thought of as a community artefact, to reflect and embody the affect of the dance floor and the community that participated in it. The series resonates with the 'explicit utopianism' contained in many house-music anthems, 'especially those with their roots in gay black America'.[34] McDiarmid employed in the fabrication of this work what was then an expensive commercial display material—holographic reflective Mylar sheeting—to evoke the sensations, seductions and illusions of the underground dance club. In a 1980 work, itself entitled *Disco Kwilt*, McDiarmid used American pioneer women's quilting patterns—in this case, the 'tumbling block' or 'baby block' pattern—to create a decorative, flashy and consciously 'shallow' work that frankly embraces the excitement of flashing lights, reflective surfaces and the visual, corporeal and spatial mobility of the dance floor (Figure 16.3).

The visual excess of the work evokes the ecstatic and utopian impulses integral to the lyrics and musicality of house music and the gay male identity politics and sociality of this heady time before the first cases of AIDS became public. Unlike the traditional familial quilt, the *Disco Kwilts* collectively proposed a 'beyond-blood' notion of kinship and community—a community that McDiarmid found in the multiracial gay male community of New York.[35] The night-time sociality of the dance club, with its intoxicating visual and aural excess and its collective expression of hip and cool, was captured in these works, which represented quintessentially the New York that McDiarmid sought and found.[36]

Figure 16.3: David McDiarmid, *Disco Kwilt*, c. 1980.

Reflective holographic Mylar foil on board, 120 cm x 160 cm. Private Collection. Reproduced with permission of the McDiarmid estate.

Conclusion

As gender theorist Elizabeth Grosz writes: 'The city is one of the crucial factors in the social production of sexed corporeality.'[37] David McDiarmid's location of himself in New York involved a commitment to the development of a mobile way of being a gay man, an artist and a cultural subject. His early interest in urban American gay culture, his extended presence in New York and his openness to allowing these to act on his performance of a 'hybrid and dialogic' subjectivity[38] engendered a personal idiolect in his art produced from 1976 until his death in 1995.

Notes

[1] David McDiarmid, interviewed by Carmela Baranowska, 1992. Transcript in McDiarmid Estate Papers, State Library of New South Wales.

[2] Meskimmon, Marsha 2004, 'Corporeal theory with/in practice: Christine Borland's *Winter Garden*', in G. Perry (ed.), *Difference and Excess in Contemporary Art: The visibility of women's practice*, Blackwell, Malden, Mass., Oxford, UK, and Carlton, Australia, p. 126.

[3] Sedgwick, Eve Kosofsky 1993, *Tendencies*, Duke University Press, Durham, NC, p. xii.

[4] Ross, Andrew 1999, 'Uses of camp', in F. Cleto (ed.), *Queer Aesthetics and the Performing Subject*, University of Michigan Press, Ann Arbor, p. 320.

[5] Barthes, Roland 2000, '*Projets de livres*—projected books', in S. Sontag (ed.), *A Roland Barthes Reader*, Vintage, London, p. 420.

[6] David McDiarmid, interviewed by Paul Canning, March 1993. Transcript in McDiarmid Estate Papers, State Library of New South Wales.

[7] Stringer, John 2002, 'Cultivating the field', in J. Smith (ed.), *Fieldwork: Australian art 1968–2002*, National Gallery of Victoria, Melbourne, p. 16.

[8] I am grateful to Billy Crawford of the Australia Council for providing a complete list of all Australian artists who have taken up Australia Council-funded residencies at these studios.

[9] Thrift, Nigel 1996, *Spatial Formations*, Sage, London, p. 295.

[10] Amin, Ash and Thrift, Nigel 2002, *Cities: Re-imagining the urban*, Polity Press and Blackwell Publishers, Cambridge, p. 23.

[11] Foster, Hal 1982, 'New York: seven types of ambiguity', in L. Appignesi (ed.), *Brand New York*, Institute of Contemporary Art, London, p. 24.

[12] Sennett, Richard 1994, *Flesh and Stone: The body and the city in Western civilization*, Faber and Faber, London and Boston, p. 355.

[13] McDiarmid, David 1972, 'Memoirs of an oppressed teenager', *Sydney Gay Liberation Newsletter*, vol. 1, no. 4, Sydney, (no page numbers).

[14] Sam Schönbaum, Typescript, in McDiarmid Estate Papers. State Library of New South Wales.

[15] Turner, Mark W. 2003, *Backward Glances: Cruising the queer streets of New York and London*, Reaktion Books, London, p. 44.

[16] Cooper, Martha and Sciorra, Joseph 1994, *RIP New York Spray Can Memorials*, Thames and Hudson, London.

[17] McDiarmid recounted later that he had known Haring socially and he acknowledged that their work intersected; he did not mention Basquiat. David McDiarmid, interviewed by Carmela Baranowska.

[18] Chauncey, George 1996, 'Privacy can only be had in public: gay uses of the streets', in J. Sanders (ed.), *Stud: Architectures of masculinity*, Princeton Architectural Press, New York, p. 259.

[19] Thrift, *Spatial Formations*, p. 295.

[20] Letter, David McDiarmid (in New York) to Peter Tully (in Sydney), 12–13 May 1977, McDiarmid Estate Papers, State Library of New South Wales.

[21] Cole, Shaun 1997, 'Macho man: clones and the development of a masculine stereotype', *Fashion Theory. Volume 3*, Berg, Oxford, pp. 125–40.

[22] Wolff, Janet 1995, *Resident Alien: Feminist cultural criticism*, Yale University Press, New Haven, Connecticut, and London, p. 139.

[23] Ibid., p. 140.

[24] Letter, David McDiarmid (in New York) to Peter Tully (in Sydney), 4 May 1977, McDiarmid Estate Papers, State Library of New South Wales.

[25] Cooper, Emmanuel 1994, *The Sexual Perspective: Homosexuality and art in the last 100 years*, Routledge, London and New York, p. 303.

[26] Mele, Christopher 2000, *Selling the Lower East Side: Culture, real estate and resistance in New York City*, University of Minnesota Press, Minneapolis and London, pp. 180–219.

[27] Ibid.

[28] Ross, 'Uses of camp', p. 314.

[29] David McDiarmid, interviewed by Carmela Baranowska.

[30] I borrow these terms from Jean Baudrillard (with Sans, Jerome) 1998, 'New York forever: interview by Jerome Sans with Jean Baudrillard', *Visual Arts and Culture: An international journal of contemporary art*, vol. 1, part 1, pp. 70–6).

[31] Gray, Sally 2007, 'Reinterpreting a textile tradition: David McDiarmid's ecstatic and utopian *Klub Kwilt*', *Textile History*, vol. 38, no. 2, November, Pasold Research and Maney Publishing, London and Leeds.

[32] Fikentscher, Kai 2000, *You Better Work! Underground dance music in New York City*, University Press of New England, Hanover and London, pp. 61–2.

[33] Currid, Brian 1995, 'We are family: house music and queer performativity', in S. Case et al. (eds), *Cruising the Performative: Interventions into the representation of ethnicity, nationality and sexuality*, Indiana University Press, Bloomington and Indianapolis, p. 178.

[34] Gilbert, Jeremy and Pearson, Ewan 1999, *Discographies: Dance music, culture and the politics of sound*, Routledge, New York and London, p. 168.

[35] For McDiarmid's idea of 'beyond-blood' kinship, see Gray, S. 2006, There's always more; the art of David McDiarmid, PhD thesis, University of New South Wales.

[36] Farris Thompson, Robert 1998, 'An aesthetic of cool', in B. Beckley (ed.), *Uncontrollable Beauty: Towards a new aesthetics*, Allworth Press and School of Visual Arts, New York, p. 372.

[37] Grosz, Elizabeth 1995, *Space Time and Perversion*, Routledge, London and New York, p. 104.

[38] Thrift, *Spatial Formations*, p. 295.

Objects of displacement

Chapter 17

Living in a material world: object biography and transnational lives

Karen Schamberger, Martha Sear, Kirsten Wehner, Jennifer Wilson and the *Australian Journeys* Gallery Development Team, National Museum of Australia

In 1989, Mrs Guna Kinne wrote to the National Museum of Australia about her Latvian national dress. 'As I have no female descendants,' she explained, 'I wish to donate the costume to an institution, preferably the National Museum.'[1] The museum, then actively pursuing the development of a migration heritage collection, gratefully accepted Mrs Kinne's offer.

As part of the donation, curator Sally Fletcher wrote to Mrs Kinne asking for information about the object and its owner.[2] Mrs Kinne replied with a letter detailing how she had begun making the dress as a teenager in Riga in the late 1930s, had taken it as her 'most important possession' when she fled the Soviet invasion of Latvia, completed it while a Displaced Person in Germany and wore it at protests for Latvian independence in Australia.[3]

It was clear that for Mrs Kinne the dress's life and her own were inextricably interwoven. The story of how the dress was made and worn was also her story, connecting Riga with Wangaratta and adolescence with old age. Further still, however, it was apparent how much the costume had shaped Mrs Kinne's experiences. Its thick and bulky fabric made her only suitcase heavy as she ran to catch the last Red Cross train from Gdansk to Berlin, and, on the day she wore it proudly for the first time, she met the man who would become her husband. She went to great lengths to make and keep hold of the dress, and each time she put it on the feelings it gave her to wear it—physically, emotionally, culturally and politically—formed an integral part of how she experienced the events in her life.

During her lifetime, Mrs Kinne assembled the story of making, wearing, keeping and giving the dress as a form of mutual biography. This was not, however, a biography in the conventional sense; it did not employ a completely linear narrative, and it was made as much from materiality as it was by words. The dress was not just a trigger to memory, it was a rich source of embodied knowledge about personal experience. Touching and talking about the dress collapsed space and time, bringing Riga in 1939, a Displaced Persons camp in Germany in 1945 and the streets of Melbourne in the 1970s together in a single moment.

From early 2009, Mrs Kinne's dress will be on display in the new *Australian Journeys* Gallery at the National Museum of Australia. *Australian Journeys* explores the transnational character of Australian experience. It traces the passage of people to, from and across the Australian continent and examines how migrants, sojourners, tourists and travellers have built and maintained connections between places in Australia and places overseas.

In developing the exhibition, the *Australian Journeys* Gallery Development Team has sought to better understand how objects participate in, shape and express transnational historical experience. We have explored how objects—understood broadly to include things, images, media and text—connect people, across time and space, with their own historical selves as well as with places here and abroad. Drawing on recent material culture scholarship, we have employed a method of 'object biography' to examine the historical agency of particular objects and collections in mediating transnational experience. We have also paid particular attention to the idea that objects generate what film-maker David Macdougall has called 'being knowledge' and what we call 'object knowledge'—embodied understandings of the world that constitute the foundation for any understanding of lived experience.[4]

In this chapter, we present two 'object biographies' that reflect complex intertwinings of the life histories of an object and a human subject. We reflect on what the process of exploring the agency of the material world through 'object biography' might reveal about the development of transnational selves and their examination through biography. We also suggest the value of attending more closely to the ways autobiography and biography might take material as well as written forms, particularly in relation to the development of museum collections and museum exhibitions.

Object biography

A focus on the flow of people, things, ideas and practices across national boundaries defines transnational scholarship.[5] Rather than seeing these flows as distinct streams, a growing body of work argues that places, people, things, practices and ideas, constantly in motion, shape each other.[6] An effort to understand better how things participate in this interaction has led the curatorial team at the National Museum of Australia to employ object biography as a method for researching collections and developing the *Australian Journeys* Gallery.

Object biography is an analytical process that has emerged within material culture studies as a way to reveal and understand object agency. As Chris Gosden and Yvonne Marshall have described it, an object biography examines an artefact's life history to 'address the way social interactions involving people and objects create meaning' and to understand how these meanings 'change and are renegotiated through the life of an object'.[7] Such a biography might include information about an object's genealogy, its manufacture, use, possession, exchange, alteration, movement and destruction or preservation, obtained from a wide variety of sources. Considering an object's life in a dynamic, active relationship with human lives raises questions about how people and things articulate in culturally and historically specific ways. One set of questions revolves around how object relationships form, form part of, perform or represent a sense of self.[8] A second set arises from arguments for the agency of objects in these processes.[9]

Object biography makes notions of self and agency more dynamic, more complex and more culturally specific. It also suggests the merits of an approach to the biography of people that engages with material culture and an individual's personal, social and cultural relationship with objects. '[E]mphasizing the manner in which things create people,' Gosden argues, 'is part of a rhetorical strategy to rebalance the relationship between people and things, so that artefacts are not always seen as passive and people as active.'[10] This is the way in which much biography, even in museums, is written. When objects feature in personal biography, they are often positioned as relics or illustrations. This diminishes or obscures objects' agency in shaping a life by restricting them to memorial or representational roles, and limiting the range of their effects to impressions on a somewhat disembodied mind, rather than a sensing and perceptual body.

Understandings of lives and events experienced across the boundaries of nations can be enriched particularly by a conversation with material culture studies, which are increasingly moving towards explorations across the boundaries of materiality and subjectivity. Gosden and Marshall, reflecting on Marilyn Strathern's study of ideas of a distributed self in Melanesia, argue that attending to the complex relationships between people and things 'has radical implications for the notion of biography. Material things are not external supports or measures of an internal life, but rather people and things have mutual biographies which unfold in culturally specific ways.'[11] Gosden's articulation of an 'object-centred approach to agency' draws our attention to 'the effects things have on people', particularly the way 'our senses and emotions [are] educated by the object world'.[12] By exploring how subjectivity is created by the material world, Gosden has shifted the debate from focusing, at least initially, on the 'meanings of objects' towards a closer reading of their effects.[13]

An understanding of how embodied experience is created by the material world opens significant possibilities for researchers exploring the lives of people and how things have moved between places that each represent substantially different material and cultural conditions. Indeed, much of the recent attention given to object agency and object biography can trace its origins to 'a broadening of research paradigms to include transnational movement and connection'.[14] In their influential articles on the social life of things, Arjun Appadurai and Igor Kopytoff proposed biography as a means to understand the agency of objects that moved through space and time.[15] Gosden's further articulation of the approach has emerged from analysis of the flows of people and goods associated with colonialism and imperialism in Papua New Guinea and newly Romanised Britain.[16]

Gosden applied his ideas about the effects of objects to a reading of change and continuity in the material culture of the period surrounding Britain's incorporation into the Roman Empire (150 BC – 200 AD). What emerged was an 'overwhelming impression…of variety, fluidity and regional difference'. This, he admits, leads naturally to an emphasis on transformation: how 'one set of forms becomes another'. This suggests that there is merit in careful readings of the 'logic' behind the creation of hybrid objects and perhaps, by extension, a hybrid self. Gosden writes:

> Overall, cultural forms always have two conflicting elements: they are often made up of bits and pieces taken from many places on the one hand, but these are quickly formed into a coherent whole on the other…We should not spend time trying to identify the original elements of a bipartite Romano-British culture, but rather look at the logics by which the pieces were combined.[17]

These comments have valuable resonances for biographers. Gosden suggests that rather than linear readings of the intersection of two worlds, we might more usefully engage with the non-linear logics that create a hybrid material world, and, in turn, how this hybridity shapes human subjectivity.

More importantly, however, he argues that we need to move beyond even that idea towards notions of transubstantiation, 'which can look at how substances, such as stone, bone, metal or clay, take on forms and qualities which transgress the boundaries between types of substance'. Gosden writes:

> Of even greater interest is that basic alchemy of human being, whereby other substances effect the flesh and blood object of the human body, thereby transmuting a series of objective qualities into subjective ones. The world changes not just in its forms but in its feelings and we can acknowledge that these two dimensions are always linked.[18]

As the boundary between people and things is conceptualised as being more fluid, as well as more various and culturally defined, a useful field emerges for the exploration of the links between 'people, things and ideas' flowing beyond national boundaries.

Object biography and *Australian Journeys*

It is from within this field that the new *Australian Journeys* Gallery will evolve. Object biography has been employed as part of the exhibition development process to make the exhibition truly object-centred, and begin exploring a material history of transnationalism in Australia.

Curators have developed object biographies that encompass the following.

- The physical form of an object and its status as an example of a style, locating the object in relation to its ancestors and exploring how it has inherited and perpetuates certain physical characteristics.
- The materials from which an object is made and the techniques used in its manufacture, and an analysis of how these embody ambitions, practices, skills and material and social conditions.
- The life history of an object, providing a diachronic account of its history that encompasses its production, circulation, use and destruction.
- The social contexts in which it has 'lived', perhaps taking the form of a synchronic slice in which an object is located within a complex of objects as a node of social relations.
- The values associated with an object and the meanings attached to it by people as they produce, use and engage with it. These might include significances, memories, identities and concepts of personhood, and might range from personal associations to broad cultural frameworks.
- The enactment or performance of an object's meaning, including those moments in an object's life when the meanings and social relationships it embodies are performed, elaborated, witnessed and reproduced within a community.

Each object biography has revealed a particular form of transnational object agency. Not all of the biographies were about artefacts with detailed provenance or things strongly linked to a particular personal biography. In some cases, however, the object biography has explored a direct relationship between a particular object and an individual.

Two of these biographies follow. Both form part of larger narratives of conflict, occupation, displacement and relocation. Both link objects and autobiography. Each, however, in its particularity, reveals something about the complex ways objects and people shape each other.

Transnational Ties

Figure 17.1: This Latvian national dress was made and worn by Guna Kinne (nee Klasons) in Latvia, Germany and Australia in the second half of the twentieth century.

Photo: Dean McNicoll, National Museum of Australia: nma.img-ci20051391-030-wm-vs1.tif.

Object biography: Guna Kinne's Latvian national dress
By Karen Schamberger

Guna Kinne was born Guna Klasons on 6 June 1923 in Riga, Latvia. Her father was a seagoing captain and accountant. Her mother was an archivist in Riga's Latvian State Archives. Guna was born and went to school during Latvia's brief period of independence between 1918 and 1939. Latvians had been oppressed by foreign rule for more than 700 years until independence was declared on 18 November 1918. As Guna was growing up, the Latvian Government emphasised the importance of Latvia's 1000-year-old heritage by teaching national dressmaking in schools.

The first part of the dress to be made was the white linen blouse, decorated with red and grey cotton cross-stitch embroidery. The material was purchased in Riga in 1937 and was cut, embroidered and sewn by Guna at high school in 1939 under the supervision of the handiwork teacher. As Guna told me in an oral history interview in 2007:

> I made the blouse at school. I had no particular feelings. It was a task we had to do, so I did it. We could actually pick what type of blouse we wanted and from which national region. I picked a particular one from the district of Nīca. But later I was really emotionally involved...I think I was seventeen years old then...my father gave me the material for the skirt, the jacket and a ready-made crown...I thought, my God, this is very rich, great gift, a national dress! But because I was at that age, I also said, 'My God, all that work which has to go into it?'[19]

The honour of having a national dress ensured Guna soon began the process of assembling its different components. She also acquired the publication *Novadu Tērpi* (*District Gowns*), which contained the patterns for the various national dresses, drawn from regional costume.[20]

By choosing the Nīca dress, Guna was continuing a regional and a national tradition. Guna made up the red wool skirt while still at high school in Riga in about 1941. The women of Nīca began making red skirts for their national dress in the nineteenth century.[21] The Nīca jacket fabric is believed to have originated during the reign of Duke Jacob of Kurzeme in the seventeenth century.[22] In this period, the creation of the costume was a way for Nīca to express its own identity. By the early twentieth century, the regional styles were established and documented during the period of independence as 'national dress' in publications such as *Novadu Tērpi*. As Guna Kinne reflected in her letter to the museum:

> The keeping 'alive' of the National Heritage seemed to assure that our nation was important enough to have a place amongst other nations. In

this light the Latvian National dress became very important, and to own and wear one showed the owner's pride in our small, insignificant and struggling nation...It became the custom to wear the national dress at any important national function but also as an alternative to an evening dress. It was the dream of any Latvian woman, specially a young girl, to own a national dress. It was very complicated to make and costly to buy.[23]

The relationship between national dress and Latvian identity, founded during the country's brief period of independence, continued to evolve throughout the period in which Mrs Kinne made and wore her dress. In the 60 years since she chose it, the Nīca dress has become a symbol of the Latvian nation as a whole.[24]

Latvia's independence would not last long. It was invaded three times in the space of five years: the Soviet Union invaded in June 1940; the Germans invaded in June–July 1941; then, between July 1944 and May 1945, the Soviet Union forcibly reoccupied the country. By the end of World War II, Latvia had lost one-third of its population: executed, killed in war, murdered in the Holocaust, allowed to die by deprivation in prison camps, deported to the Soviet Union and Germany and scattered in prisoner-of-war and displaced persons camps across Europe.[25]

Many Latvians, including Guna Klasons, fled Latvia as the second Soviet invasion was coming. Fearing her country's destruction, she took with her the remnants not only of her personal life but what she knew as the Latvian nation. The unfinished dress, pattern book and some photographs were all she took when she fled Latvia in about 1945 with her mother and sister. As she wrote:

> At that time the dress, including the Latvian jewellery, was my most important possession, sentimentally and materially, and I took the dress and the unfinished jacket with me in my suitcase on a ship to Germany [Gdansk, now in Poland] while fleeing the USSR army.[26]

Her way of preserving and continuing her nation was to preserve and continue to make her national dress. The jacket in particular was made at this time. When she had worn the unfinished dress in Latvia, she had borrowed a jacket. She was able to imagine the finished jacket and, despite her difficult circumstances, was able to draw the pattern onto the material from the pattern book and then embroider it. It was finished in 1945 in Germany in the Russian Zone, as she noted in her 1989 letter:

> It was in the suitcase also when I ran to catch the last Red Cross train carrying wounded Latvian soldiers from Gdansk to Berlin. Neither the suitcase nor the dress was harmed in the Berlin bombardments, and later I took it to Parchim, in Mecklenburg which on the close of the war became part of the Russian zone. There, desperate to find my family,

always short of food, fearing deportation back to Latvia, obtaining false documentation, forced to find new lodgings because of a Russian officer's rape attempt, I finished the jacket.[27]

Figure 17.2: The front and back of the jacket made by Guna Kinne, and the pattern book illustrations used to trace the designs.

National Museum of Australia: nma.img-ci20082088-076-vi-vs1.jpg and nma.img-ci20082088-055-vi-vs1.jpg.

The jacket is especially significant to Mrs Kinne because of the difficult and unusual circumstances in which she made it. Possibly as an expression of her individual taste and circumstances, the embroidery is slightly different to the pattern. The coiled pattern is larger and more free-flowing than that shown in the pattern book. She has also extended the pattern further up the left shoulder. Her 1989 letter continued:

> I had the completed costume in my only suitcase when I fled the Russian Zone. I was then thrown off the train at the border by Russian soldiers but in the dark, rainy night I, still holding the suitcase, fell down the railway embankment and was able to crawl back up to reach the last freight wagons of the train before it started to move and thus escape to the English Zone.
>
> I wore the dress with great pride for the first time there at the Geestacht (near Hamburg) Latvian Displaced Persons Camp dance in December 1945 and met my future husband on that day. The dress was worn at many other dances during that period in [displaced persons] camps in the English and American Zones.[28]

Performances of traditional dance and song were arranged in the displaced persons camps and in Australia as ways of continuing the traditions of the Latvian nation outside its occupied borders. The performative aspects of Mrs Kinne's national dress were to continue, albeit in a different form, in Australia.

Guna Klasons married Arturs Kinne in 1946 in a Displaced Persons camp in Germany. She and her husband left the port of Bremerhafen in October 1948 and arrived in Sydney a month later. The dress was worn again in Wangaratta, mostly at Latvian gatherings.

It was in Wangaratta that Mrs Kinne made the last piece of the dress according to her pattern book, in about 1957, when she felt too old to wear the crown. In Latvian tradition, once a woman married, her head covering changed to a head cloth or bonnet, thus completing her passage from adolescent maiden to married woman. Mrs Kinne was able to make that cultural transition by making the bonnet in Australia.

In September 1959, Mrs Kinne was invited by a Good Neighbour Council to join other 'New Australians' in national dress greeting Princess Alexandra of Kent when she visited Wangaratta. In an interview, Kinne answered my question about the events of this day:

> How did I feel when I wore my Latvian dress? Well, in a way I was proud to show off the dress, because it was unusual, being red and all. But otherwise the reception was rather boring…it was standing around for hours and waiting and waiting and then—in two minutes the princess drove past.[29]

Figure 17.3: Guna Kinne wearing her Lativan national dress in Wangaratta in 1955.

Photo: Arturs Kinne, National Museum of Australia: nma.img-ci20061760-002-vi-vs1.jpg.

Figure 17.4: The bonnet from Guna Kinne's national dress.

Photo: George Serras. National Museum of Australia: nma.img-ci20082088-086_to_087.jpg.

Figure 17.5: Good Neighbour Council group in their national costumes waiting to greet Princess Alexandra, in Wangaratta, 1959.

National Museum of Australia: nma.img-ci20061760-001-vi-vs1.jpg.

Wearing the dress in Australia also enabled Mrs Kinne to be overtly politically active when she wore the dress in two Melbourne rallies. The first rally involved walking in a procession to St Paul's Cathedral in 1968 to celebrate the fiftieth anniversary of Latvia's declaration of independence. The second rally was in the 1970s to protest against Australia recognising the incorporation of Latvia into the Soviet Union:

> [This occasion] was a lot more emotional. Again we grouped together in St. Kilda Road, but then we walked up Bourke Street. In Bourke Street there were lots of people and some cried out, 'You Nazis, you Nazis!' We were so angry. How could they call us Nazis? The Nazis occupied us as well as the Soviets.[30]

> The rally was probably worthwhile because [Prime Minister Malcolm] Fraser cancelled [former Prime Minister Gough] Whitlam's decision. Usually we felt as second grade citizens in Australia, we all stood out only in a bad way. This was sort of standing out in a good way, even if only externally.[31]

Figure 17.6: Guna Kinne wearing her Latvian national dress in Melbourne in 1970.

Photo: Arturs Kinne. National Museum of Australia: nma.img-ci20061760-003-vi-vs1.jpg.

In 1989, Mrs Kinne made the decision to finally part with her dress because 'I have no female descendants I wish to donate the costume to an institution, preferably the National Museum'. This was a poignant moment in her life and the life of the dress, given the significance she had placed on the 'putting aside of this important banner from the past'.[32]

Guna Kinne's dress connects Latvia and Australia, and the protests on the streets of Riga at the time of the Soviet invasion with protests on the streets of Melbourne 40 years later. Interwoven with her personal biography, the biography of her dress connects Riga, Gdansk and Geestacht with Wangaratta and Melbourne. Their shared biography offers insights into the relationships between occupied and displaced people, material culture and national and personal identities.

Dàn tre bamboo musical instrument created by Minh Tam Nguyen
By Jennifer Wilson

The *dàn tre*, translated simply as 'bamboo musical instrument', is the invention of Minh Tam Nguyen. Made from available materials first in Vietnam, then in the Philippines and then in Australia, the instrument was developed into its current form over 16 years. The inventive, dynamic and flexible nature of the *dàn tre*'s hybrid musical organisation is a reflection of Minh's interest in and knowledge of a number of different musical traditions.

Minh Tam Nguyen was born in Binh Dinh Province of central Vietnam on 25 November 1947. He began learning to play guitar when he was about thirteen years old, studying the theory of modern and classical music. Minh then studied music with the Redemptionist Order, a Catholic order founded in Italy in 1732. He eventually left the order and taught music theory to high school students for a number of years.

During the 1970s, Minh fought as a lieutenant with the South Vietnamese forces, known as the Army of the Republic of Vietnam. He began his service in 1968, graduating from the Political Warfare College of Dalat. He was captured by communist forces on 20 March 1975 and placed in a North Vietnamese 're-education' camp in the Central Highlands of Vietnam.

While in captivity, Minh created a musical instrument inspired by the traditional instruments of the Central Highlands, but with a greater number of strings.[33] As Minh states: 'The *dàn tre* was invented at the Tea Plantation KTK in Pleiku Province, during the time the Vietcong forced me to [do] hard labour with many other prisoners as well.' Minh later recognised the significance of making an original bamboo musical instrument in those conditions, with music being a central part of Vietnamese tradition. In his words: '[There is] a lot of music [and] folk song in Vietnam…the Communists like to make a different way…we turned back to our music.'[34]

Figure 17.7: The *dàn tre*, a 23-stringed bamboo musical instrument.

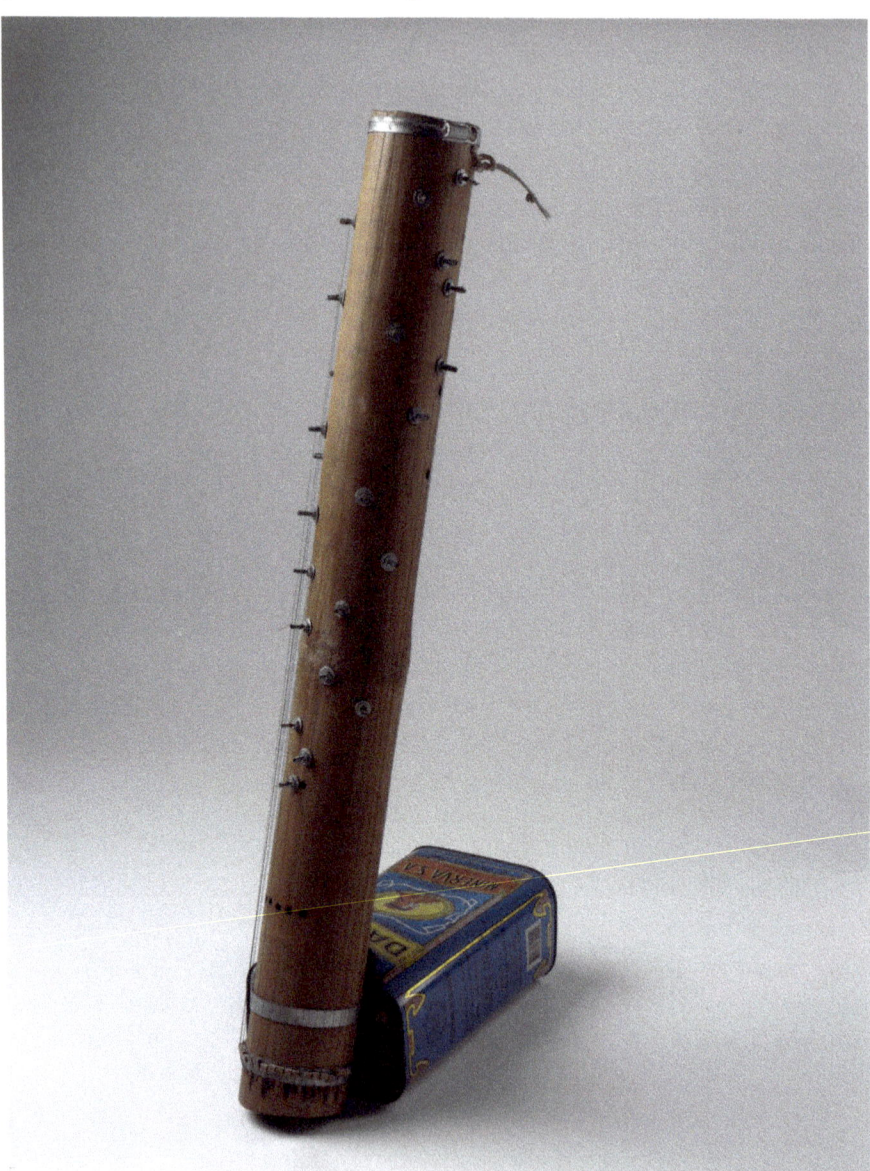

National Museum of Australia: nma.img-ci20082088-190.

A piece of bamboo, wire and a tin were used to create the first *dàn tre*. The strings of that instrument were the hard wire found inside black telephone cable used by the US Army. The instrument, as Minh explained, evolved from 18 to 21 and then finally to 23 strings. Minh was moved to a number of different camps during his time as a prisoner of the North Vietnamese. During that time,

Minh was able to make improvements to the instrument, mainly increasing the number of strings, and to teach one of his fellow prisoners how to play the *dàn tre*.

The instrument, as donated to the National Museum of Australia, features 23 strings attached to a bamboo tube, 800 mm long. A four-litre olive-oil tin acts as the resonator at the base. The number-one guitar strings are attached to metal tuning keys in the form of Australian-made stainless-steel screw assemblies. The length of bamboo is reinforced with Australian-made metal bracing (hose clamps commonly used in cars).

The *dàn tre* has been inscribed with details of the instrument's musical interpretation. Western notation is ascribed in lead pencil to each string, numbered one to 23. The complex arrangement of strings is organised into six groups and played in the C major scale.

There are many traditional and hybrid stringed instruments or chordophones in Vietnam and throughout Asia that exhibit similarities to Minh's *dàn tre*. These include the *dàn bầu*, a single-stringed instrument, and the *dàn tranh*, a 16-string zither. Minh's instrument is also similar to the *gu zheng*, a Chinese zither with 16–23 strings, reflecting the influence of Chinese forms and theory on Vietnamese music. Other possibly closely related instruments are found in Japan, Korea and Mongolia.

When speaking with the museum's curators about the *dàn tre*, Minh noted that he had made the instrument with the intention of playing Asian and European music, as he had been educated in both forms and their variations. He observed that the instruments of his reference from the Central Highlands had five knots, or strings, and the European scales had seven notes. The 23 strings of the *dàn tre* allowed Minh to cover a greater range of notes, and therefore a greater range of music, than if he had used less strings.

Interestingly, while Minh had not given a public musical performance as a student or teacher of music, during his imprisonment under the Vietcong, he performed before approximately 4500 prisoners with his *dàn tre*. When Minh was released after six years, he left that instrument behind.

In August 1981, Minh escaped from Vietnam by boat with his eldest son, Anton Nguyen, still fearing for his life under communist rule. In Minh's words: 'It was a miracle we escaped.' It was also a miracle that they made it to the Philippines by boat, as they encountered strong storms en route and the boat nearly sank twice.

Minh made his second *dàn tre* while in the Palawan refugee camp in the Philippines. He recreated the instrument from memory, again using the materials on hand: bamboo, an olive-oil tin and some electrical line. Minh initially used bamboo tuning keys in this instrument, making them from sharpened or shaped pieces that were placed through holes in the body of the instrument. There was an abundance of bamboo available at Palawan, and it was a building material utilised for a number of different purposes.

Minh and Anton lived in difficult and overcrowded conditions at Palawan for 17 months. Minh recalled that there were 7000 refugees in the camp when he arrived, with numbers increasing to more than 10,000 during his stay. Minh recalled: 'All the people were lucky, we had enough food…but the situation was so bad because we didn't have any houses to live in…we had to build our houses ourselves…make something to live in—we used trees from the forest.'

Minh acted as an information officer and translator in the camp. His knowledge of English, and the fact that he had an uncle living in Australia, helped secure his transfer with his son to Australia in December 1982. Minh was able to bring the second *dàn tre* with him, although Australian quarantine authorities held it for three weeks.

In Australia, Minh struggled to find employment, at first unable to understand the difficult Australian English pronunciation. He worked for the Commonwealth Employment Service in Brisbane and then for a law firm in Sydney.

Minh began playing his *dàn tre* at public events, and appeared on Channel 7's *State Affair* program in 1984. In January that year, he explained the making of his *dàn tre* to a conference of the Ethnic Communities Council of Queensland concerned with locating and fostering different and endangered art forms among migrant groups. Minh told his story in Vietnamese and English, commenting that he could play Vietnamese folk songs, European songs such as those by Chopin and Australian songs such as *Waltzing Matilda* on the instrument. He then performed a song from each musical style, concluding his performance with *Waltzing Matilda*.

Minh's story and his *dàn tre* earned him a certain amount of fame, and he attempted several times to patent his invention. During this period, he replaced the bamboo keys, which were prone to slipping, with Australian-made screw assemblies, also reinforcing the bamboo and replacing the tin. He was very pleased to finally place guitar strings on the instrument, believing the quality to be better than the wire he had been able to find in Palawan.

In 1985, Minh began working as an immigration consultant, assisting Vietnamese and Chinese families who were having difficulty coming to Australia. He took on a number of music students, but in order to support his family financially he was unable to concentrate on his own music.

Though Minh travelled to Australia with his eldest son, he could not be reunited with his wife and three other children for many years. Feeling loneliness and separation from his family, Minh did not wish to part with his *dàn tre*; through it, he remained connected to the life he had left behind in Vietnam. The instrument was first loaned to the National Museum of Australia for a temporary exhibition. Shortly after this initial contact, however, Minh's family—his mother, wife and three children—were able to join him in Australia. Once they were reunited, he was happy to donate the *dàn tre* to the museum.

Figure 17.8: Minh with the *dàn tre* at his home in Sydney, March 1990.

Photo: Dr E. F. Kunz for the National Museum of Australia: nma.img-ex20082168-002.

Minh feels a strong emotional attachment to the instrument that has played such an important role in his life. The *dàn tre* was, for Minh, a potent means of expression. In the mountains of Vietnam, in the Philippines and in Australia, he was able to bridge the cultural differences he encountered by modifying and adapting the instrument and his use of it, and retelling his story as he played it.

The history and cultural significance of Vietnamese music is a large area of research, beyond the scope of this discussion. Much of my research into this aspect of the *dàn tre*'s history has been drawn from the work of Vietnamese musicologist Le Tuan Hung. According to Hung, traditional Vietnamese music is based on the concept that music is 'a means for emotional expression'.[35] *Tài tử* music, the chamber music of southern Vietnam, features four modes of expression: happiness, sombreness, tranquillity and sadness.[36] Put simply, by applying certain sets of technical conventions to their music, Vietnamese musicians are able to evoke these recognisable emotions for their audience.

Originality is highly considered in the Vietnamese tradition, with performers elaborating from a given framework in their own style. According to Hung, 'Musical compositions in *Hue* and *Tài tử* traditions are flexible and dynamic entities…the act of composing a piece is a continuing process in which the performers add their final touches to the work.'[37] In the case of the *dàn tre*, this continuing process can be seen in the creation of the instrument and the performances undertaken by Minh.

There is a long history of adaptation and invention in Vietnamese music and instrument making. As Hung states, '[B]etween the 1920s and 1940s a number of *Tài tử* musicians began to experiment with [W]estern instruments in their search for new qualities and colours of sounds.'[38] Most prominent among those instruments were the acoustic guitar and the violin. Vietnamese musicians adapted the Western instruments to enable them to produce the ornaments typical of *Hue* and *Tài tử* musical compositions. Bamboo forms the basis of many of these instruments, in their historical and modern forms. In many places, the physical and musical qualities of the new instruments are explained as part of a broader cultural tradition. For example, the character of a half or flat zither is often attributed to the splitting of a tube or round zither through the act of a god or mystical being or a related event.

Of course, music itself is an active agent in the story of the *dàn tre*, be it of Vietnamese, European or Australian origin. When performing in Australia, Minh played compositions from various traditions to illustrate the musical range of the *dàn tre* and the story of the instrument that had evolved in places related to those traditions. Titles included in recordings of the *dàn tre* made by Minh are *Clementine*, *Waltzing Matilda* and various Vietnamese folk songs (including *Hòn Vọng Phu*).

When Minh made his valuable donation to the National Museum in 1990, he also provided recordings of his *dàn tre* music, an explanation of the instrument and its musical scales and an oral history outlining his story and the story of the *dàn tre*. The musical recordings chosen by Minh presented the range of the instrument and his own interests. He was proud to visit the National Museum at its temporary site at Yarramundi Reach and see his *dàn tre* on display.

As part of my research for the *Australian Journeys* Gallery, I re-established contact with Minh to learn more about the instrument and his life since the donation. He has returned to Vietnam on several occasions, maintaining contact with friends and family. Poor health and a continuing commitment to support his family have meant that he has not been able to pursue many of his musical interests. It is clear that Minh retains a strong connection with the *dàn tre* and continues to think of ways in which he could improve the quality and range of the instrument. In fact, he is in the process of making another *dàn tre*, this time using a plastic pipe and wooden-box resonator. The tradition of innovation in Vietnamese music continues in Minh's Sydney home.

Conclusion: objects make a transnational life

More than 50 object biographies have been written as part of the development of the *Australian Journeys* Gallery. Individually and together, they have revealed some of the complexities of researching, communicating and understanding the interrelated life journeys of people and things. What began in the two cases here as object biographies of a dress and a musical instrument quickly revealed themselves to be interwoven with autobiographies created by the individual donors, and then further entwined with biographies created by the museum's curators in acquiring and displaying the objects.

In both these examples, in which donors chose to part with their treasured object as part of marking a change in their lives, we had cause to consider the creation of collections as a form of autobiography. When Guna Kinne donated her Latvian national dress to the National Museum of Australia in 1989, she wrote:

> To part with one's Latvian National dress is similar to putting aside an important banner from the past. It is really not a costume because to wear your own national dress at a costume ball would be in very low taste. It is a symbol of one's ancestry.[39]

When she donated the dress to the museum, Mrs Kinne established a strong link between her own autobiography, the material history of the dress and the larger and longer history of Latvian culture. In the narrative she wrote for the museum, her description of each part of the dress was interwoven with the story of her life history. This account contrasts with her published written autobiography, which focuses more on her Latvian heritage, her flight to Germany and migration to Australia and which mentions her national dress only once.[40] Through the different media of her book and her dress, she expresses who she is as a person, a Latvian and an Australian, in different ways.

Not all of the object biographies in the gallery weave an individual's story so closely with that of an object. Objects exert agency in diverse and often interconnected ways: as repositories of memories, mechanisms for the transfer of skills, as sites for negotiating cultural frameworks, as arenas for imaginative escape, modes of connecting with lost family, or metonyms for other places or things. In every case, however, objects work as conduits for simultaneous experience, collapsing geographical, temporal and perceptual differences. As people engage with them, the objects enable them to simultaneously experience and mediate multiple times, places and modes of being.

This, we hope, will also be true for visitors to the gallery as they encounter the objects in the exhibits. The display of Guna Kinne's dress and Minh Tam Nguyen's *dàn tre* in the *Australian Journeys* Gallery will represent a very different kind of transnational biography to those conveyed here in words. Exhibition making can also be seen as a form of biography, one that is non-linear, associational and that actively involves the experiences of the visitor.[41] While preparing the text versions of object biographies, we noted how difficult it was to write so that the agency of people and objects—and the sensory and non-linear character of object knowledge—was retained within a biographical narrative. It will be instructive to compare these different biographies when the gallery opens.

The preparation of object biographies as part of the development of these and other exhibits in the *Australian Journeys* Gallery suggests that objects play a particularly important role in the shaping of transnational lives. Changes in a person's location necessarily generate new interactions between a person and a different material world. These interactions—and efforts to sustain previous interactions by continuing to use, make and treasure objects from another place—shape how a person experiences their life across multiple places. Paying close attention to how a person absorbs, rejects, accommodates and reinvents these forms reveals valuable information about the nature and meaning of those experiences.

Notes

[1] Letter from Guna Kinne to Jerzy Zubrzycki, 1 February 1989, National Museum of Australia (hereafter NMA), File 89/63, f2.

[2] Letter from Sally Fletcher to Guna Kinne, 7 March 1989, NMA, File 89/63, ff 4–5.

[3] Letter from Guna Kinne to Sally Fletcher, 23 March 1989, NMA, File 89/63, ff 6–10.

[4] See Macdougall, David 2006, *The Corporeal Image: Film, ethnography and the senses*, Princeton University Press, Princeton and Oxford, p. 6. We have explored this idea in detail in Wehner, Kirsten and Sear, Martha (forthcoming), 'Engaging the material world: object knowledge and *Australian Journeys*', in Sandra Dudley (ed.), *Museums and Materiality*.

[5] See, for example, Curthoys, Ann and Lake, Marilyn 2004, *Connected Worlds: History in transnational perspective*, ANU E Press, p. 5.

[6] Sheller, Mimi and Urry, John 2006, 'The new mobilities paradigm', *Environment and Planning A*, vol. 38, pp. 207–26.

[7] Gosden, Chris and Marshall, Yvonne 1999, 'The cultural biography of objects', *World Archaeology*, vol. 31, no. 2, pp. 169–78; Kopytoff, Igor 1986, 'The cultural biography of things: commoditization as process', in Arjun Appadurai (ed.), *The Social Life of Things: Commodities in cultural perspective*, Cambridge University Press, Cambridge, pp. 64–91.

[8] Gosden and Marshall, 'The cultural biography of objects', p. 177.

[9] Gosden, C. 2005, 'What do objects want?' *Journal of Archeological Method and Theory*, vol. 12, no. 3, pp. 193-211, esp. 193.

[10] Ibid., p. 194.

11 Gosden and Marshall, 'The cultural biography of objects', p. 173.
12 Gosden, 'What do objects want?', p. 197.
13 Ibid., p. 194.
14 Hoskins, Janet 2006, 'Agency, biography and objects', in C. Tilley, W. Keane, S. Kuchler, M. Rowlands and P. Spitzer, *Handbook of Material Culture*, Sage Publications, London, p. 75.
15 Appadurai, Arjun 1986, 'Introduction', and Kopytoff, Igor 1986, 'The Cultural Biography of Things: Commoditization as Process,' in Appadurai (ed.), *The Social Life of Things*, pp. 3-63 and 64-91. See also Tilley, C. 2006, 'Objectification', in Tilley, Keane, Kuchler, Rowlands and Spitzer, *Handbook of Material Culture*, pp. 60-73.
16 See, for example, Gosden, C. and Knowles, C. 2001, *Collecting Colonialism: Material culture and colonial change in Papua New Guinea*, Berg, Oxford.
17 Gosden, 'What do objects want?', p. 209.
18 Ibid., p. 209.
19 Interview by Karen Schamberger with Guna Kinne, Noble Park, 8 January 2007.
20 It was issued by the *Latvijas Lauksaimniecības Kamera* (Latvian Agricultural Camera) in 1939.
21 Apinis-Herman, A. 1993, *Latvian Weaving Techniques*, Kangaroo Press, Kenthurst, p. 98. This book contains a detailed technical description of the material, techniques of manufacture and diagrams of the Nīca skirt (pp. 98–104).
22 Ibid., p. 91.
23 Letter from Guna Kinne to Sally Fletcher, 23 March 1989, NMA, File 89/63, p. 3.
24 *Latvian National Costumes. Volume 2: Kurzeme*, 1997, Museum of History of Latvia, Riga, p. 357.
25 http://www.occupationmuseum.lv/lat/services/gramatu%20faili/3_okupacijas.pdf, accessed 15 November 2006.
26 Letter from Guna Kinne to Sally Fletcher, 23 March 1989, NMA, File 89/63, p. 4.
27 Ibid., p. 4.
28 Ibid., p. 4.
29 Interview with Guna Kinne, 8 January 2007.
30 Ibid.
31 Ibid.
32 Letter from Guna Kinne to Sally Fletcher, 23 March 1989, NMA, File 89/63, p. 5.
33 'Montagnard' was the French name assigned to the many ethnic groups occupying the Central Highlands of Vietnam. Minh based his instrument on the so-called 'zithers' of that region, especially of the *Gia Rai* group. Zithers in the region, such as the *din goong* (or 'new goong'), utilise local bamboo and wood, with a calabash, a type of gourd, as the resonator. Examples of the *din goong*, being of a similar size to the *dàn tre*, generally feature between nine and 13 strings. Minh also cited the 'old goong' (*goong kram*) as an influence.
34 Channel 7, *State Affair*, January 1984.
35 Hùng, Lê Tuấn n.d., *Hu and Tài Tử Music of Viet Nam: The concept of music and social organisation of musicians*, Australia Asia Foundation, ePapyrus, available from http://home.vicnet.net.au/~aaf/ch2.html#note1#note1
36 Ibid.
37 Hùng, Lê Tuấn 1998, *Dan Tranh Music of Vietnam: Traditions and innovations*, Australia Asia Foundation, Melbourne, p. 54.
38 Ibid., p. 76.
39 Guna Kinne, letter to Sally Fletcher, Acting Curator, Department of Social History, National Museum of Australia, 23 March 1989, p. 5.
40 Kinne, Guna 1993, 'Anug', in A. Markus and E. Sims, *Fourteen Lives: Paths to a multicultural community 14*, Monash Publications in History, no. 16, pp. 80–100.
41 See Trinca, Mat and Wehner, Kirsten 2006, 'Pluralism and exhibition practice at the National Museum of Australia', *South Pacific Museums: Experiments in culture*, vol. 1, no. 1, November, pp. 6.1–6.14.

Contributors

The Editors

Desley Deacon is Professor of Gender History in the Research School of Social Sciences, The Australian National University and Immediate Past President of the Australian Historical Association. She is author of *Elsie Clews Parsons: Inventing Modern Life* (University of Chicago Press, 1997) and a number of articles on 'transnationals at home' based on the career of Australian-born actor Judith Anderson, about whom she is writing a biography under an ARC Discovery grant.

Penny Russell is Associate Professor of History at the University of Sydney, where she teaches Australian and gender history. She is the author of *A Wish of Distinction* (1994) and *This Errant Lady* (2002) and co-editor, with Richard White, of *History Australia*. Her research includes the study of gender and gentility, manners and power in colonial Australia, and a biographical study of Jane Franklin and the romance of Arctic exploration in mid-nineteenth century Britain.

Angela Woollacott is Professor of Modern History at Macquarie University. Her teaching areas include Australian history, British Empire history and feminist and postcolonial history. Her most recent book, *Gender and Empire*, was published by Palgrave Macmillan in 2006. Current research projects include a study of three iconic 'Australian' women performers, race and modernity in the early twentieth century and an ARC-funded project on cultural understandings of the political and gender changes in mid-nineteenth century Australia in imperial context.

Contributors

Margaret Allen is Professor of Gender Studies at the University of Adelaide. She has published widely on feminist post-colonial histories and on Australian women's literary history. In her current project, which explores links between India and Australia in the late nineteenth and early twentieth centuries, she has focussed on Indian men living in Australia under the White Australia Policy and Australian women missionaries to India. Recent publications from this project appear in the *Journal of Social History* (2008), S. Sareen (ed) *Interconnections Identity, Representation and Belonging* (New Delhi, 2006) and *Athanor: Semiotica, Filosofia, Arte, Letteratura*, special issue 'White Matters/Il Bianco al Centro della Questione' (2006-7).

The *Australian Journeys* Curatorial Team was constituted in 2005 to develop a new permanent gallery at the National Museum of Australia that explores the transnational character of Australian experience. The team consisted of: Kirsten Wehner (Director and Senior Curator, Gallery Development), Martha Sear (Senior Curator) and curators Cheryl Crilly, Laina Hall, Susannah Helman, Lynne McCarthy, Alison Merceica, Megan Parnell, Rathicca Chandra, Karen Schamberger, and Jennifer Wilson. Exhibition making is a highly collaborative enterprise and the chapter in this volume, written by Martha Sear, Karen Schamberger, Jennifer Wilson and Kirsten Wehner reflects the contributions of the whole curatorial team, the wider museum team responsible for the gallery, and the General Manager of Collections and Content Division Mat Trinca who, with Kirsten Wehner, prepared the gallery brief.

Kate Bagnall is a historian who works as a web writer and editor at the National Archives of Australia. Her PhD, completed in 2006, explored the lives of Anglo-Chinese families in nineteenth-century Australia and China. She is currently writing a book about the travels of Anglo-Chinese Australians and their treatment under the White Australia Policy.

Mary Besemeres is a Research Associate in the School of Language Studies, ANU and co-editor of *Life Writing*. She holds an ARC Discovery grant for the project 'Anglos Abroad: Narratives of Immersion in a Foreign Language and Culture'. She is the author of *Translating One's Self: Language and Selfhood in Cross-Cultural Autobiography* (Peter Lang, 2002) and co-editor of *Translating Lives: Living with Two Languages and Cultures* (UQP, 2007).

Nicholas Brown is a senior research fellow in the History Program and Australian Dictionary of Biography, Research School of Social Sciences, The Australian National University, and in the Centre for Historical Research, National Musuem of Australia. He has published in Australian political, cultural and environmental history and is currently working on a larger project on the history of 'the international' in Australian policy and commentary (of which his essay in this collection is a part) and a biography of the rural, environmental and indigenous activist, Rick Farley.

Susan Carson is Head of Postgraduate Studies for the Creative Industries Faculty at the Queensland University of Technology. Her research areas include Australian women's writing, modernism, and teacher training in secondary English studies.

Julie Evans teaches in the School of Social and Political Sciences at the University of Melbourne. She is the author of *Edward Eyre, Race and Colonial Governance* (Otago University Press, 2005) and *Equal Subjects, Unequal Rights: Indigenous Peoples and Political Rights in British Settlements, 1830-1910* (with Patricia Grimshaw, David Philips and Shurlee Swain) (Manchester University Press, 2003). Her current ARC-funded research projects include 'Conciliation Narratives and the Historical Imagination in British Pacific Rim Settler Societies' (with Kate Darian-Smith and Penny Edmonds and industry partners National Museum of

Australia, Museum Victoria, and Tasmanian Museum and Art Gallery) and 'Beyond the Pale: Indigenous Peoples and the Notion of the "Exception" in the Constitution and Transformation of Sovereignty'.

Sally Gray lectures in Art History and Theory at the University of New South Wales College of Fine Arts. Her research interests include contemporary art, gender politics, fashion and the city in the late twentieth century.

A. James Hammerton is Emeritus Scholar in the History Program, La Trobe University. He is currently working on 'A History of British Emigration and the 'British Diaspora' since the 1960s: the "Mobility of Modernity", an Oral History', funded by the Australian Research Council. He is author of *Cruelty and Companionship: Conflict in Nineteenth Century Married Life* (Routledge, 1995) and most recently, *'Ten Pound Poms': Australia's Invisible Migrants* (Manchester University Press, 2005) with Alistair Thomson.

Mark Hearn has published widely in the field of Australian history. He was awarded the C. H. Currey Memorial Fellowship from the State Library of New South Wales for 2006 to research the fin de siècle imagination in Australia, 1890-1914. He teaches Australian history in the Department of Modern History, Macquarie University.

Ann Lane teaches at Queensland University of Technology and is an honorary staff member in the Department of English, Media Studies and Art History at the University of Queensland. Previously she was lecturer in the Department of Cultures and Humanities at Japan Women's University in Tokyo and at Nara Women's University, Japan. Her publications centre on the fictions of Joseph Conrad in the context of the late nineteenth century European Pacific. Her current research project investigates the processes of cognitive and aesthetic adjustments evident in the writings of Europeans in the 'New' New World of the nineteenth century Pacific.

Cindy McCreery teaches British and European history and Australian maritime history at the University of Sydney. She is particularly interested in the impact of the wider world on Britons living in and beyond Britain from the eighteenth to the twentieth century. She is currently pursuing two major research projects: a study of the origins and impacts of 'moral panics' in eighteenth century England (with David Lemmings and Claire Walker); and a book on Alfred, Duke of Edinburgh's world voyages, 1867-71. Her publications include *Ports of the World: Prints from the National Maritime Museum, Greenwich* (Philip Wilson Publishers, 1999) and *The Satirical Gaze: Prints of Women in Eighteenth-century England* (OUP, 2004).

Maggie MacKellar has written two books, *Core of My Heart my Country: Women's Sense of Place and the Land in Australia and Canada* (2004) and *Strangers in a Foreign Land: The Journal of Niel Black and Other Voices from the Western District*

(2008). She lives in Central Western New South Wales and is currently working on a project entitled 'In Search of Beauty: Women artists and the emergence of a national landscape'. She will take up the Blazet Fellowship at the University of Melbourne in 2009.

Nancy L. Paxton, Professor of English at Northern Arizona University, is author of *Writing under the Raj: Gender, Race, and Rape in the British Colonial Imagination, 1830-1947* (Rutgers, 1999) and co-editor with Lynne Hapgood of *Outside Modernism: In Pursuit of the British Novel, 1900-1930* (Palgrave, 2000). She edits the *DH Lawrence Society of North America Newsletter* and is working on a book on censorship in the careers and novels of Lawrence, Radcylffe Hall, and Jean Devanny.

Cassandra Pybus publishes extensively on Australian, American and transatlantic history. Her interests span Australian social history, colonial history in North America, South East Asia, Africa and Australia, slavery and the history of labour, and the history of Tasmanian Aborigines. She holds an Australian Research Council Professorial Fellowship based at the University of Sydney for the project 'Recovered Lives as Windows on the Anglo Colonial World, 1750-1850'. In addition, she heads an international team of historians and literary scholars researching 'Race and the Construction of Racial Identity at the Antipodes of Empire'. Her most recent book is *Other Middle Passages*, edited with Marcus Rediker and Emma Christopher (University of California Press, 2007).

Francesco Ricatti is Cassamarca Lecturer in Italian at the University of the Sunshine Coast. In 2007 he completed his PhD at The University of Sydney. His thesis, *Embodying Italian Migrants,* was awarded the *Premio Altreitalie*. His main research interest is the relation between body, emotions and popular culture in Italian and transnational contexts.

Alistair Thomson is Professor of History and Director of the Institute for Public History at Monash University. His publications include *Anzac Memories: Living With the Legend* (Oxford University Press, 1994) and *Ten Pound Poms: Australia's Invisible Migrants* (with Jim Hammerton, Manchester University Press, 2005). He is currently writing a collective biography with four migrant women, *Moving Stories, Women's Lives: British Women and the Postwar Australian Dream* (Manchester University Press, 2009).

Index

2BG (Sydney) 79, 87
ABC (Australian Broadcasting Commission) 87-90
Aborigines (Australian) *See also* indigenous peoples
   assimilation of 90
   attachment to land 31, 32
   'authentic' 32, 35
   as British subjects 32
   as companions on Edward Eyre's explorations 26, 31, 36 n1
   culture, breakdown of 32
   deaths in custody 36 n7
   destruction of homes of 108-109, 111, 112-113
   Edward Eyre as advocate for 30-31
   friendly encounters with 21, 31, 36 n1
   history of 36 n8
   kindness to and from 21, 31,110, 113, 113 n10
   labour of 38 n29, 100-101, 111, 113
   laws 31
   letters from 109-111, 114 n32
   on missions 109-110
   Mission, Lake Condah 109-111, 113 n11, 114 n28
   Protector of 23, 25, 31-32, 105, 106
   resistance of 104-105, 111
   slaughter of 104-106, **107**, 108, 109
   sovereignty of 30-32, 34, 35-36
   state control of 32
   women, harassment of 106-108
Abruzzese, Alberto 70
Adelaide (Australia) 21, 23, 25, 32, 61, 63, 64, 73 n28
   Observer 47
   Register 45
admiralty records 10
adventure xiii, xvi, 25, 68, 73-74 n45, 121, 136, 140-141, 145, 150-151, 155, 162, 163, 184, 186, 203, 205, 236, 246
adventurers xix, 183, 186, 187, 241
Afghans 43-45
Africa 3, 5, 9, 73 n30, n35, 140-141, 237
African-American xiii, 3-16, 269
Albany (Western Australia) 21
Albert, Prince (husband of Queen Victoria) 58-61
Alexander, Fred **85**, 86
Alfred, Duke of Edinburgh (second son of Queen Victoria and Prince Albert)
   as British prince 57-62, 71
   as German prince 60-**63**
   as possible King of Greece 60
   multiple loyalties of 64, 67, 71
   in Royal Navy 57, **58**, 67-68, 71
   and Scotland 59, **60**, 61
   and transnational experience 57, 67-68, 71
   visit to Australia xviii, 57-71
      and Australian slang 69
      attempted assassination of 66, 71
      and colonial fashion 65-66, 68
      multiple loyalties of subjects in 61-64, 66-67, 71
      transnational lives in 65-66, 67-68, 70-71
      and Victorian masculinity 70-71
allegiance xiv, xvi, 99, 233, 260
Allen, Margaret xviii, 19, 75, 82
Almost French: A New Life in Paris (Sarah Turnbull) 214, 245, 249-251
Amazon River 183, 184, 188
America xiii, 6, 7-8, 9, 13, 17 n20, 139, 229, 232, 242, 261, 260-270
American
   Alfred Deakin on 211 n43
   bank in Paris 238
   colonies 7
   critics on Eleanor Dark's *Waterway* 242
   David McDiarmid neither 'Australian' nor 'American' 259, 265
   gay culture 214, 262, 265, 270
   pioneer women's quilting patterns 269
   popular culture, influence on David McDiarmid 259-261, 264-265, 267-269
   Revolution 7-9
   women married to Chinese men 120-121
Zone (Germany) 284

Amin, Ash and Nigel Thrift 261
Anderson, Professor Francis 82
Anderson, Don 240
Andre (Andrews), Major John 5, 7-8
Anglo-Saxons, accused of vulgarity 62
'Anglos Abroad: Narratives of immersion into a Foreign Language and Culture' (Mary Besemeres) 246
Antigua 23, 27
Appadurai, Arjun and Igor Kopytoff 278
arbitration
    industrial (Australia) 52, 206-207
    of international conflict 78
archives xvi, 3, 9, 281
Arendt, Hannah xix, 213-214
arghan 188-189, **190**, 191-193
army
    British xvi, 5-8, 7-8, 46-47, 50
    Indonesian 251
    of USSR 282
    of Republic of Vietnam 289
Arnold, Benedict 7
Articles of Capitulation 8
Aryanism 55 n41
Assyrians 45
attachments xv-xvi, xviii, xix, 31, 32, 71, 95, 102-103, 138, 143, 146, 293
Auge, Marc 232-233
Australia
    art historians, and transnationalism xv
    in Asia-Pacific world xiv, 116, 205
    'Asiatics' in 48-49
    and Britain xiv, xviii, 19, 30-31, 50, 57, 59, 61, 64-71, 113, 138-140, 146
    and the Caribbean 25, 30-35
    and China 116
    Chinese community in 66, 73 n40, 120, 122-126, 129-130, 131 n13, 133 n44
    colonial xiv, xviii, 21, 24, 25, 30-33, 35, 43, 45, 48, 62, 64-65, 67-71, 75, 99, 120, 140
    Council for the Arts 260-261
    cultural diversity xiv
    and empire xvii-xix, 19, 22-24, 54, 75-76, 205-206
    experience, transnational character of 67-68
    and Germany 61
    historians in, and transnationalism xiv-xv, xvii, 35, 43, 54, 57
    history of, 'white' xvi, 21-23
    as home 99, 113, 151, 163, 215
    identity xiv, xvi-xvii, xx, 71, 98, 113, 140, 145, 200, 205
    Immigration Restriction Act (1901) 48-52, 54, 95
    and India 19
    Indians in 19, 41-54
    Irish Catholics in 66-67
    and internationalism xviii, 19, 75
    Italians in 168
    literature of 205-206, 235, 238, 253
    literary critics in, and transnationalism xv
    masculinity in 43, 45, 46, 54, 70, 71
    migrants to 5, 6, 41, 43-54, 95, 120, 122-125, 135-147, 149-163, 165-178
    museologists in, and transnationalism xv
    multiple attachments of people in xix-xx, 61-67, 71
    and national feeling xv, xvii-xviii
    patterns of authority in xviii, 19
    refuge in xviii, 70
    royal visit to 6, 19, 57-71, **109**, 34
    transnational families in 41-54, 124-126
        history of xvii-xviii, 22-23, 43, 166
        lives xiii-xx, 19, 57, 71
        ties of xviii-xx, 75
    travel to and from 67, 68, 80, 103
    typical xvii, xx
    visitors to xviii, 47-48
    'white' xviii, 16, 41, 43, 45, 46. 49, 51-54, 116, 127-130
    White Australia Policy 19, 43, 48-52, 54
        and labour movement 52, 54
    and the world xiii-xiv, xviii-xx, 19, 79

Index

Australian Labor Party 89
    and White Australia policy 52
Australian (newspaper), and Billy Blue 16
Australian National University,
    Humanities Research Centre xiv
Australian Journeys Gallery 276, 279, 295-296
'authenticity', of race 35
autobiography 5-7, 137-138, 143, 276, 279, 295-296
Aveyron, visit to Sydney 66

BBC (British Broadcasting Corporation) 86
Bhabha, Homi xiv, 168, 217-218
Bagnall, Kate xix, xx, 95-96
Bailey, Barbara (sister of Dorothy Wright) 153-154, 156-157
Bailey, Dorothy *See* Dorothy Wright
Mrs Bailey (mother of Dorothy Wright) 152-153, 163
Baldwin, James 261
Ball, Macmahon **85**, 87
Bank of England 78-79
Bareetch Churneen (Queen Fanny) 106
Barrios de Chungra, Domitila, *testimonio*, Mary Louise Pratt on 246
Barthes, Roland 168-169, 259
Bartoloni, Paolo 166
Basquiat, Jean Michel 263-264, 271 n17
Bassindale, Maurice 143-146
Bassindale, Susan (daughter of Maurice)
    mobile life of 145
Batavia (Jakarta) 41
Battle of Boyne 66
Bauman, Zygmunt 199, 208
Bean, Charles, read by Alfred Deakin 206
The Beats 261
Beckett's Budget 116
Belle Isle 5-6, 7
belonging xvii, xviii, 146-147
Benaud, L.F. 45
Bengali men, as 'effeminate' 43, 46, 47-48
Bentham, Jeremy 86
Bergson, Henri, and Alfred Deakin 181, 197-198, 201, 204, 207-208
Berry, Edith Campbell 76-77, 79
Besemeres, Mary 214-246

biography
    in *Cyclopedia of South Australia* (1909)
    and emotional memory 171
    of Henry Wickham (Joe Jackson) 184
    of Jean Devanny (Carole Ferrier) 215
    migrant 135
    in museums xv, 275-296
    national xv, xvi-xvii, 16, 35, 186-187
    and micro history 1
    object 276, 278-279
        and subjectivity 275-276, 279, 296
        and transnational lives 275-276, 279, 296
    and obscure historical actors 1
    dictionaries of xvi, 186, 187
    and global history 22-24, 25. 30. 35
    and transnationalism xv-xx, 135, 193
Black, Donald 108
Black, Niel 103, **104, 109**
    in Port Phillip district 103
    journal 103-109
    on eradication of Aborigines 104-109, **107**
    and Scotland **104**, 108, **109**
    thoughts on home 108-109
    sense of loss 108-109
black masculinity 43, 269
Blake, Bill (lover of Christina Stead) 214, 229, 232, 237-238
Blues Point 14
Blue, Elizabeth (nee Williams, wife of Billy) 11-12
Blue, Susannah (daughter of Billy) 12, 17 n1
Blue, William 'Billy' xiii, 3-16
    autobiography 5
    in Europe 3-7
    in America 5-8
    in England 8-11
    transported to New South Wales 9, 11
Bligh, Governor William 12-13
Bonetta, HMS 8, 17 n18
Bookfellow, and Henri Bergson 207
books xvi-xvii, xix, 23, 197-209, 234-256
borders xiv, 57, 130, 217, 234, 237-238, 245

Botanical Gardens 64 n2, 183-184, 188, 189
boundaries xiv, xv-xvii, xx, 19, 49, 79, 112, 118, 165-166, 181, 200, 233, 237, 259, 241, 259, 276
  between people and things xv, 277-278
  and transnational lives xv-xvi, 166-167
  and transnational history xiv, xv, 276
Bouras, Gillian xix, 214, 245, 246-249, 251, 254, 256
  A Foreign Wife 214, 245-146, 246-249
  A Fair Exchange 246-247
  Aphrodite and the Others 246-247
  A Stranger Here 246-247
  Starting Again 246-247
  emigrates to Greece with husband and children 246-247
  feeling of marginality 247-248
Bowen, Sir George, 27
Boyer, R.J.F. **85**, 90
Boyle, Kate 136
Brady, E.J., *River Rovers* 206
Brazil, Henry Wickham in 183, 184-185, 186, 187, 188, 194 n11
Brazilians, Christian Stead on 236
Brett, Judith, on citizenship 53
Breuer, Adolf (father of Agnes) 121, 122, 123, 134 n59
Breuer, Agnes (Low Mun) 118-130 , **119, 123**
  marriage to William Lum Mow 123-125
  loss of rights as a British subject 124
  in China 124, 125-127
  son William 116, 117, **119**, 123-124, 125, 126, 130
  relations with Chinese wife 126
Brisbane, Governor Thomas 5, 15
Britain
  Alfred Deakin's relationship with 200, 204, 205-209
  and Australian Aborigines' political rights 32
  anti-British feeling 62, 66-67
  and Australia xiv, xviii, 19, 30-31, 57, 59, 61, 64-71,113, 138-140, 146
  and the Carribbean 30, 32-36
  Christina Stead in 232
  class structure of 25, 70
  colonial world of 3, 19, 23-24, 30, 34-35, 41-43, 47-49, 52, 54, 76, 98-99, 183, 191
  cultural attitudes in 97, 248-249
  diaspora 95, 209
  emigrants xix, xvii, 71, 95, 99, 135-147, 147 n1, 149-164
  Government 27, 30, 34, 35, 187
  in Hong Kong 120
  imperial values of 217
  Indians as subjects of 41, 46-50, 52-54
  as Mother Country 68, 69
  Navy See Royal Navy
  and plant transplantation 183
  publishers in 219
  refugees from 68-70
  rubber industry of 183, 184-185
  and rule of law 24
  sovereignty of 31-36
  subjects of 32, 41, 46-50, 52-54, 124
  and transnational lives 57, 70, 71, 146-147
British Australian Migration Research Project 163 n1
  Honduras 184, 187, 191, 194 n11
  Malaya 191-193
  New Guinea 187, 189, 194 n1
  North Borneo 192
  royalty See also Alfred, Duke of Edinburgh; King George II; King George III; King George IV; Prince Albert; Princess Vicky; Victoria, Queen
    dissatisfaction with 58
    as Germans 59-61
    loyalty to 70-71
    and Scotland 59, **60**
  world 146
Brockenshire, Harold 117
Brooks, Barbara, on Eleanor Dark, *Waterway* 242
Brooks, Herbert 199
Brown, Nicholas xviii, 19

Brown, William Jethro, and R.G. Watt 199
Brussels World Peace Congress 80
Bulgaria, refugees in 79
Bullen Merri, Lake 106
Bureau of Social and International affairs 80, 83
Burgoyne, John 7
Burns, Creighton, on R.G. Watt 89
Burroughs, William 261
Burwood Migrant Hostel 91
Byles, Marie, 93 n33

CNN 91
Calcutta 11
Callaway, Anita, on Alfred, Duke of Edinburgh 59
Cambridge, Ada and Alfred Deakin 206
Campbell, Persia 93 n33
Canada 35, 36 n2, 37 n10, 113 n3, 120, 124, 142, 145, 147 n1
Candler, Samuel Curtis 62, 68-70, 73 n35, n42, n43, 73-74 n45
Canton 120-121
Caribbean 24-25, 27, 30-35
Carson, Susan 214
Castlemaine (Victoria), Chinese residents of 66
categories
    indigenous 44
    kinship 94 n70
    sexuality and gender 259
    suspension of 91
    and transnational biography xv
Catholic 62, 66, 88, 93 n41
    Irish, in Australia 62, 66-67, 71, 73 n32, 74 n58
Ceylon (Sri Lanka) 183, 191
Chapman, Judge (New Zealand) 25
Chauncey, George 264
Cheah, Pheng and Bruce Robbins 226 n3
China
    Agnes Breuer in **121**, 123-127, 130
    Australian wives in 115-116, 117-118, 120-128, 131 n16, 132 n36, 133 n44
    businessmen from 116-117, **122**-125, 127-128, 129, 132 n26, n32
    culture of 116, 118, 121, 124-125
    emigration from, transnational nature of 124-125
    transnational family strategies in 120, 121-125, 127-128, 132 n36
    and Japan 83, 87
    John Sleeman on 115-117, 118, 129, 130
    Kate Bagnall on xix, 95
    non-Chinese women in 120-121, 131 n21
China-Australia relationship 116, 129
Chinese-Anglo relationships in Australia 131 n17
Christian Science Monitor 86
Christopher Street (Manhattan) 267
Christopher Street 261
churches, international xv
Churchill, Winston 191
circulation, and transnational history xiv
citizen
    of empire 186
    of the world xvii, xix, 136, 181, 213, 238
citizenship xv, xvii, 49, 52-53, 145
    international 75, 78
civilisation
    and Australian Aborigines 31, 110
    European 21, 23, 33, 50, 97, 193
class 3, 14, 25, 30, 33-34, 70, 79, 83, 139, 213, 220-225, 227, 229, 233-234, 237-239, 241
    middle 137, 139, 144, 150, 218, 219, 222, 238, 246, 251, 267-268
Clinton, Henry 7
Clontarf (Australia), shooting of Alfred, Duke of Edinburgh 66
Cohen, Morris 22
Collins, Tom (Joseph Furphy), praised by Alfred Deakin 206
colonial
    discourses 43, 46-47, 54
    dividend 135
    experience, transnational nature of 98-99
    mandates, oversight of 78
Colonial Secretary
    British 11, 14-15, 18 n32

New South Wales (Henry Parkes) 66
colonialism
   and European economies and ideologies 23
   and flows of people and goods 278
   and gender 41-42
   as inherently transnational 98-99
colonials
   sense of place in world 200
   transnational lives of 98
colonies
   administration of 23, 25-26, 30, 33-35, 37 n2, 187, 205
   American 6, 7
   Anglo 3
   Australian xiv, 3, 5, 9, 11-16, 21, 24-25, 30-32, 35, 43, 45, 48, 57-71, 97-113, 120, 183-193
   British 19, 23, 34
   Caribbean 25, 27-30, 32-34
   governance of 19, 21, 23-25, 30-35, 75, 197
   New Zealand 25-26
   Papua New Guinea 184, 189-190, 278
   patterns of authority in xviii, xx
   plantation 30, 32-35, 183-193
   settler xiv, 9, 15, 21, 22-23, 30-32, 34-36, 44, 46, 50, 75, 97-113, 186
   Sierra Leone 9
   'trans-colonial' careers in xvii, 19, 25-30
   violence in 23, 30, 34-35
colonisation 36 n7, 112
colonised people 23, 32, 41-42, 43, 246
Committee for the Relief of the Black Poor (London) 9
Commonwealth Department of Information (Australia) 89
Commonwealth Department of War Organisation and Industry 89
Communism, and internationalism 82, 213, 217-218, 226
Communist Party 215, 217-218, 221, 226, 232, 240, 289-291
communities xv
comparative method 24-25

The Comparative Imagination (George Frederickson) 24
Condah (Condon), Lake 100, 101-103, 110-112, 113 n11, 114 n28, n32
conference
   Ethnic Communities Council 292
   Fourth National Homosexual 264
   Imperial, London 205
   Institute of Pacific Relations 81
   International Women's, Workers
   International Relief Organisations 217
   League of Nations 82, 85
   League of Nations Union **85**
   on postwar reconstruction 86
   Paris Peace 75
   'Transnational Lives' xv
connection xiv-xv, xx, 19, 95, 99, 101, 103, 124-125, 205, 276, 278
Conor, Liz, on modern women 219-220
Conrad, Joseph and Alfred Deakin 201
Continental Catholic Migrants Welfare Society 88
convicts, transported to Australia xiii, 9, 11, 15, 67
Cooke, Alice Margaret (nee Chambers) (wife of Samuel Winter Cooke) 113 n1
Cooke, Arbella (nee Winter) 97
   travel to Van Diemen's Land 99
   in the Wimmera District 99
   at Lake Condah (Condon) station 100-103, 113 n11, 114 n28
   letters to sons 100
   loss of intimacy 101
Cooke, Cecil Pybus (husband of Arbella)
   letters to sons 100-101
   relations with Aborigines 100-103, 112-113, 113 n10
Cooke, Edmund (son of Arbella and Cecil) 101-103
Cooke, Herbert Pybus (son of Arbella and Cecil) 102, 113 n15
Cooke, Samuel Winter (son of Arbella and Cecil) 97
   ideas of home 97, 100, 102-103
   at school in England 100-102
   and European cities 97

Cooke, Trevor (son of Arbella and Cecil) 102
Cooke, William Winter (son of Arbella and Cecil) 100-103, 113 n8
Cooper, Emmanuel 267
Copland, Douglas 85
cosmopolitanism 76, 95, 97, 112, 181, 213, 215-226, 226 n3, 237-238
  and transnationalism 213, 215-226, 233
Cornwallis, Lord 7-8, 13
country 98, 110-112
'Credo' (Sir Walter Murdoch) 80
Critchett, Jan, *A Distant Field of Murder* 106
critical thinking, and imagination 213
crossings, and transnational history xiv, xx, 97
culture xx, 78, 97, 166-178, 234, 247, 234, 249-250, 259-270
  Aboriginal 112
  shock 154, 155
  universal 78
cultural
  custodians, Italian women as 169
  displacement 178
  others 246, 256
  zones, liminal 260
curiosity, and transnationalism xvi, xix, 181
Curthoys, Ann xiv, 200
Customs
  Australian 49-52, 115, 117, 123-124, 127-128, 134 n59
  Brazilian 184-185

Daily Mail (Brisbane) 117, **119**
Daily Telegraph (Sydney) 91
dàn tre xiii, 289-296, 290, 293
dance club 269
Dark, Eleanor (nee O'Reilly) xix, 213-214, 229-234, **231**
  Slow Dawning 232
  Waterway 232-239
    on class 239, 241
    critique of gender relations 233, 236, 238-240, 241

  critique of global financial exploitation 232-233, 238-239
  resistance to nationalism 233, 235, 239
  support for internationalism 236, 239
  The Timeless Land 229-230, 235, 242
  trip to New York 229, 235-236
  promoting Australian literature 235
  as 'exile at home' 232
  as regional writer 214
  Susan Carson on 214, 229-242
Dark, Eric (husband of Eleanor Dark) 229, 232, 235
Dark Palace (Frank Moorhouse) 76
Darling, George 12
Dawson, James, and Bareetch Churneed (Queen Fanny) 10
Deacon, Desley (with Penny Russell and Angela Woollacott)
  on the transnational subject 217
  Transnational Lives 36 n1
Deakin, Alfred **198**
  ambivalence towards Britain 205
  and Australian literature 205-206
  and the 'Australian settlement' 197
  as citizen of the world 181
  Conciliation and Arbitration Act 206-207
  correspondence of 199-200
  as cosmopolitan 181
  cultural affinity with Britain 200
  and French literature, 181, 200, 202
  Mark Hearn on xvii, xix, 181
  and idealist philosophy 203-205
  Imperial Conference, London 205
  and imperial federation 205
  and reading 197-209
  and the United States 204-205
  friendship with Walter Murdoch 199-200, 201, 202, 203
  visits the Webbs 205
  in *London Morning Post* 199
Deen Biroo (son of Khair Deen) 51-52
Deen, Khair 51-52
Deem, Marm 49
Department of Home Affairs 127-129

Department of the Interior 128-129
Delany, Samuel 61
Deptford (England) xiii, 8-11
Devanny, Jean, New Zealand novelist **216**
   The Butcher Shop 218
   Lenore Divine 218
   Dawn Beloved 218
   Riven (*Unchastened Youth*) 218
      appeal to cosmopolitan audience 218, 226
      published in US 218
      treatment of modern female sexuality 218-221
      and transnational subject 220
   The Virtuous Courtesan
      published in New York 221
      and class 221-226
      and gender relations 221-226
      and race 225-226
      transnational perspective 222, 225-226
   Sugar Heaven (1936) 226
   and Australia 213, 215-218
   in Berlin 217
   Carole Ferrier on 215
   and Communism 217-218, 221, 226
   as cosmopolitan writer 217-218
   and critique of gender relations 214, 215, 218-226
   Drusilla Modjeska on 215
   in England 217
   between home and away 213-214, 218
   and imagination 213-214
   leaves New Zealand 215
   Nicole Moore on 215
   as popular romance novelist 217, 218, 221-224, 226
   Susan Sheridan on 215
   in Soviet Union 217
   as transnational subject 215, 217-218
   on Wellington (New Zealand) 215, 217, 218-221
diaspora
   British 95, 135, 209
   and identity 205
   of the imagination 200, 202, 208
   Indian 43
   Ann Curthoys on 200
   queer xix-xx, 259-270
   and transnational history xiv
   of white race 205
dictionaries of national biography xvi, 186, 187
Didion, Joan, *Salvador* 246
disarmament 76, 78
Dirks, Nicholas, 23
Disco Kwilts (David McDiarmid) 269-**270**
displacement 178, 279
   of previous occupants 99, 113
   and transnationalism xiii, 95, 98
distance xviii, 71, 86, 98, 99, 101-103, 149-150, 167
   cultural 249, 255
   and independence 163
Distant Field of Murder, A (Jan Critchett) 106
domestic crafts 269
domesticity, flight from 70-71, 219
Dongguan (Guangdong province, China), emigration from 120
Dorfman, Ariel, *Heading South, Looking North: A Bilingual Journey* 245
Doss, Nunda Lall, as effeminate Bengali 47-48
Dreiser, Theodore, *An American Tragedy* 220-221
Duffy Land Selection Acts 114 n28
Duncan, Constance 80, **85**, 87
Duke of Genoa, visit to Tasmania 65-66

Eagleton, Terry 35
East, J.B. 16
East Yorkshire 25
economic progress, international standards for 78, 90
economy, global 21, 185
education 77, 78, 82, 87, 101-103, 139, 147 n4, 203, 219, 247
eighteenth century 1, 3, 5, 18 n39, 60, 109, 186, 251
emigrants *See also* emigration, migrants, migration
   British 97-113, 135-147, 149-163
   as citizens of the world xvii

    describing their life 135-147
    marital and family relations 135, 136, 140-147
    motivations 135-136, 138-140
    'Thatcher refugees' 138
    as transnationals 67, 135-136, **137**, 138, 140-147
    and transnational marriages 136, 138, 140-147
  from South Africa, to Australia 142
  Chinese 120, 124-125, 292
  Indian 41, 44
  Italian xix, 95, 165, 166, **167**, 169-178
  and 'lens of migration' 95, 136, 138, 143, 146, 165-166
  Punjabi 41, 43-44
emigration
  as adventure 68, 74 n45, 95, 120-121, 136, 140-141, 145, 150-151, 155, 162-163
  change in 135, 140, 143, 146
  and corporate employment practices 140
  as family strategy 44-45, 120, 124-125, 135-136, 138-140
  history xiv, 165-168
  and loss of family support 155-156
  and mass air travel 140
  and reinvention of self 70
  and working holidays 140
empathy, enlarged xix, 208, 213
empire *See also* colonial, colonies, Britain, colonial world of
  builders 191
  citizen of 186
  concepts of 75, 76, 82, 88, 112
  diaspora of 205
  'families' 76
  German 64
  'intimate' (Gillian Whitlock) 6-7
  legacies of 23
  of literature xix
  and metropole 23
  ties of 205
  and transnationalism xiv, xix, 19
England 6, 8-9, 17 n20, 21, 23, 25, 27, 30, 34, 36 n1, 37 n12, 69, 72 n6, 103, 109, 111, 118, 120, 215, 219, 220, 226, 232, 234, 236
  education in, of colonial children 101-103
  as home 86, 99, 113
  and identity 62, 97-98
  importation of tropical plants to 184
  landscape of 137
  and migration 138, 141-147, 149-163
  publishers in 217-218
  readers in 219
English language 71, 91, 110, 213, 217-218, 248, 253, 292
  global reach of 245
  travel books in 245-246, 255-256
  writers in 242
English Speaking Union 84
English Zone (Germany) xiii, 284
Enterprise, HMS 9-10
entrepreneur, imperial xix, 181, 186-188
Equiano, Olaudah (Gustavus Vassa) 5
Ernest of Saxe-Coburg Gotha, as King of Greece 60
ethnicity xx, 43, 169, 226
Eucken, Rudolf read by Alfred Deakin 203-204
Europe, 9, 73, 86, 87, 120, 193, 203, 204, 229, 233, 236, 237, 241, 242, 246, 249, 262
  as centre of culture 97, 203, 260
  civilisation of 21, 23, 97
  and the colonies 23, 24, 30, 31-35
  economies and ideologies of 23
  expansion of 23, 24, 30
  replaced by New York as centre of art 260, 268
  understandings of sovereignty 35-36
Europeans
  in Canton 120
  as cosmopolitans 76
  in Hong Kong 120
  and Indians 47
  in Macau 120
  refugees 88
  women married to Chinese men 120
Evans, Julie xviii, 19, 75, 82
Evatt, Dr H.V. 'Bert' 89, 242

exchanges, and transnational lives xiv, xvi, 238, 277
exile, and transnational lives xiv, xv, 110, 245
'exiles at home' (Drusilla Modjeska) 232
expatriates 121, 136, 140, 144-145, 246-256
Experiment 11, 12, 18 n32
exploration
   of Australia xviii, 21, 23, 25, 31, 36 n1, 206
   of ideas 198, 200, 202, 213
   of identity 260
   of sexuality 262, 264, 265, 267
explorer, historiography 21, 30
Eyre, Edward John 19, 21, 27, **28**, **29**, 30
   as explorer 21, 23, 25, **26**, 30, 31
      dependency on Aboriginal knowledge **26**, 31, 36 n1
   Journals of Expeditions of Discovery 30-31
      advocacy of Aboriginal sovereignty 30-31
   as Resident Magistrate and Protector of Aborigines 25, 33
   Manners and Customs of Aborigines and the State of their Relations with Europeans 31-32
      rejection of Aboriginal sovereignty 31-32, 34-36
   as Lieutenant Governor, New Zealand 25-27, 33
   as Lieutenant Governor, St Vincent 27, 32
   as Lieutenant Governor, Antigua 23, 27
   as Acting Governor, Jamaica 27, **28**, 33-35
      repression of freedpeople 32-34
   and Morant Bay rebellion 27, 34
      and strategic significance of race 32-35
   recall to England 27
   retirement to Devon **29**, 30, 34
   as transnational figure 21-24, 25-30, 34-35
'Eyre controversy' 23

family *See also* kinship
   avoidance of 70, 138, 262, 268
   and emigration xix, 135-147, 167, 246-249
   global 80
   networks xv, 3, 6, 120. 129, 132 n32, 151, 155-156, 162
   separation from xiii, xix, 44-45, 49-51, 69, 97-101, 111-113, 126-130, 149-163, 262-263, 291-293, 295
   strategies 44-45, 120, 122, 124
   transnational xvii, 95-96, 99, 124-125, 145-147, 149-150, 162-163, 294-295
fantasy, and memory 95, 168, 169-170, 178
   and transnationalism xx, 261
Federal Australian League of Nation's Union, and R.G. Watt 78
Federated Malay States 191-193
Feminine Mystique (Betty Friedan) 162
femininity, black and white 43
feminist 90, 206, 217, 219, 260
   historians, post-colonial 41-42
feminism 76, 82
Fenian conspiracy, suspicion of 66
Ferguson, Niall 23
Ferrier, Carole, on Jean Devanny 215, 226 n2
fifteenth century 23
Findley, John, *The Imperial Conference of 1911 from Within* 205
Fiorani, F. 65-66
first love, migrants' memories of xix, 95, 165-178
Fisher, Andrew, and Alfred Deakin 205
Fitzgerald, Shirley, on John Sleeman's *White China* 116
Flinders Ranges (South Australia), Eyre expedition to 25
Florence (Italy), as centre of culture 97
flows, of objects and people 276, 278
   and transnational history xiv
fluid, boundary between people and things 278
forgetting, and 'active recollection' 166
A Foreign Wife (Gillian Bouras) 214, 245-249
Foster, Hal 261

France 1, 5, 9, 65, 181, 197, 200-202, 237-238, 249-251, 255
Franco-Prussian war 64
Franklin, Miles, read by Alfred Deakin 205-206
Frederickson, George, *The Comparative Imagination* 24
freedpeople (Caribbean) 32-35
Freeman's Journal (Sydney) 62, 65, 66
French Jew 237
Friedan, Betty, *The Feminine Mystique* 162, 219
frontier 99-100, 103-113
violence 34, 104-106, 108
Furphy, Joseph, read by Alfred Deakin 205-206

Galatea, HMS, and Alfred, Duke of Edinburgh 59, 61, 67, 73 n28
Gallery Development team xiii-xiv, xv, xx, 276
Garibaldi, visit to Tasmania 65-66
Gawler, Governor 25
gay
    couples 218
    culture and art 259-270
    diaspora 262, 264
    men 213, 214, 223
Gay Liberation Newsletter (Sydney) 262
gaze, romantic, and migrant memories 172-178
gender
    and the city, Elizabeth Grosz on 270
    and class identity 226, 229, 238-239
    colonial discourses on 43, 75
    and feminist post-colonial historians 41-42
    liminal spaces of 260
    and migration 136, 146, 149-163, 169, 176
    and new imperial history 41-42
    and politics 267-268
    and queer theory 259
    and transnational subjectivity xv, xx, 82, 213, 214, 218, 221-222, 225
'geometry of order' 199
George II 5-6

George III 5-6, 17 n7
George IV 59, 72 n6
German Emergency Fellowship Committee 88
Germany xiii, 5-6, 187, 226 n2, 237, 275-276, 280, 282-284, 295
    Alfred, Duke of Edinburgh, as Anglo-German 59, 60-64, **63**, 67, 72 n16, n22
Ghurkas, as martial race 46
Ginsberg, Allen 261
Glenormiston 106-109, **107, 109**
global
    community of ideas xiv-xv, xvi
    conflict 200, 214
    cultures xx
    diaspora of gay men 262
    English 245
    history, and biography 22-24, 25, 34-35
    identity 19
    and local xv, 34-35, 208, 233, 241-242
    market xvi, 21, 136, 186-187, 214, 222, 233
    mobility, and migration 136, 146-147
    networks xx
    political and social change 229
    transformation, and internationalism 75
    world xvii
Gosden, Chris and Yvonne Marshall 276-278
Good Housekeeping Baby Book (UK) 152
Gore-Brown, Governor Thomas 70-71
Gosford (Australia) 77
governance, colonial 19, 21, 23-25, 30-35, 75, 197
graffiti, influence on David McDiarmid 263-264
Grand Days (Frank Moorhouse) 76
Greece 60, 79, 246-249
Greenish, R.P. 90
Gregg, Robert 3
Grewal, Inderpal, on travel writing 245
Grey, Sir Edward 83-84
Grey, Governor George (New Zealand) 27
Groom, Littleton 78
Grosz, Elizabeth 270

313

Guardian (Manchester) 86
Gustin, Lena, letters to, in *La Fiamma*, 165, **167**, 172-178, 179 n11

habit, of allegiance xviii
Haggis, Jane 41
Hall, Catherine 43, 48
Hall, Radclyffe 220, 227 n6
Hammerton, James, on British diaspora 5, 7, 95, 135-147, 147 n1, 165-166
Hanoverians, on British throne 60-61
Harbin (China), Janet Mitchell in 81
Haring, Keith 263-264, 267, 271 n17
Harris, John, and Billy Blue 12
Hawaii, women married to Chinese men 120, 132 n33
Heading South, Looking North: A bilingual journey (Ariel Dorfman) 245
health, international standards for 78, 90
Hearn, Mark, on Alfred Deakin's reading habits xvii, xix, 181, 197-209
Hedges, Leonard 139-140
Henry Lawson Labour College 90
Herald (Melbourne) 86
Hevea brasiliensis 183-185, 189-191
Hibbert Journal 207
hierarchy xv, xviii, 19, 88, 259
    of masculinities 45
Higgins, Henry Bournes (Bourne) 199
Hill, Margaret writing life story 140
Hillgay (Victoria) 111
Hinder, Eleanor 8, 81, 82
Hindus, in South Australia 45, 47
historians
    of Alfred Deakin 197
    audience for xiv, xvii
    Australian xiv
    feminist post-colonial 41-42
    oral 136
    transnational xv, xviii, 16
    at 'Transnational Lives' conference xv
history
    of Africans in Anglo-colonial world 3
    Australian 160, 187
    and Indian settlers 41, 54
    and biography 3, 21-22, 24, 25, 35-36

communal 269
comparative 24-25, 30, 34
dynamic xiv
and gender xx, 41-43
global 22, 24, 34
imperial 23
of Latvian culture 295
life 135-137, 143-144, 276-277, 279, 295
literary 232
material 295
and memory 3
micro 3
and narrative 3
national xiv, xv, xvii, 16, 21-24, 30, 36
new imperial 41-43
oral 136, 147 n1, 163 n1, 281, 294
postcolonial 22-23
of sovereignty 35-36
transnational xiv-xv, xvii, xx, 21-22, 43-44, 57, 91, 165-168, 200, 279, 296
of Vietnamese music 293-294
'white' Australian xiii, 41
historiography
    of explorers 21
    imperial 22
    of migration 165
    of the Morant Bay rebellion 30, 34
Hobart (Tasmania) 11
Hobsbawm, Eric 82
Hoffman, Eva, *Lost in Translation* 245
Hogan, Mr, at Lake Condah Mission 110
Holland, Patrick, on travel writing 245
Holmes, Rear Admiral Charles 6, 17 n10
home 97-99, 149-151, 160, 162-163
    Australia as 145, 151, 163, 215, 217
    and away 213-214, 229, 232, 238
    ambiguities of 95, 99, 100, 103, 112-113, 130, 137
    Bill Blake as Christina Stead's 214
    China as 125
    destroyed by colonialism 95, 99, 103-105, 108-113
    as emblem of new attachments 95
    'exiles at' 232

and imagination 104, 234, 242
    market place as 238
    New York as 259
    yearning for 95, 104, 108
homelessness, spiritual 203
homesickness 121, 141-142, 151,154-155
Hong Kong 115, 117, 118, 120-121, 125-127, 130
Hornsea (East Yorkshire) 25
Howe, General William 5, 7
Hudson River (New York) 7-8
Huggan, Graham, on travel writing 245
Humanities Research Centre, Australian National University xv
Hungarians, in New South Wales 66
Hunt, Atlee 49
hybrid xiv, 237, 238, 265, 278, 289, 291
    self 215, 218, 223, 225, 261, 270, 278

Iacovetta, Franca 169
idealist philosophy, and Alfred Deakin 203-204
ideas
    of 'America' 264-265
    as bridges to the world xviii
    fin de siecle 197, 208
    flow of xv, xvi, 276
    of home 99
    international community of 234
    of internationalism 213
    about masculinity 43
    national 242
    networks of 8
    about race 24
    transnational 278
identity 57, 200, 203, 204, 205
    Ann Curthoys on 200
    Australian xiv, xvi, 71, 140, 145, 200
    class 221-223, 225, 226
    dual 61-62, 71
    ethnic 66, 222, 225, 226
    formation 269
    Homi Bhabha on 168
    hybrid 225-226
    imperial 213, 218
    and language 245
    multiple 168, 260, 261

    national 82, 98, 113, 225, 281-282
    new 225
    politics 260, 269
    as 'repetition with a difference' 168, 178
    sexual 221-223, 225, 226, 259-261, 265
    transnational 82, 98, 113, 135-136, 138, 142, 146-147, 178, 200, 225-226
Illustrated Sydney News 66
il primo amore See first love
Il Salotto di Lena, letters to 165-178, **167**
imagination 22, 24, 104, 151, 167, 170, 200-208, 213-214
    and transnational life xiv, xviii, xix-xx, 181, 197-209, 213-271
immersion narratives 245-256
immigration policies (Australian) 19, 43, 48-51, 95
Immigration Restriction Act (1901) 48
imperial
    adventuring 181
    authorities 50, 187
    conference 205
    culture xx
    enterprise xix, 23, 181, 183, 205
    federation 205
    historiography 23
    history, new 41-42
    identity 213, 218
    loyalty 19
    romance 213, 218-220, 222-224, 226
    values 217
Imperial Eyes (Mary Louise Pratt) 214, 245, 246
Indian Ocean 229
Indians
    in Australia 19, 41, 45, 48-54
    in Australian history 41, 44
    and Australian Labor Party 52, 54
    in Batavia (Jakarta) 41
    Bengalis 43, 46, 47-48
    in British army 46-47, 54
    as British citizens 41, 45, 46-47, 54
    in British Mounted Police 41, 46
    as businessmen 41, 52-54
    common Aryan origin 47

diaspora 43
emigration of 44-45
Ghurkas 46
loyalty to British Raj 46-47
masculinity of 43, 45, 46, 47-48, 54
plantations in 191
as problematic term 43-44
as property holders 46
from Punjab 41, 43-44
and race 45
surveillance and regulation of, in Australia 48-52, 54
protests against restrictions in Australia 49, 52
Sikhs 46-47, 55 n32
in Sumatra 41
and 'white standard' 50
indigenous peoples *See also* Aborigines (Australian) 22, 35-36, 37 n10, 105
Indonesia 245-246, 251-256
inequalities, and biography 22
Institute of Pacific Relations 81, 83
institutions
    British 57, 70
    cultural xvi, 109, 268
    imperial 205
    international 75
    political xvi
    transnational xiv, 181
intellect, ties of xiv, xv, xviii, xix, xx
    and transnational life 77-79, 181, 233-234, 237, 238, 239
intellectuals xix, 237, 267
The Interesting Narrative of Olaudah Equiano The African 5
international
    book market 213, 217, 218, 222, 241-242
    business 187, 214, 232, 233, 237-239
    causes 77-80, 82
    citizenship 75
    communities xvi, 65, 79, 234
    discursive power of 75
    gay life 260-261
    intellectualism 239
        and the League of Nations 77
        and League of Nations Union 78
    Labour Organisation 78
    law (law of nations) 31, 32
    management 89
    migrant self-image as 136
    and national xiv
    new modes of 75, 77-78, 89, 91-92
    opportunities 81, 82
    organizations 75
    politics 234
    and pursuit of democracy 90
    relations 76, 80, 89
    as sociability 80, 84-85, 88, 90
    society, idea of, Akira Iriye on 75
    transition from 'empire' to 76-77, 88
    travel 217, 245
    and language travel 245
    woman 76
    Women's Conference of the Workers International Relief Organisations 217
internationalism
    communist 82, 213, 236, 239
    feminist 82
    and ideology xviii, 19
    and imperialism 79
    and modernity 82
    and nations 84, 87, 89. 91
    politics of xviii
    and R.G. Watt 19, 75-92
internationalist, David Stead as 78
interracial marriage and relationships 115-130, 132 n33, 136, 213, 218, 267, 269
    as transnational 125, 130
Interview 261
intimacy xx, 13-14, 101, 167
    and transnational lives xviii, xix, 95-96
investors 21, 188, 194 n17
Irish 62, 66-67, 71, 74 n58. 97, 99. 201
Ismail, S.W.S. 52
Italian xix, 65, 95, 165-178,166-178, 247-249

Jacks, L.P. 207-208
Jackson, Joe, on Henry Wickham 184-185
Jacobs, Jane, *The Death and Life of Great American Cities* 261

Jamaica, Edward Eyre acting governor of 23, 27-30, **28**, 33-35
James, William, read by Alfred Deakin 181, 204, 208
Japan, and China 83, 87
Japanese, in Australia 53
Jebb, Richard, *Imperial Conference* 205
Jewish Welfare Society (Australian) 88
Johnson, Amanda, review of John Mateer, *Semar's Cave* 255
Jones, Sir Henry 23
journeys
    home 51, 53-54, 69, 99, 100, 103, 111-112, 117-118, 120, 125,189, 232, 234
    of objects 275-196
    official scrutiny of 128-130
    and transnational history xiv, 276, 295-296
Juicy Fruits: Ralph, Joe, Frank . . . (David McDiarmid) 265, **266**
justice, international standards for 78

Kaiping (Guangdong province, China), emigration from 120
Kalamata, Greece, Gillian Bouras in 247
Kangaroo Island 41, 46, 51-53
Kangaroo Island Courier 46
Kaplan, Caren, on travel writing 245
Kent, William Saville 190
Kent Assizes 11
Kessinger, Tom, on Punjabi emigration 44
Kew Botanical Gardens, Royal 183-184, 187-189, 191, 193 n1, 194 n14
Khan, Joe 51
Khan, Jumee 54
Khan, Rahma 53-54
Kipling, Rudyard, and Alfred Deakin 181, 205
King of Greece, Alfred, Duke of Edinburgh as possible 60
King, Governor 11
Kingscote, Kangaroo Island 41, 42, 51, 53
Kinne, Guna 1, 275-276, 280, 281-289, **285, 287, 288**, 295, 296
kinship, 'beyond-blood' 269 *See also* family
Kor, Harman (wife of Gola Singh) 50

La Condamine, Charles-Marie de 246
La Fiamma 165, **167**
labour, international standards for 78, 234
labour force 9-11, 30, 32-33, 39 n29, 52, 54, 100, 113, 186, 187, 221
Lady Jane Halliday 11
Lake Bullen Merri 106
Lake Condah (Condon) 100-103, 110-113,113 n11
    Aboriginal mission and reserve 110-112, 114 n28, n32
Lake, Marilyn 43, 37 n15, 204-205, 208
Lambert, David xvi
land
    concessions, in colonies 186, 187, 191, 192
    control of, in Australia 30, 32
    in British New Guinea 189-190
    Indians purchasing in homeland 41, 44
    'knowing', and Aboriginal companions 30
    'of the mind and the soul' 204
    replacing indigenous peoples on 22-23, 24, 30-32, 34, 103-113
    rights 22-23
    use, primitive 21
landscape
    cultural 246, 260
    and home 108, 112, 137, 232, 233-236
    and the 'spectator-traveller' 233
    and travel writing 245
Lane, Ann 181
language
    Bahasa Indonesia 252
    body 248
    borders 245
    Cape Malay 251
    and emigration 125, 246-251
    foreign 202, 241, 245-251, 255
    French 160, 181, 197, 200, 202, 249-251, 297 n33
    Greek 77, 246-249
    hybrid 238, 265
    of internationalism 90
    Italian 165, 168-169, 171-172, 179 n11, 247-249

and the self 245, 249, 253
shared xix, 47, 214, 217, 255
travel xix, 214, 245-256
Latvia xiii, 275, 281-284, 287, 289
national dress 275, 280-289, **280, 281, 283, 285, 286, 287, 288**, 295
law 9, 19, 31, 24-25, 27, 31-35, 84, 93 n41, 95
Leadbeater, Charles read by Alfred Deakin 203
League of Nations 19, 76, 77-78, 83-84, 86-87
League of Nations Union 75-92 *See also* United Nations Association of Australia
and arbitration of international conflict 78
and disarmament 78
and equitable distribution of economic progress and access to justice 78-79, 83
and oversight of colonial mandates 78
and public lectures and meetings 79-81, 84-88, 91
and R.G. Watt 77-92
and refugees 88-89
and standards and conditions for labour, health and migration 78-79
Stuart Macintyre on
and world citizenship 78
Lester, Alan xvi
letters
as connection to family 7, 68, 95, 97, 99, 100-103, 126, 130, 149-163
to *Il Salotto di Lena* xix, 165-178, 179 n11
as reflective space 95
from traditional custodian 109-113, 114 n30, n32
in transnational relationships 7, 95, 99, 113, 147 n12, 162-163, 165-166
Levan, Larry (DJ, Paradise Garage) 269
Levine, Philippa, and masculinity 41-42
Lewis, D.C., on Henry Wickham 186-187
Li Yunying (first wife of William Low Lum) 122, 126

Liberian coffee 188, 194 n14
Liedertafel 61, 65
life stories
and authority 19
and dictionaries of national biography xvi
of emigrants xvii, 95, 135-147, 149-163
and history xv
and intimacy 95-96
in motion xviii
and social structure 22-24
transnational xv-xx, 19, 95
life writing, as therapy 103, 138-139 198-199
Lindsay, A.D. read by Alfred Deakin 207
Listener (BBC), and R.G. Watt 86
literary criticism xv, 197, 202
literature
Alfred Deakin as lover of 202
Australian 205-206, 235, 238
beyond national boundaries xx
empire of xix
French 181, 197, 200, 202
Hollywood 264-265
Indonesian 254-255
Italian 170-174, 178
travel 232, 245
Little York (Virginia) 5-8
Liu, William, 116-117, 129, 130, 132 n32
Live Aid 91
lives
of Africans in the Anglo-colonial world 3
Australian xvii-xx
far-flung xiii
divided 19
expatriate 246
individual, significance of 21-24, 25
narratives of 95, 135-147, 165-176
of objects 277-280, 295-296
regulation of 31-32, 48-52
and the storyteller 213
subaltern 19
transnational xiii-xx, 19, 45, 57, 71, 82, 130, 149, 166-167, 176, 181, 225-226, 229, 296

local xv, 3, 24, 82, 112, 208, 214, 218, 233
London 8-11, 18 n25, 47-48, 49, 187, 191, 192, 194 n17, 205, 209, 217, 218, 222, 232, 237, 242
   Morning Post, Alfred Deakin in 199
   Times, and R.G. Watt 86
loneliness 151, 154, 155, 158-159, 178, 292
Lord, Simeon 15
Lost in Translation: A Life in a new language (Eva Hoffman) 245
Lougher, Ann (wife of Albert) 139
Lougher, Albert 139-140
Louisbourg, seige of 6
love xviii-xx, 118, 120, 123, 129-130, 168-171, 177-178, 179 n13, 214, 259-260
   'world' 78
Low Mun *See* Agnes Breuer
lower Herbert River, North Queensland, Henry Wickham at 187-188
loyal addresses 66, 73 n30
Loyalists 8, 17 n18
loyalties
   to Australia 140, 146
   to Britain 15-16, 19, 46-47, 53, 61, 64-67, 71
   contingent 146
   multiple, in Australia 61, 64, 66-67, 71, 74, 74 n58, 206, 218, 236
   The Philosophy of Loyalty 204
   'reprioritised' 82
Lum Mow (father of William Lum Mow)
   migration from China to Australia, two-way nature of 120, 124-125
   transnational family strategies 125, 127-128
   Townsville business 117, 122
   disapproval of William's marriage 125-126, 129
Lum Mow, Norman (brother of William) 123, 125, 127, 129, 132 n32, 133 n52
Lum Mow, Thomas (brother of William) **122**, 123, 129
Lum Mow, William (Lum Wie) 117, **119**, 121
   Townsville education 122
   in family business **122**
   Chinese wife, Li Yungying 122-123, 126
   marriage to Agnes Breuer (Low Mun) 123-124, 125-126
   legal status 124, 127-130
Lum Mow, William jr (son of William and Agnes) **119**, 123-124, 126-127, 130, 134 n29

McAleer, John, on popular romances 218
McCreery, Cindy xviii, 19, 41, 75, 82
McDiarmid David 259-270
   Alphabet City 262, **263**, 264
   Disco Kwilt series 269-270, **270**
   and New York 259-270
   as gay political artist 264, 269
   and liminal cultural zones 260
   multi-faceted identity 259-260, 261
   'mobile and located' art xx, 214, 259
   as Australian and American xx, 214, 259, 261
McKay, Daniel, and Billy Blue 12
McKeown, Adam 124
McKillop, G. 106
Macgregor, Sir William 187, 189
Mackellar, Maggie xix, 95, 97-113
Macquarie, Lachlan xiii, 13-15, 16
Macau, non-Chinese women in 120-121
Madras, ships from, in Sydney Harbour 11
Malaya 183-185, 188-189, 191-193
Magistrate, Resident, Edward Eyre as 23, 25, 31
Man who Loved Children (Christina Stead), and 'monoman' 78
Manhattan, occupation of 7
Mar family 129, 132 n32
Mar Leong Wah 132 n32
Mar Sun Gee 132 n32
markets xvi, xxi n9, 21, 222, 233, 237
marriage
   and Australian immigration laws 127-130
   between Chinese and Anglo-Australian xix, 95, 116-118, 120, 123-126
   critique of 218-226, 232, 239-241
   delayed, in Australia 70
   inter-racial 132 n32, 136
   of migrants 136, 138, 140-147, 150-151

transnational 138
volatile 136
Marshall, Yvonne and Chris Gosden 276-277
martial
    Indians, and masculinity 43, 46-47
    law, and Governor Eyre 27, 34
masculinity
    in Australian colonies 43, 45, 46, 51-54
    black, Catherine Hall on 43
    in *House of all Nations* 240
    of colonised men 43
    hyper- 265
    imperial 41-42
    of Indian men xvii, 19, 43, 45, 46-48, 50-54
    Marilyn Lake on 43
    Mrinalini Sinha on 43
    Philippa Levine on 41-42
    Victorian 71
    white 41-42, 43, 46, 52, 54
    and the White Australia Policy 43, 50-52, 54
    Richard White on 43
Mass Observation collection 163 n1
Massola, Aldo, *Aboriginal Mission Stations in Victoria* 112
Mateer, John, *Semar's Cave* xix, 214, 245-246, 251-256, **252**, 257 n26
    in South Africa and Australia 251
    writer-in-residence, North Sumatra and Java 251, 256 n26
    and Cape Malay language 251
    and translation 253
    and cultural differences 246, 254-256
    as transnational 252-253, 255
    Mary Besemeres on 7, 214, 251-255
material culture scholarship 276-278
    and object biography 276-279, 289, 295-296
    and transnational biography 275-278, 289, 295-296
Matthews, Jill xv
Mead, G.R.S. read by Alfred Deakin 203
Meehan, Surveyor, and Billy Blue 14
Melanesia, distributed self in 277

Melbourne (Australia) 59-70, 72 n7, n22, 73 n43, n45, 97, 102, 108, 197
    Chinese community 66
    Club 68-70
    Herald 86
    Round Table 83
    University 85
men
    all-male environments 70-71
    Australian 43, 46, 49, 52, 54, 68-71, 262
        unemployed 221, 223
    Chinese 118, 120-121, 124-125, 128, 131 n13, n16
    colonised 43
    and flight from domesticity 70, 71
    free 6, 11
    gay 262, 264, 265
    governing 19
    Indian 19, 41-54
    Italian 169-178
    non-white 118
    and reinvention of self 68, 70
    white 41-43, 46, 49, 52, 54
    and intellect and authority xx
    young 21, 71, 140
memory xiii
    as 'active recollection' 66
    'emotive organization of' 170
    and fantasy 165, 168, 169-170, 178
    of *feuilleton* 170
    of first love 166-178, 179 n11
    and forgetting 166, 171
    of former homeland 108-109, 111-113
    of migration 7, 95, 99, 135-146, 155, 163 n1, 165, 167, 168-178, 179 n11, 275-296
    in transnational perspective 165-167
Meredith, Louisa Anne 65-66
Metcalf, Thomas R. 46, 55 n32
metropole, new ideas from 205
migrant *See also* emigrant, emigration, migration
    British xix, 95, 135-147, 149-163
    Chinese 120, 125
    as 'citizen of the world' 136
    as cosmopolitan 95

families 143-147, 149-163, 166-167
gentlemen 68, 71-72
German 64
Hostel 91
ideas of home 95
identities 135-136, 138, 140, 143, 178
Indian 41, 44-45
as international 136
interviews with 147 n1, n5
Italian 7, 95, 165-178, **166**
letters 147 n5, n12, 165-178, 179 n11
marriages 136, 140-147
memories 9, 95, 135-147, 165-178
mobile 135-137, 140-147
and money-making 136
motivations 138-147
as nomads **137**, 140-147
from non-English background 166-167, 245
to non-English countries 245-241, 255-256
serial 95, 135, 140-147, 147 n1
self-improvement 135-136, 140, 147 n4
as 'Thatcher refugees' 138
as transient workers 144
as transnational xvi, xix, 67, 135-136, 140, 146-147, 149, 178, 276
war brides 136
welfare 88
women, agency of 143, 155, 162-163
and working holidays 140
migration 225 *See also* emigration
as bridge to world xviii
as centre of life story 135-147
colonial context for 98
and families 44-45, 97-113, 120-122, 124-125, 136-147
and fantasy 95, 168, 170, 178, 261
global context for 146
international standards for 78
and intimacy xix, 95. 99
and language xix, 214, 245-251, 255-256
'lens of' 95, 135-147
and loss 95, 100-103, 109-113, 155, 247

and marriage 136-147
and nostalgia 95
of objects 275-298
and rupture xviii, 95
schemes 140, 151
urban, and gay sexuality 262
Miller, J.D.B., on R.G. Watt 80, 94 n75
Millers Point (Sydney), and Billy Blue 14
Mills and Boon, imperial romances 219
Mills, C. Wright, on biography 22
Minorca, and Billy Blue 11
missionaries 33-34, 47-48, 128, 120-12, 129, 187
mission, Aboriginal, at Lake Condah 110-112, 114 n28
Mitchell, Janet 81-82
Mitchell Library 133 n53, 165, 179 n11
mobility xvii, xviii, 135-147, 217, 237
of modernity 75, 135, 146-147
restricted xviii, 48-52
modern
    Australia 235-236, 239
    consumerism 218-219, 238-239
    female sexuality 218-226
    intellectuals 237, 239
    migrants 135-136, **137**, 139, 140, 146-147
    post- 259-260
    urban life 215-226, 235-236, 261
    world xiv, xvi, xvii, 22, 37 n12, 135-136, 201, 203-204, 208, 233-235
modernism, Zygmunt Bauman on 208
modernity
    and internationalism 75, 78, 82-83, 233-234, 237, 239
    technologies of xvii, 233, 235
    and transnationalism 229
Modjeska, Drusilla 215, 232
Mohmad, Sher 49
monarchy, British, transnational nature of 71
Montefiore, Abraham 192
Moorhead, Arthur, and R.G. Watt 87-88
Moorhouse, Frank 76, 79
Moorunde (South Australia) 25, 36 n1
Morant Bay rebellion 30, 34, 38 n26

321

Mori, Kyoko, *Polite Lies: On Being a Woman Caught between Cultures* 245
movement
    of ideas xiv-xvi
    international 89, 123, 262
    memories of xiii
    of money 237-238
    of objects 277-178
    of people xiv, 138, 143, 238
    political 19, 66, 238, 260, 262
    social 75, 77, 84, 88, 139, 147 n4, 160, 260, 262
    and transnational history xiv, 278
Moving Stories: British Women and the Postwar Australian Dream 163 n1
Mrs Macquarie's Chair, and Billy Blue 16
Murdoch, Sir Walter 80, 199-203
Murndal homestead 97, **98**, **100**, 109-112, 114 n30, n32, n34
Muscio, Mildred, and R.G. Watt 90
musical instruments xiii, 289-295
museology, and transnational biography xv

narratives
    of Anglo-Chinese marriages 118
    of Australia's place in the empire 206
    of class, gender and race 229, 238-239
    of quest xvi-xvii
    of adventure xiii, xvi-xvii, 136-137, 241
    immersion 245-256
    of migrants 95, 136-138, 145, 146-147, 168, 169, 170, 173, 177
    national 3, 21, 43, 168, 232
    and objects 275-276, 279, 295-296
    transnational xv-xvii, 21, 43, 91, 118, 186, 232-237, 275-276, 279, 295-296
nation xiii, xv, xvii-xviii, xx, 19, 24, 30, 35, 49, 57, 60-67, 71, 75, 77-79, 83-84, 87, 90-91, 97-98, 112-113, 118, 127, 130, 140, 168, 181, 186, 194 n11, 205, 208, 232-224, 242, 252-253
    and audiences xvi-xvii
    and biography xvi
    loyalty to 146
    and markets xxi n9

Patrick Wolfe on 98
    and publishers xvi-xvii
    for the white race 43, 48
national
    apology 37 n10
    Archives (UK) 9, 233
    borders 236, 276
    Council of Women 90
    dress xiii, 275, 280, 281-289, **285**, **286**, **287**, **288**, 295-296
    heritage 281-282
    history xiv, xv, 16, 21-24, 30, 35-36, 36 n8, 41, 187, 193
    identities 213, 214, 218, 225, 229, 282, 284, 289
    literature 235
    narratives 3, 22-23, 36 n8, 41, 43, 168
    Maritime Museum 9-10
    Museum of Australia xiii, 275, 288, 291-294, 295
        Australian Journeys Gallery xiii, xv, 276-279, 294-296
    stereotypes 237, 249, 255-256
National Life and Character (Pearson) 205
nationalism, and internationalism 75, 233, 235, 239, 241
nationality 124, 237, 254
nations, law of 31
Navy *See* Royal Navy
networks xv, 9, 84, 90, 151, 155-156, 162, 262
    and transnational history xiv, xv, xx
New Guinea (British) 184, 186, 187-190, 194 n11 *See also* Papua New Guinea
'new imperial history' 41-42
New South Wales (NSW) 3, 9, 11, 16, 45-46, 50-51, 53, 66, 77, 81-83, 85, 88-90
New Woman 219
New York xiii, 3, 6-8, 13-14, 17 n1, 214-215, 218, 220-222, 229, 232, 235-236, 241, 259-270
New Zealand 22-26, 33, 35-36, 120, 124, 147 n1, 213, 215, 217-226, 254
Nguyen, Minh Tam xiii, 289-296, **293**
Nielsen, Niel on Hindu settlers 46
Niemeyer, Sir Otto 78-79, 289-90
nostalgia xviii, xix, 95, 178

novelists xix, 206, 213-214, 215-226, 229-242
Nullarbor Plain, and Edward Eyre 21, 25

object biography xiii, xv, 276-279, 295-296
    and transnational lives xv, 276, 278-279, 295-296
officials xviii, 19, 34, 49-52, 87, 115, 118, 124, 127-129, 133 n44, 192, 253
Old Bailey online 10, 18 n25
Old Commodore (Billy Blue) 4, 9-10, 14, 15-16
Oliver, Pam 53
Omissi, David, on Indian masculinities 46
On the Plantation, Cultivation, and Curing of Para Indian Rubber (Henry Wickham) 184
Orange Protestants, in Australian colonies (Orangemen) 66
O'Reilly, Dowell (father of Eleanor Dark) 234
Ormond, Adelaide (Ada) Fanny (wife of Edward Eyre) 25, 27, 30
O'Shanassy, John, Premier of Victoria 59
The Oxford History of the British Empire 23
The Oxford Dictionary of Biography 186, 195 n24

Pacific Ocean 2, 73 n30, 186, 187, 189, 205, 229, 236
Pakistan, Punjabis in 43-44
Palfreeman, A., on Indians in Australia 41
Pang, H. Louey 127, 133 n44
Pamamull, Rochimull 49
Papua Act 1905 189-190
Papua New Guinea 184, 278 *See also* New Guinea (British)
Para rubber tree 183-185, 188-189
Paradise Garage (New York) 269-270
Parents (UK) 152
Paris Peace Conference 75
Parks, Tim, *An Italian Education*, and language difference 247-248
parochialism xiv, 138, 233, 235
pastoral expansion 21, 34, 109

and rule of law 30-32, 34-36
Paterson, Banjo, read by Alfred Deakin 206
Pax Britannica, and Prussia 64
Paxton, Nancy xix, 213
peace, cause of 76, 78, 80, 84, 88, 207, 236
Pearl River Delta region 120
Pearson, Charles, friendship with Alfred Deakin 199, 202, 205
periphery, cultural 267
Persians 45
personal, as political 267-268
Peters, A.R. 128
petitions, by Indians in Australia 49
Philippines, Minh Tam Nguyen in xiii, 289, 291, 293
photographs xix, 48, 163 n1
pioneers, British 103, 109, 183, 186, 193
Piper, Edwin 12
plantations
    Ceylon (Sri Lanka) 191
    colonies (Caribbean) 11, 30, 32-35
    Indian 191
    Malayan 184, 185, 189, 191, 192-193
    New Guinea 184, 186, 190
    Queensland 188, 189
    rubber 183, 185, 189
    Santarem 188
    Sumatra 41, 185
political
    affiliation xv, 236
    artist 264, 268
    boundaries xiv, 78, 88, 206, 213, 226
    causes 83, 219, 225, 226, 229, 237, 261
    ideologies 19, 267
    maturity 76
    movements 19, 81, 238-239
    and personal 267-268
    rights 32, 109-110
politicians, and transnational history xiv, xviii
policy 19, 43, 49-52, 54, 205, 206-207
Polite Lies: On Being a Woman Caught between Cultures (Kyoko Mori) 245
Pollitt, Sam, in *The Man Who Loved Children*, as portrait of David Stead 78
Polynesia 186-187

Poms, ten-pound 135, 137
popular culture 168-174, 178, 217-221, 259-268
Porter, Dennis, on travel writing 245
Portuguese army, and Billy Blue 7
post-colonial historians, feminist 41-42
power xviii, xix, 43, 48, 75, 79, 82-83, 214, 237, 240, 241, 246, 247
powerlessness, sense of 141
Pratt, Mary Louise, *Imperial Eyes* 214, 245-246
Premier of Victoria 59
press-gang, and Billy Blue 6, 10, 18 n25
Princess Vicky (daughter of Queen Victoria) 61
Protector of Aborigines 23, 25, 35, 105, 106
Providence, ships from in Sydney Harbour 11
Prussia 61-62, 64, 67
publishers xvi -xvii, 218, 220, 221, 226, 227 n12, 242
Punch (Melbourne and Sydney), on Prince Alfred 59, 73 n32
Punjab, and Pakistan 43-44
Punjabi Sikh, Otim Singh as 41
Pybus, Cassandra xiii, xx

Quebec, Battle of, and Billy Blue 6-7
Queensland 52, 184, 187-189, 226 n2
queer diaspora xix-xx, 259-270
quilting 269
Quinlan, F.J. 129
Quinlan, Judith 18 n32
Quota Acts (England) 10

Rabinow, Paul, on the 'in-between' 218
race xv, xviii, 24, 25, 30, 32-36, 43-54, 74 n45, 80, 98, 118, 205, 221-222, 225, 229, 237, 260, 267-269
Racial Hygiene Association 84, 90
radio, and R.G. Watt 79-80, 86, 89, 90, 91
'Radio Nations' (UNO) 86
Rand Daily Mail 141
readers xvi-xvii, 160, 165, 172, 181, 199, 202, 205, 213, 217, 220, 221, 226, 229, 238, 240, 245, 252-253

reading, and transnational ties xvi-xvii, 7, 86, 160, 181, 197-209, 262
Redman, Chief Constable John 12
refugee camp xiii, 291-292
refugees 9, 35, 79, 88-89, 138
reinvention, and emigration 70, 166, 296
religion, 43, 168, 203-204, 254
'remembering forward' 166
repression 33-35
residence, length of, and being 'Australian' xvii
Resident Magistrate, Edward Eyre as 23, 25, 31
revolution 3, 7-8, 75, 217, 232, 241
Revue Latine, read by Alfred Deakin 202
rhizome 186-187, 193, 193 n1
Ricatti, Francesco xix, xx, 95
Richardson, Henry Handel, *The Getting of Wisdom*, read by Alfred Deakin 206
Richmond River Times (NSW) 45
ricordo di feuilleton 170
Ridley, Sir Henry on Henry Wickham 189
Riley, Alexander and Edward 15
Riven (Jean Devanny) 215, 217-226
Roberts, Lord 205
Robinson, George Augustus 106
The Rocks (Sydney) 11-12, 18 n28
Roe, Michael, on Bergson 204
Rolland, Romaine, read by Alfred Deakin 202
Rooney, Brigid on *House of All Nations* 237
Ross, Andrew, on the new politics 268
Rowley, Hazel. on Christina Stead
Royal Botanical Gardens, Kew 183-184, 187-191, 193 n1, 194 n14
Royal Institute of International Affairs 83
Royal Navy (British) 6, 8-10, 17 n19, 57, 61, 67-68, 70
Royce, Josiah, friendship with Alfred Deakin, Marilyn Lake on 204-205
rubber xix, 89, 183-185, 187-188-189
rule of law 19, 24-36
Russell, Dr 101, 110, 111 (Russel)
Russell, Penny 70, 227 n6
(with Desley Deacon and Angela Woollacott)

on the transnational subject 217
Transnational Lives 36 n1
Russian Zone (Germany) 282-284

sailors 6, 8-10, 17 n19, 65, 194 n17
Salvation Army 115, 126
Santarem (Brazil) 184, 188
School Magazine 80
Schleswig-Holstein affair 61
Schomburg, Dr 64
Schreiner, Olive 181, 206
science xix, xx, 78, 84, 236, 207-208
Scofield, Susannah (granddaughter of Billy Blue) 17 n1
Scotland 59-61, **60**, 72 n6, 97, **104**, 108, **109**
Seeley, J.R. 37 n12, 205
self
    distributed 277
    hybrid 278
    improvement 135-136, 139-140, 147 n4, 199
    independent 163
    language and 245-246, 247, 249, 255-256
    mobile and transnational 135, 138, 143, 146, 225
    and objects 277-278
    performance of 269
    reading and 199, 204
    as 'repetition with a difference' 168
    transformation 197-198, 208-209, 278
    and transubstantation 278
Semar's Cave: An Indonesian Journal (John Mateer) 214, 245-146, 251-256, **252**
Sennett, Richard, and Jane Jacobs 261
settler societies xiv, xix, 21-24, 30-32, 35-36, 38 n29, 44, 46, 49-50, 75, 97-113
Seung Hang (China) 120
Seven Years War 5, 7, 13
sex 118, 206, 219, 220, 221, 223-226, 240-241, 264-270
sexuality 215, 218-226, 261-262, 268-270
    discourses of 259-260, 267-268
Shaw, George Bernard, read by Alfred Deakin 201
Shekki (district of Zhongshan, China),

Agnes Breuer in **119**, 120, **121**, 125-127
Sheridan, Susan, on Jean Devanny 215
shipping 187, 234
Shue, Davi Louey 133 n44
Sierra Leone 9
Sikhs 41, 44-54
Singapore Botanical Gardens 189
Singh, Golar 50
Singh, Isher 44
Singh, Naraung 44
Singh, Otim **42**
    in Australia 41-54
        masculinity of 43, 46-47, 54
        and Punjabi family 45
        and racial prejudice 51
    in Batavia (Jakarta) 41
    in British Mounted Police 41, 46
    in Sumatra 41
    transnational life xviii, 19, 41, 45
Singh, Sirdar 50-51
Singh, Sowar Saut 45-46, 49
Singh, Susannah 51
Singleton (NSW) 46-47
Singley, Carol, on Edith Wharton 203
Sinha, Mrinalini 43, 46
Sino-Japanese crisis 83, 87
slaves 5, 6, 30, 32-34, 251
Sleeman, John, *White China*, and Agnes Breuer 115-118, 129-130
Smith, Chris and homesickness 141-142
Smith, O. **85**
Smith, Ros, and homesickness 141-142
sociological imagination, and biography 22
sojourners 140-141, 276
South America 120, 183-184, 188, 189, 191 193, 237
South Australia 25, 45-47, 50-51, 64
South Pacific Commission 91
sovereignty 23, 24, 30-36
Soviet Union xiii, 217, 275, 282, 287, 289
sport, and Australian identity xv
St Lawrence River 6
St Vincent (Caribbean) 23, 27, 33
Standish, Frederick 68-70
State Library of New South Wales 165, 179 n11

State Library of Victoria 97, 103
Stead, Christina **230**
    as wanderer 232, 233, 234, 235, 236, 237
    lover Bill Blake 232, 237, 238
    and socialism 232-233, 239
    at Travelers' Bank, Paris 238, 239
    House of All Nations 229, 232-233
        on cosmopolitanism 233
        on international banking and crime 232, 233, 236-238
        on racial and national stereotypes 237
        critique of marriage 233, 237, 239-240
        Susan Carson on 214, 229-235, 236-238, 241-242
    as transnational writer xix, 213, 229, 232, 233, 235, 238, 241, 242
Stead, David (father of Christina) 78, 81, 83, 234
Stewart, John McKellar 207
storyteller, and imagination 213
Strathern, Marilyn 277
Streeter, Caroline 138
Stringer, John 260
subaltern lives xviii, 19, 43
Sydney (Australia) xiii, 5, 9, 11-15, 47, 53, 66, 61, 62, 64, 74 n58, 77-84, 129, 132 n32, 139, 144-145, 150-163, 213-226, 229, 232-236, 238-242, 259, 262, 264-265, 268, 284, 292-295
Sydney Gay Liberation Newsletter 262
Sydney Gazette, on Billy Blue 11-16
Sydney Punch, on Alfred, Duke of Edinburgh 59, 73 n32
Sydney *World* 115, 117
Sumatra 41, 46, 185, 251, 253-254

Tasmania 64, 67, 68, 70-71
Taishan 120
Taylor, Captain, (*Galatea*) 69
Taylor, Frederick, and violence towards Aborigines 106
Taylor, Henry 27
teachers of Australian history xvii

tears, and migrants' memories of first love 176-177
telegraph, underwater 187
Telegraph (Brisbane) **119**
Telia (Punjabi for Australia) 44
Ten Pound Poms (Alistair Thomson) 138
'ten-pound Pom' 135, 137, 151
Teo, Hsu-Ming, on popular romances 218
testimonio 246
testimony, oral, of British migrants 138, 47 n1, n5, n12
Thames xiii, 9-10
'Thatcher refugee' 138
Theroux, Paul 214
Thief at the End of the World, (Joe Jackson) 184-185
Thomson, Alistair xix, 95, 138, 147, n5, n12, 163 n1, 166-167
Thrift, Nigel, 261
Times (London) 186, 86
topoi, and memory 168-169, 175
Tosh, John 70
Townsville (Queensland) 115, 120-125, 127-129, 134 n59
    Evening Star 117, 133 n37
tradition, 'invention of' 59
'trans-colonial' 23, 75
transnational
    lives xviii-xx, 65, 67, 70-71, 77, 79, 82, 124-125, 135-138, **137**, 178, 186, 217, 218, 220, 225-226, 229, 251-253, 270
    and archival fragments 3, 5-7, 9-10, 11, 13-14, 15, 16
    and authority xviii, 19, 22-30, 34, 45, 57, 75
    and class 221-222, 225
    and ethnicity xx, 221, 225
    and gender xx, 215, 218, 220, 221-222, 225
    and imagination xix-xx, 213-214
    and intellect xix, 181
    and intimacy xviii-xvix, 95, 118, 130, 136, 138, 140, 146-147, 149-150, 162-163, 165-168, 225
    and material objects 275-279, 295-296

history xiv-xvii, xx, 43
   and national narratives xiv-xvii, 3, 5, 16, 22-30, 41, 71, 91-92, 97-99, 112-113, 118, 127, 130, 146, 166-168, 200, 214, 215, 217, 229, 232-233, 236-241, 252-253, 255-256, 275-279, 295-296
transnationalism
   and biography xiii-xx, 22-30
'Transnational Lives' xv
transportation (convict) 9, 11
travel, language 214, 245-255
   through literature 232
   writers 214, 245-246, 249, 250
travellers xiii, 7, 71, 120, 193, 214, 236, 276
   Aboriginal 36 n1
   as 'seeing-man' 246
   'spectator-' 232, 233, 241
Turnbull, Sarah xix, 214, 245-246, 249-251, 255-256
Turner, Graeme, on CNN 91
Turner, Mark, on gay urban migration 262

United Nations Association of Australia 90
United Nations Organisation 19, 89
United States of America 35-36124, 204-205, 218, 220, 221, 229, 232, 235, 259, 260, 264, 265, 267
University
   Australian National xv
   of Melbourne 85
   of Sussex 163, n1
   of Sydney 77, 81, 82
   of Western Australia 86
urban migration 262

Vassa, Gustavus (Olaudah Equiano) 5
Vasta, Ellie 169
Victoria (Australia) 45, 66, 68-69, 71, 80, 83, 97-113,160
Victoria (British Columbia) 145
Victoria, Queen 57-61, 72 n6, 187
Victoria League 84
Victoria Station (London) 242
Vidal, Gore 261

Vietcong 're-education' camps xiii, 289-291
Vietnam xiii, 289, 291, 293-295
Village Voice 261
violence 23-24, 27, 30, 31, 34-35, 71, 105-109
Virginia, Billy Blue in 7-8
Vilyatpur, Punjab 44
von Hügel, Baron, and Billy Blue 16

Walkowitz, Rebecca 226 n2
Wannon 101, 110-112, 114 n32 *See also* Murndal
war xv, 5-9, 13, 19, 50, 53, 61, 64, 75, 77, 83, 88, 89, 214, 230, 233, 236, 282-283, 289
'war brides' 136, 143
Warhol, Andy, *Interview* 261, 267
'Watchman' (ABC), and R.G.Watt 87
Watt, Alan (brother of R.G. Watt) 82, 91
Watt, Eileen (wife of R.G. Watt) 80, 82
Watt, R.G. 75-92, **85**
   advocate for international causes xviii, 19, 77-91
   as transnational 82, 91
   and NSW League of Nations Union 77
   and Australian League of Nations Union 78, 80, 83
   and International Labour Organisation 78
   and Worker's Education Association 79-80, 81, 89
   and Refugees Emergency Council of New South Wales 88-89
   and United Nations Organisation 89
   and United Nations Association of Australia 90
   and Burwood Migrant Hostel 91
   and South Pacific Commission 91
   Creighton Burns on 89
   and David Stead 78, 81, 83
Way, J.P. (Hong Kong Anzac) 127
Wells, H.G. 75-76, 87, 201, 205
   and Alfred Deakin 200-201
Wentworth, D'Arcy, and Billy Blue 14
Western District (Victoria) xix, 45, 95, 97-113

traditional owners 100, 102, 103-109, 110-113, 113 n10, 114 n28, n32
Wharton, Edith 202-203
White, Edmund 261
White, John (Jacky) 109-112
White Australia Policy 19, 41, 43, 49-54, 27-128
White China 115-116, 118, 129, 130
white men xviii, 45, 46, 115, 118, 129, 130
White, Richard 43
Whitlock, Gillian xviii-xiv
Wickham, Sir Henry Alexander 183-193, **185**
   as citizen of empire 186-187
   as transnational 186-187, 193, 194 n11
   as rhizome 186-187, 193
   in Brazil 184, 187, 188
   Rough Notes on a Journey Through the Wilderness 188
   and *Hevea brasiliensis* (rubber) 183, 184-185, 187, 188
   and Royal Botanical Gardens, Kew 183-185, 186, 188, 191, 194 n14
   in British Honduras 184, 186, 191
   in Queensland 186, 187-188, 189
   in New Guinea 184, 186, 187, 188, 189-190
   On the Plantation, Cultivation, and Curing of Para Indian Rubber 184
   adviser to Arghan Company 188, **190**, 190-193
   failures 186, 189-190, 193
Williams, Elizabeth *See* Blue, Elizabeth
William, John 187
Williams, Richard, on Alfred, Duke of Edinburgh 61-61
Wills, Sara, on 'unsettled settlers' 99
Wing Lun, Thomas 126
Wing Sang & Co, Sydney 129
Winter, Arbella *See* Cooke, Arbella
Winter, George (brother of Arbella, Samuel and Trevor), in Van Diemen's Land 99
Winter, Samuel Pratt 98
   to Van Diemen's Land 99
   at Murndal homestead **98**, 100

Margaret Kiddle on 109
   letters from John (Jacky) White 109-112, 114 n32
   instructions for Aboriginal burial 112
Winter, Trevor (brother of Arbella, George and Samuel) 99
Winter Cooke collection, letters from Aboriginal, Jackie White 109-112
Wolfe, General, and Billy Blue 5-6, 17 n10
Wolfe, Patrick 30, 98
Wolff, Janet 267
women
   colonial 59, 70
   colonised 41, 48
   Conference of the Workers International Relief Organisations 217
   and consumption 218-219
   Indigenous 106-108
   Italian 166-178
   in the League of Nations Union 84, 93 n41
   migrants, letters of 147 n5, n12, 149-150, 162-163, 163 n1, 166-178
   National Council of 90
   'New' 219
   rights of 75, 79, 90, 206, 217 236, 260
   sessions on ABC 87
   in Sydney
      in Eleanor Dark, *Waterway* 239-240, 241
      in Jean Devanny, *The Virtuous Courtesan* 218 221-226
   and suburbia 162
   transnational 67, 71, 149-150, 162-163, 166-167, 178, 217, 220, 225-226, 229-232, 236
   in Wellington, New Zealand, in Jean Devanny, *Riven* 218-221, 222
   white 41, 118, 120-121, 125, 131 n13, n16
   and intimacy and imagination xx
Woollacott, Angela 41, 218
   (with Desley Deacon and Penny Russell)
   on the transnational subject 217
   Transnational Lives 36 n1
Workers Art Club (Sydney) 223

Workers' Education Association 79-80, 81, 89
Workers International Relief Organisation, and Jean Devanny 217
workers' rights, and Eleanor Dark 236
world
    Ambassador to 86
    citizen of xvii, xix, 84, 136, 181, 213, 238
    Congress of Workers 217
    education 87
    government 78, 89
    modern 22, 82, 136
    peace 78, 80
    regulation 75
    transnational 241
World (Sydney) 115-118, 130
World War I 75, 77, 200
World War II 53, 79, 88-89, 241, 242, 264, 282
Wright, Bridget (Biddy) (daughter of Dorothy and Mike) **150, 155**, 151-154, 156-159
Wright, Dorothy (nee Bailey) **150, 155**
    emigration to Australia 151
    loneliness 151, 154, 155-156, 158-159
    homesickness 155
    and 'culture shock' 155
    as 'Pommie' 159
    and swimming 160-161, **161**, 162-163
    personal transformation 162-163
    and transnational family 149-150, 162-163
    letters of 95, 149-163, 163 n1
    migration memoir of 154-156 163 n1
Wright, Mike (husband of Dorothy) 150, 151, 153-154, 156, 157-160, 163
Wright, Nicholas (son of Dorothy and Mike) **150**, 151, 152-154, 156-159, 163
writing
    and connection 103, 162-163, 175
    as space for reflection 136-138, 143, 149-151, 158, 159, 198, 199

Yarwood, A.T. 41
YellertPerne, at Wannon (Murndal) 111
York River (Virginia) 8

Yorktown (Little York) (Virginia) 8
Young Women's Christian Association 81

Zengcheng (China), emigration from 120
Zhongshan district (China), emigration from 120

www.ingramcontent.com/pod-product-compliance
Lightning Source LLC
Chambersburg PA
CBHW042336230426
43664CB00046B/2937